Use of the Telephone in Psychotherapy

Use of the Telephone in Psychotherapy

EDITED BY
JOYCE K. ARONSON

JASON ARONSON INC.
Northvale, New Jersey
London

This book was set in 11 pt. New Aster by Alpha Graphics in Pittsfield, New Hampshire and printed and bound by Book-mart Press, Inc. of North Bergen, New Jersey.

Library of Congress Cataloging-in-Publication Data
Use of the telephone in psychotherapy / edited by Joyce K. Aronson.
    p. cm.
    Includes bibliographical references and index.
    ISBN 0-7657-0268-1 (alk. paper)
    1. Telephone in psychotherapy. I. Aronson, Joyce K.
  RC489.T42 U84 2000
  616.89'14—dc21   00-041618

Printed in the United States of America on acid-free paper. For information and catalog write to Jason Aronson Inc., 230 Livingston Street, Northvale, NJ 07647-1726, or visit our website: www.aronson.com

For Alex, Brian, and Paul

CONTENTS

III
With Parents, Children, and Adolescents

IV
In Different Therapeutic Modalities

V
With Different Diagnostic Disorders

VI
Other Issues

ACKNOWLEDGMENTS

I thank the contributors to this book for their thoughtful chapters on the use of the telephone in clinical practice, an area that up to now has not been openly addressed. I am grateful to Judy Cohen, my editor at Jason Aronson, for her excellent editing, to Eve Golden and Diana Siskind, for their suggestions on the introduction, and to Norma Pomerantz, for her attention to many of the details involved in this project. On a personal note, I thank my husband, Jay, for his support and encouragement during the process of producing this book.

CONTRIBUTORS

Joyce K. Aronson, Ph.D., is on the faculty of the Center for the Study of Anorexia and Bulimia in New York City. She received her doctorate in clinical social work from Smith College, where she has been an adjunct faculty member. The editor of *A Guide to the Dynamic Psychotherapy of Anorexia and Bulimia*, Dr. Aronson is a graduate of the New York University Postdoctoral Program in Psychotherapy and Psychoanalysis, and the Freudian Society. She is a member of the International Psychoanalytical Association and is in private practice in New York City.

F. Diane Barth, CSW, is a faculty member, senior supervisor, and training analyst at the Psychoanalytic Institute of the Postgraduate Center and the National Institute for the Psychotherapies. She also teaches at the Center for the Study of Anorexia and Bulimia and leads private study groups for therapists. She is the author of Daydreaming: Unlock the Creative Power of Your Mind, and is in private practice in New York City.

Karl Heinz Brisch, M.D., a training psychoanalyst at the Psychoanalytic Institute "Stuttgarter Gruppe," specializes in child, adolescent, and adult psychiatry, neurology, psychotherapeutic medicine, and psychoanalysis. He is head of the department of psychosomatic medicine at the Children's Hospital at the Ludwig-Maximilians-University of Munich. Dr. Brisch's research field is the development of infants and children with high-risk conditions and the development of attachment and its disorders. The author of *Attachment Disorders: From Attachment Theory to Therapy*, Dr. Brisch leads research projects on attachment disturbances and early psychotherapeutic interventions.

Luanna E. Devenis, Ph.D., was a presidential fellow at the State University of New York at Albany, and received her doctorate in counseling psychology in 1994. Dr. Devenis has had extensive experience working in open residential treatment centers and college settings. She specializes in working with young adults and conducting psychological assessment and research and is in private practice in Williamstown, Massachusetts.

Sue N. Elkind, Ph.D., is the author of Resolving Impasses in Therapeutic Relationships. She is a member of the Institute for Contemporary Psychoanalysis, Los Angeles and Dean of Candidates at the Psychoanalytic Institute of Northern California. Dr. Elkind is in private practice in Orinda, California, specializing in consultation to therapists and patients in serious impasses.

Jerome D. Levin, Ph.D., is Director of the Alcoholism and Substance Abuse Counselor Training Program at the New School University in New York City, where he also serves on the humanities department faculty and as co-director of the joint masters program in psychology and substance abuse treatment. He is also an adjunct associate professor of social science at New York University. Dr. Levin has authored eleven books on such subjects as the history of ideas, narcissism, addiction, and contemporary affairs. He maintains a psychotherapy practice in Manhattan and Suffolk County, New York.

Marsha H. Levy-Warren, Ph.D., is a clinical psychologist and psychoanalyst who writes, teaches, lectures, and consults nationally and internationally. She is currently Associate Director of the Institute for Child, Adolescent, and Family Studies in New York City and a faculty member and supervisor in New York University's Postdoctoral Program in Psychotherapy and Psychoanalysis. Dr. Levy-Warren is also a training and supervising psychoanalyst in the New York Freudian Society and the International Psychoanalytic Association. She is the author of The Adolescent Journey and numerous articles on adolescence, culture, and gender.

John A. Lindon, M.D., Ph.D., was the first candidate accepted for training by the Southern California Psychoanalytic Institute in 1950. He went on to become a faculty member, supervising and training analyst, and president of the Institute. Dr. Lindon was one of the twelve founding members who in 1991 started the Institute of Contemporary Psychoanalysis in Los Angeles, where he is a faculty member and a supervising and training analyst. He is president of The Psychiatric Research Foundation and has published widely.

Hindi T. Mermelstein, M.D., is Senior Assistant Attending Psychiatrist, supervisor, lecturer, coordinator of postgraduate training in emergency psychiatry and psychiatry, and director of adult ambulatory services and emergency room psychiatry services at the North Shore University Hospital in Manhasset, New York. She is also assistant professor of clinical psychiatry at the New York University School of Medicine. Dr. Mermelstein has published widely on such subjects as psychotherapy with cancer patients, depression in the medically ill, and related topics.

Ira L. Mintz, M.D., was a supervising child psychoanalyst at the Columbia University Psychoanalytic Training Center and associate clinical professor of psychiatry at the New Jersey College of Medicine. He was also a consultant at Hackensack Medical Center, a member of the Psychosomatic Study Group of the Psychoanalytic Association of New York, and former president of the New Jersey Psychoanalytic Society. Dr. Mintz co-edited Fear of Being Fat and Psychosomatic Symptoms.

Jane Plummer, Psy.D., is co-director of Massachusetts Psychotherapy Associates in Westborough, Massachusetts, where she specializes in the treatment of eating disorders. She received her training at Massachusetts General Hospital and Harvard Medical School, and is former director of the Eating Disorder Treatment Program at Westwood Lodge Hospital, a private psychiatric hospital outside of Boston. Dr. Plummer is in private practice.

Claire Rosenberg, MSW, has been a researcher in the Follow Along Study, a massive research project studying the value of long-term psychoanalytic treatment. Ms. Rosenberg has presented on family work for the American Group Psychotherapy Association and the Western Massachusetts and Albany Association for Psychoanalytic Psychotherapy. A graduate of the Smith College School for Social Work, she is currently a clinical social worker at the Austen Riggs Center in Stockbridge, Massachusetts.

Sylvan Schaffer, J.D., Ph.D., is an attorney and a clinical psychologist. He is Clinical Director and Coordinator of Training at North Shore University Hospital, Manhasset, New York, Department of Child and Adolescent Psychiatry, attorney for the New York State Psychological Association and other mental health associations, and Associate Clinical Professor of Psychiatry at New York University and Albert Einstein Medical Schools. An adjunct faculty member at Hofstra Law School, Downstate Medical Center, and Yeshiva University, he is also affiliated with the Department of Psychiatry at Lenox Hill Hospital in Manhattan. Dr. Schaffer's psychology practice includes psychotherapy and psychological testing for children and adults. His legal practice focuses on mental health concerns and related business and litigation issues.

Diana Siskind is a psychoanalyst and psychoanalytic psychotherapist in New York City whose practice includes adults and children. She is the author of numerous articles and three books: The Child Patient and the Therapeutic Process, Working with Parents, and A Primer for Child Psychotherapists. Mrs. Siskind is a member and Distinguished Practitioner of the National Academy of Practice.

Nechama Sorscher, Ph.D., is a clinical psychologist in private practice in New York City whose areas of specialty include pediatric and adolescent individual and group therapy as well as neuropsychological assessments. She has worked as a school psychologist and has taught adjunct courses on assessments and group therapy on the undergraduate and graduate levels. Dr. Sorscher's postdoctoral training was completed at Columbia Presbyterian Medical Center in pediatric psychiatry. She is currently completing a postdoctoral degree in psychoanalysis at the Postdoctoral Program in Psychotherapy and Psychoanalysis at New York University.

Robert H. Spiro, Ph.D., received his doctorate in 1973 from Yeshiva University. He completed postdoctoral and advanced postdoctoral fellowships in clinical psychology at the Austen Riggs Center, Stockbridge, Massachusetts, where he remained on staff until 1982. A fellow of the Academy of Clinical Psychology, Dr. Spiro holds a diplomate in clinical psychology from the American Board of Professional Psychology. He is currently in private practice in Williamstown, Massachusetts.

Martha Stark, M.D., is a psychiatrist/psychoanalyst in private practice in Newton Centre, Massachusetts. She is a teaching analyst at the Boston Psychoanalytic Institute and a teaching and supervising analyst at the Massachusetts Institute for Psychoanalysis. Dr. Stark has a teaching appointment at the Harvard Medical School and is on the faculty of the Center for Psychoanalytic Studies at Massachusetts General Hospital. She is the author of Working with Resistance, A Primer on Working with Resistance, and Modes of Therapeutic Action.

Herbert S. Strean, DSW, is Distinguished Professor Emeritus, Rutgers University, and Director Emeritus of the New York Center for Psychoanalytic Training. In his forty years of professional practice, he has trained more than 4,000 therapists. Author of thirty-five books and over one hundred papers, Dr. Strean has been on the editorial boards of Psychoanalytic Review, Clinical Social Work, and Analytic Social Work. He maintains a private practice in New York City.

Joan G. Tolchin, M.D., is a clinical assistant professor of psychiatry at Cornell University Medical College. She is a past president of the New York Council on Child and Adolescent Psychiatry, current secretary of the American Academy of Psychoanalysis, and serves on the editorial board of the Journal of the American Academy of Psychoanalysis.

Judith J. Warren, Ph.D., received her doctorate from U.C.L.A. She is a clinical psychologist and a candidate in psychoanalysis at the New York University Postdoctoral Program and has been a high school consulting psychologist at the Dalton School since 1997. Dr. Warren is currently secretary of the Media Division of the American Psychological Association and is a public speaker on the issues of divorce, depression, and finding the right life partner. She has been in private practice since 1986, first in California and now in New York.

David S. Wilson, Ph.D., immigrated to the United States from Canada in 1979, after a business career in electronics and sound reproduction of more than thirty years. He earned his masters and doctoral credentials from Yeshiva University and The Union Institute respectively. Dr. Wilson has taught at the New York University School of Social Work, is a graduate and faculty member of the Center for the Advancement of Group Studies, and is a graduate of the MidManhattan Institute for Psychoanalysis. He is co-author of "Psychologics," a highly efficient PC-based professional practice management program.

INTRODUCTION
The Evolving Use of the Telephone in Clinical Practice

JOYCE K. ARONSON

*T*he telephone has quietly slipped into clinical practice, and many practitioners have by now adopted its use. However, this development is rarely discussed or written about, and the familiar instrument is seldom recognized as the important treatment tool it is. This book will explore the value and use of the telephone in clinical practice.

The increasing complexity of our social structure and consequently our patients' lives has resulted in an expanded use of the telephone in clinical work. Once confined to crisis situations, telephone contact now serves a multitude of therapeutic functions, and maintaining ongoing treatment when distance or other factors prevent in-person sessions is only one of them. The telephone can promote object constancy, provide a transitional space, or build a working alliance with the parents of child patients—and these are just some of the ways that it can enable and enhance the psychotherapeutic process.

My own participation in this process began when a dangerously ill anorexic with fifteen years of previously failed psychotherapies began treatment with me, but became so afraid of the needs that might be aroused in the contact between us that she refused to come in to see me. Instead she began to call me on the phone. She also left long messages on my answering machine. For her this was a transitional space in which I was both "there" and "not there." In it she could enact some of her early developmental needs, and gradually

become able to give up her masochistic and omnipotent anorexic defenses.

Some anorexic patients, at the low-level borderline and
psychotic end of the diagnostic spectrum like this one, are not
treatable with traditional psychotherapeutic approaches. I
believe that her use of the telephone allowed my patient to
maintain the illusion of omnipotent control over me, and that
by allowing her to engage with me in this way, I helped her to
internalize gradually another way of relating, one that recognized the other as a separate person. I think that my flexibility
about the phone was essential for this patient's survival. And
after I presented this case for the first time (Chapter 7, this
volume), a number of colleagues approached me and con-
fessed, with some hesitation, that they too had been doing
psychotherapy by telephone.

Sometimes unconscious reluctance to address an issue
takes the form of psychosomatic symptoms and cancelled appointments. By the time of the next appointment the conflict
is no longer as emotionally available. A telephone session can
prevent this crusting over and consequent resistance, keeping
the conflict and feelings more accessible. When the request for
a phone session is initiated by the patient, she is likely to be
less defensive, and therefore freer to explore her concerns. A
patient of mine called to say that she was feeling exhausted
and sick, and asked if we could have our session by phone. In
the course of that session she spoke more directly than usual
about how upset she was about her husband's repeatedly failing her. This enabled her to recognize her anger at him, which
she had previously experienced as global hopeless feelings
about her life.

Sometimes a patient requests a phone session when she
needs to distance herself emotionally. Over the course of her
summer vacation, a bulimic patient of mine who was success-

fully controlling her bingeing and vomiting after several years of our working together, learned that her husband had lost his job, and that they might have to leave the city, in which case she would not be able to continue to see me. She did not come to her session, but called to tell me how upsetting and disruptive the move would be to her life. However, she said, her husband's needs should come first, as he was the breadwinner. In our work by phone we came to understand that she was reluctant to see me in person because it had taken her so long to trust me. To see me would evoke the loss she anticipated with her husband's plan to move, and arouse feelings that she feared would be too painful. She also realized that moving again would be a hardship for her in many ways at that point in her life. Eventually she was able to express to her husband how devastating a move would be, and he took her needs into account.

The telephone can be used to bridge geographic distance in many kinds of situations. A patient with a history of panic attacks asked to continue our sessions by phone when she went back home to work for her father's company. Having had the opportunity to develop and reflect on a newfound understanding of her parents in her therapy, it was productive for her to see and experience firsthand her father's pervasive narcissism. Knowing that she would be able to speak to me by phone allowed her to process her feelings about him as they arose, without the panic attacks she had previously suffered.

It is not unusual for therapists nowadays to maintain treatment with patients by telephone while the therapist is on vacation, or with adolescent patients away at college, to name two common situations.

By now, the use of the telephone in psychotherapy is so widespread and popular that it was the subject of the charming closing moments of the movie *Analyze This*. At the beginning of what is to be an eighteen-month incarceration in Sing Sing prison, Robert DeNiro (whose psychotherapy with Billy Crystal has led to his decision to leave mob life and live in accordance with the awakenings that his therapy has yielded) asks "the Doc" during a visit to the prison if they can continue to have sessions while he is in jail. Billy Crystal answers, "Sure. I can come up on Saturdays or we can have sessions over the phone." DeNiro looks at him quizzically and Crystal says, "I do that when I have a patient who's out of town . . . or in federal prison."

Yet all of this potential notwithstanding, serious consideration of the therapeutic implications of telephone contact between patients and therapists has lagged behind the actual practice. And although the telephone has long been accepted in crisis intervention and suicide hot lines, it has rarely been addressed as a viable option in traditional psychoanalytic treatment.

Until recently the psychoanalytic community in the United States seldom considered treatment by telephone. The traditional approach was to focus on the exploration of the unconscious intrapsychic determinants of behavior. Consequently, the blank screen provided by the silent analyst was considered indispensable. A colleague of mine, now in her late fifties, told me her analyst was absolutely silent during the five-year psychoanalysis she undertook in her twenties, except to tell her every few weeks that she wants a penis. Then there is the apocryphal psychiatrist who asks his training analyst how he is doing after six months of total silence from the analyst. "Aferage," the analyst replies in his thick German accent. A blank screen doesn't work over the telephone. But as contemporary psychoanalysis has taken a broader view of the analytic interaction, the phone has become a viable means, at least in some cases, of analytic communication.

Another factor that accounts for the increasing use of the telephone is the growing number of female psychotherapists and psychoanalysts. Men often confine their telephone use to the accomplishment of specific tasks, and women are usually more comfortable in relating over the phone. Eugene Kaplan (1997), in his paper on psychotherapy by videotelephone, addressed his own reluctance to use the telephone: "I have never enjoyed protracted telephone conversations; I feel sensorially deprived and become impatient after about twenty minutes. It may be that patients who might have requested telephone sessions were deterred by my negative reaction" (p. 240). The videophone provided the visual experience that Kaplan needed to do his psychotherapeutic work. Perhaps with the growing availability of videophone technology we will see its increasing use by male psychotherapists.

The paucity of literature on the subject, the absence of open discussion among colleagues, and the lack of information available in graduate and postgraduate training programs led me to bring together the chapters in this book. I hoped that the effort would leave professionals feeling less hazy in their understanding of the practical, theoretical, and technical implications of the increasing use of the telephone in psychotherapy. The authors—twenty-one chapters' worth—were pleased to have this opportunity to discuss their experiences, and some make clear that they find their work by phone not only useful, but indispensable.

John Lindon was way ahead of his time, a pioneer in the use of the telephone in psychoanalysis. His paper "Psychoanalysis by Telephone" appeared in 1988, when most traditional psychotherapists and psychoanalysts considered work by phone as supportive therapy, only justified for suicidal, borderline, or psychotic patients. He describes his initial experiment with this modality, his expectation that only supportive work would be possible, and his surprise at how easily psychoanalytic work could be continued on the phone if the analyst keeps up his analytic mode of listening. That is, the analyst sets the tone by listening and responding as a working analyst. After addressing the question of the use of the phone for emotional distancing, he describes a case in which physical separation made it easier for his patient to experience strong, intimate feelings toward the analyst without fear of engulfment, which had been his childhood experience with his mother.

Sharon Zalusky, in her chapter, "Telephone Analysis," reviews the literature on the use of the telephone in psychoanalysis which, she acknowledges, emphasizes the positive aspects of treatment by phone. While it is often a therapeutic compromise, she notes sometimes in a particularly sensitive or transitional phase of a psychoanalysis continuation of treatment by phone may be the best available option. Under these circumstances, *not* to offer this continuation may itself be a transference–countertransference enactment. Using the term *analysis* in the broad sense for any intensive treatment that focuses on the analysis of transference and resistance, she emphasizes the conflictual nature of telephone analysis, not because she is opposed to it but because she believes that by recognizing its inherent complexities we can add to its potential effectiveness. In a case example she examines in depth some of the basic issues surrounding telephone analysis: the continuous interplay among real logistical considerations, the patient's and the analyst's transference–countertransference resistances, and the unconscious meanings that they attribute to them. In this thoughtful and complex case study, Zalusky considers initial resistances by both patient and analyst, the issues and indicators involved in the decision to continue psychoanalysis by telephone, the complexities and paradoxes of telephone work, and the termination phase. Building on John

Lindon's work she explores the complexities and paradoxes involved when only data from the verbal realm is available. Her chapter raises many questions, in accord with her goal of opening communication about the use of the telephone in psychoanalysis.

Robert H. Spiro and Luanna E. Devenis, in "Enhancement of the Therapeutic Process," argue that telephone therapy is not only comparable to face-to-face meetings, but may be superior as a form of treatment in its own right when used by a skilled practitioner. Without visual distraction the therapist can develop increased sensitivity to listening, and not being looked at seems to enable some patients to express sensitive concerns that they might not reveal under the scrutiny of a therapist's gaze. Therapists' lack of experience in this modality may lead them to slip into a social rather than therapeutic mold, to feel anxious and frustrated about not being able to see the patient, or have difficulty handling silences in the absence of visual clues. The authors discuss the indications and contraindications for the use of the telephone. It is important that treatment by phone be initiated by the patient and used in the interest of the patient, and not for the convenience or financial benefit of the therapist. If this modality is being used defensively by the patient, its defensive function should be considered in making the decision to use it.

In a practical and helpful chapter, "Skills in Dealing with the First Telephone Contact," Herbert S. Strean points out that a transference begins with the first phone call. With this dynamic understanding he suggests how to deal with questions: about the therapist's qualifications, the therapeutic modality, fees and fee policies, and the therapist's theoretical positions. He also covers the handling of calls from individuals who are not calling voluntarily or who are calling on behalf of someone else. Even in the initial phone call, when the patient's disappointment, resentment, and criticism of the therapist are listened to, his questions explored but not answered, mistrust recedes and the therapeutic alliance begins.

"Long-Term Therapy by Telephone" by Jane Plummer and Martha Stark, describes Plummer's fifteen-year treatment of Rachel, a depressed, quietly desperate, 19-year-old woman who was raised by an unrelentingly abusive mother and a father who could not protect her from her mother's outrageously provocative behavior. For the first three years sessions were conducted face-to-face, but work was continued by phone after Rachel moved to the Midwest to attend law school. At first it did not occur to Plummer to offer Rachel the option of continuing treatment by telephone, and Rachel found a therapist with whom she initially felt comfortable. Eventually, however, as this therapist pressured her to find ways to reconcile with her family, she began to feel increasingly uncomfortable and misunderstood. With reservations, and after consultation with colleagues, Dr. Plummer made herself available for ongoing phone sessions. We come to understand how, in the course of her long-term treatment by phone, Rachel developed from a desperately depressed, helplessly victimized girl into an actively engaged, emotionally available adult who derives pleasure from love and work. In this complex case, the defensive functions of the phone are also addressed.

My chapter, "Use of the Telephone as a Transitional Space," reports on therapeutic work with a severely disturbed, extremely masochistic, anorexic patient, where telephone sessions and the telephone answering machine were used to create a flexible therapeutic hold. Her deficits in dyadic experiences with early attachment figures had left her unable to tolerate face-to-face contact in ongoing psychotherapy. Since she had to be allowed to titrate the amount of contact she could tolerate, parameters were used: telephone sessions, the therapist's answering machine as a transitional space, the therapist's availability by phone to help her deal with the overwhelming anxiety aroused by new experiences, and telephone contact during my vacations. The parameters became unnecessary as the patient grew emotionally.

F. Diane Barth elaborates on the use of the phone as a tool in the therapeutic negotiation of separation and connection in her chapter, "Using the Telephone to Negotiate an Optimal Balance between Separation and Connection." The process of negotiating separations while simultaneously remaining connected to important others is, for some patients, one of the most important aspects of the therapeutic work. Using clinical examples from her work with families and individuals she shows how balancing this tension is an ongoing process for every individual, and how phone therapy can, when used thoughtfully, enhance this developmental process.

In her chapter, "When the Therapist Moves," Judith J. Warren describes the guilt she felt when she left her patients in Los Angeles to move to New York. For some patients brief telephone work eased the transition to a new therapist, or lessened the pain of what felt like an intolerably abrupt ending. Some needed to unburden themselves of hurt, angry, and disappointed feelings, which they were able to do by telephone. One patient found the phone a safer way to express pent-up longings for her as well as his disappointment that she would no longer be there for him. Warren found that the telephone functioned as a transitional object for some of her patients, and as a long-distance umbilical cord for others. Moreover, it was helpful to her as well, enabling her to meet the needs of her patients and also ease some of her own pain on leaving them.

Herbert Strean's flexibility and willingness to continue by phone the treatment of a patient who was afraid of seduction was a key factor in her developing the ability to trust him, and eventually the understanding that enabled her to face her own seductive wishes. In his chapter, "Psychotherapy with a Patient Who Was Afraid of Seduction," Strean expresses the fact that had he not provided the experience of the telephone she would have continued to feel like a helpless victim with men, and would not have matured.

How many child therapists stop working with children because of the frustration of dealing with parents who terminate treatment when threatened by the therapist's relationship with their child? Until Diana Siskind's recent book on this subject, *Working with Parents* (1997), little had been written addressing psychotherapeutic work with parents. In her chapter, "Use of the Telephone in Work with Parents of Children in Psychotherapy," Siskind acknowledges the centrality of the parents in the treatment of their children. There is general agreement that the relationship between the child's therapist and the child's parents can become mired in rivalries and lead to premature termination. With specific clinical examples she illustrates how contact by phone, used wisely and sensitively, can provide the vital link between the child's therapist and the child's parents and go a long way toward building a working alliance with the parents. She describes how contact by phone can be used productively in the evaluation stage, in short-term interventions regarding developmental lags, and with parents of very disturbed children whose ego deficits make them unable to deal with the ordinary frustrations of daily life. She makes it clear that the real power of telephone contact between therapist and parents comes out of the therapist's concern for the parents, from her continuous effort to understand the effect of the child's treatment on them, and from her ongoing effort to engage them respectfully in a therapeutic alliance.

In "Telephones, Teens, and Therapy," Marsha H. Levy-Warren and Nechama Sorscher describe the developmental differences among early, middle, and late adolescents, and consider the telephone as a potential adjunct to the therapeutic process when teenagers are in treatment. Case anecdotes are included for each subphase. The authors also discuss the use of the phone as an important adjunct to collateral in-person contact with the parents of adolescents.

As Joan Tolchin says in her chapter, "Telephone Psychotherapy with Adolescents," the telephone is a natural and useful tool in working with this challenging and rewarding population. With specific clinical examples, she shows how adolescent patients can benefit from knowing that the therapist can be reached by phone, and how availability helps develop a positive working alliance. She feels that the work by phone was a key factor in her depressed and anxious patient's ability to go off successfully to college after a summer in treatment. In another situation she considers the importance of the therapist as a real object, demonstrating her concern for her alcoholic and drug-using adolescent patient by offering her continued telephone contact. Therapists' availability by phone can also help strengthen the internal controls of self-destructive youngsters. Tolchin discusses monitoring depressive symptoms, including suicidal ideation, by telephone.

F. Diane Barth, in "Couples Therapy by Telephone," discusses her initial ambivalence about using the telephone in therapy, and her even greater resistance to using it in work with couples. However, telephone work almost immediately changed the therapeutic process. The loss of visual cues led to a greater sensitivity in both partners to their own and the other's communications. The couple was able to use the phone and the distance it provided to step back and observe their interactions in ways they had not done before. They also began to say things that they previously had expressed only in body language. The telephone sessions established boundaries that allowed them to be connected and yet separate from one another.

David S. Wilson, author of "Group Therapy by Telephone," had thrust upon him the opportunity to experience and study group therapy by telephone when his neurologist ordered him to bed, horizontal and immobile. Faced with the alternative of canceling his group practice, knowing the value of continuity in group treatment, and weighing the limitation of the loss of the powerful component of body language in human communication, he was surprised to learn that group therapy, facilitated by a leader on the telephone, can be beneficial in developing progressive emotional communication and in accelerating group coalescence.

In "Family Work by Telephone with the Hospitalized Patient," Claire Rosenberg describes the value of working with families by phone as both a diagnostic and a treatment option when on-site work is impractical, actively avoided, or too intense for a patient's defensive system. She describes how escalated acting-out suicidal behavior can be modified with phone intervention: the telephone provides space to listen and to talk that may feel less threatening than on-site work, allowing for insight while remaining respectful of the family's and the patient's defenses. Work by phone can also be a motivation factor for later participation in an on-site family therapy. With specific clinical examples, including process material, she demonstrates how phone work can open perspectives in treatment and create the potential for less defended communications among family members.

"Dealing with Substance Abuse Crises by Telephone" had me laughing out loud at Jerome D. Levin's remarkably honest description of his male response to the telephone: having trouble maintaining his focus during a telephone session one day, he found himself thinking of Lacan, his least favorite psychoanalytic thinker, because of Lacan's advocacy of the short session. Levin experiences silence in person very differently than over a phone line where it is "tense, awkward, and unproductive." He says, "It is probably no accident that the vast majority of the chapter authors of this book are women." Yet he ultimately concedes that the telephone has its uses in therapy with substance abusers, and that it can be a lifesaver as well as a necessary evil. He makes a case for the use of the telephone with substance abusers from a theoretical and clinical perspective, and considers especially patients struggling through the early days of sobriety. He reminds us of the strong correlation between substance abuse and suicide. Although we cannot completely protect our patients from hazards by telephone or by any other means, we can be reachable when the patient is in danger, and we can intervene appropriately. The pressure of managed care makes it harder to get patients who are in potential danger admitted to hospitals, and telephone therapy is for that reason more central to treatment than ever.

Another flexible and thoughtful pioneer of telephone therapy in the 1970s was Ira L. Mintz. Although his chapter, "Adjunctive Use of the Telephone in Therapy of Severe Anorexia," does not focus exclusively on his telephone work, it was essential in the psychoanalytically oriented long-term therapy with a severely anorexic patient who came to him after years of failed treatment. Initially she was hyperactive, agitated, and close to death. During her hospitalization she would become enraged during sessions, swear and curse at Mintz, and terminate the treatment. He would phone her afterwards, alluding to their difference of opinion during the session, and attempting to resolve it. This demonstrated to her that he could tolerate her hostility without retaliation. In the three weeks following her discharge from the hospital, he saw her daily, and following stressful sessions she would call him in the evening. Contact served to contain her separation anxieties, promoted a sense of trust in the therapist, encouraged her dependence on the treatment, and diminished her tendency to sudden regressions. It also allowed her to utilize her ability to think incisively and self-reflectively and contributed to her continued progress. Mintz's capacity to use the phone creatively allowed this therapy to succeed where more rigid approaches had failed.

In his chapter "Use of the Telephone in the Treatment of Attachment Disorders," Karl Heinz Brisch summarizes the basics of attachment theory and attachment-oriented psychotherapy. With that as a background, he delineates the seven basic forms of attachment disorders and demonstrates, with compelling clinical examples, how psychotherapeutic work by phone can facilitate more secure attachment. The telephone can open up a transitional space to maintain the relationship between patient and therapist, especially with patients who have a highly avoidant or clinging enmeshed pattern of attachment disorder. In phases of very affect-laden negative transference, the phone gives the patient the ability to stay in contact with the therapist and to be distant at the same time, eventually helping the patient become more open about aggressive affects in face-to-face contact with the therapist in sessions.

Hindi T. Mermelstein, in "Use of the Telephone in Psychotherapy of the Medically Ill," points out that patients require frequent contact with their therapists, but are often unable to come to an office on a regular basis. Mermelstein presents four cases: a woman with endometrial cancer who needed psychotherapy for help in dealing with her anxiety and depression, a young woman with Hodgkin's Disease who knew intellectually that she had a potentially curable condition but was unable to comply with treatment procedures, a woman with a recurrence of breast cancer who had symptoms of chronic depression that probably predated her illness, and an elderly man with Parkinson's Disease whose wife had recently died. Mermelstein comments that the phone equalizes the power between patient and therapist. The patient doesn't have to come to a strange office. This anonymity may allow patients with paranoid tendencies to feel more at ease. Although there is a loss of visual and nonverbal cues, the telephone is nevertheless accessible and effective in providing psychotherapeutic interventions.

Sue Elkind specializes in consultation to therapists and patients in serious impasses. Her use of the telephone for impasse consultations was as experimental as the consultations themselves, and has become a large part of her professional work. Her priority is to intervene as quickly and efficiently as possible, an approach facilitated through work by phone. In her chapter, "The Use of the Telephone for Impasse Consultations," she discusses the advantages and limits of the phone, noting that human beings are adaptable and that when visual cues are unavailable, auditory sensibility is sharpened.

In "Legal and Ethical Issues," Sylvan Schaffer discusses licensure for therapeutic contacts that cross state lines, the ethics of telephone psychotherapy, and malpractice liability. Growth of telephone work has been so rapid that ethical standards for its practice are still evolving. Licensure is the exclusive preserve of the states, and requirements vary from one to another: Kansas, for example, requires that anyone treating a patient located in Kansas must have a Kansas medical license. Schaffer suggests that psychotherapists limit their liability exposure by getting written informed consent from the patient, and by being careful in the type of patients they select—avoiding, for example, suicidal patients. They should seek consultation in difficult cases, maintain treatment records, and make sure that telephone psychotherapy is covered in their liability insurance.

The theory and technique of psychotherapy has to keep pace with changes in social structure and patient population. The way we live now is very different from how things were when psychotherapy was in its infancy. We see these changes in work, in family life, and in the culture of childhood. The telephone, once used only to make appointments and handle crises, now serves a multitude of therapeutic functions. The chapters that follow will illustrate the clinical breadth and value of the telephone as a therapeutic tool.

REFERENCES

Kaplan, E. (1997). Psychotherapy by telephone, videotelephone, and computer videoconferencing. *Journal of Psychotherapy Practice and Research* 6:227–237.

Siskind, D. (1997). *Working with Parents*. Northvale, NJ: Jason Aronson.

I

GENERAL ISSUES IN INDIVIDUAL THERAPY

1

Psychoanalysis by Telephone*

JOHN A. LINDON

Although the use of the telephone for psychotherapeutic work is reported in the literature (Chiles 1974, Freud 1912, Grumet 1979, Miller 1973, Robertiello 1972–1973, Rosenbaum 1974, 1977, Saul 1951), most authors have considered it 'supportive therapy. Most phone calls reported were ad-lib, brief, and the patient was not charged for the time. Some authors thought use of the telephone for psychotherapeutic work was justified only for suicidal, borderline, or psychotic patients. Some thought that use of the telephone was related to a patient's unresolved mourning due to separation from an analyst who had moved away. One analyst who had made a geographic move thought he took the phone calls because of his own guilt feelings about abandoning his patients.

Two authors were the exceptions, reporting analytic work via the phone. Saul (1951), in a short note, reported doing full-fledged analytic work by phone; he considered the telephone a "technical aid" and a parameter to enable a borderline patient to better work on her intense transference. Saul also described a patient with an intense hostile transference who used the telephone to proceed when all else seemed stalemated.

---

*An earlier version of this paper was presented to the Southern California Psychoanalytic Society, November 19, 1984.

Robertiello (1972–1973) also wrote a short note describing his few months of experience of conducting analytic sessions over the telephone with two patients, one who had to take a writing job out of town for four months, and another whose archaic transferences were too painfully intense when in the therapist's office.

Now that I have had more than 30 years of experience using the phone to continue ongoing psychoanalysis, I want to share my experiences. I have done psychoanalysis by telephone with many patients for short periods, with several patients for more than three years, and with one patient for more than five years. This option has allowed continued analysis when otherwise it would have been disrupted for weeks or months, or involved transfer to new analysts (which the patients preferred not to do), or been prematurely terminated. In addition, the increasing complexity of our society and of our patients' lives causes many occasions when, except for the telephone, sessions would be truncated or missed entirely because of unforeseeable difficulties.

DEVELOPMENT OF THE MODALITY

In 1964, at the urgent suggestion of a patient, I started experimenting with this modality. My patient, a vivacious, sensitive man with a Ph.D. from a prestigious university, had been in analysis with me for three years when his career as a rock-and-roll singer took off. Suddenly he was "hot," which meant many one-night stands, and he often did not know which of the fifty states he was in. In part, this confusion was because of his routine: flying into the cities where he was to perform, staying in almost identical hotels, and being sheltered and rushed around by limousines from the hotel to the auditorium and then back to the hotel. He was further confused because of his heavy use of drugs, his acting out with the faceless groupies who pleaded for sexual contact with him, and other aspects of a frenetic, fast-lane lifestyle. He knew he was in trouble, and when he was in town between engagements he persuaded me to try telephone sessions. I agreed because his reasons made sense and because he and I both feared his psychotic disintegration.

Looking back now, I think it is fortunate for the development of psychoanalysis that patients continue to educate their analysts as they have done since the time of Freud's first patient, who essentially told him to dispense with his hypnotic suggestions and just listen to her. My patient and I agreed to schedule regular sessions, and he would telephone at the appointed times after clearing the room of hangers-on and sycophants. I entered into this arrangement with open but benign skepticism and at first thought I would do only supportive therapy via the telephone, but when the patient presented material that I thought I understood, I cautiously began to interpret it. (I made interpretations in part because at that time I believed that when a patient presents material clearly enough for the analyst to understand, it indicates that the patient is ready for the interpretation. Also, I have always believed that a therapist can be most supportive and helpful to a very anxious patient by interpreting the underlying causes of the anxiety, thereby reducing or relieving it. Just naming the unnameable terror reduces anxiety.)

The patient was in town only about one week per month, and we conducted telephone sessions when he was away. After several months, the work we were doing by phone, including analyzing his dreams, seemed to be as effective and analytic as the work we did in the office. (At that time, 1964, I was not aware of Saul's 1951 "A Note on the Telephone as a Technical Aid"; it was yet the only reference in the literature.) At this time, I did not have the experience to determine whether the patient's positive response resulted from the pressure of his fragmenting anxiety or whether this unique approach might be effective for other patients. However, after considerable experience with this method with numerous patients, I have been surprised at how easily the psychoanalytic work can be continued using the telephone *if the analyst continues the mode of analytic listening*. Analysis by telephone is analogous to seeing the patient face to face; that mode of relating can lead to diluting the analysis or to treatments other than psychoanalysis; but whether the patient is sitting up or lying down need not determine whether it is psychoanalysis or not, if the analyst sets the tone by continuing to listen to the material and to respond as a working psychoanalyst.

Several years ago, a patient who had been in analysis with me for one year suddenly learned that his work would require him to travel to various cities on the East Coast. After considering whether to transfer him to an analyst in one of those cities, we decided to continue the analysis on his regular schedule by telephone when he was out of town. When he returned, he came to the office for his regular sessions four times a week. This arrangement continued for a year or so, but gradually his work required him to be away most of the time. Consequently, for almost five years our only contact was our regularly scheduled telephone sessions. Two years ago he returned for a week. During the sessions that week, I paid particular attention to his reactions and mine, and I noticed that each of us greeted the other warmly. I was glad to see him in person, and he reported his pleasure at seeing me. He noted that it was as if he were reinforcing his visual memory of me, concentrating in particular on details of my physical appearance.

I paid close attention to the patient's dreams and other analytic transactions. As far as I could determine, the analytic sessions prior to his visit (when we both knew he was coming), during the week he was here, and after his departure seemed indistinguishable (except, of course, for the visual aspects). Some months later I learned from my patient that he had also been curious about whether the in-person sessions would be different from the telephone sessions and had also found them indistinguishable.

Recognizing that I could be missing some differences between the two modalities, I presented detailed process notes to various study groups without mentioning that the psychoanalytic sessions were conducted by telephone. The microscopic analysis of the notes did not lead any of the participants in the study groups to detect anything unusual.

For some years, I have recommended psychoanalysis by telephone to colleagues, and their feedback indicates that they, too, have found psychoanalysis can continue by telephone. Some years ago, a colleague whose analysand was worried about coordinating her analytic appointments with a new job tried conducting some sessions by telephone before it became geographically necessary. He reported that despite his patient's initial doubts, she expressed surprise at how easy it was. In fact, this sensitive analyst reported that adjusting to the new procedure was more difficult for him than for his patient. They now conduct four in-person sessions and one telephone session each week, and the telephone session seems as productive and analytic as the others.

When one knows in advance that there will be some interference with appointments, I recommend a trial period with some telephone and some in-person appointments so that both parties have the opportunity to test the new method. Patient and analyst can then explore the patient's subjective experience of the phone sessions and their transference meanings during the in-person analytic sessions. In a conversation with Joseph Sandler (personal communication 1983), I asked about his arrangements while traveling between London and Israel when he was Sigmund Freud Professor of Psychoanalysis in Jerusalem. Our experiences were remarkably similar, including our insistence on having speaker phones.

CHARACTERISTICS OF TELEPHONE SESSIONS

Telephone sessions, of course, deprive the analyst of visual, olfactory, and tactile clues. The therapist cannot see the patient's face, posture, clothing, or movements. I have found that patients are fully aware of this situation, and the co-operative patient reports physical responses that I have no way of knowing. One patient told me, "Tears are rolling down my cheeks"—she knew her voice gave no clues to that response. Another patient said, "You know, I suddenly became aware that after I told you that dream, I started clenching my fists." We then explored the implications of that gesture. Another patient advised me of his nervous reaction to a particular subject; he had become aware that he was drumming his fingers on the chair, something he did only when he was quite anxious.

Theoretically, the telephone could be used by patients to distance themselves from the analyst and the fears associated with closeness. One colleague who, at my suggestion, used the telephone to continue analysis for a year with a patient who was out of town reported that when his patient returned, she experienced her fears of her erotic feelings toward him more intensely than she did during the phone sessions. This analyst thought it would be difficult to fully engage the patient's fears of intimacy with a man via phone sessions; her fears might be worked through with other men, but not necessarily in the transference, when only the phone was used.

This is what I had anticipated when I started—that all transference fantasies with intense affects such as love, direct sexual feelings, shame, anger, murderous hatred, guilt, and humiliation would be diluted or "distanced out" of the analysis. Of course, the phone can be used by the patient for distancing or diluting *but so can anything else, including reporting dreams or free associations* (Lindon et al. 1972). However, I have not found that the telephone sessions *automatically* lead to being used as a distancing mechanism. Patients who are working well make use of what is available to bring the material into the transference, including strong affects. For example, when I asked my East Coast patient to repeat a statement during a telephone session, he reacted with annoyance. Why hadn't I heard it the first time? Suddenly he was filled with intense anger, disgust, and contempt toward me. Exploration revealed that the transference had shifted and the patient was experiencing me as he had experienced his father, as the incompetent shell-of-a-man who could never understand him. Other patients have experienced such strong anger that they reported wanting to physically "deck" me or "beat the shit out of" me. At times, the patients and I have thought that the emergence of such intense affects was facilitated by the phone and the physical separation.

One patient who had taken a summer home wanted to continue his analysis, although it meant driving two and a half hours each way; he was certain analysis by telephone could not work for him. I made clear the choice was his, but suggested that he try it once before committing himself to five hours of driving a day, especially since he was going away to have time for writing his novel. He reluctantly agreed, "although I feel certain that I will not even be able to relate to you on the telephone." He and I were both astonished at the results. During the five years of analysis with me and his four years earlier with another analyst, this analytically sophisticated man had experienced a transference neurosis manifested as "absolutely no transference" to me or to his previous analyst. Therefore we were both surprised when, from the first telephone session on, he reported various transference experiences involving me. We found that in his case the physical separation made it easier for him to experience strong, intimate feelings toward me without the fear of being engulfed and enslaved as was his childhood experience with his mother.

It takes time for both patient and analyst to accommodate to this new modality. Interestingly, in my experience and that of many others whom I have recommended this method to, the analyst initially seems more ill at ease than the patient. For example, it is common for analysts to talk more during the first few phone sessions than they would in the office. For a time, analysts tend not to allow the same amount of silence as they would with patients in the office. However, as analysts gain experience, they feel more at ease. For example, with my East Coast patient, there have been periods of absolute silence lasting four to five minutes—a long time when all sensory input has been cut off. During this time, both the patient and I have felt quite at ease. This patient's report of his experience of the silence reminded me of Winnicott's (1958) paper, "The Capacity to Be Alone"; my patient was experiencing what he had missed genetically: the capacity to be alone with the silent-but-holding-environment presence of the mother. All this occurred by phone, with 3,000 miles between us.

PRACTICAL CONSIDERATIONS

In almost all instances, I let the patient call me at the prearranged times so that the patient can choose to be late, in much the same way as if coming in person. Sometimes a patient wants to change the appointment time, which I do if I can, just as I would with an in-person psychoanalytic patient.

The patient needs encouragement to try analysis by phone, and an analyst who is willing to try it. Patients must have access to telephones where they will not be overheard. On rare occasions when something has interfered with a patient's privacy, the session has become superficial and chatty or ended prematurely.

I have found a speaker phone almost indispensable for the analyst because the ambience becomes much the same as when the patient is in the office. Of course the analyst needs a quiet and private area, too. When I am away on vacation and need to conduct an emergency session, I can work with a regular phone, but I strongly urge analysts to use a speaker phone when conducting a serious trial of the telephone-analysis process.

ADVANTAGES AND DISADVANTAGES
OF PSYCHOANALYSIS BY TELEPHONE

Analysis by telephone can be useful for patients with geographical or other obstacles to regular appointments, those with unexpected interferences such as car trouble or a sick child, and those who are hospitalized or confined to bed. Analysis by telephone may be the only treatment option for some patients, such as borderline patients or severely regressed patients who refuse to come to an office because of paranoid fantasies or as a defense against a longed-for fusion with the analyst.

Some patients who would terminate analysis if they were required to come in to the office may be willing to continue analytic work by telephone. I had one such patient who absolutely refused to come in, or even to let me know where he was staying (he changed motels daily because of his fear of me), but he continued the analytic work by telephoning me each day at his appointment time. These telephone sessions continued for eight months until this revived transference psychosis was worked through.

Any difficulties one can have with a telephone (e.g., disconnections, crossed wires, static) can occur during the phone sessions; fortunately, they happen infrequently. In a profession where the analyst, too, must endure abstinence, the patient's physical absence is further deprivation. I recognized the intensity of this emotion with the patient I had not seen during three years of telephone sessions. When I heard he was to be in town for a week, I experienced much anticipatory excitement and pleasure. I had missed seeing him more than I realized. I felt some sadness and loss at the end of that week because we were already approaching the termination phase of his analysis and I did not know when I might see him again.

Given the option, I cannot imagine electing to work by telephone because of my own needs and because I have so much more experience with in-person psychoanalysis. However, psychoanalysis by telephone is a valuable second-best method when the best method, for whatever reason, is not available. I could not conceive of working *only* by telephone, without having first physically met the patient. Yet, even as I was writing this paper, I could imagine being contacted by telephone by a complete stranger who had heard that I work this way, and *if*, via the telephone, that person were able to engage my interest, I wonder if perhaps I might be willing to try it as a research experiment.

REFERENCES

Chiles, J. A. (1974). A practical therapeutic use of the telephone. *American Journal of Psychiatry* 131:1030–1031.

Freud, S. (1912). Recommendations to physicians practising psycho-analysis. *Standard Edition* 12:111–120.

Grumet, G. W. (1979). Telephone therapy: a review and case report. *American Journal of Orthopsychiatry* 49:574–584.

Lindon, J. A., Lewin, B. D., Balint, M., et. al. (1972). Supervision by tape: a new method of case supervision. *Psychoanalytic Forum* 4:399–452.

Miller, W. B. (1973). The telephone in outpatient psychotherapy. *American Journal of Pschotherapy* 27:15–26.

Robertiello, R. C. (1972–1973). Telephone sessions. *Psychoanalytic Review* 59:633–634.

Rosenbaum, M. (1974). Continuation of psychotherapy by "long-distance" telephone. *International Journal of Psychoanalytic Psychotherapy* 3:483–495.

———. (1977). Premature interruption of psychotherapy: continuation of contact by telephone and correspondence. *American Journal of Psychiatry* 134:200–202.

Saul, L. J. (1951). A note on the telephone as a technical aid. *Psychoanalytic Quarterly* 20:287–290.

Winnicott, D. W. (1958). The capacity to be alone. *International Journal of Psycho-Analysis* 39:416–420.

2

Telephone Analysis

SHARON ZALUSKY

THE TELEPHONE IN CLINICAL PRACTICE

For most analysts in private practice the telephone is often the first introduction to their patients. It is the beginning of the assessment process. Before patient and analyst ever meet, the potential for a therapeutic relationship is already being considered. Each party is responding to the other's voice, verbal demeanor, and ease at establishing an appointment time. Initial transference–countertransference reactions and enactments are set into motion. Both analyst and patient hypothesize consciously and unconsciously about the availability of the other to engage. All this happens prior to either party's laying eyes on the other. Information gained on the telephone is then used to facilitate the initial face-to-face encounter. We take all this for granted. We even rely on it.

The telephone has long been accepted outside analytic circles as an important therapeutic tool in its own right. Its use in crisis intervention, suicide prevention, and community hot lines is well documented (Brockropp 1976). It has been discussed in the literature as an emotional safety valve. The telephone has also been considered in treatment with severely anxious, regressed, and unstable individuals who find therapy in person too threatening (Grumet 1979). It has been found to be effective with adolescents who would not ordinarily come in for treatment (Zalusky 1988).

Apart from a few notable exceptions (Lindon 1988, Robertiello 1972, Saul 1954), use of the telephone in psychoanalysis has not been discussed as a viable treatment option. As analysts, our attitudes about the telephone in clinical practice are often quite complicated. We each have a private, if not public, position on use of the telephone and its limitations. Some analysts encourage telephone calls between sessions, others accept them, and some refuse all telephone contact except for scheduling purposes. Each analyst, if asked, presumably has a considered theoretical rationale for use of the telephone as an auxiliary analytic function between sessions. The same analyst, however, may be more conflicted about its use for entire sessions at times when either patient or analyst cannot physically attend because of illness, is away on prolonged business trips, is unable to come into the office during or after pregnancy, or has moved and wishes to continue the analysis.

The use of the telephone in clinical practice evokes many feelings and raises a number of important issues, for both patient and analyst, which have not adequately been addressed in the literature.

Privately one hears, in an almost matter-of-fact way, "I can't talk to you now. I'm about to have a phone session with a patient." However, that seems to be the extent to which this matter is ever discussed. It is as if telephone sessions may be revealed only to one's closest friends and colleagues. The subject of the telephone in analytic practice is not brought up in seminars and is rarely ever written about in case studies. One can easily get the impression from its absence in discussion that telephone work does not exist except in the rarest of circumstances. My experience with colleagues, however, suggests otherwise. Use of the telephone in psychoanalysis, though certainly not an everyday occurrence, does take place far more than the literature would suggest.[1]

Those who do write about the telephone in psychoanalysis portray its use in a primarily positive light, while neglecting its more problematic aspects. Both Saul (1954) and Robertiello (1972) report using the telephone as a technical aid in actual psychoanalyses with patients whose intense regressed transferences precluded productive analytic work during sessions. Both believe that without its use analytic work would have been terminated. Lindon (1988) records the most extensive use of psychoanalysis by telephone. His experience spans over twenty years. Lindon reports that most of his patients who were analyzed by telephone chose that option because their work made it impossible or impractical for them to come for sessions in his office. Without use of the telephone, these analyses would have to have been disrupted, transferred, or terminated.

Like most who write about psychoanalysis or psychotherapy by telephone, Lindon was surprised how easily analytic work could proceed over the telephone as long as the analyst perseveres in the mode of analytic listening. In many cases Lindon believes the analytic material is indistinguishable from an analysis taking place in his office. He reports recommending psychoanalysis by telephone to colleagues who con-

---

1. Though I did not conduct a formal survey, I presented a draft of this chapter at the American Psychoanalytic Association's fall meeting in 1996 and at various local societies. During these presentations, analysts in the audience related their own personal experience conducting intensive analytic treatments over the telephone. It seems to me that the more one talks about telephone analysis, the more one hears about its practice.

curred that analysis can continue by telephone. He states that often it is more difficult for analysts to adjust than it is for analysands. Though he does not elaborate why that may be the case, it is my hypothesis that the analyst's unanalyzed loyalty to past traditions may continue, at least initially, to exert its influence.

Building on Lindon's work, I will attempt to explore the complexities and paradoxes involved when analysis is conducted with only data from the verbal realm available. I agree with Lindon that it is often impossible, given verbal transcripts of sessions, to differentiate a telephone analysis from one occurring in the office. However, that does not mean that the two experiences are the same for the participants. There are essential differences and unique challenges, each deserving of consideration.

I start with the premise that telephone analysis most often represents a therapeutic compromise. Rarely, if ever, is it the treatment plan of choice. In fact, more frequently than not, patients who leave town interrupt the treatment, terminate, or transfer to another analyst and the question of continuing the analysis by telephone is never actually considered. I also recognize there are some analysands and some analysts for whom psychoanalysis by telephone may represent a resistance to experiencing the emotions created by absences. Under these circumstances such a form of treatment may not be well advised. However, it is my belief that there exists a group of patients who may be in a particularly sensitive and transitional phase of an analysis where a continuation of the analysis on the telephone may very well be the best treatment available at that time. Not to offer or to at least explore a modified continuation of the analysis by telephone may at times amount to a transference–countertransference enactment.

I choose to emphasize the essentially conflictual nature of telephone analysis, not because I am opposed to this therapeutic modality, but because I believe that by recognizing its inherent complexities we can add to its potential effectiveness. It is my belief that embedded in the communications of both analyst and analysand is often a recognition, conscious or unconscious, of what each gains and loses by doing the analysis by telephone. I hope to show that transference–countertransference feelings evoked by the differences, when analyzed, often yield insight into the internal world of the analysand.

Below I present a case of telephone analysis. This patient had been repeatedly traumatized, throughout both childhood and adulthood, by emotionally unavailable parents. I hope to show that a continuation of treatment on the telephone represented a needed holding environment. The ability to maintain consistent emotional contact with the same analyst, rather than interrupting or terminating treatment, created an analytic space where the patient's transference could be analyzed and worked through. The work on the telephone helped the analysand develop greater object constancy, which has had a beneficial impact on her developing sense of self.

CASE STUDY

I offer the case of Annie. Because the telephone and all the fantasies evoked by its use often became the central focus of this analysis, our work together offers a unique opportunity to examine in depth some of the basic issues surrounding telephone analysis.

The decision to continue her psychoanalysis by telephone was not an easy one to make. It evolved over time. I will present material from four different periods to illustrate (1) the poignancy of our initial telephone contact, (2) the conflicts associated with the decision to continue psychoanalysis by telephone, (3) the complexities and paradoxes of telephone work, and (4) the termination phase.

Throughout there was a continuous interplay between the real logistical considerations in doing psychoanalysis by telephone, our transference–countertransference resistances, and the unconscious meanings attributed to them. We grappled with many of the implications, both positive and negative, of this form of treatment.

Our task was facilitated by the unique attributes that this particular analysand brought to the work. Annie was a child of divorce, and thus was used to telephone communication with one parent or another. She had a highly developed verbal self, which was coupled with an unusual sense of openness and trust. She was committed to the analytic process and devoted to understanding her unconscious.

The Poignancy of the First Telephone Contact

Annie, 41, was a bright, energetic, enthusiastic African American woman who came to treatment before breaking up with her boyfriend of many years. During our first session, which took place the day after our first telephone contact, Annie reported the following dream:

> I am at the seaside. I dive into the water and deep underneath there is a box that I bring to the surface. I look inside. There is this weird frightening creature. I want to close the box. Then I see this woman who is a marine biologist. I take it to her. She isn't frightened by what she

sees. She tells me, "I'll help you look inside. You don't have to be frightened of it either." She seemed curious about its nature. Next, I'm with her and my family and we are in the desert. Off in the distance is this miniature house which I recognize as my house from childhood. It's not entirely constructed. We all go together to take a look.

I present this dream to underline, from a psychoanalytic perspective, the poignancy of our first telephone encounter. Prior to having ever set eyes on each other, Annie and I were already beginning to respond to each other's tone of voice, choice of words, and general level of responsivity. Reassessing this initial dream, with the benefit of our having worked together for many years, I suspect that during our brief telephone conversation prior to our meeting, I must have responded to Annie's distress in such a way that allowed her to know that she could create me as a guide to take her on an analytic journey into the depths of her unconscious and back to her childhood in order to finish the "construction of her house." Transference–countertransference fantasies were being stimulated in anticipation of our first session. Presumably, a sense of hopefulness arose from the telephone contact and linked up with Annie's need for a caring maternal figure, thereby generating the dream. In like manner, our initial contact must have encouraged in me a certain receptivity to be the guide for whom she was searching. Verbal contact alone was a powerful medium that activated these fantasies.

In our first session together, we both knew that her dream had significance, and we have repeatedly returned to it. What we were unaware of at the time was that our way of verbally relating to each other might already have been predictive of our ability to conduct a psychoanalysis by telephone.

The Decision to Do Psychoanalysis by Telephone

Through the analysis, Annie became aware of her needs and desires. She discovered a personal passion—a career she wished to pursue. With the same intensity and dedication she employed in the analysis, she prepared herself to apply for graduate school in a field in which she had no prior experience. Through sheer perseverance, she prevailed much sooner than either of us would have predicted and was accepted into a prestigious university in another city, long before her analysis could be completed.

The possibility of this important, perhaps monumental, change created in Annie a state of intense conflict. Within three months she would have to leave a job, a home she had created for herself, and an analyst to whom she was deeply attached. This was particularly problematic for Annie, given an early and repeated history of emotional deprivation and loss, which manifested itself early on in the transference by an acute and continuous sensitivity to my presence and availability. As she prepared to leave, memories of a repetitive childhood nightmare of being left in the care of a phantom returned. These memories were reminiscent of the opening phase of her analysis, when she could barely count on my physical presence. During that time, at the end of each session Annie would take out her date book and reconfirm the next day's appointment with me. When this pattern was explored, we discovered that she was afraid that if she did not actively remind me of her sessions day by day, I might not remember to come. Deeper still, Annie feared I might not remember that she existed.

After many years of intensive work, it was no wonder that Annie experienced her acceptance into graduate school as a mixed blessing. It represented a tremendous sense of fulfillment and personal growth. However, it also meant that she would have to leave her analysis. Together we analyzed the meaning of her early termination. I paid a great deal of attention to my countertransference feeling of pride in her achievement. I wondered whether I was reenacting an old family theme of hers, overglorifying her academic accomplishment, while insufficiently weighing the emotional toll it might take.

We examined what going to graduate school meant to her and what it meant in the transference. But in the end Annie was convinced that she had finally found a career that resonated with her view of herself. The opportunity was too great to miss. If it proved to be the wrong decision, it would not be irreparable and she could return. We both, however, recognized that she was in the middle of an analytic journey. We were confident that one day she would continue her analysis, either with me or with a new analyst. At that time neither of us considered psychoanalysis by telephone—it was not an option.

As the move became imminent, Annie's anxiety mounted, bringing forth childhood memories of repeated location changes. With each change, she remembered, both she and her mother had withdrawn deeper and deeper into a depression, but one that was masked and never discussed.

As her excitement shifted to fear, Annie asked if we could have twice-a-week telephone sessions while she traveled to her new destination. She told me that she did not want to submerge her feelings this time. She wanted to do something different. She wanted to stay connected to me. Hesitantly, without time to analyze in depth the meaning of telephone contact, I agreed, but only as a transitional phase. I told her I had my concerns. Because I had never done telephone sessions, I wondered whether I would be able to maintain a sustained connection over the telephone. I knew how much she relied on my emotional availability and how sensitive she was to any deviation from the optimal. I told her I did not want to re-create the phantom of her childhood nightmare. However, I did not want to abandon her either. Having considered the options, we both agreed to give it a try, recognizing that she might be disappointed.

In an ideal analytic world we would have had the opportunity to either terminate our work in a more timely fashion or to analyze in depth what her request meant.[2] Unfortunately, that is not always possible. Today, because analyses spread over many years, life intervenes in our work. Actors get roles. People become ill. Pregnant women have complications that require immediate and prolonged bed rest. Spouses need to move for business purposes. People lose their jobs and need to relocate. As analysts, we must take the patient's needs into account. Sometimes we must offer creative solutions to such exigencies. And that is what I tried to do.

We worked out a schedule where she would call me twice a week at a regular appointment time. Very shortly it became clear that Lindon (1988) was right. The tone of our sessions was almost indistinguishable from our previous work. Her transference to me did not disappear because we were talking on the telephone. Instead, ironically, I was more present to hear the nuances of her associations. Because I had no visual interference, I could more easily follow Freud's recommendation (1912) to turn my "own unconscious like a receptive organ towards the transmitting unconscious of the patient"

---

2. Now that I accept a continuation of psychoanalysis by telephone as part of my therapeutic repertoire, I am sure that today I would have handled her short termination phase in a different manner. The possibility of continuing our work on the telephone would have been discussed much sooner. But at that time we were forging new ground.

(pp. 115–116). Interestingly, it is in this very passage that Freud uses the metaphor of the telephone: "He [the analyst] must adjust himself to the patient as a telephone receiver is adjusted to the transmitting microphone" (p. 116).

With only my auditory sense available, I was able to hear her differently. Annie's basic good nature, her enthusiasm, and her delight to be in the room with me could no longer mask the depth of her pain, her loneliness, and her depressed affect. The telephone tended to facilitate unconscious-to-unconscious communication. Annie, too, became more sensitive to my moods and commented on changes in the tone of my voice, longer or shorter periods of silences, and the like. We were able then to explore what these shifts meant to her. Through these telephone sessions we were refining our level of attunement to each other. It was surprising how easily affect was transmitted through the telephone lines.

In fact, I have found some other advantages to doing work over the telephone. Like Freud (1913), who felt the couch freed him from the gaze of patients, I too was at liberty to walk around my office with my phone. I suffer from a back problem and while sitting all day am always faintly aware of my pain. Paradoxically, walking around, I was more able to be there with her. I also felt a greater responsibility to be present. If all I had to give her in that regard was my mental attention (without my physical presence), I quickly became aware when my mind would wander and would analyze my countertransference. Our analytic work was indeed continuing. Annie was still associating and I was still analyzing.

However, I began to notice something curious. Though we both valued our sessions on the telephone, neither of us had broached the topic of formally continuing, by telephone, the four-day-a-week analysis. I began to question why I was not offering her a continuation of a treatment from which she had greatly benefited and why Annie was not asking for it. It was clear that she wanted more and more telephone contact between sessions, but not sessions themselves. I wondered: Were we in the midst of a particular transference–countertransference enactment, was there something about telephone analysis itself that we were both resisting, or were the two somehow inseparable at this moment?

At first I attempted to examine my countertransference. The predominant affect I was defending against seemed to be guilt. It was, however, complex. On the most superficial level my guilt seemed to be about violating some unspoken analytic rule: you do not analyze by telephone—you transfer. I wondered what my colleagues would think. Would they assume it was I who was encouraging Annie to stay tied to me in a regressed, dependent way? In fact, Annie would often raise that possibility herself, but she did so hoping that I would need her as much as she needed me. But was there truth to it? Or was that concern part of a complex transference–countertransference paradigm that prevented me from offering her what she could not ask for herself?

I thought at times I should try harder to get her to transfer to a local analyst. When I would bring up the possibility, Annie would tell me how disruptive that would be. As we continued to investigate her feelings, she spoke of how much she had already lost: her friends, the home she had created, the consistency of her daily life. She would tell me that she could not bear to lose me too, not now. If she saw another analyst, she said, all she would talk about would be her loss of me, and what she needed was help dealing with everything else going on in her life. Annie explained that she did not need just any analyst to be there with her; she needed her own trusted analyst. Analysts were not like goldfish. She insisted that now was not the right time. I sensed she was right. Transferring patients in the best of circumstances is often complicated. But in this particular case, where there had not been an adequate termination phase, I felt ending the treatment would be experienced as if I were abandoning her just as she began to experience her own autonomy. To transfer her because I felt guilty about transgressing some abstract analytic norm would have been an enactment on my part.

Though I knew she needed more than twice-a-week therapy, I still did not suggest increasing our telephone sessions. I continued to examine my own resistance. Doing so, I realized I felt guilty for other reasons—reasons I considered purer. Would I not be depriving her of a full analytic experience? Because I recognized and valued the importance of the nonverbal aspects of analysis, I knew we would be missing a very essential component of our work.

I raise the issue of my guilt because I believe I am not alone in having these feelings in relation to telephone work. Otherwise I suspect that we, as analysts, would be more open to talk with our colleagues about a phenomenon that is not altogether rare. I think most analysts who consider telephone work must contend with the guilt of depriving the patient of visual contact and many of the routines that have become a part of analytic work. There is something comforting and reassuring for analysands in knowing that the analyst is behind them, literally seeing them through the difficult process. There is the routine of carving out a special time each day for oneself, of traveling to the office, waiting in the waiting room, settling into the couch, and then getting oneself together to leave. All this is lost in a telephone analysis.

As analysts, we are used to providing a safe environment, both physically and emotionally, for our patients. But during telephone analysis we must rely on our analysands to provide this for themselves, and sometimes they may have difficulty doing so. In addition, our contact, though still vital and important, is nonetheless indirect. We are dependent on technology. Our voices first need to travel through cables or optic fibers. These are not insignificant concerns.

Analysts who portray telephone analysis as almost indistinguishable from analysis in the office may also be defending against feelings of depriving their patients. When we call the work indistinguishable, it seems we are reassuring ourselves. There is no way around the fact that we offer a compromise when we do telephone analysis. If we are not open to that fact, it will be difficult to analyze the meaning of that compromise to our patients, and the feelings it stirs up. I believe that the fact that we are making compromises or accommodations is not as deleterious to the analysis as the denial that we are doing so would be. Accommodations at the right moments are a part of any healthy relationship. They are unavoidable. Not to be able to adapt to special needs is a form of rigidity. It is a way of elevating principle over context.

As I became clearer in what was blocking me from offering an analysis by telephone, I began to realize that my ambivalence was perhaps depriving my patient of something more profound—the possibility of what for her was the best treatment possible at this particular time. In many ways the situation is not that dissimilar from what children and parents of divorce must contend with. Annie may not have had me in full sight, but I was still there as an emotionally available person who was not abandoning her during her difficult and stressful journey. We would both have to learn to be there for her in new and different ways in order to help her continue to grow

(Zalusky 1995). In retrospect I recognize the fact that while I was there struggling alongside her, trying to decide what was right for her and for me, we were creating a new experience that contradicted Annie's old transference belief that neither she nor her needs would be considered.

Now that I had shifted internally, I was free to help her analyze what was behind her resistance to psychoanalysis by telephone. We both could "see" that she did much better when she was in contact with me four days a week, even if two of the calls were just to touch base between sessions. I think it is important to clarify that it is not only the number of days a week that makes a treatment an analysis. Analysis is about analyzing transference, countertransference, and resistance. In Annie's case, she needed the consistency of four days a week to create a safe holding environment in order for us to do the work of analysis.

As we explored her resistance to increasing the number of telephone sessions, the following emerged. Annie feared that her family would interpret her attachment to me as disloyalty to them. As she was a child of divorce, the transference implication was clear. She also feared that they might view her dependency on me as a sign of weakness and so be disappointed in her. Annie then began to acknowledge that not only her family but she too was disappointed in herself for not being able to function as well as she wished without consistent contact. If guilt is the affect with which the analyst is struggling, its corresponding emotion in the patient may very well be shame over continuing dependence on the analyst.

I interpreted to Annie that it may seem threatening to her to acknowledge her own needs when they seemed to diminish her in the eyes of those on whom she relied. She denied her needs even to herself in order to maintain a sense of safety within her family, but she was suffering. It became clearer that we were both involved in an elaborate transference–counter-transference enactment. Because of my own unanalyzed guilt, I was colluding with her in her denial of her own needs. I was like her parents, who did not want to see the extent to which their divorce (like my absences) caused her pain and disorganization. Unable to acknowledge this, they failed to provide her the help she needed. By talking to her two days a week instead of four, I was reenacting her experience of her mother's moving emotionally farther and farther away.

Certain that her move had triggered a regression, I still did not see her wish to stay attached to me as a sign of pathological dependency. She simply needed to feel the consistency of our established relationship to help her through an important life transition. We both recognized that it was because of the considerable work Annie had done in the analysis that she was able to push ahead with her life and take on new risks.

Once four-day-a-week analysis was resumed by telephone, our work deepened. We were able to deal with issues surrounding her parents' divorce, which heretofore we had discussed only intellectually, in an affectively charged way. The telephone itself took on new meaning. Annie could remember the many intimate moments she had spent with her father on the telephone. We were beginning to deal with what it felt like not to have her father physically present. She described how she had experienced his moving out as a tremendous loss, as it was with him that she felt most alive. After the divorce, Annie remembered feeling dead inside. She remembered pictures she had drawn at that time of a little girl peering into and out of a coffin. It was only through her analysis that it was becoming clear how little stability there had been in her life, and how she had

had no one to help her appreciate what suffering she had endured because of it.

Our work on the telephone seemed to represent a powerful holding environment for her. No matter where Annie was, even in a distant city, she could always maintain connectedness to an emotionally present person, her analyst. Our contact on the telephone paradoxically enhanced her belief in my availability, which corresponded to what seemed an increasing sense of object constancy. The contact had an impact on Annie's sense of self, and she became increasingly more resilient.

Regardless of Annie's improvement, however, I wondered whether we might not at times be involved in a folie à deux, in an attempt to deny our loss, or in the reenactment of an early childhood trauma. This is one of the things that makes telephone work difficult. As analysts, we inevitably face the question whether we are appropriately analyzing the material or simply colluding with the patient in the service of avoidance. In telephone analysis, however, this conflict has the potential for being omnipresent and may be experienced by either party. Because as analysts we want to offer the best treatment possible, the feelings evoked are not unlike the feelings of working mothers or divorced parents who are constantly balancing gains and losses.

The Complexities of Telephone Analysis

What is most interesting theoretically about work on the telephone is that in various ways it focuses and condenses such basic analytic issues as separation, loss, availability, the needs of both patient and analyst, and the analytic frame and deviations from it. The following brief vignette from my work with Annie sheds light on the paradoxes and complexities of telephone analysis in two areas: (1) the needs of the analyst and (2) the transference and its special significance in this modified form of treatment.

Recently, after a period of time during which Annie spent much of the analysis dealing with her intense longing to see me, wondering what I now looked like, and fantasizing about me, she told me that she was going to visit a friend in a city not very far from Los Angeles, but made no mention of wanting a session in person. A bit surprised at this, I found myself unable to explore this contradiction with her. I knew us both well enough to understand, by the way I felt blocked, that we were involved in a transference–countertransference enactment. Embedded in it was the usual interplay between her dynamics and mine, as well as realistic logistical considerations regarding telephone analysis.

The issue of acknowledging needs had always been a focal part of Annie's analytic work. As I began to unravel this issue, however, I realized that I was having difficulty exploring it with her, as I did not want to impose my needs on her. I tried to play with the idea, asking myself what it would mean if I wanted to see Annie and she had no need to see me. Beyond the personal meanings, it would raise an interesting technical consideration in doing telephone analysis. Could it ever be a necessary consideration that the analyst may need to have sessions in person, even if the analysand does not? I imagine it is possible. As analysts we often have needs that are gratified (Renik 1993), but usually they have been integrated into the formality of analysis itself: a need to be helpful, a need for a consistent schedule, for a certain fee that is paid on time, and so forth. As analysts, we rarely think about them. We accept these needs as part of the frame. But in telephone analysis the need to see the patient would have to be openly acknowledged for what it is. Ordinarily, we interpret to the patient that coming to sessions is for the benefit of the patient, but here, paradoxically, it may be a necessary condition for the analyst to be able to continue the work.

Bacal and Thomson (1998) offer a convincing rationale for accepting this as a potential condition when they speak of the analyst's need for optimal responsiveness by the analysand. They contend that the notion of reciprocal sustenance is at the core of any viable therapeutic process. Once I could accept this possible need of mine to see her as legitimate, I was able to wonder out loud about the transference implication of Annie's making no mention of coming for an office visit. It freed me to explore her needs. As we examined her feelings about her upcoming visit to California, layers of meaning were discovered. The first was her conscious anxiety that she would have to see too many people in too short a period. But just beneath the surface was her fear of seeing me. Annie described feelings she had had during a previous visit. In fantasy, she explained, "we are always extremely close. Then when I see you, you are different from the person who is on the telephone with me. There is, paradoxically, an intimacy of physicality on the telephone. I don't mean sexual, but a profound personal sense of closeness. We are like wallpaper on the wall, familiar, when we talk without seeing each other. But then I see you and you don't look like you, the perfect you I have created." Our office sessions would stir up a hunger, a longing, a knowledge that Annie could not see me when she wanted. She would feel like she was missing out. Annie finally revealed that she was afraid of feeling greedy because she truly wanted to see me all the time. That evening, after our telephone session, she dreamt that she was having sex with a woman. The erotic components were analyzed, along with the sexualization of hunger for contact.

I introduce this material because it speaks to the complexity of the transference. Telephone analysis can at times serve to intensify rather than dilute the transference, as has often been suggested it does. Naturally, before she moved away, Annie's hunger and longings had always been part of her analysis. Our work on the telephone, however, seemed to amplify her experience, giving her a vehicle to express these powerful feelings more directly. If, as Freud (1913) suggests, the couch induces a regression in which the analyst as a person does not interfere with development of the transference, then the telephone should be a vehicle par excellence in this regard.

However, over the telephone reality seems to play less of a role in mitigating the internal world of the analysand. Without the visual presence, the fantasy of the analyst may be untethered, lost in inner space. In a regular analysis, if an analysand should fantasize that his analyst is as sexy as Marilyn Monroe, he may not, as he arrives or leaves the session, be able to escape the fact that she looks more like Hillary Clinton. Again, if the same analysand should become enraged with his analyst, when he leaves the session he must notice at some level that his analyst continues to survive his attacks intact and may even have a smile on her face when he arrives for his next session. Such nonverbal perceptual knowledge may very well be essential to the resolution of the transference.

Transference, though intensified, may also be more hidden in telephone analysis, as we have no visual cues to alert us. Though some have implied that the erotic component of the transference may be diluted, it too has the potential to be intensified, yet concealed. Certain possibilities for acting out (e.g., coming to session drugged, naked, etc.) without the analyst's knowledge are also created.

The unique challenges posed by telephone analysis were not insurmountable, but I found that they required an adjustment in technique. It seemed to enrich the experience when I took a more active and inquisitive stance. When applicable, I asked more questions regarding possible transference implications. For example, I often actively inquired about Annie's setting. Where was she when we spoke? In what room of the house and under what conditions? Did she have fantasies about where I was or what I was doing? She often volunteered her fantasies regarding my setting. At times Annie dreamt that we were both in bed together in the dark, whispering in each other's ears. Once when I was particularly silent, she had the fantasy that I was distracted, browsing through a Victoria's Secret catalog. We used this information, as we would any other, to gain insight into important genetic material.

Without visual input I needed to rely more heavily than I ordinarily would on my own intuition or feelings. In doing so, I offered my interpretations in a spirit of collaboration. I found this helpful, and it has influenced my work in general. In addition, I discovered it was important that if Annie noticed something in my voice like sadness, after exploring her fantasies with her I would tell her, to the best of my ability, whether I was actually feeling as she had thought. I often added verbally the visual cues she could not see, and she tended to do the same. Annie would inform me, "I'm crying now. Tears are running down my cheeks. *You can't see me.*" Then she would begin to sob. Her pain, I learned, had more to do with my not being able to look at her than her not being able to see me.

Often when we talk about a lack of object constancy, we are referring to the analysand's inability to maintain a mental representation of the other. But it is my experience that patients frequently do hold on to an image of the analyst. The tremendous pain, however, comes from the analysand's belief that during separations the analyst ceases to remember that the patient exists. The result of such a fantasy is a sense of extreme isolation and at times fragmentation. Telephone work offers a unique opportunity both to elaborate on the fantasy that the analysand ceases to exist for me outside my gaze and, inadvertently, to create a corrective emotional experience. My analysand learned concretely that she continued to exist for me. She understood that though she was out of sight, she was not out of mind. There was something powerful about hearing my voice, visualizing me while I was physically not present which, I believe, aided in Annie's developing the ability to maintain a mental representation of a caring other.

The analysis continued for several years on the telephone. During that time Annie married, had a pregnancy fraught with complications, gave birth to beautiful twin boys, lost a parent, completed her qualifying exams, and, most important, grew to have confidence in her own self. As Annie grew more secure, she was able to experience anger in a direct way. Instead of retreating into fantasy, she learned to go after what she needed and wanted, and to recognize when she was disappointed.

Finally Annie began to talk about the possibility of terminating. She experienced the thought no longer as an abandonment, but rather as a sign that she had grown. Annie told me she knew that she had me inside her, which made the thought of separation possible. This time, however, we had the benefit of our prior experience and gave ourselves a year to do the work of termination. We agreed that during the year we would have intermittent office visits and that the last week of the analysis would take place in person in my office.

Termination

Termination in telephone analysis raises its own set of complications. As with most aspects of this unique form of treatment, if one were to read the verbal transcript, termination on the telephone might seem indistinguishable from a termination taking place in the office. Yet there are nuanced differences to keep in mind.

First, there is the added potential for premature termination over the telephone, especially if the analyst continues to be conflicted about telephone work. Premature termination can happen at any time during an analysis by telephone. For example, if an analyst experiences boredom, he or she may feel the telephone work is the problem and may encourage the analysand to transfer rather than exploring what that boredom means at that time with that particular analysand. The analysand, too, may at times want to terminate prematurely. The decision to change analysts or leave treatment altogether, though appearing to be a practical decision, may very well be in the service of resistance. Until we are comfortable with this form of treatment, we may need to remind ourselves of the obvious: these are communications that need to be understood first and not acted upon.

With Annie, however, premature termination was never an issue. Throughout the analysis her fantasy had been that she would never want to be independent of me. So it came as a surprise that initially I had more difficulty with the termination process on the telephone than Annie did. It seemed that she was dealing openly with her sadness, her fears, her loss, her pride, and her accomplishments. I, by contrast, had to keep reminding myself that this analysis was ending. It was not simply her fantasy that she was leaving. It was a reality.

Embedded in my problem with termination were Annie's and my usual transference–countertransference resistances. However, I was also certain that there was something about the use of the telephone that reinforced a sense of timelessness. Unlike office visits, which are reserved almost exclusively for time-limited professional endeavors, repeated and long telephone conversations are generally saved for friends and family, with whom there is no set termination point. The telephone crosses the boundaries of these intimate relationships. In general, I think there is something about telephone work that is more directly linked to the timelessness of the unconscious.

The telephone analysis terminated in my office as planned. Our scheduled office visits were an essential part of the termination process. They underlined for both of us the finality of the treatment. They were bittersweet, because they also reinforced our conviction that Annie was indeed stronger and ready to be on her own. During her last week, Annie gave me a gift she had made. I recognized it immediately. It came from her first dream—the box she had pulled from the sea.

Annie told me the box represented our work together. But now, unlike the situation in the dream, she was no longer frightened by its contents. Annie was happy to discuss her interpretations of the gift. In fact, that was her gift to me. She decorated the box with seashells, which had many meanings for her. Naturally, they reflected the sea, a metaphor for her unconscious, she explained. The shells also represented an outside, a skin that developed over the course of her analysis. Annie explained that when she came to treatment she had no protective shell. She used to walk around feeling exposed. But that was no longer the case. Annie then described the inside of the box and how she had debated whether or not to line it in velvet. She chose instead to leave it in natural wood to express that she, herself, was more natural, no longer needing to glorify her experience. She could accept who she was. Annie also told me she chose to leave the box unfinished to represent that, though the analysis was ending, she still saw herself as a work in progress.

During the final week she turned to me and asked, "How did you change by knowing me?" The way she asked the question signified her growth. It was not tentative. The tone of her voice implied a certainty that she was important to me. It represented a knowledge that no two people could go through something so powerful and not both be changed in the process. As I reflected to myself, I realized that she had helped me in my own process of individuation as an analyst. Because of her, I had allowed myself the freedom to try something new, to separate from my past traditions and prejudices in order to find a treatment that met her special needs. Annie had indeed had a profound impact on my development as an analyst and on me as a person (Kantrowitz 1996). We had both changed in the process.

Discussion

Though it is impossible on the basis of one case alone to make generalizations about the efficacy of telephone analysis, clearly for Annie it was an effective form of treatment. I believe it worked for a number of reasons. She had had a strong commitment to our work prior to leaving and had benefited considerably. In fact, without the analysis to that point, it is doubtful whether she would have felt secure enough to have moved forward with her life goals. Leaving represented progress, not defeat. It also, however, stirred up tremendous depressive anxiety.

Annie was then in a particular stage of her analysis. She was in a transitional phase, having moved from a preoedipal position toward one in which she was beginning to view herself as a separate person, an initiator of her own experience (Winnicott 1953). Initially, our work on the telephone served as an adaptive defense against separation anxiety. It allowed her a safe place in which to analyze the impact of her many traumatic losses, even as she was moving forward.

In addition, I believe Annie's treatment was successful because the work on the telephone was supplemented by occasional office visits. These visits served as an analytic frame. Fantasies were allowed to ripen without visual interference over the telephone until we would finally meet again in person. Transference distortions would then stand out in bas-relief, which made them easier to analyze. The unique interaction between our memories of each other, the anticipation of seeing each other again, and the actual office visits served to keep our analytic work grounded.

INDICATIONS FOR TELEPHONE ANALYSIS

Certainly most patients who leave an analysis rarely consider a continuation of treatment by telephone. However, for those who do, a commitment to the analytic process is the primary indicator. In assessing the viability of telephone analysis, it is essential first to consider the overall nature of the pre-telephone relationship. A sufficiently developed working alliance seems a necessary precondition for sustained analytic work to occur over the telephone. Second, the analysand's need for contact must be appraised. Undoubtedly there are some patients whose intense need for contact would preclude this form of treatment. For them, telephone analysis is likely to be experienced as too depriving. On the other extreme, telephone work would not be indicated for many analysands who have serious issues with intimacy. The risk here is pseudointimacy. This treatment modality could potentially reinforce the analysand's pathological defenses. On the other side, however, for these severely traumatized people it may allow a necessary space in which to begin to tackle the fears associated with intimacy.

It is also important to determine the reasons for leaving. Once it has been assessed that leaving is either necessary or promotes the analysand's well-being, it is important to appraise whether the continued relationship on the telephone will serve to advance the analytic work or whether it will be used for defensive purposes (e.g., as a magical defense to deny the loss). Obviously, the stage of the analysis at the time of leaving must be considered. It would be difficult to justify telephone analysis during the opening phase of an analysis, unless the person is moving to a remote area where there are no analysts. If that is the case, frequent office visits would be advised. Telephone analysis is highly suitable for many analysands whose intense or regressed transferences make it impossible to terminate or transfer without causing some degree of harm. It may also be extremely important to patients whose early life was characterized by inconsistent and emotionally unavailable caregivers. To have *one* special person witnessing one's life through disappointments and victories can be extremely meaningful.

Telephone sessions may be beneficial for people who travel often on business. It allows the work to continue more smoothly. Without this option, patients who have difficulty with self-regulation may find it difficult to maintain a connection either to the analyst or to themselves. In such cases, telephone sessions may serve as a safeguard to allow the analysis to continue. Finally, for patients who defend against their own dependency needs, the desire to have telephone sessions when traveling may be seen as an indicator that the work is progressing and the relationship with the analyst is deepening.

Obviously, telephone analysis is not without its problems. However, due to life's exigencies it may be the best treatment possible for a particular patient at a particular time in the treatment.

CONCLUSION

We are living in a changing and highly mobile culture. Often, if our analytic work is helping, patients will have options available to them that they had never dreamed possible. Under ordinary circumstances there often is sufficient time to terminate with a patient. But in the case described above, that was neither possible nor desirable. Having telephone analysis as a viable treatment alternative allowed my analysand to have a more adaptive and meaningful transition into a new phase of her life while being able to continue her analysis.

Annie's case raises many questions about telephone analysis. In the most fundamental way it pushes our notion of intimacy. When the psychoanalytic process is channeled exclusively through the verbal realm, it challenges us to rethink our familiar analytic concepts and to reformulate our technique.

Obviously, one chapter cannot address all of the issues such analyses raise. However, there is a font of information out there. Until now, those of us who do telephone work have been doing so in isolation, without benefit of discourse with our colleagues. By bringing this topic out into the open, we will be able to refine our technique and better assess the implications of this type of work.

REFERENCES

Bacal, H. A., and Thomson, P. G. (1998). The psychoanalyst's self-object needs and the effect of their frustration on the treatment: a new view of countertransference. In *Progress in Self Psychology*, ed. A. Goldberg, pp. 17–35. Hillsdale, NJ: Analytic Press.

Brockropp, G. W. (1976). *Crisis Intervention and Counseling by Telephone*, 2nd ed. Springfield, IL: Charles C Thomas.

Freud, S. (1912). Recommendations to physicians practising psycho-analysis *Standard Edition* 12:111–120.

———— (1913). On beginning the treatment. *Standard Edition* 12:123–144.

Grumet, G. W. (1979). Telephone therapy: a review and case report. *American Journal of Orthopsychiatry* 49:474–584.

Kantrowitz, J. L. (1996). *The Patient's Impact on the Analyst*. Hillsdale, NJ: Analytic Press.

Lindon, J. A. (1988). Psychoanalysis by telephone. *Bulletin of the Menninger Clinic* 52:521–528.

Renik, O. (1993). Analytic interaction: conceptualizing technique in light of the analyst's irreducible subjectivity. *Psychoanalytic Quarterly* 62:553–571.

Robertiello, R. C. (1972). Telephone sessions. *Psychoanalytic Review* 59:633–634.

Saul, L. J. (1954). A note on the telephone as a technical aid. *Psychoanalytic Quarterly* 20:287–290.

Winnicott, D. W. (1953). Transitional objects and transitional phenomena. *International Journal of Psycho-Analysis* 34:89–97.

Zalusky, S. (1988). Social responsibility and empathy in adolescent volunteers. Unpublished doctoral thesis, California School of Professional Psychology at Los Angeles.

———— (1995). Analyzability from an intersubjective perspective. Unpublished doctoral thesis, Southern California Psychoanalytic Institute.

3

Enhancement of the Therapeutic Process*

ROBERT H. SPIRO
LUANNA E. DEVENIS

*C*hange does not come easily to psychodynamic work, in spite of its commitment to scientific principles and self-exploration. At its best, psychodynamic psychotherapy is a system that demands intelligence, thoughtfulness, reflection, and overwhelmingly compelling reasons before any parameter can be altered. This conservatism ensures order and safeguards the body of our work, so that it is not easily influenced by fads or whims. Clients benefit from this stability, and acting out, when disguised as attempts to deviate from the rules, is detected early and analyzed. As we practitioners zealously watch for our clients' deviations from the rules, however, we can lose our own flexibility to test and explore new methods for fear that we might act out as well. Opting for safety through rigidity, we often choose to do nothing rather than assume the risk

---

*An earlier version of this paper was presented at the annual meeting of the American Psychological Association, Boston, MA, August 1990. In order to preserve the intimate, first-hand feeling of the clinical work and the authors' initial doubts about the use of the telephone to provide psychodynamic psychotherapy, the first person is used to convey the senior author's therapeutic experiences.

of being proven wrong. Although this cautious attitude may minimize acting out, it also diminishes the likelihood of pursuing innovation and thereby prevents our work from evolving into new areas. Efforts to effect legitimate modifications are frequently not examined but are rejected out of hand simply because they advocate change. At these moments, scientific scrutiny is suspended while an emotional attack, disguised as intellectual rigor, is brought to bear until such endeavors are satisfactorily driven away. Any new direction, thus stripped of meaning and value, can then be safely discarded. When such values prevail, the quest for true scientific knowledge is not served; rather, the practice of psychodynamic psychotherapy is protected from thoughtful challenge and insulated from meaningful change.

When I was first asked to use the telephone to provide psychotherapy sessions seven years ago, for example, I did not seriously imagine it to be a real possibility. During a span of approximately six months, three clients approached me, all for different reasons, asking if I would consider telephone sessions. One had an injury that left him bedridden for approximately one month, another was moving to attend college, and the third would be out of town for an indefinite period of time because of work commitments. I had been working with each of them for over one year in two to three times weekly psychodynamic psychotherapy. Their requests were for regularly scheduled, fifty-minute psychotherapy hours that would begin and end at a predetermined time and for which I would be paid my usual fee. Instinctively I refused, although I was neither eloquent nor particularly clear about my reasons. I told them, "it just was not done" or "this really works best face-to-face," allowing that the telephone was suitable for changing an appointment or dealing with a crisis, but not for ongoing therapy. In other words, the telephone was appropriate for going over highly specific information in order to arrive at a temporary course of action, but was not well suited to an open-ended, exploratory psychotherapy session. In retrospect, I think one of the most disturbing aspects of how I handled my clients' requests to continue our work on the telephone was that I firmly dismissed them without reflection. It is, therefore, in the spirit of open and honest discourse that we will explore the use of the telephone, both historically and currently, in conducting psychodynamic psychotherapy.

THE TELEPHONE AND PSYCHOTHERAPY: HISTORICAL AND CURRENT USES

In describing the technique of psychoanalysis and the necessity for the analyst to maintain "evenly suspended attention" in listening to the patient, Freud (1912) used the analogy of the telephone receiver:

> He must turn his own unconscious like a receptive organ towards the transmitting unconscious of the patient. He must adjust himself to the patient as a telephone receiver is adjusted to the transmitting microphone. Just as the receiver converts back into sound waves the electric oscillations in the telephone line which were set up by sound waves, so the doctor's unconscious is able, from the derivatives of the unconscious which are communicated to him, to reconstruct that unconscious, which has determined the patient's free associations. [pp. 115–116]

Thus, Freud recommended that the analyst "use his unconscious in this way as an instrument in the analysis," but it did not occur to him, or to others until years later, to use the telephone instrument itself as an aid to psychoanalytic and psychodynamic technique.

Despite the fact that the use of the telephone has been reported in the psychoanalytic and psychotherapeutic literature for the past four decades, there continues to be widespread confusion and controversy surrounding its use for psychotherapeutic purposes. Most often viewed by clinicians as an adjunct to face-to-face therapy or a substitute for in-person sessions, the telephone has been employed generally in psychotherapeutic work as a means of providing support to clients on an episodic or short-term basis. Usually, such phone conversations are unplanned, unstructured, and engaged in on an as-needed basis with no charge to the client. The primary use of the telephone in conducting long-term, psychodynamic psychotherapy, however, is a topic that has remained relatively unexplored until recently. Given the numerous potential benefits and few drawbacks to this new mode of providing psychotherapy, it is surprising that so little attention has been paid to telephone therapy.

Traditionally, the telephone has been used for initial contact (MacKinnon and Michels 1970); additional contact and support between sessions (Chiles 1974, Miller 1973); emergency contact (Grumet 1979, Miller 1973); crisis intervention (Lester 1974); follow-up contact (MacKinnon and Michels 1970); maintaining contact after termination of office visits (Rosenbaum 1974, 1977); and supportive psychotherapy over the short term (MacKinnon and Michels 1970).

Two early authors, however, described psychoanalytic work with the telephone. Saul (1951) was the first to report "full-fledged analytic work" using the telephone as "an instrument of technique" that aided his work with clients whose intense transference and negative therapeutic reactions made it impossible for them to come to the office. Whereas Saul (1951) took clients' phone calls on an unplanned, on-demand basis, Robertiello (1972–1973) conducted regular analytic sessions over the telephone. Both of these analysts worked on the telephone for a limited period of time until their clients were able to return to their offices to meet in person.

More recently, the telephone has been employed as the primary treatment modality in a structured, planned manner to conduct both supportive and psychoanalytic psychotherapy over the longer term (Hymer 1984, Lindon 1988, Ranan and Blodgett 1983, Shepard 1987, Tolchin 1987). Yet these clinicians continue to view telephone therapy as a second-best method when the best method, for whatever reason, is not available (Lindon 1988).

Thus, the telephone has been advocated for use with special classes of patients, characterized by physical, geographical, or emotional limitations, who would not otherwise get to a therapist's office: bedridden or incapacitated clients (MacKinnon and Michels 1970); clients separated from the therapist by geographical distance (Hymer 1984, Lindon 1988, Robertiello 1972–1973, Rosenbaum 1974); clients who prefer to stay at home because they either express themselves better in their own surroundings, feel threatened by the therapist, or fear a loss of control in the therapist's office (Miller 1973); clients who have intense transference or negative therapeutic reactions (Robertiello 1972–1973, Saul 1951); distressed and desperate clients (Chiles 1974); highly anxious and unstable clients (Grumet 1979); self-destructive or suicidal clients who may require additional monitoring (Tolchin 1987); depressed, withdrawn, and isolated clients (MacKinnon and Michels 1970, Miller 1973, Rosenblum 1969, Shepard 1987); phobic clients (MacKinnon and Michels 1970, Ranan and Blodgett 1983, Rosenblum 1969); clients with intense dependency needs, separation conflicts, and "distance-relatedness" issues (Hymer 1984, Miller 1973, Rosenblum 1969); manipulative, hostile, and borderline clients (Miller 1973; Ranan and Blodgett 1983); severely disturbed, paranoid, and schizophrenic clients (Grumet 1979, Hymer 1984, Miller 1973, Ranan and Blodgett 1983, Rosenbaum 1974, Rosenblum 1969); and adolescent clients living away from home (Tolchin 1987).

ADVANTAGES AND DISADVANTAGES
OF TELEPHONE THERAPY

Although the use of the telephone for psychotherapeutic work has thus far been suggested only in circumstances where face-to-face meetings are impractical, uncomfortable, or impossible, a multitude of benefits has nonetheless been noted by practitioners. The following therapeutic benefits are especially noteworthy: avoiding interruptions due to geographical obstacles or physical impairments (Lindon 1988, Robertiello 1972–1973, Tolchin 1987); avoiding transfer or premature termination (Lindon 1988, Rosenbaum 1974); overcoming client resistance or negative therapeutic reaction (Saul 1951); maintaining continuity and preventing self-destructive behavior (Tolchin 1987); and aiding clients who are in crisis or in transition (Grumet 1979). In addition to these advantages, numerous emotional benefits to clients have been reported, such as: increased control (Grumet 1979, Lester 1974); safety and security (Grumet 1979, Lester 1974); privacy and "intimacy at a distance" (Grumet 1979); accessibility and immediacy (Lester 1974); promoting the formation of an internalized image of the therapist that can be more easily "held" between sessions

(Hymer 1984); providing an "emotional safety valve" or outlet for the client's frustration, anger, and anxiety (Chiles 1974, Grumet 1979); greater freedom and openness, thus allowing more difficult material to emerge (Lester 1974, MacKinnon and Michels 1970); the absence of social cues serving to trigger unconscious material (Hymer 1984); and equalization of power and control in the therapeutic relationship (Lester 1974, Ranan and Blodgett 1983).

In discussing the transference, some clinicians have reported a dilution or diminution of the intensity of the client's reaction when the therapist was not present visually (Grumet 1979, Robertiello 1972–1973, Saul 1951, Shepard 1987), whereas others have reported the potential for intensified transference due to an increase in client fantasy (Hymer 1984, Lester 1974). However, in spite of disagreement on this point, it is generally agreed that the effect of the telephone on the transference provides an enhancement to the therapeutic process. Given the numerous advantages described in the literature on telephone therapy in specific circumstances and with particular groups, it is unfortunate that no greater effort has been made to implement and test its use in a wider variety of circumstances and with a broader range of clients.

Nevertheless, some potential problems of telephone therapy cited by critics include the absence of nonverbal cues, therapist boredom, and lack of therapist training in and research on the method (Buie 1989). Thus, therapists unfamiliar with this technique may react with feelings of anxiety and frustration due to the decreased control and increased responsibility they may experience as a result of not being able to see the client (Miller 1973). Critics have also charged that the technique has no proven long-term curing potential and that providing telephone therapy was stringing clients along, offering them a band-aid when they could need surgery—as, for example, when a client misrepresents a serious health problem such as anorexia or obesity (Buie 1989). Yet defenders of the use of the telephone have noted its essential similarity to in-person sessions and benefits such as its easy accessibility to clients who have physical disabilities or emotional problems that may prevent them from going to a therapist's office, as well as the increased safety and comfort that clients experience during telephone sessions as compared to face-to-face meetings (Buie 1989).

The argument that we will advance is that telephone therapy is not only comparable to face-to-face meetings, but may be superior as a form of treatment in its own right. The use of the telephone as a therapeutic tool in an analytically oriented setting may act as a catalyst, intensifying and enhancing psychotherapeutic processes such as client self-discovery and empathic listening on the part of the therapist. Telephone therapy is not a specific method or technique. We believe that it is how the telephone is used in the service of understanding the client that determines the type and quality of the psychotherapy. The telephone acts merely as a technical aid (Saul 1951), providing a novel modality by which to conduct psychotherapy (Lindon 1988). Just as face-to-face therapy does not automatically indicate an interpersonal relationship orientation on the therapist's part, neither does telephone therapy automatically indicate a conversational tone to the work. We maintain that the problems that exist with telephone therapy do not result from the use of the telephone per se, but from therapists' lack of training and experience in this modality (Lester 1974), which may lead them to slip into a social versus therapeutic mode, to feel anxious and frustrated about not being able to see the client, or to have difficulty handling silences in the absence of visual cues.

EVOLUTION OF THE USE OF THE TELEPHONE
AS A NEW THERAPEUTIC MODALITY

Until about 1984, my use of the telephone in treatment was confined to initial contacts, making or changing appointments, effecting cancellations and, on rare occasions, dealing with an emergency in which the client felt that he or she could not wait for the next regularly scheduled appointment. My first attempt to use the telephone to continue therapy that was already in progress was the result of tireless and seemingly endless efforts put forth by a bright, articulate, persuasive and desperate young borderline woman with whom I had been working for approximately two years, three sessions weekly. When Laila transferred from a local college to one away from home, she insistently pleaded with me to continue her sessions on the telephone. I gently refused, explaining that she really needed to work with a therapist in person, and suggested that she consult the Psychological Services Center at her new college. Although I did not really have a good rebuttal when she challenged my notion that meeting face-to-face was essential for psychotherapy to work effectively, I was nonetheless unwavering in my insistence. Some months went by and, since I did not hear from her, I assumed that she had found a new therapist and their work was proceeding. I soon found out, however, that this was not true. I received several letters in rapid succession, then a phone call, and finally a phone call from her mother stating that Laila was "losing it." After several attempts to begin work with a new therapist had failed, Laila found herself on the verge of panic, confused, sleeping and eating poorly, and increasingly unable to concentrate and do her schoolwork. When I was asked once again to schedule sessions with her on the telephone, she was feeling so desperate that there was really nothing to lose, and I finally capitulated.

In retrospect, this initial endeavor was tainted from the outset because, although I reluctantly agreed to do therapy on the telephone, there was a tacit assumption on my part that talking on the telephone was really only a substitute for meeting face-to-face. This approach was, therefore, better than nothing, but not something that could hold significant promise on its own. In spite of the cloud of doubt that hung over our continued work—and my stubborn belief that an inferior but necessary technique was being employed under adverse circumstances—I was surprised now and again that good therapy was in fact being done. As we continued to work on the longstanding issues that had brought her into treatment, Laila's feelings of panic diminished, as did her distractibility, and she was able to begin to apply herself to her schoolwork again. I was surprised how easily and smoothly continuity was established between the work that was done before treatment was interrupted and after we resumed therapy on the telephone. The intensity was diminished, however, since we were talking only once a week. It was my belief at the time that the telephone could provide only an interim solution until she returned home for the summer and we would meet again in person, three times weekly.

As planned, we did meet over the summer and then continued once weekly telephone sessions during the next academic year. I continued to be surprised, although less so as I gained more experience working on the telephone, that good therapeutic progress could be maintained with telephone sessions. The following summer, our main focus was termination because Laila and her family were moving to a remote area in the Far East after her graduation from college. She joked that she could call me only if she had two tin cans and a very, very long piece of string, since that would be more sophisticated than the local phone system. As a result of our work, both on the telephone and in person, Laila had matured significantly, gained a solid footing in establishing her own identity, and could separate from her mother without fear of destroying her. Over the years, I have received several letters in which she expressed appreciation for our work on the telephone and described a reasonably good life that she has made for herself.

Although still dubious about the effectiveness of the telephone in conducting psychotherapy, I was pleasantly surprised by these results and reluctantly suggested its use on several occasions over the course of the next year. One woman, with whom I had been working twice weekly for several years, was unexpectedly called out of town on business for an indeterminate length of time. Betsy was very distraught, since the anniversary of her husband's death one year earlier was approaching, and she did not want to miss her sessions; yet she did not feel she was in a position to refuse to go on the trip. I suggested that we could set up regularly scheduled appointments and talk on the telephone during the time she would be away. I volunteered that I already had some experience doing this and, in spite of my initial doubts, it seemed to work fairly well. Again, I presented the telephone as an interim solution, and asked how she would feel about talking once weekly until she returned and could resume our regular appointment schedule. When Betsy unexpectedly asked to continue talking twice weekly, I was surprised and, with some reluctance at the thought of requiring more from the telephone than it could reasonably be expected to deliver, I agreed.

We worked on the telephone, maintaining a twice weekly schedule, for nearly three months—far longer than either of us had expected. Periodically, we assessed the work to ensure that therapy conducted over the telephone was at least reasonably effective. Although some compromise in quality would have been acceptable as long as it was not too great, we were both surprised by the continuity of the material and the absence of any adverse change. Gradually, it became apparent that psychotherapy over the telephone was continuous with, and not noticeably different from, our face-to-face encounters, except for the occasional session where Betsy reported feeling safer and more comfortable discussing some subject where she neither had to be looked at, nor did she have to make eye contact in return. For the first time, I began to wonder whether working on the telephone might not be comparable to working face-to-face, rather than being a lesser, although acceptable, substitute when circumstances required it. Because this change in modality seemed too radical a departure from the rather traditional work I had done up until this point, such thinking made me anxious. However, constant examination and comparison of both modes of treatment not only failed to reveal the shortcomings I had expected to find with telephone work, but instead served to reinforce my growing sense that this new modality might indeed turn out to be comparable to working face-to-face.

During the remainder of that year, I had several other experiences conducting telephone therapy with clients I had already been working with face-to-face for some period of time. One was ill and unable to leave the house for several weeks; another, a college student, lost the use of his car for a few days; and a third, an adolescent attending prep school, wished to continue his sessions over the summer when he would be living at home with his parents. Had I not already acquired a sufficient base of experience to offer therapy on the telephone as an option in these three instances, we just would have accepted these interruptions as inevitable occurrences and weathered them in the best possible manner. Although none of these breaks was sufficiently long either to jeopardize treatment or to be intolerable, it was most helpful to be able to offer these clients flexibility with regard to the continuity of their treatment.

As I was gaining experience using the telephone to provide psychotherapy, I nonetheless remained skeptical that it could actually take the place of working in person. Based on my experience thus far, I was beginning to be convinced that it might be a very adequate substitute for periods of short duration, ranging from a few days to several months. I continued to be uncertain, however, about the adequacy of the telephone as the primary modality of treatment that was both intensive and long term. At the end of that summer, a new opportunity to assess the effectiveness of therapy over the telephone on a long-term, intensive basis presented itself with a young woman I had seen in my office for a relatively short amount of time. We will present this case in detail, since it was my first experience where I clearly took a position recommending that the telephone be used as the primary means of providing such treatment. Prior to working with this client, I only had offered to use the telephone as a stopgap measure between in-person sessions and had not advocated its use for ongoing, intensive work.

CASE ILLUSTRATION

Emma, who had just turned 18, was referred to me at the beginning of the summer following her graduation from high school because she felt extremely anxious about making the transition to college. She stated that change, especially when it involved separation, was very troublesome, although she had little understanding as to why this was so. Emma was frightened that if she did not gain some understanding and mastery of her fears of change and separation, then her attempt to begin college a significant distance from home would most likely fail.

Because she had some acquaintance with psychodynamic psychotherapy through friends who had been in treatment, Emma expressed a desire to work intensively for the three months that remained before her classes started. When I enquired as to why she did not pursue therapy earlier, she said that she had been too frightened, and now she was too frightened not to enter into it. In an effort to make some headway in what appeared to be a rather formidable undertaking, we agreed to meet three times weekly. I pointed out that it might be difficult terminating with me at the end of the summer, when she planned to continue with a therapist at school, especially in light of her already known sensitivity to separation. Emma agreed, but nonetheless wished to push on, suggesting that perhaps we could spend some time examining her anticipated separation from me. I concurred and, with that, our work began.

When she was 5 years old, Emma was left in the care of her father after the mother ran off with her guru in order to find herself, attain enlightenment, help humanity, and ultimately become a healer in her own right. According to the father, the mother's leaving was totally unexpected. Since the family had moved from a large city to the country a year after Emma's birth, he believed that they were happily pursuing a better and more peaceful life . According to Emma, the moment of her mother's departure was as dramatic as it was unforgettable. While the father, an attorney, was working late at his office one summer evening, she revealed her plans. At dusk, the mother brought Emma out to a deck at the back of the house, disrobed, and told her that she was leaving as she had come into this world, was going on a spiritual journey, and would return someday. She then kissed her on the forehead, climbed down the stairs, and walked through a field of tall grass before finally disappearing.

When her father returned home, Emma was crying hysterically. It has been almost impossible to reconstruct how much time she was alone, but it was most likely somewhere between one and three hours. The father, thinking the mother was just having some harmless fun and would soon return, dismissed her absence as a prank. Apparently she was always doing odd things, although even to him this seemed a bit extreme. The police were called when she did not return after several days. Then, on the following day, they received a letter that basically restated what the mother had told Emma a little less than a week before.

The father, who was above all else a practical man, immediately made arrangements for a live-in maid to cook, clean, and take care of his daughter. Because he insisted on order at home as much as he did at the office, he was most unsympathetic to Emma's poor appetite, fits of crying, hysterical outbursts, and frequent nightmares. As his frustration over not being able to soothe and control her grew, his words became harsher, and mild admonishment soon gave way to teasing and ridicule in more desperate attempts to silence her grief and confusion. She was told to grow up and act like a big girl, stop crying over what she did not have, and learn to appreciate all the good things she did have. He would tell her horrifying stories about little girls who were abandoned by both parents, only to be left to caretakers who would commit various forms of physical and emotional abuse. Finally, his message struck home, and Emma realized, at least outwardly, what a lucky girl she was to have a father who did not beat her and provided so well for her physical comforts. Under the oppressive weight of his insistence on her gratitude, her symptoms seemed to disappear, and she eventually threw herself into projects and schoolwork to prove to him that she could be the girl he wanted.

During the first year of her mother's absence, Emma sporadically received postcards, each mailed from a different town crisscrossing America. Not surprisingly, she took an interest in geography and drew a very detailed map, inserting stick pins into every place from which her mother had sent mail. She later told me that if she connected every town her mother went to with a different colored line, it would look like a Jackson Pollock painting. Recently, upon rereading the postcards that she had saved, Emma was most struck by how little interest her mother expressed in her child's well-being. Instead, she mainly focused on how good it felt to be free, to travel, and to meet interesting people who, like herself, were spiritually united in their quest for an inner vision.

Eventually, the mother and her guru parted company, but there were other men who came and went, some lasting a brief time and others for relatively long periods. All were given only a line or two on a postcard, as was Emma, while the mother reserved the bulk of the text for herself. Meanwhile, the father's business grew, and he merged his law practice with that of another attorney. Busier and more prosperous than ever, he had virtually no time for his daughter. Hired help assured that Emma's physical needs were met, while her almost inaccessible father praised her continued achievements in school. If she ever inquired about her mother, Emma was made to feel so guilty that she almost forgot about her—at least she tried. Although she became withdrawn from friends, this passed unnoticed because her father assumed that she was intentionally isolating herself so that she could devote more time to her studies.

The next several years seemed to pass in a blur. What Emma most clearly remembers about this period is her bedroom, where time stood still while she spent endless hours studying. She was aware of little else and had no recollection of whether or not her father dated or how frequently her care-takers changed. One vivid recollection, however, was fixed in her mind. Her father had taken her to a museum, where she saw an ancient beetle trapped and frozen in yellowish, trans-parent amber. "That was me," she later told me, "I knew it then, only I couldn't put it into words. I could only feel it. I was des-perate and helpless, but had no one to turn to. I was completely alone." Emma's state of lifelessness was punctuated occasion-ally by a postcard from her mother, which momentarily filled her with sadness. "At least it was a feeling," she said, and so she knew she was still alive.

In the summer of her ninth year, Emma's mother ap-peared as mysteriously and suddenly as she had disappeared. A few friends were visiting for a Fourth of July cookout when an old car, with all kinds of things tied to the roof and trunk, pulled into the driveway. Emma later remarked that the car reminded her of photographs of sharecropper families headed to California to escape the dust bowl, but there was only one person in it. "I'll never forget it," she said. "This lady with a weird expression on her face got out and started walking to-ward the picnic table where we were all sitting. She stopped about ten feet away and said, 'It's me, honey, your mother. I'm home.' I don't remember anything else, except what they told me years later. I guess I ran into the basement and hid. I wouldn't come out until hours past dinner when I was too starved to be scared anymore."

Only nine years later, when she began psychotherapy, could Emma begin to question, in the most tentative manner, how seamless and bizarre her mother's re-entry into the house-hold was. Her departure four years earlier was scarcely men-tioned, nor was what had transpired in all of their lives during the intervening years. The father and mother acted as if nothing had happened, and Emma, taking her cues from them, behaved similarly. Gradually, she forgot the strangeness of it all, as well as her hurt and anger over unanswered questions about how it was possible for a mother who loved her only child and husband to abandon them, and a loving father to silence her tears, deny her grief, and act cheerful in the face of such turmoil and despair. Aided by her parents' uniform front that since the past was behind them all that mattered now was the future, she began to wonder whether or not it ever really happened at all. The giant tear in Emma's life resulting from her mother's quest for enlightenment was being forcibly sealed shut. In a final effort to make this process of denial complete, the mother announced that she was pregnant after being home only four months.

Jason's birth, eight months later, marked the anniversary almost to the day of the mother's return. The parents made little effort to conceal the fact that the baby's presence represented a new beginning for the family, a chance to start over and erase the events of the past four years. Now 10 years old, with her brother as the focus of attention, Emma sensed that her very existence was an annoying reminder of something gone wrong. Feeling like an impediment standing in the way of her family's happiness, she tried to become even more invisible by being as compliant and studious as possible. In an effort to deny her jealousy and win the approval of her parents, Emma assumed the role of Jason's protector and caretaker. That she could have felt anger toward her parents or her little brother was almost unimaginable. Her investment in being a good girl was so enormous that she tried to mask or disown any thoughts, feelings, or actions that did not conform to this image.

When we began meeting in three times weekly psychotherapy eight years later, this was still very much the state of

affairs. Filled with anxiety centered on her anticipated departure for college, Emma felt blank when it came to understanding either herself or her family. She nevertheless became intensely involved in therapy from the outset, expressing both
relief and pleasure at finally being able to voice her feelings
and having someone interested enough to listen. The summer
passed rapidly, and the work progressed well. Initially, the
therapy was focused primarily on examining her relationships
with peers, with the result that two patterns emerged. Emma
observed that because she felt stifled by men, she had never
engaged in a long-term relationship, but had only a series of
brief affairs lasting a month or two at the most. She was attracted to males who were emotionally abusive, constantly
criticized her, demanded perfection, and showed little interest in her except as a narcissistic extension of themselves. Although she tried her best to act compliant and fulfill their
wishes, Emma eventually shut down and withdrew into herself, causing the men to become frustrated and ultimately leave
her. Predictably, her relationships with women were different.
She had a group of female friends with whom she engaged in
a variety of activities, but shared no real emotional closeness.
Although she liked to be with them, and felt comforted by their
presence, she was much more quiet with women than she was
with men.

Yet, whether or not she was with girlfriends or boyfriends,
Emma continued to complain of an enormous sense of emptiness that never seemed to leave her. Any attempt on my part
to steer her, no matter how gently, toward looking at her family history in order to begin to understand the source of this
emptiness was met with extreme resistance. Toward the end
of the summer, Emma acknowledged, ever so tentatively, that
her mother's leaving may have been more significant than she
had thought previously. At this point, however, our sense of

accomplishment at having gotten off to such a good start was tempered by frustration at having to end our relatively successful, but short-lived venture. Although I did make some efforts to deal with termination, my resolve was easily overcome in favor of helping her gain some understanding of the underlying family dynamics.

Time moved forward, and soon only one week remained before Emma had to leave for school. She was tearful and distraught, fearing that the progress she had made would not be sustained working with another therapist. While I did not feel indispensable, I did feel that the work had progressed extremely well and that it was most unfortunate to terminate at this juncture. For several weeks I had entertained the notion of continuing therapy on the telephone, but did not share my thoughts with her because I felt uncertain about recommending it. Up until then, it was generally my clients who made the request to use the telephone and, after much deliberation, I either agreed to go along with it or suggested using it for limited periods of time. The use of the telephone in this case would be for an extended period because it would be almost ten months before Emma would return for the summer to resume our work in person. Then, if all went well, we could continue on the telephone again at the end of the summer. Perhaps these thoughts were somewhere in my mind all along and, as a consequence, I did not push harder to work on termination. When I finally did recommend that we continue working together over the telephone, getting the words out was not easy. I had to force myself to say them once I had made up my mind to offer telephone therapy. It felt strange to actively recommend what I still experienced to be a significant departure from the way I was used to working.

Since that moment of intense discomfort two years ago, Emma and I have continued to work three times weekly, nine months on the telephone and three months in person, except for vacations and other occasional interruptions. As I have slowly gained a clear sense of what can be accomplished on the telephone, I have actively recommended and heartily endorsed its use, with the result that I presently spend approximately twenty hours per week working on the telephone.

Clinical Material

In order to give the reader a first-hand feeling for long-term, intensive, psychodynamic telephone work, we are including process notes for one week of three times weekly psychotherapy presented at six-month intervals since I began working with Emma. What we find most striking about the work presented below is how similar, in terms of both process and content, it is to face-to-face material.

Six months: Emma reported feeling anxious and abandoned after her roommate got drunk and passed out. She was bothered by her roommate's loss of control, as well as her emotional absence while in this state. Emma reported a nightmare in which she had to perform some complicated task but couldn't and felt helpless. She feels responsible for taking care of those around her and making them well, even if it is not in her power to do so.

Emma is worried about her grades. She wants her family to be proud of her, but is afraid she will let them down. She feels phony and dumb, and wonders if her school made a mistake in admitting her. She believes everyone else is so smart and resolves to work harder. Emma mentioned some slight apprehension about going home for Christmas, but felt stuck and could not explore this feeling further. She is feeling extremely inadequate without the presence of external achievements.

Emma expressed interest in a male student. She reported some thoughts that she regarded as odd, such as the feeling of wanting to visit his family instead of her own at Christmas. For the first time, Emma felt slightly annoyed at having to arrange her plans to accommodate her family. She felt guilty and confused at the end of the session. She is beginning to sense that she has needs and is questioning for the first time why her needs always have to remain in the background.

One year: Emma reported a dream in which she had to be sexually provocative in order to get the attention of a man. Her associations led to her father and me, as she expressed fears and concerns that she will have to be exploited in order to achieve closeness with men. She feels that if she cannot do something special for a man, she will be seen as profoundly unattractive, both physically and intellectually, which will result ultimately in her abandonment. Emma also had a dream in which she appeared as a child covered with feces in a bathtub. Strangers wandered by, but no one seemed to notice.

Emma feels very distressed over an increased awareness that she needs to be the star academically or athletically in order to maintain other people's interest in her. She is now beginning to realize that she must repeat this pattern over and over again for fear that she will not exist if she is not a stellar performer. Emma is beginning to look at what price she must pay in order to get attention and to examine her fears that she will be neglected if she is not pleasing to others.

Emma talked about how she continues to feel extremely vulnerable when she risks making her needs known for fear that those upon whom she depends will withdraw, leaving her feeling empty and humiliated. She expressed the wish to talk with me more often and then became afraid that this would lead me to feel burdened and overwhelmed. She then wondered if her demands for attention as a child forced her mother to leave. Emma started crying and expressed the fear that I will go away and not come back. She wondered if I am resentful of her. I have been seen both as her mother and father in the transference this week. First as her father, who will reject her if she does not please him, and then as her mother, who will abandon her if she is too demanding.

One and one-half years: Emma got into a number of arguments with her mother and father over the weekend. This stirred up earlier feelings of having to submerge herself in order to be close to them. She expressed her fear of me and of therapy because I would help her to *not* submerge herself, and then she would alienate her family and be left all alone. Emma is afraid that her family does not want to see her true self, only the false self that she had to create in order to win their love and approval.

Emma spoke about critical feelings toward her mother, father, and brother. She felt that they would do or say anything just to get along. She believes that they only want to see the good in things and minimize conflict. When her mother said that "everything always happens for the best," Emma got angry and asked, "How was it for the best when you left us?" Her mother did not answer. Although she is feeling more confident with her own voice and point of view, Emma is sad and angry that her family is so unaccepting of her perceptions.

Emma is feeling upset about being on the periphery of her family because of her differences of opinion with them. She feels that people are responsible for their own actions and the effects that they have on others. She also insists on the importance of the past and vehemently disagrees with her parents' view that "what is past is past" and only the future is important. In spite of her feelings of increased independence, she voiced fears of losing her sense of self if she agrees with them in order to fit in and be accepted. As the hour progressed, Emma was able to regain her sense of self and became clearer about her own boundaries and opinions about herself and her family.

Two years: Emma spoke about the struggle she is engaged in with her mother because she refuses to acknowledge how damaging it was to leave her when she was 5 years old. Her mother insisted that it was right at the time and that, had she stayed, she would have been so unhappy that she wouldn't have been a good mother anyway. Emma said that an unhappy mother was better than no mother at all and adamantly stated that even if her mother did what she felt was necessary, she shouldn't pretend that it had no effect on her and thereby silence her feelings. Emma finally told her mother, "You can go away, but you can't take my feelings away." A real sense of self has begun to crystallize and make its presence known.

Emma spoke about feeling good about the last session and liking therapy, but then became fearful that if she felt free to express these feelings, I might leave her. She made the connection between seeing me as her mother and realized that she equated openness and vulnerability with abandonment. For the first time, Emma looked at photographs taken before her mother left home. She described herself as looking defeated, empty, and depressed. She is far more open to her feelings about her mother now. Her response to my recent week-long vacation was to feel deadened and believe that I no longer mattered to her. This led to a deeper re-examination of her mother's leaving and its impact, as well as its manifestations in the transference.

Emma now realizes that she has many feelings of hurt and anger toward her mother for leaving. She had to deaden herself when her mother left and tried to replace her need for affection from her mother with that from her father, which was only forthcoming if she was good and excelled in school. She is beginning to understand her true self as it is emerging and why, in order for her to survive as a vulnerable child, she had to hide it and construct a false self in its place.

DISCUSSION

What struck us as most unusual about the clinical material presented above is that it is no different from the material that emerges in long-term, intensive, psychodynamic psychotherapy that takes place face-to-face. In fact, we would go so far as to speculate that if the material were presented as a part of any other paper except this one that specifically deals with telephone therapy, it would not occur to a reader that the work took place almost entirely over the phone. It is not the point of this paper, however, to demonstrate that psychotherapy on the telephone is as good or the same as face-to-face psychotherapy. Instead, our contention is that in very specific ways the use of the telephone actually enhances the psychotherapeutic process and is therefore at least as good as, and oftentimes superior to, face-to-face work. Having made such a bold assertion, we would like to offer our understanding as to why we believe this is so.

For a little more than the past one and a half years, I have averaged twenty hours per week of psychotherapy on the telephone, which amounts to approximately 1,500 hours. Another 300 or so hours could be added to this figure for less systematic work carried out in the years prior to the past one and a half. Eighteen clients, whose ages range from mid-adolescence to elderly, have worked with me in this manner. Their occupations are diverse, including student, professional, business, arts, and entertainment. All had worked with me in face-to-face psychotherapy before beginning work on the telephone, some for as long as several years and, in one case, for as little as six weeks.

It is from this reasonably diverse data base, compiled over several years from nearly 2,000 clinical hours, that we would like to offer our observations about the benefits and viability of long-term psychodynamic psychotherapy over the telephone. Issues handled in telephone therapy have been comparable in every way to those encountered in face-to-face psychotherapy, including dealing with crises and working through acutely suicidal behavior. In one instance, I arranged for a client's leave of absence from college and subsequent hospitalization. Making these arrangements necessitated talking to parents, psychiatrists, social workers, and administrators, who repeatedly asked me if I felt comfortable working on the phone during this difficult period. After carefully considering the question, I realized that I would have done little else differently if we were meeting face-to-face. Although I would have met with the client in person, all other arrangements would have been made over the telephone.

In order for any psychotherapeutic medium to be mastered and used to its best advantage, its parameters must be clearly defined and respected. We view the telephone as a parameter in exactly the same manner as the couch is characterized in classical psychoanalysis. Like the couch, the telephone provides an enhancement to the psychotherapeutic process when properly used. This means that psychotherapy is conducted in a structured therapeutic frame in which the telephone is included as a parameter, and every communication must be analyzed in this context. While there may be an exchange of social pleasantries or occasional small talk, their meaning must be understood in the larger scheme of defenses and resistances, just as it would in face-to-face meetings. Similarly, a regular appointment schedule is set up with each appointment lasting fifty minutes; the client is responsible for calling on time, paying for the call, canceling in advance, or being charged for the missed appointment.

It is essential to understand, however, that as a parameter, the telephone's performance as a therapeutic tool is a direct result of how it is used or misused. The couch can be an enhancement to psychoanalytic treatment by facilitating the process of free association and thus the emergence of unconscious material, but it is the analyst's skilled use of the couch that is essential to this process, not just the presence of a couch per se in the hands of any practitioner. This same skill and sensitivity must be brought to bear when using the telephone in conducting psychodynamic psychotherapy. The therapist must learn to listen in an analytic manner and not use the telephone in a conventional way for social conversation. The ease with which the therapist can fall into this trap has been commented on by Lester (1974), who correctly concluded that many of the problems that occur with the use of the telephone are not the fault of the modality, but result from a lack of professionalism on the therapist's part. In addition, therapists who are either inadequately trained or insufficiently experienced in providing psychodynamic psychotherapy over the telephone, or both, may easily wander into a conversational mode as a result of their own lack of clarity about what they are doing and how they should proceed using this new parameter. Working on the telephone requires intense concentration, oftentimes more than in person because the therapist operates without visual feedback from the client. While this refined focusing of therapeutic attention can result in increased awareness and sensitivity in the therapist, any lack of skill or resolve can easily lead to a straying from the work at hand. It is not the fault of the telephone that this can happen; rather it is the responsibility of the therapist who uses it. If an analyst misuses analytic technique and allows a client to free associate for an entire session without intervening so that real interpretive work is avoided, it would be inconceivable to attribute the problem to the couch. It is simply inferior therapy and the therapist, not the parameter, must bear that responsibility.

The absence of visual cues provides one of the significant enhancements offered by this parameter. Unlike the use of the couch, where the client is looked at but is unable to return the therapist's gaze, the telephone ensures that both participants are equal with respect to sight. There are several distinct advantages of both participants being unable to see each other, although this state of visual abstinence has overwhelmingly been cited by critics of telephone therapy as creating such an insurmountable disadvantage that meaningful work cannot proceed. We therefore wish to address this point in some detail since our position is such a radical departure from the consensus opinion. Sight is relied upon so disproportionately to process information that most of us find it difficult to imagine functioning without it. Such heavy reliance upon vision understandably leads to dependence and results in overvaluation of it under certain circumstances where sight may not only be nonessential, but may actually interfere with receiving and processing data. We believe that face-to-face therapy is one such situation, and it is only after we examined many hours of work on the telephone that we began to be aware of how dependent therapists are in adjusting their behavior to the social demands and interpersonal reality of working face-to-face. We mislead ourselves if we think that we are observers who are not equally dependent upon feedback from our clients, as they are from us, for reassurance and well-being. The absence of sight eliminates this source of interference, of which we are frequently unaware, because it operates in an unconscious or semi-conscious realm. It must be noted, however, that whereas the majority of clients feel freer expressing themselves under these circumstances, some clients will experience the loss of visual contact with the therapist as a threat to their psychic integration. We believe such clients, who have not developed the "capacity to be alone" in the presence of another (Winnicott, 1958), may become intensely anxious while fending off threats of disintegration.

In addition to reducing interference, the loss of visual contact with the client has the beneficial effect of enabling hearing to become acutely sensitized. Not only is more information heard, but it is organized in a new way, permitting the listener access to a world materially different from one in which there is both visual contact and sound. Processing information in a different way through a newly refined sense of listening, the therapist gradually becomes aware of information whose existence was previously not known. In the course of conducting psychotherapy over the telephone, the client's voice becomes broader, and therapists hear new dimensions of enriched sound—tones, intonations, sighs, pauses, and silences—which can provide them with material equal, and often superior, to that which is perceived through both vision and hearing when meeting in person. Not being seen can also lessen the pressure to react either verbally or nonverbally, so that a space is created giving the therapist more time to listen and reflect before responding.

It was only after working on the telephone, for example, that I was finally able to understand significantly more about a blind client with whom I had once worked. His sightless world of sound had seemed so rich to him but so flat to me. It was only after re-evaluating my work with him and better understanding the quality of work that can take place in the absence of visual cues that I began to think about the blind psychotherapists who are trained by accredited institutions to engage in clinical practice. We doubt that these institutions believe that they are turning out therapists who are "nearly as good as" or "the next best thing to" therapists with sight, and it makes us wonder if not using sight is criticized only when one elects not to use it. If true, this seems neither rational nor scientifically founded.

Just as increased sensitivity in listening is an advantage for the therapist, clients too have voiced several distinct advantages that they have experienced. These include a sense of increased comfort and safety due to the fact that they are able to speak in a setting that is of their own choosing where they are not observed. Not being looked at seems to be especially freeing in enabling clients to express highly sensitive concerns that would have been much more difficult to reveal under the scrutiny of a therapist's gaze. Moreover, because the work takes place as much in the client's setting as it does in the therapist's, a greater sense of equality has also been reported. Since we rarely question that we meet in our own offices, we do not stop to examine the issues of power and control that are conveyed by the setting alone, which is not a common ground but a place where the therapist is seen as being in charge. Perhaps opponents of telephone therapy, who have charged that the absence of visual cues may enable clients suffering from eating or depressive disorders to conceal their conditions from their therapists, have not reflected on these issues of power and control because it is also true that a client may choose to withhold significant material in face-to-face psychotherapy. We maintain that it is not the function of the therapist to corner clients in order to prevent them from "getting away" with concealment; to do so is a misuse of the therapeutic relationship and an abuse of power. The client must determine the content and pace of disclosure, while the therapist's presence is to facilitate this process, not to force it. Resistance must be worked through, and the therapist must respect and work with what the client chooses to present.

This same mentality that advocates policing clients' behavior is responsible for the criticism that the therapist might not be attending fully while listening to the client on the telephone, but may be arranging items on his or her desk or thumbing through a catalog instead. The client, too, might be engaged in various forms of distraction. These critics fail to examine this issue from an analytic framework, where such straying from the work is understood as countertransference and transference reactions and, as such, is not to be rigidly prevented. Analysis of transference and countertransference forms the backbone of psychodynamic work, regardless of the setting or parameters employed. Although at times I have been distracted while working on the telephone, this has occurred no more or less than when working in person with a client. Distractions are part of the analytic process and provide valuable information about the work in progress. They are also inherent in the unfocused, free floating of attention that is essential to permit unconscious material to come to the fore, while at the same time, the therapist maintains concentration in a highly focused manner. These methods of attending coexist simultaneously.

A more relevant question, however, concerns not the issue of distractibility, but whether transference and countertransference dynamics are more accessible while working on the telephone or in person. Opinion is divided on this issue, with some clinicians suggesting that the absence of visual feedback promotes fantasy formation and more intense transference reactions on the part of the client, whereas others feel that the elimination of visual stimuli leads to a minimization of the transference. My own experience is that the role and formation of transference and countertransference depend almost entirely on the unfolding of dynamics between the client and therapist, and is least dependent upon the presence or absence of visual cues.

Moreover, therapists' need for control, which may also be expressed through their insistence that the client be observed in their offices, often has more to do with countertransference issues relating to therapists' insecurity and rigidity than with promoting good psychodynamic work (Giovacchini 1985). Thus, while working on the telephone, therapists may feel less in control of the therapeutic interaction, leading them to assert themselves in ways that are countertherapeutic. Requiring that the client accommodate to the therapist's setting may promote false self organization (Winnicott 1960) and its maintenance in those clients for whom the need for approval and acceptance is especially strong. Just as the client may feel pressured to conform to the therapist's needs and expectations, the therapist may also respond to pressures to conform to the client's expectations, as well as the social demands of a significant relationship. Our self-esteem, sense of professional competence, and income depends upon our clients' continued presence, so that our sensitivity to nonverbal cues is not only used to understand them, but is also used unconsciously in our efforts to be liked, valued, and win our clients' approval. Thus, the elimination of visual and nonverbal cues will likely diminish social pressures that distract from the goal of understanding.

CONCLUSION

We have presented the use of the telephone as a new parameter in conducting psychodynamic psychotherapy. We believe this modality provides distinct advantages that enhance the psychotherapeutic process when used by a skilled practitioner. With the distractions present in face-to-face work minimized, the therapist is introduced to a new and enriched realm of listening that permits heightened responsiveness to the needs of the client. This, coupled with the client's greater sense of equality with the therapist, leads to increased feelings of intimacy and presence in the work. Feeling safer, more secure, and in control, the client experiences a new openness and freedom in revealing and examining sensitive material.

It is important to emphasize that the use of the telephone need not affect the therapist's technique. Telephone therapy is simply a change in modality, and when the telephone is used properly as a parameter, it should enhance the psychotherapeutic process. However, this modality is not appropriate for everyone, particularly clients and therapists who become highly anxious in the absence of visual feedback, as well as therapists who lack experience and training in psychodynamic psychotherapy.

We hope this chapter will stimulate a serious interest in understanding and analyzing the impact of the telephone as a parameter of psychodynamic treatment, so that rich and informative material may emerge to further refine the psychotherapeutic process. It is only by evaluating this modality openly and honestly, however, that a clearer understanding will be brought to bear on the use of the telephone in conducting psychotherapy, hopefully eliminating the confusion and prejudice that currently surround it.

REFERENCES

Buie, J. (1989). Therapy by telephone: Does it help or hurt? *American Psychological Association Monitor* 20(3):14–15.

Chiles, J. A. (1974). A practical therapeutic use of the telephone. *American Journal of Psychiatry* 131(9):1030–1031.

Freud, S. (1912). Recommendations to physicians practising psycho-analysis. *Standard Edition* 12:111–120.

Giovacchini, P. L. (1985). Countertransference and the severely disturbed adolescent. *Adolescent Psychiatry* 12:449–467.

Grumet, G. W. (1979). Telephone therapy: A review and case report. *American Journal of Orthopsychiatry* 49(4):574–584.

Hymer, S. M. (1984). The telephone session and the telephone between sessions. *Psychotherapy in Private Practice* 2(3):51–65.

Lester, D. (1974). The unique qualities of telephone therapy. *Psychotherapy: Theory, Research and Practice* 11:219–221.

Lindon, J. A. (1988). Psychoanalysis by telephone. *Bulletin of the Menninger Clinic* 52:521–528.

MacKinnon, R. A., & Michels, R. (1970). The role of the telephone in the psychiatric interview. *Psychiatry: Journal for the Study of Interpersonal Processes* 33:82–93.

Miller, W. B. (1973). The telephone in outpatient psychotherapy. *American Journal of Psychotherapy* 27:15–26.

Ranan, W., and Blodgett, A. (1983). Using telephone therapy for "unreachable" clients. *Social Casework* 64:39–44.

Robertiello, R. C. (1972–1973). Telephone sessions. *Psychoanalytic Review* 59:633–634.

Rosenbaum, M. (1974). Continuation of psychotherapy by "long-distance" telephone. *International Journal of Psychoanalytic Psychotherapy* 3:483–495.

——— (1977). Premature interruption of psychotherapy: Continuation of contact by telephone and correspondence. *American Journal of Psychiatry* 134(2):200–202.

Rosenblum, L. (1969). Telephone therapy. *Psychotherapy: Theory, Research and Practice* 6:241–242.

Saul, L. J. (1951). A note on the telephone as a technical aid. *Psychoanalytic Quarterly* 20:287–290.

Shepard, P. (1987). Telephone therapy: an alternative to isolation. *Clinical Social Work Journal* 15:56–65.

Tolchin, J. (1987). Telephone psychotherapy with adolescents. *Adolescent Psychiatry* 14:332–341.

Winnicott, D. W. (1958). The capacity to be alone. In *The Maturational Processes and the Facilitating Environment*, pp. 29–36. New York: International Universities Press, 1965.

——— (1960). Ego distortion in terms of true and false self. In *The Maturational Processes and the Facilitating Environment*, pp. 140–152. New York: International Universities Press, 1965.

4

Skills in Dealing with the First Telephone Contact*

HERBERT S. STREAN

*T*he first contact between therapist and patient is usually over the phone. Despite the ubiquity of this event, the dynamics of the first encounter are rarely discussed at clinical conferences or in the professional literature. Because there are few dynamic principles on which practitioners agree regarding the first phone contact, clinicians' responses to it tend to be idiosyncratic and subjective. Some therapists have lengthy discussions with prospective patients, eliciting many facts, a great deal of history, and other data; others have a very brief conversation and try to schedule a consultation interview as soon as possible.

In my supervisory work and in my discussions with colleagues, I have learned that many cases are lost during or right after the first phone conversation. A large number of clinicians tend to minimize not only the importance of this event for patient and therapist, but also can underestimate how very anxious, ambivalent, and apprehensive most prospective patients are when they finally make a decision to ask for professional help. Moreover, therapists frequently are not fully aware

---

*This chapter was originally published in 1998 as "A Good Therapist Is a Good Telephone Operator," *Don't Lose Your Patients*, by Herbert S. Strean, published by Jason Aronson Inc.

of how they themselves feel and appear over the phone when talking to prospective patients.

The decision to pick up the phone and ask a therapist for a consultation is rarely, if ever, a spontaneous act for most individuals. Many patients, after they have been in treatment for several months, report having started to call a therapist for the first time and then putting the phone down even before hearing the therapist's voice. This same scenario can be repeated many times. Particularly in American culture, where autonomy is championed (Kardiner 1945) and dependency is demeaned, individuals often consider it a sign of weakness or failure when they reveal their need for professional help with their psychological and interpersonal problems.

Although few prospective patients directly state over the telephone how frightened they feel and how dubious they are about receiving therapeutic help, the way they conduct themselves over the phone often tells us how agitated they are. A barrage of questions about how therapy works, how long it takes, what the practitioner's qualifications are, what the therapist's theoretical predilections may be, and how much she charges, usually reflect how uncertain the prospective patient feels about undertaking treatment. If the therapist is not sensitive to the fact that requests for information usually are a reflection of the applicant's anxiety and therefore cannot be answered factually but must be explored instead, the prospective patient will not feel very well understood by the therapist.

I recall when I was a beginning practitioner, I received a phone call from a prospective patient who asked, "Can you tell me the times you can *not* see me?" Unaware that her query revealed an unconscious wish *not* to meet with me, I answered her question directly and told her when I was occupied. The applicant never arrived for an appointment. At least one of the reasons for this was that I did not show her I understood that a big part of her did not want to begin therapy with me.

Clinicians soon realize that, despite the pain and anguish that prospective patients endure, they have enormous fears about altering the status quo. These fears or *resistances* to being helped are manifested from the first phone call right through termination of treatment.

Many clinicians, especially beginners, are so determined to get a prospective patient into therapy, particularly if they are in private practice, that in their eagerness and enthusiasm they fail to relate to the applicant's resistances (Strean 1990) and, instead, doggedly attempt to set up a consultation. This rarely brings the consciously desired result.

Another situation that I flubbed as a beginning practitioner was when a man called me and made a most revealing slip over the phone. He said, "I'm desperately in *need of trouble!*" He wanted to say he was "desperately in need of help," but instead revealed his unconscious wish to stay in trouble. Eager to get him into my office, I bypassed his wish to maintain the status quo, and he never did become a patient.

I believe that because many clinicians are so eager to get applicants to become their patients and very fearful of losing this opportunity, they provide too much reassurance over the phone, answer too many questions, and then can cause an intimidated, ambivalent prospective patient to feel too overwhelmingly anxious and very unprepared to begin therapy.

The sensitive, empathetic clinician shows in her attitude over the phone that the caller does not have to make a commitment to arrange an appointment pronto. She is not in a rush to bypass resistances by answering questions readily, nor is she tempted to provide a lot of reassurance, which usually looks suspicious. Instead she is interested in sounding receptive, and, without getting involved in a long dialogue over the phone, suggests to the prospective patient that the caller *might consider* meeting her face to face so that questions, concerns, and doubts, which always exist, may be discussed in a consultation. I have found that most prospective patients respond positively to this approach, and if they insist on having their demands gratified over the phone, in all likelihood they are not really ready to begin psychotherapy.

Too frequently, therapists impose conditions for therapy over the phone that only serve to alienate the prospective patient. To tell an apprehensive applicant that he should consider twice-a-week therapy when he wants to come once a week or less only compounds resistances. When the applicant wants to come alone to the consultation to discuss a marital problem, but the therapist says that he should bring his wife with him, this only induces feelings of anger, rejection, and alienation. Prospective patients make many outlandish requests— desires to meet a mate or to receive sexual stimulation, opportunities for sensitivity groups, changes to their religion or gender, or many other fantastic demands. The sensitive clinician does *not* say over the phone that she does *not* render the service requested, but invites the prospective patient into her office to discuss the request further, so that the prospective patient can feel better understood eventually. A maxim from social work that is pertinent to all of psychotherapeutic practice is "Begin where the client is" (Hamilton 1951). This means that regardless of the client's request over the phone (or later), the request is empathized with and studied, rather than rejected or gratified. When the applicant observes that the therapist is trying to understand, he usually feels more willing to become a patient.

Inasmuch as the vast majority of prospective patients are individuals having difficulty liking themselves, they are very ready to feel misunderstood or rejected. Consequently, the more the therapist asks questions over the phone, the more possibility there is for the applicant to find something offensive. If a clinician wants the applicant to become a patient and appear in her office, she should listen to his requests patiently, suggest that questions about schedule, fee, the therapist's qualifications, and so forth, could be discussed in more detail face to face, *if the prospective patient would like this*, and then see how the applicant responds to this invitation. If the prospective patient responds with doubt or uncertainty, the therapist can empathetically show that she understands the prospective patient may have some doubts about meeting her. Then, feeling understood, most prospective patients do make an appointment. In those cases where they don't, prospective patients can be warmly told that they may wish to call back at a later date. Often this stance does eventually bring them back.

I want to focus sharply on those issues that usually pose difficulty for prospective patients and prospective therapists that emerge during the first telephone contact. The case illustrations that we will be discussing are real examples of real telephone contacts. Names and identifying data are disguised.

DEALING WITH THE REQUEST

There are some prospective patients who can pick up the phone and tell the practitioner that they would like to meet with her to have an interview as soon as possible. When the clinician offers a time, place, and date for an appointment, she then has her first opportunity to ascertain how the prospective patient feels about therapy. Well-motivated individuals, those who may be compliant and/or cooperative, and those who feel they are in crisis frequently accept whatever appointment time is offered and do come in for an interview. This, of course, does not mean that resistances to therapy will be absent in the first interview or the last.

I have found that if the applicant is ready to accept the appointment as presented, I can then give him instructions to get to my office and tell him that I am looking forward to meeting him on the designated date. I ask no further questions nor do I make any further remarks. I have plenty of time to hear about the prospective patient's situation when he comes to my office.

If the prospective patient has difficulty adapting to the times offered by the practitioner, this is usually a sign of his anxiety. I have found that after a couple of appointment times are rejected by the prospective patient, it is not productive to offer more. Rather, it is more helpful to the applicant to make some empathetic remark about his difficulty in arranging an appointment time.

> Andrew, a man in his early thirties, called Ms. B., a private practitioner, for a consultation because he had "difficulty establishing relationships with women." Although Ms. B. offered Andrew several possible appointment times, he had many reasons why none of them was convenient. Insensitive to his anxiety and not dealing with his resistance, Ms. B. gave Andrew a date and time that he thought he "might be able to make." Andrew did not show up for his appointment nor did he call to cancel. Andrew and Ms. B. never met each other.

When an applicant for psychotherapy finds it difficult to work out an agreement about an appointment time, invariably we know that a big part of him does not want an appointment.

It's too scary! In the above case of Andrew, we could antici-
pate his reluctance to make an appointment. He had "difficulty
establishing relationships with women." Consequently, he was
not going to establish a relationship with Ms. B. easily. Ms. B.
did not realize that sooner or later all patients usually relate
to the therapist the same way they relate to others. A transference begins with the first phone call (Strean 1990).

> When Andrew called another therapist three weeks later,
> he again had difficulty finding a proposed time and date
> convenient for him. However this therapist, Ms. C.,
> handled the situation differently. After Andrew turned
> down three proposed appointments, Ms. C. said warmly,
> "It's awfully difficult coming to a therapist. Most people
> feel uncomfortable right before they have their first ap-
> pointment. Would you like to wait a while before you
> make an appointment?"
>
> Hearing Ms. C.'s nonthreatening and accepting re-
> marks, Andrew felt understood and did make an appoint-
> ment, which he kept. He stayed in therapy with Ms. C. for
> over two years.

One of the most common errors that clinicians make during the initial phone interview is to experience the applicant's
request too literally. Many prospective patients hear from others and/or tell themselves that they need something like sex
therapy, or group therapy, or family therapy, psychoanalysis,
or possibly marital counseling. What they say they need may
or may not turn out to be an accurate assessment. However,
all too often therapists are ready to tell these patients what they
need is what the practitioner specializes in—turning a deaf ear
to what the patients say they need.

Many cases are lost over the phone when the clinician does not "begin where the client is." Professional staff from social agencies and mental health centers are often inclined to tell applicants over the phone that they do not work with particular modalities and thus alienate prospective patients right away. It is perfectly ethical and is good therapy to accept whatever the patient is interested in doing and suggest that he come in for an appointment and discuss it in further detail.

> After Daisy, a single woman in her thirties, had called three therapists requesting "a sexual cohort" and was either told she needed psychotherapy or was rejected altogether, her fourth telephone call yielded more satisfying results. Dr. E., when he heard what transpired in the previous telephone calls, tried to be more related to Daisy's request. He told her that he was interested in discussing her need for a sexual cohort in more detail. Feeling accepted, she made an appointment and kept it.
>
> When Daisy met Dr. E. she told him of severe sexual inhibitions and an intense dislike of sexual intercourse. As Dr. E. tried to understand the roots of Daisy's difficulties, she gradually moved into intensive psychotherapy. Her desire for a sexual cohort quickly dissipated.

Although many therapists respond too literally to their applicants' requests and alienate them, as we have already suggested, other therapists respond with too much eagerness to their patients' requests. Over the phone, therapists often tell prospective patients that they are experts in the modality requested and are very sure they can be of much assistance. Although they are not always consciously aware of it, prospective patients feel manipulated when they are promised a great gift after barely being acquainted with the therapist.

Frank was a senior citizen who called an intake worker of a social agency in order "to expand my social relationships inasmuch as they are currently too superficial." Ms. G., the intake worker, told Frank that she was sure she could help him. Her agency had many groups for senior citizens and there were many people who would be glad to meet him. Although Frank seemed to accept the idea of coming for an intake interview, he never arrived at the appointed time.

When another worker at the same agency, Mr. H., called Frank a couple of weeks later to try to find out what had happened to him, Frank's statements were very revealing and instructive. Averred Frank, "That lady sounded too interested in having me. I kind of felt I was with an insecure salesperson. She boasted of her product so much, I thought she was protesting too much."

RESPONDING TO THE
REFERRAL PARTY'S PRESCRIPTIONS

Most individuals who seek out mental health practitioners are recommended to do so by friends, family, colleagues, or other professionals. Usually these referral parties have their own diagnoses and treatment plans for the prospective patient and frequently have convinced him of their validity. When the prospective patient calls for help, he may be so well indoctrinated that he requests a special type of therapy for a very specific condition.

Although it may be that the referral party knows what he's talking about, he may not. Very often, because the applicant is ambivalent about help, he can unconsciously arrange for the referral party and the prospective therapist to get into a real or imagined argument. By externalizing his ambivalence about receiving therapeutic help, the prospective patient can rationalize away his need for help, feeling that those who are supposed to know are really all mixed up. Therefore, in his mind therapy and therapists become unreliable.

Isabella, a woman in her forties, was referred by her physician to Mr. J., a therapist in private practice. Isabella had severe migraine headaches, gastrointestinal difficulties, as well as phobias, compulsions, and other neurotic problems.

Over the phone, Isabella told Mr. J. that her physician felt she was suffering from severe anxiety and needed intensive therapy. Eager to reassure Isabella that her condition was not so awful, Mr. J. told her that she probably could be helped by having weekly therapy. To his surprise, Isabella told Mr. J., "If my doctor says one thing and you say another, I don't know what to believe. I'll have to think this over." Isabella never did make an appointment with Mr. J.

Following her phone call with Mr. J., a few days later Isabella called Ms. K., a psychologist in private practice. On hearing about the disagreement between Isabella's physician and Mr. J., Ms. K. tried something else. She told herself that inasmuch as Isabella had a closer relationship with her physician than she did with Mr. J., it would be a good idea to reinforce the physician's diagnosis and treatment plan.

When Ms. K. told Isabella that she knew her physician, thought well of him, and tended to endorse his prescriptions, she, too, received a response that surprised her. Said Isabella, "If you and Mr. J. in the same field can't agree, what am I supposed to do?" Attempts to get her to make an appointment were futile.

The case of Isabella, who was very ambivalent about help, teaches us that most of the time it is unwise to take any stand over the phone. Because most prospective patients are ambivalent about requesting help, when the clinician reinforces one side of the ambivalence, the prospective patient is inclined to take the other. If either Mr. J. or Ms. K. had told Isabella in a neutral but friendly manner that it may be a good idea to come in and discuss the doctor's recommendation together, the results may have been different.

In some research I did on the dynamics of referring a patient for psychotherapy (Strean 1976), I learned that all referrals contain an unconscious message emanating from the referral source to the recipient of the referral. I said:

> Referrals may be expressions of love, hate, or ambivalence; they may be manifestations of rivalry and competition or defenses against these drives. Inevitably they reveal something about the psychodynamics of the referring party and his transference to the person to whom he is referring the prospective patient, and to the prospective patient himself. A resistance to the understanding of the personal and interpersonal forces operating in the referral transaction may lead to patient dropout and to the compounding of patient resistance and [therapeutic] counterresistance. [p. 131]

As I have studied the referral process further and discussed it frequently with colleagues, I have concluded that referral sources can be categorized. There are some referral sources who are almost always dependable—the individuals they refer almost always become patients. There are other sources whose referrals hardly ever show up. Finally, mixed results emanate from referral sources who are ambivalent toward us.

Just as children often express the unconscious feelings of their parents, prospective patients frequently reflect the unconscious affects of those who have referred them. It is a good idea to find out over the phone who referred the applicant to us and remind ourselves of the referral source's track record with us.

A therapist in private practice, Dr. L., reported to his colleagues in peer supervision that a former supervisor of his referred prospective patients to him frequently. The only trouble was most of the individuals that the former supervisor recommended never called and those who did never showed up.

When Dr. L. discussed this situation with his former supervisor, he learned that the supervisor envied Dr. L.'s success as a practitioner, resented that he did not need the supervisor any more, and unconsciously sabotaged the referral process.

Dr. Murray Sherman (1966), over thirty years ago in *Psychoanalysis in America: Historical Perspectives*, said something about the dynamics of the referral process that is still pertinent:

Over a period of time, a particular therapist may develop a particular type of practice built upon his past successes, failures, and sources of referral. The referral process itself would likely be most resistant of all to scientific appraisal, but there is doubtless a subtle social interchange that occurs but receives little attention in terms of the psychological and even unconscious significance involved. A determined researcher would find this a most rewarding field of investigation. [p. 20]

DEALING WITH THE
PRACTITIONER'S QUALIFICATIONS

By far, the most frequent question asked by a prospective patient over the telephone is "Could you tell me about your qualifications?" What practitioners often fail to appreciate is the obvious—when the prospective patient makes this query *he is questioning the therapist's qualifications*. He wonders whether the therapist can or will help him.

When a prospective patient is wondering about the possibility of being helped, and therefore is suspicious of the helping process, the most wonderful professional qualifications are not going to reduce his anxiety. Rather, this applicant needs to be told in an empathetic manner that perhaps he is not sure whether the practitioner can help him.

What clinicians often overlook when they are on the phone with someone applying for help is that most prospective patients have been told about the practitioner's qualifications prior to the phone call. Furthermore, the referral source has usually recommended a therapist of whom he has spoken positively. I have made an axiom of psychotherapeutic practice for myself: When a prospective patient questions my qualifications, I try to explore his doubts about me. If I don't do this, he probably won't become a patient.

Mary, a 40-year-old married woman, was referred to Ms. N. for marriage counseling. Over the phone, Mary asked Ms. N., "Do you know anything about bad marriages and how to fix them?" Ms. N. responded to Mary's question by telling her of her long experience working with all sorts of conflicted marriages and that she was an expert in individual therapy, conjoint marital therapy, and family therapy. Sounding impressed, Mary nonetheless said that she wasn't ready to make an appointment and never did with Ms. N.

One of the pitfalls in stating one's excellent qualifications is that the prospective patient can feel intimidated by a professional who has so much stature. When the applicant for psychotherapy calls a prospective therapist, at a time when he is feeling low himself, he is looking for compassion (Lewin 1996) and empathy, not somebody who flaunts her superiority. Hearing about outstanding qualifications often induces in the applicant the feeling of being a second-class citizen. If one feels like a second-class citizen, a means of coping with this ignoble position is to attempt, albeit unconsciously, to make the therapist feel vulnerable. This can be done by rejecting the therapist, as Mary did to Ms. N.

Mary, in the above case illustration, called Ms. O. a week later. She asked Ms. O. if she knew anything about marriages and how to fix them. Ms. O. replied, "Usually when people ask me about my qualifications, they have some questions about me. Would you like to come in and see for yourself how we do when we talk about your marriage?" Mary, after a moment's silence, said, "I like your approach. You're not a braggart. The last professional I spoke to tried to impress me with her great qualifications. I concluded she was desperately trying to get new patients!" Mary made an appointment with Ms. O. and stayed in treatment for several years.

Sometimes a prospective patient is very insistent about knowing about the professional's background and doesn't take "no" for an answer. Although the applicant may appear intimidating, this is no cause for the therapist to capitulate. I have learned that the prospective patient who is insistent, provocative, and intimidating, although belligerent at first, welcomes a firm response primarily because the therapist who does not capitulate is considered somebody one can respect.

> Peter, a man in his forties, sought help from a mental health center in his local community. On the phone he told the intake worker that he had a lot of sexual problems but he wasn't sure that the intake worker, Mr. Q., was able to handle "a tough case" like his. When Peter learned that Mr. Q. would be his therapist if he came to the mental health center, he asked Mr. Q. over the phone, "Are you familiar with the latest sexual therapy techniques?" Mr. Q. said, "I get the impression you are not confident that I have the stuff to help you." Brusquely, Peter retorted, "I'm *not* confident that you have it. That's why I'm asking you a question." Then he inquired again, "I want to know, do you have the knowledge to help me?" Mr. Q. responded, "I could tell you about some of my knowledge but I think it would help you more if we met and you could see for yourself if you were helped." After a silence, Peter said, "I'll think it over and call you back if I decide to come in."
>
> Peter called Mr. Q. to make an appointment two days later. In the initial consultation, he told Mr. Q., "When I saw that you didn't get ruffled by me, I knew you knew your stuff."

THE USE OF MODALITY

As we have already suggested, many prospective patients, influenced by others and/or by their own biases, often suggest over the phone what kind of therapy they need. In our current mental health scene there are literally dozens of therapeutic modalities for sale and dozens of theoretical orientations being utilized. Prospective patients often have some strong convictions about what they need or don't need. But what happens when the prospective patient says over the phone to a Freudian clinician who specializes in intensive individual therapy, "The one thing I don't want is a Freudian who does that long-term stuff!"? Or what if the prospective patient wants conjoint marital therapy and that is the practitioner's first love? Should she share that information over the phone?

I believe the two most common errors that mental health professionals make on the phone are stating that what the prospective patient desires they can't provide or pointing out that what is requested is exactly what is available. The reason these stances turn out to be errors is that, as already implied, what people feel they want, they may not need. Somebody wanting short-term treatment may need many sessions. A man who wants to acquire some new sexual techniques may need to talk about his fear of and hostility to women. A woman who wants individual treatment may get more from a group.

Because requests that contain the prospective patient's preferred modality need to be studied in one or more interviews, I believe it is always more helpful to the prospective patient not to have the therapist's theoretical predilections revealed over the phone. First of all, it is the rare clinician who can be sure about what a patient needs before meeting him. She has to study his request thoroughly and get to know more about his history, current modus vivendi, and a host of other factors before formulating a treatment plan. Second, I have found that most prospective patients feel much better understood and more supported when the therapist says, "I think it might be a good idea for us to get to know each other better so that we can decide together what's best for you. At this point I don't think I can be sure. How about coming to my office and talking it over with me?"

WHO SHOULD COME TO
THE FIRST INTERVIEW?

Many cases are lost over the phone because the therapist is too inclined to state dogmatically who should come for the initial interview. If she is a specialist in long-term individual treatment, the therapist might too quickly tell a woman who is fighting daily with her husband, and desperately wants marriage counseling, to come alone to see her. Or the therapist who is a specialist in family therapy or conjoint marital counseling may fail to recognize that the individual who is speaking to her over the phone may very much want a confidential one-to-one interview.

Although all clinicians are entitled to have their preferred methods of working—with individuals, couples, families, or small groups—in order to avoid losing patients over the phone, they have to be able to begin where the client is.

As the therapist listens to the phone applicant describe his problems and situational difficulties, she can often infer correctly if the caller wants and needs a one-to-one interview. For example, if the caller talks exclusively about himself, the chances are quite high that he needs a private interview. On the other hand, if he constantly refers to his wife and/or his child, the chances are greater that he may need a conjoint or family interview.

In most cases, the individual who can answer the question "Who should come to the first interview?" with the greatest degree of accuracy is the caller himself (Maroda 1994).

Furthermore, if the individual making the phone call is consulted on this issue, diagnostic material of pertinence often becomes more available.

> Rhoda, a woman in her forties, called Dr. S. and told him over the telephone of her very conflicted marriage of ten years. She mentioned that she and her husband, Sam, had continual arguments "about so many things—money, sex, the children," that her married life seemed very much like a war.
>
> As Dr. S. listened carefully to Rhoda, he was quite sure that she and Sam needed conjoint marital therapy and that this would be Rhoda's preference. However, when Dr. S. asked Rhoda if she would like to come for an interview with Sam, or alone, she strongly responded, "I must see you alone. There are a lot of things I don't want Sam to hear about. Seeing you alone is a must! Is that okay with you?"
>
> Dr. S. assured Rhoda that he could see her in a one-to-one interview, and did so. At this interview, Rhoda revealed she was having an extramarital affair that she did not want to discuss with Sam, who was not privy to this information.

Sometimes clinicians who feel they do not have any expertise in working within a particular therapeutic modality are reluctant to have a consultation that involves an interview outside their area of expertise. Yet, if the prospective client is the best judge, it is helpful to adapt to his preferences and see what happens in the consultation interview.

> When Tom, a 30-year-old man, requested that he and his wife be seen in conjoint treatment, the therapist, Ms. U.,

although working exclusively in one-to-one therapy, agreed to Tom's request. As Tom and his wife felt very much individualized and empathized with, at the end of the consultation, they both requested individual therapy with Ms. U., which worked quite well.

What happened with Tom and his wife in the above illustration does not always occur; that is, the patient chooses the modality at which the therapist is an expert. Sometimes it is necessary for the therapist, after a face-to-face consultation, to refer the prospective patient to a colleague who has expertise in a modality in which the therapist does not. Usually a prospective patient can accept a referral with more confidence after he has had a favorable experience with a therapist in consultation. The important point I wish to emphasize is that telephone applicants for therapy are more apt to accept the idea of a meeting if they are consulted on the matter of who should come for the initial interview. If their ideas are respected, they are more inclined to remain in treatment with the therapist or accept referral to a colleague.

THE INVOLUNTARY PATIENT

If it is difficult for individuals who voluntarily seek psychotherapy to reveal themselves to a stranger, imagine how vexing it is for an involuntary patient to call up a therapist! Yet many prospective patients have been commanded to see a therapist by a boss who threatens to fire him, a spouse who threatens to divorce him, or a fiancée who will not marry him unless he undergoes treatment. Although the criticized spouse or lover, troubled student, or adjudicated criminal may initially welcome treatment rather than face the alternative of divorce, being thrown out of school, or being sent to prison, he usually resents being forced into treatment (Strean 1991). Because the involuntary patient often cannot tell anybody this, the skillful clinician knows that unless the prospective patient's resentment is faced and discharged, therapy will have a limited effect or none at all.

As suggested earlier, one of the essential tasks of the therapist on the phone is to determine who referred the prospective patient and how he is responding to the referral. By confronting this task we will usually learn if we have an involuntary caller. If so, we have to be able to demonstrate to him over the phone that we are compassionate and can empathize with his dilemma. Showing compassion for the difficult position he is in often animates the phone conversation (Lewin 1996).

> Victor, a college student of 19, phoned Dr. W., a private practitioner, and told him that he "must have therapy." When Dr. W. inquired why Victor "must" the latter told him that he would be thrown out of college if he didn't get into therapy right away. On Dr. W.'s asking Victor how it felt to be forced into therapy, Victor replied, "It's okay." When Dr. W. quizzically said, "Really!" Victor said, "I have no choice."
>
> Dr. W., sensing how trapped Victor felt, compassionately stated, "It's damn tough to be forced into something—particularly something like therapy, which can go on for a while." Sensing that Dr. W. was a possible ally, Victor said, "You seem to understand how much of a jam I'm in. I'd like to meet you."

Much of Victor's therapy with Dr. W. involved looking carefully at Victor's readiness to submit to authoritative pronouncements without realizing how much he resented capitulating. Had Dr. W. not related over the phone to the predicament that Victor was in, the therapy would not have gotten off to the excellent start that it did.

I have found that therapy never works when the patient feels under legal, moral, or psychological coercion. If an empathetic, non-authoritarian attitude is shown to the patient from the first phone call on through the treatment, therapy has a much better chance of succeeding.

CALLS ON BEHALF OF A PROSPECTIVE PATIENT

A difficult phone call for the therapist to cope with is from the individual who is calling on behalf of a prospective patient, instead of the patient himself. Often a wife phones a therapist to arrange treatment for her husband, or a parent may do the same for a child. Often therapists are recipients of phone calls from sons and daughters who want to make appointments for their parents. I have received many calls from men and women who want to make appointments for their friends.

Often, when the therapist asks the caller to have his spouse, child, parent, or friend call the practitioner, the person never calls. When an appointment is made by one person for another, the appointment is frequently broken by the person for whom it was made.

When one person calls a therapist for another, the person calling is often, albeit unconsciously, asking for help for himself. Most of the time the spouse, parent, child, or friend who calls for someone else does not feel free to ask directly for therapy and finds it easier to ask for help for someone else. However, if the caller's unconscious wish is interpreted over the phone and he is told he is indirectly asking for treatment for himself, the caller will probably deny it. Therefore, to respect the caller's latent wish for help and concomitantly respond to his resistance to therapy, the sensitive therapist will ask the person making the call to come in and discuss his child's, spouse's, or friend's problem. Many parents, spouses, and friends welcome the possibility of an appointment for such purposes, and if empathetically responded to by the therapist, they often become patients in their own right.

> Yolanda, a single woman in her thirties, called Dr. Z., a female therapist in private practice, to discuss her friend, Alice. Over the phone, Yolanda told Dr. Z. that Alice was a very insecure person who needed much therapy but found it difficult to ask for it. On being asked by Dr. Z., "What do you suppose is in Alice's way?" after a long pause Yolanda responded, "She can do for others but she can't take care of herself."
>
> Dr. Z. noted to herself that Yolanda's description of Alice as one who does for others but can't help herself might also apply to Yolanda. After all, Yolanda was doing for others by calling up Dr. Z. and asking for her friend to be helped.
>
> When Dr. Z. asked Yolanda how she would feel coming in to see Dr. Z. and discuss Alice some more, Yolanda seemed surprised. She said, "I'm only interested in help for a friend, but . . . if that's what you want, I'll try it."
>
> After Yolanda met with Dr. Z. for two interviews and spent a lot of time talking about Alice, she was able to ask for help for herself. Dr. Z., realizing that Yolanda's statements about Alice were self-descriptions, handled her responses empathically but deliberately.

FEES

Almost as frequent as queries about the practitioner's professional qualifications are questions about fees and fee policies. Many clinicians believe that the phone caller has "a right to know" the fee before making an appointment and do tell him when asked over the phone. I do not subscribe to this point of view, for several reasons. First, many prospective patients may think the fee mentioned over the phone is too high and either turn away from the practitioner or try to bargain with her. When two people who have never met face-to-face are in a bargaining situation, they are not likely to resolve it easily and therefore it does not seem to be a good way to begin a relationship. Second, the fee offered over the phone could sound too low to the applicant, and then he may begin to have doubts about working with the practitioner who does not value herself enough. Third, as is true with many of the issues we have discussed in this chapter, prospective patients and therapists have a better chance to determine what the fee will be after they have had a warm face-to-face interview. Many issues between two people have a better chance to be resolved in the flesh than over the phone.

When a prospective patient asks me over the phone what the fee will be, I tell him that I'd like to determine that with him when we meet. Most prospective patients seem to respond positively to this suggestion and do come in. Like most practitioners, I have a pretty good idea about what I want my fees to be, but I try to keep the fee arrangements flexible. Even if the therapist is adamant about the fee she is going to charge, she is usually much better off discussing it in a face-to-face interview. Very often, after a reluctant prospective patient meets the therapist, he is more inclined to accept the fee that is asked.

Bob, a 30-year-old man, called Ms. C. because he needed help so he could "give up my single status." On Ms. C.'s suggesting that he come in and discuss it further, Bob said he would very much like to do that but needed to know Ms. C.'s fee. When Ms. C. told Bob that her fee was $100 a session, Bob said it was too high and did not make an appointment. Despite the fact that Ms. C. said she would be glad to reconsider the fee, Bob remained adamant about not making an appointment.

Two weeks later Bob called Dr. D., a male therapist. When Dr. D. was asked over the phone what his fee was, he told Bob that he would like to determine that with him when they met. Bob came in for an interview, discussed his problems, and shared some of his history. At the end of the interview, Dr. D. said, "My usual fee is $100." Bob willingly accepted.

Money is a highly cathected subject in our culture. Many people's self-esteem is based on how much they are worth financially. Furthermore, how we value other people often depends on their financial assets. That is why the issue of fees needs to be explored sensitively and empathically in the therapeutic situation.

One reason that motivates people to seek psychotherapy is a wish to have a loving relationship with a parental figure. To pay for this opportunity often conjures up associations in the patient's mind that he is visiting a prostitute or someone similar.

Erik, a married man in his forties, phoned Ms. F., a therapist in private practice, because he wanted help for his "shaky marriage." After a mutually pleasant phone conversation, Erik asked Ms. F., "How much do you gals get for this stuff? I know you don't believe in free love!" When Ms. F. told Erik she had the impression that he had some questions and feelings about paying for her help, he replied, "I feel like a fool paying to be serviced."

Money and fees, like most of the issues we have been discussing in this chapter, do not cease to be concerns after the first phone conversation between therapist and patient. Money and fees are of concern to both parties throughout the entire treatment process.

HOW MUCH DOES THE THERAPIST
DISCLOSE ABOUT HERSELF?

Throughout this chapter one of the central themes has been how much the therapist discloses about herself. Does she tell the prospective patient what her professional credentials are? Does she discuss her fee policy? Does she reveal her preferred therapeutic modalities or her theoretical predilections?

Self-disclosure has become a much discussed and controversial subject among contemporary therapists (Goldstein 1997, Raines 1996). While I believe that there are times when it can help the patient and advance the therapy if a therapist shares some aspects of her life and/or selected countertransference reactions with the patient, I am wary of doing so at the beginning of treatment, either during the initial phone call or in the first interviews. The reasons for this are several. When we don't know the patient well, we can't be certain how he will react to our disclosures. Further, questions about the therapist's life, as we have indicated, are usually an expression of the prospective patient's doubts and anxieties about therapy and the therapist, and therefore should be explored as to their meaning rather than immediately answered.

One of the problems in answering personal questions at the beginning of treatment is that the patient then has "the right to have encores." Why shouldn't patients whose questions about the therapist are initially answered assume the right to have all questions answered throughout the whole treatment process? By answering personal questions at the beginning of treatment, we can make it more difficult for the patient to absorb the inevitable frustrations that will come later.

It has been my consistent observation that therapists who answer personal questions at the beginning of treatment are frequently doing so to ward off the patient's anger or wish to reject the therapist. I have also found that when therapists do not need to protect themselves this way and can listen to the patient's disappointment, resentment, and criticism of the therapist when his questions are explored and not answered, as hostility is discharged in what begins to look like a safer environment, mistrust recedes and a therapeutic alliance begins.

REFERENCES

Goldstein, E. (1997). To tell or not to tell: the disclosure of events in the therapist's life to the patient. *Clinical Social Work Journal* 25(4):41–59.

Hamilton, G. *(1951). Theory and Practice of Social Casework.* New York: Columbia University Press.

Kardiner, A. (1945). *The Psychological Frontiers of Society.* New York: Columbia University Press.

Lewin, R. (1996). Compassion: The Core Value That Animates Psychotherapy. Northvale, NJ: Jason Aronson.

Maroda, K. (1994). *The Power of Countertransference*. Northvale, NJ: Jason Aronson.

Raines, J. (1996). Self-disclosure in clinical social work. *Clinical Social Work Journal* 24(4):351–377.

Sherman, M. (1966). Psychoanalysis in America: Historical Perspectives. Springfield, IL: Charles C Thomas.

Strean, H. (1976). Some psychodynamics in referring patients for psychotherapy. In *Crucial Issues in Psychotherapy*, ed. H. Strean, pp. 53–63. Metuchen, NJ: Scarecrow Press.

—— (1990). *Resolving Resistances in Psychotherapy*. New York: Brunner/Mazel.

—— (1991). *Behind the Couch*. New York: Continuum.

5

Long-Term Therapy by Telephone
The Patient Who Cannot Let Go

JANE PLUMMER

MARTHA STARK

*T*he following case vignette covers fifteen years of psycho-therapy—the first three in face-to-face meetings and the last twelve over the telephone. The patient, Rachel, and I (JP) have had planned face-to-face sessions at various times over the years, but the treatment has been conducted primarily by telephone. Both Rachel and I believe that the ongoing treatment relationship has been life-sustaining for her—far outweighing whatever negative impact there might have been from the loss of face-to-face contact.

What follows is a fairly detailed narrative of our work together as Rachel and I have negotiated the various twists and turns that are to be expected in any long-term therapy relationship.

PRESENTING PROBLEM

Rachel is currently 34 years old, and she and I have been working together for fifteen years. During her sophomore year, Rachel referred herself to the counseling center of an intensely academic college in the Boston area, reporting that she was feeling depressed and lonely, as she had been her entire life.

She denied any prior treatment history. Rachel was petite and childlike, with a soft voice and a self-deprecating manner. She had beautiful, large eyes and thick, curly hair. Rachel observed that the things upon which she had always relied to calm and to soothe herself (like going on shopping trips to Boston to buy herself gifts, listening to music) were no longer helping. She experienced herself as damaged inside and paralyzingly handicapped. With much anguish, she expressed her desperate desire to become all that she had secretly dreamed of becoming as a child—dreams that had sustained her during her traumatized early years.

Rachel presented with chronic suicidal ideation but had no intent or plan and no history of prior gestures or attempts. She talked at length about her boyfriend, with whom she had been involved for over nine months, a relationship that provoked feelings of desperation and aloneness because he was such a disappointment to her. Rachel at the same time as she felt her relationships with women were mistrustful, emotionally distanced, and unfulfilled, experienced them as often vicious and intensely competitive. At one point, she told me she actually hated women, although she was aware that she would seek out men who had feminine, maternal, nurturing qualities.

Rachel was an excellent student, was involved in some campus activities, and felt generally comfortable at school. It is noteworthy that despite her long history of low-level depression and her enduring sense of alienation, Rachel had nonetheless managed to get by for years without revealing to anyone her quiet, internal desperation.

FAMILY HISTORY

Rachel rapidly introduced her early childhood experiences into the treatment. By the fifth session she had brought reams of material that she had written as a young girl. In one letter, she had poignantly written:

> I can't function like a normal person. I'm looking for something I can't find. But if I don't find it I'm going to die. . . . Everyone uses me. I have no friends. I have no parents. I'm all alone, and I'm so tired of being alone.

Rachel's father was a brilliant academician at a well-known university. He had been doted upon as a child and success had come easily for him. In his early twenties, he had met and immediately fallen in love with a beautiful woman, who soon became his wife. They had two children. Rachel's sister (three years younger than she) was dismissively described by Rachel as emotionally immature, demanding, entitled, and "like my mother." The family relocated several times. The father held several academic positions and finally moved the family to Boston, where he was offered a tenured position.

Rachel's mother never worked outside the home. She was emotionally labile and was, at one point, diagnosed as bipolar. Her behavior was erratic, bizarre, and unpredictable. When Rachel was young, her mother was verbally abusive and physically assaultive. With eerily flat affect, Rachel described horrendous episodes of being entrapped in the basement and of having Mother pinion her to the floor while she repeatedly beat Rachel's face. Mother was intrusive, not allowing Rachel and her sister any privacy, either in their bedrooms or in the bathroom. Not only would Mother barge in while Rachel was showering, she would also fling back the shower curtain and demand to see how her daughter was developing physically. Periodically, Mother would rage at Rachel and her sister, calling them whores and blaming them for all her misery.

Mother was particularly jealous of Rachel and, believing that Rachel was a direct competitor for Father's attention, would scream obscenities at her. Any attention Father paid Rachel would precipitate rageful outbursts from Mother. When Mother was particularly enraged, she would shriek at Rachel, would toss her belongings out her bedroom window, and would then eject her from the house. Father would come home from work, would find this chaos, and would shuffle off to a chair, claiming that he was too tired to deal with it. He would then fall asleep, even while Mother was flinging pots and pans around the house and screeching at Rachel to stay out.

One incident powerfully demonstrates Father's inability to deal with his wife and children in an effective way. Mother had hit Rachel on the head with a skate, cutting her scalp with its blade. Rachel had appealed to Father upon his return home, showing him her bleeding wound. His response was to tell her that her head was not bleeding, and he had then gone off to bed.

Meal times were described as agonizing; to this day, Rachel remains a restrictive eater and is highly squeamish about many foods. For dinner, Mother would cook bizarre concoctions that were inevitably charred; she would then insist that her daughters eat every last morsel.

Mother was also capable, unpredictably, of being warm, humorous, generous, and loving. She had been quite good with Rachel and her sister when they were infants and toddlers; it was when they began to separate from her that she fell apart. Mother perceived any attempts they made to be autonomous as brutal personal attacks, to which she responded with rage and vituperation.

Father, although avoidant, could also be very witty and was well known for his wonderful stories about his worldwide travels. Father was able to be charming, however, only if his needs were being met. Rachel learned early on that if she were attentive to "Daddy," literally bringing him his slippers, listening to his woes about work or his chronic dissatisfaction with his wife, she would be rewarded by his staying awake.

Father and Mother's marriage was like the rest of Rachel's upbringing: chaotic and unpredictable. They would get along famously for a few hours but would then fight savagely until Father once again withdrew. They would often have intercourse with their bedroom door open. Rachel also remembered being as old as 10 and being taken into their bed (where they both lay nude) and then being cuddled by Mother.

During Rachel's formative years, Mother's family played a major role. Her maternal grandfather had been a famous classical musician, and her grandmother had come from a famous musical family. With much fondness, Rachel remembered going to see these grandparents, and she recalled in particular the delicious food Grandmother always prepared whenever Rachel visited. Poignantly, she related that she had always longed for them to be the parents she had never had, yearning, above all else, for them to be loyal to her. The reality, however, never measured up to her dreams. Grandmother would become embroiled in vicious arguments with Rachel's mother. Meanwhile, Grandfather was sexually molesting Rachel and her sister (a fact that Rachel repressed until several years into her treatment with me). Grandfather was a tyrant and was very cruel to Rachel, but he was revered and beloved in the community of musicians. There was as much disorder at her grandparents' house as there was at her own.

Rachel grew up in a home that was unpredictable, violent, abusive, and traumatizing. As she noted in a journal she was keeping: "As soon as I stepped back and examined my relationship with my family—whether it be grandparents, aunts, mother, or father—I was left holding smoke. It was nothing. No one came to me when I was needy and troubled. No one supported me. No one bothered getting involved. I was always alone."

PSYCHODYNAMIC FORMULATION

When Rachel first presented, she was a depressed 19-year-old, a quietly desperate, highly defended, passively dependent young woman who quickly delivered her despair and her hopelessness into the treatment relationship and looked to me for the good mothering she was denied early on. She needed continuous reinforcement from external objects, whom she experienced as necessary for her very survival. Although it was difficult for her to express anger directly in relation to her family, she was filled with outrage about the many injustices in the world around her and was the constant champion of the underdog. Rachel had little positive to say about her mother but was obviously devoted to her father. She was deeply aggrieved that even though he was intensely attentive at times, he would constantly retreat from engagement both unpredictably and abruptly.

COURSE OF PSYCHOTHERAPY

Rachel and I have now worked together for fifteen years in both weekly and twice-weekly psychotherapy. For the first three years, sessions were face-to-face. After she moved to the midwest to attend law school, we continued our work by telephone and now we do regular weekly sessions by telephone (with two to three times per year face-to-face double sessions when Rachel is in town).

The First Three Years of Treatment

Our work started at the beginning of Rachel's sophomore year of college. In her first year of treatment, Rachel made a sudden, impulsive suicide attempt by overdosing on several medications in a low-risk, high-rescue gesture. She was admitted to the psychiatric unit of a general hospital. This was the first suicide attempt she had ever made, but she had long lived with intense feelings of aloneness and desperation. Several months after her release, Rachel was able to tell me that early on the day of her suicide gesture, she had called the counseling center in a panic because I had cancelled her appointment. The secretary had indiscreetly disclosed that I was at home taking care of a very sick daughter. Rachel had not known that I had children; she felt that her "bubble" had suddenly "burst"—and she was utterly devastated. Rachel had fantasized that I was the good mother for whom she had been yearning and she felt very displaced knowing I had a daughter. After much hard work to process her disillusionment, we ultimately recovered our equilibrium.

There have been subsequent disruptions in our relationship. Each time Rachel has experienced me as abandoning, but we have managed to work through her disenchantment and, in the process, to modulate the intensity of her need for the people in her world to be perfectly available. In retrospect, Rachel and I recognize that her suicidality arose out of her desperate need to make absolutely sure that I understood just how much she needed me—a need about which she felt much shame during the early years of our treatment.

Initially, my stance was primarily empathic, and Rachel, within the context of the safety she experienced by way of my "holding" of her, elaborated more and more details about her early years. What became increasingly clear was that she had been raised in a family where there was no surcease from extreme disorder and cruelty. I would listen intently and offer comfort when Rachel spoke about her many conflicts with her friends and the terrible disappointments she had suffered when people were thoughtless or insensitive, which she inevitably experienced as extreme harshness. As best I could, I would help her to become calm when she was severely anxious about her school performance and would validate her experience of upset, hurt, and anguish at the hands of her extended family.

Whenever Rachel would permit it, I would attempt at least to name the longings she experienced in relation to me. But what soon became clear to us both was that my making explicit her attachment to me left her feeling humiliated and diminished. Nonetheless, Rachel reported that my capacity to tolerate the intensity of her desire for me was tremendously reassuring and enabled her, over time, to deliver other shameful secrets into the therapeutic relationship. Rachel was looking for someone who would be diametrically opposite to her family, somebody who would be kind, gentle, and loving. In finding me, she felt that she had at last found the comfort and consistency for which she had been searching her entire life. Her gratitude was palpable, though we both knew she preferred that we not make too big a deal of it.

In the first years of therapy, I began to focus my interpretive efforts on Rachel's extreme sensitivity to disappointment. She spoke often, and with much anguished affect, about her conflicted relationships with friends, and we focused on her tortured relationships with the men she was now dating. Rachel would build her world around whatever man she was seeing at the time; any disruption in that relationship would precipitate profound despair, depression, and panic.

Gradually, Rachel came to understand just how destroyed she had always felt by her mother's emotional abuse and just how betrayed she had always felt by her father's passivity and unwillingness to intervene on her behalf. Of note was the fact that though devastated, Rachel never expressed outrage: her fury was unleashed only years later once she began to acknowledge, first to herself and then to me, the degree of deprivation and cruelty to which she had been exposed as a child and the extent of the emotional damage that had resulted. Year by year Rachel was letting herself know, in incremental bits, the horror of what she had been subjected to during her formative years. She would often wish that she could find in the present that person who would be able to provide for her in the ways that her parents had never done—to offer her the opportunity both to realize her potential and to come into her own personally, professionally, and romantically. Unfortunately, despite Rachel's recognition that her parents were toxic, she insisted on maintaining fairly regular contact with them. All the while, they, were completely oblivious to the impact on her of their continued outrageous behavior.

During her senior year of college, Rachel was accepted at a midwestern law school. She and I were acutely aware that, despite the good work we had accomplished in identifying some of her core issues and in developing her capacity to tolerate some degree of disappointment, there was still much more work to be done. Although I sensed that it would be exceptionally hard for Rachel to let go of me after our three years of difficult but intensely rewarding work, she herself was not able to admit just how much she feared going off on her own. I offered her my telephone availability on an as-needed basis until she was able to make a good connection with someone in the counseling center at her new school. Rachel and I talked about what she would want in a therapist, and, though she said she would want somebody just like me, it never occurred to me to offer her the option of continuing our treatment by telephone in regularly scheduled weekly sessions.

Our termination work lasted six months. During that time, it became increasingly clear that Rachel had a limited internal capacity to regulate her self-esteem and that she could only feel good about herself if she were treated "specially" by the other. Because of how dependent she had become on me, it made her very anxious to acknowledge how profoundly attached she was and how deeply important I was to her.

Treatment during the Law School Years

Rachel headed to law school in search of further therapy. Interestingly, she did find a female therapist with whom she initially felt comfortable. In time, however, she felt increasingly uncomfortable as this therapist (in an effort to be helpful) began to encourage her to find a way to reconcile with her family. In October, Rachel called me late one evening reporting that she was really frantic; she adamantly insisted that she was no longer willing to work with this new therapist because she was feeling pressured and misunderstood.

It suddenly occurred to me that perhaps I could offer Rachel my own availability by telephone on a regular weekly basis until her winter break in December, at which time she and I could review the situation and make a decision about our future. I had some reservations about making myself available for phone sessions in this ongoing way, but after consultation with several colleagues, I decided to give it a try. I offered her my proposal, which she eagerly and with much relief and gratitude accepted. In fact, we were easily able to pick up where we had left off, focusing in particular on her feelings of inadequacy in relation to her fellow students, her more general sense of alienation and estrangement, her desperate attempts to find a new boyfriend, and her yearning to be back home with her parents—and with me.

When I saw her during her winter break, Rachel admitted that she had known all along that it would be impossible for her to work with any other therapist and that she had gone to the other therapist only because I had strongly encouraged her to seek treatment once she arrived at law school. Interestingly, this was the first time Rachel had openly expressed her need for me and her faith in me. She pleaded with me to allow her to continue our work for an indefinite period of time by telephone. So I put aside my own anxieties about venturing into uncharted territory and about what my colleagues might say were they to find out what I was doing and resolved to make the best of it.

In the years since, I have encountered therapists who, though often reluctantly, have acknowledged their own use of telephone treatment for those patients with whom they have felt particularly connected and with whom there was a particular need. When Rachel and I contracted to do our sessions by telephone, we agreed that she would commit to doing all she could to ensure that we would have face-to-face sessions during her school breaks and summer recesses. She returned to school greatly relieved and I, too, was aware of feeling relief. Part of what enabled me to feel comfortable enough to offer the telephone contact was Rachel's exceptional reliability and my faith in her and in her capacity to deal with losing the face-to-face contact.

Over the course of the next two and a half years, while Rachel completed law school, interestingly—and perhaps to the surprise of us both—our work took a new direction and seemed, if anything, to deepen and in time to free Rachel to be more expressive of how frightened and alone she had always felt. There was now something more intimate about our conversations and, paradoxically, we both felt closer, despite the geographical separation, than ever before. It was as if the loss of face-to-face contact offered Rachel the safety, the security, and the freedom to be more herself and to express more of her vulnerability, her yearnings, and her pain.

With the containment provided by our twice-weekly telephone therapy, Rachel finished her three years of graduate
study with honors. She was able to be focused on her academ-
ics and to manage her anxiety about her school performance.
She did, however, become embroiled in a devastatingly ruin-
ous relationship with a fellow graduate student and once again,
found herself feeling suicidal and unable to go on. This man
had offered her the tantalizing hope of intimacy and kindness
but, ultimately, was quite cruel and emotionally unavailable.
The relationship with him recapitulated for her both the abu-
siveness of her mother and the abandonment by her father.
Despite the insight she gained about why she found this man
so compelling, Rachel nonetheless suffered terribly and might
well have required hospitalization had she not been able to
maintain her connection with me. (There were several weeks
when we spoke four or five times by phone.)

During the summer before her final year of law school
(and in our fifth year of treatment) Rachel and I were meeting face-to-face as per our agreement. She was offered a very
prestigious summer internship in Boston, but she became very
depressed and despondent because she could not get along with
the senior members of the firm. She found them to be harsh,
critical, mocking, and disdainful, and she found it very difficult to perform well under these all-too-familiar circumstances.

I needed to be vigorously interpretive with Rachel in order to help her understand the extent to which her sensitivity
to rejection and her tendency to experience others as rejecting were determined, in large measure, by her family history.
Interestingly, once she came to appreciate just how impactful
her early experiences had been, Rachel was able to achieve
some distance and managed to complete her internship. Also
of note, as Rachel became more outspoken about the actual
abuse on the job, she began to speak up to her mother about

how unacceptable Mother's behavior was. She returned to school after the summer and finished well.

Years Six through Ten of Treatment

After her third year of law school, Rachel moved to New York, taking the only job she had been offered. Fired for poor performance almost immediately, she was then unemployed for the next two years. At this juncture in her life, Rachel's hypersensitivity to insult and to the degradation that were the daily fare at her Wall Street law firm made it impossible for her to accomplish the duties of her new job, despite her recognition of the part played by her vulnerabilities to this kind of familiar atmosphere. After she lost her job, Rachel went into a profound regression and was unable to return to work because she could not face dealing with people. It was clear that Rachel experienced the work place the same way she had experienced her home life: unpredictable, emotionally brutalizing, and utterly depleting. She felt vulnerable to disappointment and attack at every moment. It also became increasingly apparent that she was choosing people who not only were unable to provide her with emotional support and consistency but also were directly demanding, exploitative, and assaulting. In short, she continued to recapitulate in her contemporary relationships the dysfunctional dynamic that had characterized the relationship with her parents.

In the eighth year of therapy, after much hard work, Rachel succeeded in landing a job with the government (one she actually maintains to this day), a job that affords her both financial and emotional security and, though extraordinarily challenging at times, is something she can manage. Since she secured her position, our work has focused primarily on her need to set limits with people's intrusiveness (which she unwittingly allows and sometimes even encourages) and on emotional abuse (which she tolerates). For the first time, Rachel reported being able to terminate conversations with mother when the latter was being particularly provocative and, in her relationships with co-workers and people in positions of authority, being able appropriately to disengage when situations became intolerably disrespectful and intrusive.

In the ninth year of our treatment, Rachel met her husband-to-be, Jason, a very bright medical student who had come from a family as dysfunctional as Rachel's. Jason's mother had been intrusive, abusive, and vicious; his father had been passive and withdrawn. Together, Jason and Rachel attempted to create an island of sanity away from the cruelty, intrusiveness, and disorder of their families.

Admitting that the bond she experienced with me lent her a certain confidence and faith, Rachel was able to fall deeply in love with Jason, almost as if the closeness and the security she had discovered in our relationship was giving her the courage to expose her own vulnerability and her own desire to this man. Jason and Rachel were married after she and I had been working together for ten years, and they remain close and loving to this day. Even though there have certainly been difficulties, mainly because of their similar histories and backgrounds, both of them work exceptionally hard to make their marriage viable.

Inspired by Rachel, Jason entered treatment while still in New York as a medical student with a woman with whom he continues (by telephone!) since he and Rachel moved to Los Angeles in the tenth year of Rachel's therapy with me. In a conversation with Jason's therapist, I learned that what had given her the courage to accept Jason's proposal that they continue their treatment sessions by telephone was the fact that Rachel was doing so well in her work with me. Furthermore,

Jason and Rachel have now been in couple therapy for the past five years in face-to-face treatment and not by telephone (although it is noteworthy that they have had conference calls with their couple therapist when they were in crisis). Now that Jason has finished his medical training, he and Rachel are attempting to become pregnant. Both recognize that they are at risk for transmitting intergenerationally the traumatizing dysfunctionality of their families of origin, but they are hopeful that their awareness of that potential will enable them to avoid repeating with their child what was done to them.

Years Ten through Fifteen of Treatment

During the last several years of her therapy, Rachel has come to feel better and better about herself and her capacities and, as a result, has been able to secure much more respect and even admiration from both her peers and her supervisors. Although she still finds herself drawn into potentially abusive situations, she nonetheless consistently demonstrates an ability to extricate herself before there is bloodshed. Painfully for Rachel, however, remains the fact that she quickly shifts from anger to despair when she finds herself disappointed by the objects in her life. With Jason especially, she feels entitled to complete availability, absolute understanding, and total empathic resonance with her feelings.

With respect to her mother's verbal assaultiveness, Rachel has been increasingly able to hold her own and even to provide some containment when her mother is uncontrollably screaming and shouting.

In her relationship with Jason, she has been more frequently able to give voice to her needs and expectations and has insisted that he be held accountable for any disrespectful behavior.

In her relationship with me, Rachel has become increasingly comfortable articulating both her yearning for me to gratify and her outrage at being denied that gratification. Whereas during the first years of our work together Rachel was unable to express just how much I mattered to her, in these last years she has become able increasingly to verbalize her heartfelt gratitude and her appreciation for my unrelenting efforts on her behalf. Most recently, she has even been voicing her love for me and her increasing identification with me.

Despite Rachel's knowing that her family will never change, she finds herself continuing to long for a loving family, a longing that places her at risk because it consigns her to a lifetime of continuous disappointment and heartache. Periodically, she will try to entice her mother into caring for her lovingly and gently, and to coax her father into relinquishing his self-involvement. Obviously, Rachel is doomed to fail. Although she knows it in her head, she does not yet fully know it in her heart.

TOWARD THE FUTURE

Clearly, Rachel still has work to do. She has been in therapy a good many years yet still cannot fully grieve her loss of good, gentle, consistent parenting that she never had or will ever have. It may be that the telephone serves a defensive function for her and allows her to avoid her need to engage me in a more negative transference. I remain highly idealized and it is Rachel's way of feeling she has found in the present what she never had in the past. Not seeing me face-to-face may make it too frightening for her to allow her rage at being disappointed by me because I can never make up for her loss of good parenting. I believe that so much of what transpires for more primitive patients in the re-introjective processes of therapy is grounded in the reality of the therapist's physical presence. Rachel is deprived of these reality testings by the telephone. I believe that to accomplish this work I would need to see her face-to-face and hope that we will at some time have the opportunity to do this work because at this point Rachel has directly stated that she intends to be in therapy forever. Without working through the negative transference she cannot leave because she has grief work to do in our relationship, as well.

Over the course of our fifteen years, Rachel has transitioned from a desperately depressed, achingly lonely, helplessly victimized girl-woman into an actively engaged, emotionally available, and firmly assertive professional adult who derives pleasure from both work and love. She now has access to a broad range of affects and is able to harness her passion in the pursuit of what she desires and what she knows she deserves. Our work goes on and will probably continue indefinitely—until there comes a time when Rachel feels that the damage done at the hands of her parents has been repaired and she has become the person she had always wanted to be.

II

SPECIFIC ISSUES IN INDIVIDUAL THERAPY

6

Use of the Telephone as a Transitional Space

JOYCE K. ARONSON

INTRODUCTION

How do you work with a patient who refuses to come in to see you? This chapter is about a dangerously ill anorexic who began therapy and became so afraid of her needs—of what might be aroused in the contact between us, the possible threat to her schizoid withdrawal into anorexic preoccupation, and her unconscious fear of the inevitable disappointments in the potential intimacy between us—that she refused to come in to see me. However, she discovered the use of telephone sessions and the answering machine as a transitional space. On the machine she could hear my voice in an absolutely predictable way and establish an illusion of my constant availability. She could be as needy as necessary. This regressive experience allowed her to enact early developmental needs and begin to give up masochistic and omnipotent anorexic defenses. The holding qualities of this safe transitional space facilitated a relationship with a new attachment figure, and allowed a developmental thrust that eventually made these parameters unnecessary.

WORKING WITH THE
SEVERELY DISTURBED ANOREXIC

Patients with anorexia exhibit a broad range of ego functioning. Their capacity for object relations can vary considerably,
as can their developmental deficits (Aronson 1986). Chassler
(1994) has suggested that the starvation of the anorexic elicits
caretaking behaviors from significant others and is an expression of an unconscious hope to repair unfulfilled needs with
important early attachment figures. Consequently, the therapist must be flexible, responding to where the patients are and
to what their needs may be.

Diagnoses range from psychoses through character disorders to neuroses. Some patients, like this one, are at the low-
level borderline and psychotic end of this spectrum and are
not treatable within the traditional psychotherapeutic framework. These are patients who are unable to engage in a therapeutic relationship, don't get into treatment, avoid hospitalization unless forced by the family, avoid contact with hospital
staff, and, although they comply with refeeding, upon discharge resume defensive anorexic patterns and remain
chronically and dangerously emaciated. These patients flirt
with death and sometimes die.

This chapter reports on therapeutic work with a seriously
disturbed, extremely masochistic, anorexic patient, and the use
of telephone sessions and the telephone answering machine
to create a flexible therapeutic hold. Winnicott (1951) used the
terms *transitional objects* and *transitional phenomena* to describe an intermediate area of experience created by the infant, a way station in the transition from inside to outside,
"between the thumb and the teddy bear." This concept of transitional space between mother and child is useful in understanding this patient's use of my telephone. She created this

transitional space out of her needs; it was not something I suggested. On the machine the therapist's voice was always present in a totally predictable way and the illusion of constant availability could be maintained. Speaking aloud to the machine was entirely under the patient's control. Used between sessions, in states of depression or excitement, it helped her discover what she was thinking and feeling. Since she could not tolerate face-to-face contact, the telephone sessions and the answering machine allowed an intermediate area of experience in the therapeutic relationship.

In recent years, the work of infant researchers has made us aware of the impact of mother–infant dyadic interaction in the first years of life. Highly restricted patterns of self- and mutual regulation can occur in infancy and be minimally transformed through adult experience. Kiersky and Beebe (1994) describe how understimulation in infancy may result in the lack of a sense of mutuality and effectiveness in dyadic exchange and subsequent avoidance of mutually regulated affective contact. For some severely disturbed anorexic patients, there has been a paucity of the interactional sensory-motor experiences that are the precursors of psychic structure. These deficits in dyadic experience can lead to the inability to tolerate face-to-face contact in ongoing psychotherapy. This patient had to be allowed to titrate the amount of contact she could tolerate.

Interpretations were meaningless to this patient. For example, I could tell her that she wanted to have me endlessly, but it had no effect. She needed to enact it for a mutual engagement to evolve. Since she found a face-to-face encounter overwhelming, the following parameters were used: permitting telephone sessions, allowing the therapist's telephone answering machine to be used as transitional space, letting her limit the time of sessions and set limits on the therapist's affect, being available to help the patient deal with the immediate and overwhelming anxiety aroused as she tried new experiences, avoiding hospitalization insofar as there was no threat to life, and having telephone contact during vacations for the first four years of treatment. Each parameter became unnecessary as the patient grew emotionally.

PRESENTING PROBLEMS

Ms. K. was referred to me for outpatient psychotherapy. I first saw her in preparation for her discharge from a hospital, where she had been for two months. She had had many previous hospitalizations. Ms. K. is a 4' 10", 80 pound, 26-year-old with a strikingly high-pitched, childish voice. She was dressed in odd, shabby clothing. Physically she looked prepubertal. She has never menstruated and has no breast development. She has lovely features—big dark eyes and waist-length black hair, which is unkempt, with large, bloody scabs visible on her scalp. She looked painfully thin and delicate. Her weight had been as low as 54 pounds. Her speech was pressured and she jumped from one topic to another without completing any thought. She seemed very anxious and timid, averted her eyes, and spoke with false hopefulness about her discharge plans. I felt as if I were talking to a poorly functioning 11-year-old child as far as her social judgment was concerned. The one thing she talked about in an affective way was her love of skating. She had taken lessons as a child, but her parents had not let her train as an adolescent.

Ms. K. lived an isolated, schizoid life alone with her cat, who she felt shared her human feelings; she was preoccupied with hurting him emotionally if she wasn't affectionate. She had money available to her from the family, but she felt that she had no control over it, had to save it for her old age, and lived like a bag lady, dirty and in old clothes. Her apartment was hot, dirty, disorganized, and rat-infested. The television was always on. Most of her time was preoccupied with what she could or would not eat, and with her upset stomach or diarrhea. Ms. K. would spend her time exercising or stretching, sometimes sitting in a split for hours chewing on ice cubes, her legs aching. If she did a good split she believed that the cars outside were honking their approval. If lights went off in a neighboring apartment, she thought that neighbor was watching her disapprovingly. At times she would search for and listen to music with lyrics that expressed her mood. Her hyperactivity, exhaustion, starvation, and pain kept her empty of thoughts and feelings most of the time. She was terrified that neighbors could see her, hear her, or know her thoughts and they would be angry. She frequently heard voices saying disapprovingly, "She's an anorexic." Unwashed and unkempt, she lived in an autistic, sensory-dominated mode (Ogden 1989). She was agitated, incapable of reflective thinking, and frightened of human contact.

PREVIOUS TREATMENT

Socially isolated throughout her childhood, Ms. K. developed anorexia at 11. She was treated by a psychiatrist who was also her parents' friend. As part of the treatment, he came to family meals and encouraged her to eat. She recalls following his advice, eating voraciously, gaining thirty pounds, feeling out of control, and resuming her anorexic behavior. At 17, her anorexia became worse. She saw a therapist five days a week for five years. She described him as often silent. She too was silent. She said that her parents insisted she go and she complied. She recalled how she hated him and her pleasure in defecating on his chair. She was in and out of the hospital during this five-year period, often hospitalized when he went on vacation, although she denied that his going on vacation had anything to do with her hospitalizations. During the last year of treatment, it was suggested to the parents that they hire someone to watch her eat—which they did for one year. At age 22, she adamantly refused to see him. For the next two years she was seen by the internist who had worked collaboratively with this psychiatrist. Ms. K. said that she went to his office several times a week, he ate with her, and told her that she had to get well because he cared for her. Eventually he became enraged when she didn't gain weight and refused to see her. For the next two years she was in and out of the hospital on medical units, at times close to death. Eventually she was so malnourished that she had to have a surgical hip replacement. She also had surgery to correct her severely crossed eyes, which she had had from birth. After this corrective surgery she was hospitalized on an eating disorders unit because her weight was dangerously low. While hospitalized, Ms. K. avoided contact with other patients and with staff. For the most part she would stay in her room, isolated, and come late for activities. When she met her goal weight of 80 pounds, she was referred to me for outpatient therapy.

I thought that with such serious developmental deficits she should be seen three times weekly; she should also see an internist regularly to follow her physical condition, and a psychiatrist for medication. She agreed. Her parents were to be seen monthly, but after a year of this, the parents' therapist refused to work with them because of the father's rages.

EARLY LIFE

In the course of treatment it emerged that Ms. K. is the middle daughter of five children. The siblings are three years older, two years older, three-and-a-half years younger, and five years younger.

Born with severely crossed eyes, which were later corrected, she started out at some disadvantage in face-to-face experience. The mother had told the patient that she was preoccupied with the care of her other children, especially one who was continuously ill, and that after the first few weeks Ms. K. refused the breast and had to be bottle fed. She was left alone a great deal, and was a quiet baby who never cried, even when wet or hungry.

The family moved during her first year, a change that was anxiety-provoking for both parents, making them even less available. They said she was such a good, undemanding, quiet baby that they could take her to restaurants and she wouldn't make a peep. At 1½ Ms. K. was diagnosed with failure to thrive.

It is probable that with her crossed eyes and her mother's unavailability, the patient had experienced very little dyadic, face-to-face gazing and vocalization—the interactional sensory-motor experiences that are the precursors of psychic structure. In this mother–child dyed there was little mutual gazing, mutual smiling, and sharing of excitement. Consequently there was attachment disorder with psychosomatic symptoms (Brisch, this volume). This was not only true in infancy but was an ongoing deficit throughout her childhood. The paucity of affective dyadic interaction came across poignantly when the patient told me that she had never had fun with her mother. She remembered going to the playground and watching a child holding a penny and playing a game on a swing where, as she came close to her mother, she excitedly gave her mother the penny, then swinging back and forth exchanging the penny, laughing together. She asked her mother to play the game but her mother was so affectively bland that it was no fun.

In our sessions, Ms. K. was unable to engage in conversational dyadic interaction. In her high-pitched, pressured voice she didn't converse. She often spoke whenever I began to speak, and she would rarely complete a thought. There was no eye contact. She seemed extremely vulnerable to overstimulation in face-to-face contact.

Ms. K. described herself as "very quiet" during her childhood, spending most of the time in front of the TV while her mother was in the kitchen. A recurring memory is of her younger brother being held by a nanny who was employed to take care of him while she sat alone with the TV. The parents were often out, leaving the children with babysitters.

At 11, she became anorexic and dressed in rags. She reported that for one year she didn't bathe, and her parents said nothing. When she became dangerously cachectic, they were very responsive. Mother went to school everyday to feed her. Father became enraged at her for not eating, seeing her as a willful, rebellious, defiant child who refused to take on his intellectual pursuits.

A test report at age 12 noted she was an estranged, depressed, fragile girl with borderline features, whose love for ice skating contained elements of desperation. "It keeps this estranged girl alive and also serves as a medium for human contact, however tenuous and impersonal."

PSYCHOTHERAPY

Initially she came to some sessions, although very late. She had a difficult time just organizing her daily life, shopping, eating, and getting to my office. Terrified of the unexpected, she was totally preoccupied with others' perceptions of her, and often heard voices saying, "She's an anorexic." She expected rageful responses if she asked for anything.

In this beginning phase, she talked about her love of skating, and gradually, with enormous anxiety and fear of criticism for being too thin and not being perfect, she started taking skating lessons again. Terrified of any new experiences, she would come home flooded with feelings and leave lengthy messages on my answering machine. She was obsessed with being criticized, felt people could read her mind, were calling her sick and anorexic, and were silently denigrating her skating.

I went on vacation for a week. Although I did preparatory work, telling her months in advance, she handled the impending separation with denial, increased psychosomatic problems, and overt psychosis. She was hospitalized and, although I saw her regularly during her hospitalization, after discharge she refused to come to sessions but would call me during the time we were scheduled to meet, often at the very end of the hour. At other times she would leave messages or ask desperately that I return her call. I often spoke to her on an as-needed basis until she calmed down (sometimes it took a half hour or more), and then I'd suggest we talk further at the next scheduled session.

Ms. K. felt that if she came to see me in person there was something very wrong with her; she did not want to be aware that she needed me. She would rarely call at the beginning of a scheduled phone session. She would do exercises and then decide when she wanted to initiate the contact. For the next three years most of our sessions were by telephone.

I did insist that we meet in person once a week, but most of the time she would come to the last fifteen minutes of the session. She would spend the first five minutes in the bathroom and, after leaving, would return to the bathroom for ten minutes. She sometimes missed even those weekly sessions and expected a rageful response from me. In session, if I was animated or used my hands, she asked me not to do so. In a similar way she became afraid to go to the movies and would only watch films on television. She was generally afraid of being overwhelmed by positive as well as negative affects.

Although ostensibly seeking help, for the first few years this patient was totally absorbed in hopelessness and self-destructive activities: starvation, hair pulling, creating bloody scabs on her scalp, drinking large amounts of bitter coffee, excessive and exhausting exercise, obsessive rumination about her life, and cutting herself off from all relationships and from therapy. This behavior produced in me a sense of hopelessness, despair, and ineffectiveness, which I had to contain during the several years I worked with her by phone. This countertransference gave me an awareness of her own hopelessness, despair, and ineffectiveness.

Betty Joseph (1982) states, "It seems to me the near destruction of the self takes place with considerable libidinal satisfaction" (p. 450). These patients are enthralled by the pain. No ordinary pleasure offers such delight as exciting self-annihilation. The analyst is the only person who is actually concerned about progress. The patient pulls back into deadly passivity. The wanting parts of the patient are split off and projected. The patient goes over and over her failures and attempts to induce the analyst to become critical, despairing, and hopeless. Joseph (1982) says that these patients lacked warm early contact and often had a violent parent. This was true of Ms. K. Her early life was remarkably bland and void of positive affect. The major emotional intensity in the family was her father's rageful reactions. Her parents' primary experience of her was as their dangerously sick child. Elliott Markson (1993) described how shared suffering is the essential emotional connection in families of the masochistic patient.

The classical position is that failure of infantile omnipotence forces the child to turn to reality. My experience with this patient is in line with the Novicks' (1991) view that the failure to achieve competent interactions with others forces the child to turn to omnipotent solutions. They argue that masochism can best be understood as the result of a multi-determined, epigenetic sequence of pain-seeking behaviors, which start in infancy and result in fantasies, modeled on the beating fantasy. The Novicks (1991) note that transitory beating fantasies can be seen in some form in all children. Fixed beating fantasies are derived from disturbances in the first year of life. In a sample of ill children indexed at the Anna Freud Center, there was a mutual lack of pleasure on the part of mother and baby in the earliest months of life in those children with a fixed beating fantasy. This patient's beating fantasy took the form of a constant preoccupation with a man who was unpredictable and enraged at her. This fantasy, often kept her terrified and immobilized. For several years, it was the head of the skating school, who once commented on how strange she looked. The beating fantasy also included her coach feeling sorry for her, comforting her, sticking up for her, and reprimanding the head of the school.

The infancy of the severely masochistic patients the Novicks (1991) saw was marked by significant disturbance from the first months of life. They point out that self-esteem, confidence, and effectance are rooted in the child's real capacity to elicit the appropriate response from the mother. All of their masochistic cases had parents who were intermittently caring, but in response to the parents' needs, and in a way that gave the children little confidence in their ability to evoke a response. Ms. K.'s parents, too, were intermittently caring. Ms. K. recalls being scheduled to be with her father a few hours one Saturday every month, but this was often canceled. The Novicks speculate that externalization of hated, devalued aspects of the self onto the child serve as the mother's main mode of relating to the child who later develops masochistic pathology. Ms. K.'s mother's main need in relation to this daughter was to see her as a poor, sick, helpless, anorexic child.

These patients used the experience of helpless rage and pain magically to predict and control their chaotic experiences. The early repetitive traumata forced the child into an imaginary world where safety and omnipotent control were magically associated with pain. When Ms. K. was a toddler and young child, her mother was available only when this child was sad, unhappy, sickly, or in pain. Moves toward autonomy and self-assertion were not encouraged. Mother was also physically intrusive, demanding to see her bowel movements up until latency and preoccupied with cooking and feeding. This physical intrusiveness contributed to the child's inability to integrate body and self.

She had a poor capacity to tolerate anxiety, as well as little ability even to begin to organize her cognitive and emotional responses to situations to which she was exposed. If she put off talking about her immediate experience it was lost to her. She could not hold it in her mind and talk about it later during a session. The immediate contact with me through the answering machine was used to explore both what she was experiencing and the tentative and fragile possibilities for connectedness and separateness from me. She could not begin to let herself experience anything new unless she had a means by which, on an as-needed basis, she could organize her life. She used my answering machine to do this.

In the first year of treatment she was hospitalized during my two vacations. After that I realized that she needed ongoing contact. For the first three years it was impossible for her to handle lengthy separations without psychotic withdrawal into a self-contained state. A treatment relationship could only begin to be established once the patient was assured that ongoing phone sessions would be maintained during vacations.

Even with phone sessions, Ms. K. was scheduled to come to a session after one vacation. Instead, she called and said she had been sleeping. There was no way she could get there. It was only on the phone that she discovered she was angry at me for having been away on vacation. "I didn't know I was angry until now that I'm saying it." Even with that awareness she did not hold onto it. She also missed her next session. She came at the last few minutes of the hour, expecting me to be angry.

Several years later, after much discussion, we agreed that she would not contact me in person on vacation but could leave phone messages on my machine and I would call in to receive them every few days. I found myself enraged at the repetitive, endless rambling, unlike her usual messages. I felt nothing was enough for her, that she was endlessly demanding and insatiable and had no notion of what was reasonable to expect. I found myself talking out loud—furious, impatient, feeling that she'd drained me dry. Phone messages lasted for almost an hour. She was angry at me for leaving and was putting her anger into me, a characteristic pattern for her. I could detect it first in my countertransference, and only then help her express it to me.

This patient attributed magical omnipotent power to her own feelings and fantasies, and consequently carried around a terror of her anger. A key element in treatment was for her to be able to express anger at me and experience my tolerating what the original objects couldn't.

ENACTMENT AND COUNTERTRANSFERENCE

Christopher Bollas (1987) has written:

> By permitting himself to be used as an object the therapist facilitates the patient's sense of self. . . . We are made use of through our affects, through the patient generating the required feeling within us. In many ways, this is precisely how a baby "speaks" to its mother that either inspires some action in her on the baby's behalf or leads her to put the baby's object usage into language, engaging the infant in the journey towards verbal representation of internal psychic states. [pp. 203–204]

As a therapist, what I said did not matter as much as what I did. It didn't help to tell Ms. K. that I felt she wanted me available unconditionally. Interpretation of this was not meaningful. I had to be available as much as possible to maintain the illusion of optimum availability. I did not charge for phone time since I was being paid my full fee for three sessions a week. Ms. K. needed to feel that I wanted to talk to her for nothing in order to maintain the sense that I cared for her—a prerequisite for the relationship. She later spoke of her skating instructors, who stayed with her a few minutes more at the end of her lesson, as possibly caring. Eventually I addressed this in the transference. Initially, and for several years, it was essential to the treatment that this illusion of caring availability, which she had never experienced with her mother, be enacted over a long period of time.

In much the same way as the mother of an infant is first all available on demand feeding, and then the sound of her voice can let the infant know that she will be available later to soothe and help the baby contain and delay the satisfaction of its needs, I initially spoke at length to Ms. K. when she called (mostly to clarify affects and help her organize her thoughts). When later it became possible, I would put off a lengthy phone contact to when we could talk during our next scheduled session. For the first two years this patient would call, leaving lengthy messages several times during the middle of the night and as much as ten to twenty times over weekends. I arranged to listen to these at my convenience, or else I would have found it an unbearable intrusion. At many points early in treatment, I would come to the office and find that a dozen messages had been left for me during the night, all from Ms. K. Often there was more than a half hour of messages. At times I found myself angry at this intrusion. Did she feel she was the only person in my life? Was she testing to see if I'd be sick of her? Intellectually, I knew that as she gave up the anorexia more of her infantile demandingness and rage would come out. It helped me to contain my annoyance to know that she needed the answering machine as a transitional space in which to organize her thoughts, fears, feelings, and fantasies. If she asked that I call her back, I did so at a time that was comfortable and leisurely for me.

I had to be able to live through her pain, despair, depression, self-destructiveness, and demandingness. There was a period of several months where I felt that she was trying to provoke the kind of rage response that was typical of her father. It became apparent with Ms. K. that the major affective response from her parents was related to her illness. They came running when she was hospitalized, although expressing rage that she was ill. After years of illness, when she gave a public performance, preparing months in advance and telling them about it, the parents not only didn't come, but didn't even ask her about it. This is consistent with Markson's (1993) findings. With severely masochistic patients, pleasurable states are ignored by the parents.

Understanding my anger as a countertransference guide to what's going on has helped me to contain it. After a successful and satisfying skating lesson, Ms. K. came to our session forty-three minutes late, terrified that I would be enraged at her "like my father would be." She walked into my office cowering, saying she expected "the wrath of God." I had felt angry at her lateness, but knowing that this was connected with her terror of success, the anger dissipated. I told her that when she is satisfied and has a sense of accomplishment it seems to be followed by a barrage of uncertainty. She defended against this frightening uncertainty by trying to provoke the only thing she could count on in her family, an angry response. Over time we came to see that every successful interaction was followed by some self-destructive incident. Ms. K. would eat only melon, causing diarrhea, take the wrong subway, or overflow her bathtub.

Many traditional theorists (Wilson et al. 1983), emphasize the self-destructive behavior in anorexics as aggression turned against the self out of fear of expressing it directly. In addition, this patient had a childhood of bleak emotional monotony, where anger was the only emotional response that she could be sure of evoking. When she had some slight success, she became anxious, feeling that she could not believe it was happening or would continue to happen. It was unlike her familiar experience and she returned to home base by a masochistic provocation.

When Ms. K. started to come to full sessions about three years after treatment began, I found myself dreading our meetings. In anticipation of seeing her, I wanted to eat something to store up energy so I wouldn't feel depleted. I had the fear that I wouldn't be able to get rid of her, that she wouldn't leave. I felt burdened, tired, as if I'd be drained. This countertransference feeling put me in touch with the voracious neediness for human contact, which she had been keeping at bay.

Ms. K. attempted to maintain a sense of constant availability of the object (therapist) while denying dependency on or need of the object. By actually physically coming to sessions and then leaving, she experienced both her need and then her loss. She would start to talk and then have to tear herself away when contact was satisfying. After sessions she would exercise in the waiting room for fifteen minutes before she left. Only recently was she able to say that if she has a good feeling with me she wants to stay as long as she wants to and not have to leave. She would rather not feel that she wants than to feel that she wants and can't have. This is true for food as well. She would eat only cold food, because hot food smelled so delicious.

THE PATIENT'S GROWTH

In the sixth year of treatment, Ms. K. began to face her hopelessness, despair, depression, the bleakness of her childhood, and the emotional emptiness she experienced with her parents. She's been able to become aware of her hatred, envy, and aggression. She came to each of her three sessions a week, and rarely used the telephone. When she faced an experience that she anticipated she would have difficulty handling emotionally, she scheduled a telephone session after it, for which she paid. She said this helped her calm down and put things in perspective.

There was a shift in her capacity for more human relatedness, which could be seen in her move from the isolated, controlled world of skating to the dyadic world of ballroom dance. Initially she only worked as an instructor with the elderly because she was sure they would be responsive to her and they didn't engender envy in her.

CONCLUDING COMMENTS

As the reader will recall, in the past this deeply troubled patient had attended for five years all of her five-times-a-week therapy sessions without apparent change. It was the regressive experience of the treatment described herein that allowed improvement to occur. Regression allowed an enactment of developmental needs and growth. The emotional availability and the holding qualities of the therapist facilitated a relationship in which the patient could feel understood and begin to give up her masochistic, omnipotent, anorexic defenses.

In this treatment situation we can see, in particular, the way in which a carefully planned parameter can be usefully employed to advance the treatment of certain patients. Ms. K.'s use of the telephone answering machine to speak to me whenever she wanted to allowed her to speak to me as if I were present and as if I were her omnipotent creation. It served as a transitional object that enabled her to build up an internal object. As she became able to talk to me in her mind, her voices disappeared.

Winnicott (1971) embedded the idea of the transitional object in a developmental theory of object relations. Initially, the subjective object is created with no independent existence by the infant. Then there is an omnipotently controlled object, perceived as outside the self, existing as a pole for identifications and projections. Finally, there is a movement to an object that is an independent part of external reality. According to Winnicott, this transition is the result of the subject's fantasized destruction of the object and the object's survival.

In keeping with Winnicott's ideas, Ms. K. had a version of me that belonged to her like a teddy bear. She could be as destructive as she needed to be. She would call me via the answering machine at 2:00 A.M. and talk to me for as long as she wanted. Just as with a teddy bear, there was the illusion of the responsive object. She could be as needy and as greedy as was necessary, and got to use me without using me up. The answering machine provided a transitional space that was uniquely under Ms. K.'s control. It allowed her to play with being connected, and to explore what she was thinking and feeling as she was experiencing it.

This patient could not tolerate the usual comings and goings of the treatment situation, which impose an experience of separateness. She needed the possibility of having me endlessly, which she could do by talking to my answering machine as if she were talking to me, and she could do this in an abusive, provocative way without destroying the relationship.

The transitional object is a possession used by the child to negotiate the area between the experience of inner and outer reality. Transitional objects are used, as the telephone was in this case, in the development of reality acceptance. In this transitional space Ms. K. could accept therapy while rejecting it, accept the therapeutic relationship while at the same time rejecting the terrifying closeness to another person. Just as a transitional object becomes unnecessary and is relinquished in the course of development, in time this patient no longer needed to use the telephone as a transitional space.

Treatment of anorexic, severely masochistic patients is long and difficult because the self-destructive nature of the psychopathology has its roots in every developmental phase. Ms. K. continued to retreat to the magic of pain, but it was possible in the context of an ongoing relationship for her to put her experiences into words.

The telephone as a transitional space was not suggested by me. It was found by the patient, arising out of her deep, unmet needs.

REFERENCES

Aronson, J. K. (1986). The level of object relations and severity of symptoms in the normal weight bulimic patient. *International Journal of Eating Disorders* 5:669–681.

Beebe, B., and Lachmann, F. (1988). The contribution of mother–infant mutual influence to the origins of self and object representations. *Psychoanalytic Psychology* 5:305–337.

Bollas, C. (1987). *The Shadow of the Object: Psychoanalysis of the Unthought Known*. London: Free Association Books.

Chassler, L. (1994). "In Hunger I am King." Understanding anorexia nervosa from a psychoanalytic perspective: theoretical and clinical implications. *Social Work Journal* 22(4):397–415.

Joseph, B. (1982). Addiction to near death. *International Journal of Psycho-Analysis* 63:449–451.

Kiersky, S., and Beebe, B. (1994). The reconstruction of early nonverbal relatedness in the treatment of difficult patients: a special form of empathy. *Psychoanalytic Dialogues* 4(3):389–408.

Markson, E. R. (1993). Depression and moral masochism. *International Journal of Psycho-Analysis* 74:931–940.

Novick, J., and Novick, K. (1991). Some comments on masochism and the delusion of omnipotence. *Journal of the American Psychoanalytic Association* 9:307–331.

Novick, K., and Novick, J. (1987). The essence of masochism. *Psychoanalytic Study of the Child* 42:353–384. New Haven, CT: Yale University Press.

Ogden, T. H. (1989). The autistic-contiguous position. In *The Primitive Edge of Experience,* pp. 47–81. Northvale, NJ: Jason Aronson.

Wilson, C. P., Hogan, C., and Mintz, I. (1983). *Fear of Being Fat: The Treatment of Anorexia Nervosa and Bulimia.* New York: Jason Aronson.

Winnicott, D. W. (1951). Transitional object and transitional phenomena. In *Collected Papers: Through Paediatrics to Psychoanalysis.* New York: Basic Books.

——— (1971). The use of an object and relating through identifications. In *Playing and Reality.* New York: Basic Books.

7

Using the Telephone to Negotiate an Optimal Balance between Separation and Connection

F. DIANE BARTH

*A*s I note in another chapter of this volume, I came slowly and with significant resistance to the idea of telephone therapy. Even now that I use it fairly regularly, I consider it, as I do many therapeutic tools and techniques, to have both positive and negative aspects. To name just one of the more obvious negative ones, many therapists feel that the telephone deprives us of important visual cues that are often a key part of the work. On the other hand, this very lack of visual contact can lead to greater efforts in the sphere of verbal communication, thereby actually enhancing the therapeutic process. In this chapter, I would like to address an aspect of doing psychotherapy on the telephone that highlights the two-sided nature of this experience: that is, the use of the phone as a tool in the therapeutic negotiation of separation and connection.

For many years, psychoanalysts agreed with Mahler (Mahler et al. 1975) that separation was a major developmental achievement and a significant goal of therapy. When I was in psychoanalytic training, if a client left therapy to move to another locale (which at that time happened far less often than it does today), the move was frequently viewed as reflecting resistance to the psychoanalytic process. Once this dynamic was explored, and if they did not change their plans, clients were referred as a matter of course to a therapist in their new hometown. A therapist who tried to maintain telephone or written contact with the client after the therapy was ended was considered to be having difficulty with separation and was encouraged to address the problem in her own analysis and supervision. The world has changed dramatically since I was in training, and analytic theory has changed along with it. Stolorow and Lachmann (1980), among others, have questioned the concept of termination and "resolution of transference." Kohut (1971) and Stern (1985) have suggested that the capacity to be connected to another is, in fact, an even greater feat than the ability to separate.

Today, with mothers and fathers traveling for work, families traveling for pleasure, and moves not only to new towns, but to new states and countries commonplace, it appears to me that many people come into therapy with difficulty in both of these spheres of experience. While the Internet and electronic communication are accused of promoting isolation and disconnection, they also provide contact with people all over the world. An article in the *New York Times* (Gross 1999) expressed concern about a growing trend among college students to stay in close contact with parents by cell phone. The author worried that cell phones "tether" these adolescents to their parents in an inappropriate and unhealthy manner. My own experience has been that cell phones can be utilized to avoid not only separation, but also the development of genuine intimacy with others. One young woman, for example, was so terrified of intimacy that she regularly carried on conversations on her cell phone while out on dates. On the other hand, these amazing gadgets can also be used as tools for enacting conflicts about boundaries, as was done by a young man who regularly, but without conscious intent, allowed the battery on his cell phone to lose its charge, making it impossible for his well-meaning but intrusive mother to get in touch with him.

The telephone itself, I would suggest, has come to represent one of the most important psychological conflicts of our age: what Benjamin (1992) has described as the struggle to find an optimal balance between separation and connection. This struggle is, I believe, a crucial key both to healthy, lively relations with others and to what Stolorow and Lachmann (1980) have described as a cohesive, positively colored sense of self and ongoing aspect of the psychoanalytic process. Furthermore, as Benjamin has pointed out, this is not a finite process with a single, observable ending. The balance between separation and connection, and negotiations to find and maintain a working balance between any two people, go on throughout the lifecycle of both the individuals and the relationship.

Not surprisingly, therefore, I have come to believe that the process of negotiating separations while simultaneously remaining connected to important others is, for some individuals, one of the most significant activities of the therapeutic work, and it is one in which the telephone can play an extremely important role. In my work with eating-disordered college students, I often find that a key part of the work I do involves actually coaching the family in the process of connecting and separating. Parents and their adolescent children often have complementary difficulties being in touch without being intrusive or clingy, and of being separate without being disconnected. Both struggle with fears about what it means for a child to grow up, about coping with their changing roles, and about managing the emptiness they experience at times of separation. Recently, for example, after meeting with the out-of-town parents of Debbie, a college junior, I began having telephone family sessions with her and her parents. Debbie, who was mildly anorexic, sat with me in my office, where we used a speaker phone to communicate with her parents, who were also using a speaker phone at their home in another state. The work was fascinating and productive as I became the mediator of their attempts to negotiate a mutually acceptable balance between separateness and connectedness. In one particularly touching moment, Debbie, who had been talking to me individually about her father's overprotectiveness and her mixed feelings about it (on the one hand, she felt loved and protected, on the other, smothered and infantilized) turned to me and mouthed, "This is what I mean!" I nodded, smiled supportively, and gestured to her to speak to him.

"Daddy," she said in a little girl voice I had never heard before, "you're making me into a baby."

"But you are my baby," he said in a booming voice.

My interventions for several weeks had been along the lines of the family's difficulties coping with Debbie's growing up and moving away. Something in this interchange reminded me that they also needed help learning that they could be connected to one another, perhaps not in the old, familiar ways, but in a new and, as Loewald (1956–1957) has put it, "mutually satisfying, rewarding relationship" (p. 395). Almost immediately after I began to put this into words with them, Debbie's voice turned back into that of a twenty-year-old woman, and her father's took on a quieter tone. This does not mean that the problems ended with this intervention, but the idea that they could find a way to be connected as well as separate was a completely new one to them. Once they understood that we were working toward that goal, rather than toward one in which they would be disconnected and separate, the process went much more smoothly for all of them.

Individuals with eating disorders are one of the groups with whom I found myself working by telephone first. This is a population that often has clear difficulties finding an optimal tension between connection and separation, and for them the telephone can be a useful medium for working on this dynamic. Yet, while I now find myself working on the telephone with several clients with different diagnoses, I do not offer this therapy to everyone. In some cases, I decide to end the work rather than give up the in-person contact. It has become clear to me over time that there is no single, simple, or arbitrary answer to the question of when and why to use telephone therapy. I believe it is, a decision that must be made with a patient's participation, and this exploratory process itself can be the basis for fascinating and often extremely important therapeutic work. In the following clinical examples, I will try to tease out some of the factors that, in my experience, have led to useful telephone therapy, and some that have made it more beneficial to make a referral to a new therapist. As will become clear, I think that each decision has to be made individually and tentatively, with ongoing evaluation of whether or not, in the opinion of both therapist and client, the process is working.

Because these guidelines have grown out of my own work, I will offer three clinical examples with the hope of illustrating some of the issues that can emerge in this process, and some of the pitfalls and surprises that can accompany the work. Many of the disadvantages are obvious, but some of them are quite surprising. For example, while I was aware, as I noted earlier, of the double-sided nature of the loss of visual cues, I was not prepared when one patient arrived in my office for one of the occasional face-to-face meetings that I require when I do extended telephone work. She was not only many pounds heavier than she had been when she left, but her hair, which had been a rather striking black, was now bright purple. Noticing what must have been a somewhat stunned expression on my face, she said, "But I told you I'd gained weight . . . and I also told you I'd dyed my hair." What was fascinating was that she had not reported any of what it turned out were extremely significant changes in her experience of herself and others' experience of her, but what we gradually understood was that even if she had talked about these changes, I would not have understood the drama—and therefore the meaning— they had for her without seeing her in person.

It is important for therapists working by telephone to take into account the fact that there are unknown occurrences that are playing a significant role—outside of our vision, so to speak—in the lives of our clients, whether we are working with them by telephone or in person. To my mind, this very awareness is a crucial component of the separation–connection negotiation. The capacity to keep something to oneself, *not* to talk about it with one's therapist, is sometimes as much of an achievement as is the capacity to talk freely. One guideline I find myself using for deciding about phone therapy is a person's ability to let me know when she feels I am pushing her too hard or am invading her boundaries. This is how it worked with Alice.

CASE EXAMPLE: ALICE

Alice is a thirty-two-year-old woman who has been in psychotherapy with me for five years, twice a week for the most part. She had been greatly helped in many ways by a male therapist with whom she had worked for about four years before seeking a consultation with me. However, she sought me out because they had not been able to make a dent in her long-term bulimia. The following summary cannot do justice to either Alice's fascinating and complicated dynamics, the depth of confusion that we both felt at many different times in our work together, or the richness of the relationship as it evolved over time. I will simply focus here on the ways in which phone therapy both utilized and enhanced Alice's nascent ability to recognize her need for boundaries with me and with others in her life.

A brilliant woman who had just received a law degree from a prestigious university when we began working together, Alice had always been the "adult child" in her family, but had never felt truly "grown up." In fact, it seemed that one of the difficulties she had recently encountered in her work with her previous therapist was related to her new position in the world as a professional woman. While Alice still felt like a needy child, she experienced her therapist as pushing her to be more "adult." Furthermore, she felt that he was unhappy that she had taken a job in a high status law firm rather than doing legal aid or working in the district attorney's office. Yet she didn't feel strong enough to follow her own desires against his will or to discuss her feelings with him. Her need to escape from situations in which she felt that her boundaries were not being respected became a central theme in our work.

Alice spoke often of her feeling that her therapist was angry at her for making the choices she was making, but she could neither examine her own related issues nor make room for a discussion of the therapist's issues or dynamics. With my encouragement, she did at least go back to the therapist and explain her reasons for leaving, and, to her surprise, got some confirmation of her perceptions and a blessing of sorts to leave. The therapist also told her that he thought it was a good idea for her to work with a woman therapist so that she could address her gender identity issues. Alice's explanation of this instruction was that she had some "bisexual" feelings; as I soon discovered, Alice was living with a man and having an affair with a woman.

The work with Alice was peppered with enactments. She often arrived late at sessions, missed others, and frequently failed to call me to explain. At the same time, however, it was quickly apparent that she felt understood by me and helped by my approach to the work. I saw her behavior as a reflection of what Guntrip () has called the "schizoid dilemma": a wish to be close that can become a terror of merging, and, at the same time, a wish to be separate that can become a dread of isolation. I encouraged her to try to talk to me about her need for space, her fears of my pushing her in a direction that might not be where she wanted to go, and her anxieties about getting close to me. None of this was easy for Alice, and for much of the time we worked on other, less threatening aspects of her life. Over time, Alice began to show evidence of improvement. Her binges occurred less frequently. She started to arrive at more sessions on time and with more regularity. She began to talk to me about her anxieties rather than to act on them. She began to give me a more complete picture of her life, her family, her relationships, and she gradually became dependent on me to help her through painful moments for which she had previously used food to help her cope.

As we continued to look at how Alice could both set and accept limits, she became more comfortable in relationships and eventually became involved and monogamous with a man a few years younger than herself. Her sexual relationships with women ended and her sense of herself as a "whole, complete human being with a right to live" increased. After they had been living together for nearly a year, Alice's boyfriend was offered a job in another part of the country. He asked her to marry him and move with him. Alice was thrilled, but devastated at the idea of leaving therapy. "I've just begun to manage to hold onto a sense that you're there for me when I need you, even if I'm not actually in the room with you," she said. "I'm not ready to start trying to do that with someone else. I'm sure there are other fine therapists out there. But you're mine."

I, too, felt that Alice was at an important stage in the therapy, and I hated to think of her having to start again with someone else, even though I knew that a new therapist would build on all the work she had done so far. I told her this and offered her the possibility of phone therapy, but also repeated that I thought she could certainly start with another therapist from where she was, if need be, and make significant gains in the process, just as she had done with me. Alice was immensely touched that I would even offer this possibility to her. She had felt that by leaving, she was disconnecting from everyone and could not expect anyone to even try to keep a connection going.

Not surprisingly, Alice missed her first telephone session and did not call me to explain what had happened. When we finally did make contact, she told me that she had been bingeing and purging, that she was having difficulty getting to work, and that she had not returned any phone calls from her family or friends, although she had received numerous messages from all of them. "I'm afraid that they'll all stop caring about me if I don't call them back, but I don't have anything to say to anyone." We talked about these feelings for some time, looking at the ways they reflected old feelings about both separation and connection, as well as fears that both she and the people who were important to her could not maintain an image of one another in the absence of physical and visual contact.

In the course of our telephone work, Alice developed a greater capacity to be alone, to explore her own dynamics, to process painful experiences with her husband, and to develop new and extremely important relationships—in other words, we continued the process much as we had been working prior to her move. At one point, when I asked her about her feelings about working with me without seeing me, she commented that she was lying on her bed, letting her mind wander, and just watching to see what was coming up. She made the analogy to meditating. I thought she sounded remarkably like an analytic candidate on the couch. She and I both agreed that this form of therapy only worked for her now because she did have a sense of ongoing connection with me. Her capacity for object constancy had improved markedly. As she put it, "I can imagine what you look like and even what expressions you have on your face—which I couldn't do in the old days even five minutes after I left your office." But there was more: she trusted both me and herself to respect her boundaries, her need for separateness, without letting her drift off into the ether world of isolation. It seems that the work we had done prior to her leaving the state had helped make the telephone work possible. At the same time, the actual experience of remaining connected to someone in the intense, emotional manner that she remained connected to me even while she was physically far away was a powerful antidote to her previous experiences of separation equalling total loss.

For these reasons, I tend to prefer not to work with a new client on the telephone. I cannot always gauge the relationship, nor do I trust my ability to assess accurately the dynamics that the individual is struggling with on the telephone. Yet sometimes one does not have a choice. In these cases, I believe it is useful to make a probationary agreement. I usually say something like, "We'll try this out for a month and see how it works for both of us."

CASE EXAMPLE: LAINE

Laine came to see me the summer after her junior year of college. A breakup with her boyfriend of two and a half years had left her feeling sad, hopeless, and helpless. Her grades had fallen and she was considering dropping out of school altogether. Although her parents were encouraging her to take antidepressant medication, Laine decided to try psychotherapy first. She quickly developed a positive relationship with me, and, although she maintained a touch of cynicism about the therapeutic process itself, she did quite well over the course of the summer. We talked about the meaning of the relationship; her sense of loss not only of the connection with her boyfriend, but also of many aspects of her identity that had been tied to him; and her concerns about returning to school without him. We also discussed her plans for the future and her fears about graduating and "being on my own."

By the time Laine returned to school that fall, she was feeling significantly better and decided to end the therapy, which had lasted less than two months. However, shortly after classes began, her depression returned and she called and asked me if we could talk on the phone. This was the beginning of a long-term therapeutic relationship that covered not only several years, but also a number of states and even continents, as Laine moved into graduate and then postgraduate studies. As I do whenever I do work by telephone, I encouraged her to come for face-to-face appointments whenever possible. Laine came to see me in person during vacations and breaks, but once she began graduate school, she spent most of her summers out of the country. We had occasional phone sessions during these trips, but in general summers provided important breaks in the therapy, during which Laine attempted to work on her own on many of the issues we had been discussing in therapy.

The therapeutic work uncovered a long-term, generally well-hidden separation anxiety that had been activated in the breakup with her boyfriend and then again on her return to her last year of college. As with Alice, I felt that a crucial component of the therapeutic process was her learning to be able to be separate from yet connected to another. The telephone therapy allowed us to negotiate the ongoing tension of these two poles in a concrete and regular manner. As Laine gradually began to count on my ability to be present even while "not there," she, like Alice, also gradually began to build a sense of object constancy, an ability to remember the sound of my voice and to soothe herself with memories of my words. She also started to imagine what I might say in a given situation, that is, to carry with her an internalized sense of me, and as she did so, she began to feel more capable of connecting to her own experience as well as to the others who were an important part of her life. Thus, although we had only worked together for a brief time before we began to use the telephone, the phone therapy provided her with an opportunity to work through a crucial aspect of her dynamics that could not have been done if I had either demanded that we meet in person or that she see a therapist in any of the places in which she set up short-term residences over the course of the years we worked together.

WHEN TO USE THE TELEPHONE
AND WHEN NOT TO

There are, of course, times when telephone therapy is not a productive tool and, in fact, can be somewhat destructive. It has been my experience that it can be used to maintain a status quo, as when an individual uses the telephone to resist the therapeutic relationship or, conversely, to preserve merger fantasies without using them in the service of therapeutic progress. People with no capacity for object constancy at all may find it disturbing or distressful to work by telephone, as they truly cannot conjure up a visual image of the therapist to accompany the verbal contact, and those individuals who tend to lie, manipulate, or conceal important information can be expected to use the telephone for this purpose. Because of the need for diligent monitoring by the therapist, I generally will not work by telephone with someone who is dangerously anorexic, using drugs or alcohol, or actively suicidal. However, a supervisee of mine, a talented young therapist, recently undertook a period of telephone therapy with Sam, a recovering alcoholic who "slipped," with excellent results. I would suggest that there were two important factors that made this work possible: first, the supervisee insisted that Sam work closely with a collateral professional during this time, and second, but certainly equally, if not more important, they had a long-standing, strong working relationship, and this was the first time he had started drinking in several years.

CASE EXAMPLE: SAM

Sam was not only a recovering alcoholic but also an occasional drug user who was required to be out of town for several months for work. His therapist and he decided that this was not a good time for him to miss so much therapy, so they agreed to meet by telephone on a once-a-week basis. Within two weeks, Sam informed the therapist that he was drinking heavily and didn't care. The therapist insisted that he go to an

Alcoholics Anonymous meeting that day, whether or not he intended to stop drinking, and she also insisted that he see an alcoholism counselor in the area. The therapist made a referral and spoke directly with the counselor (with Sam's permission), explaining that she would be continuing to work with him by phone, but that he needed more direct contact, structure, and support during this time of separation from his therapist and other supports. Sam initially agreed to go to AA but refused to see the alcoholism counselor. The therapist insisted, telling him that he did not need to stop drinking, but that she, the therapist, needed to be sure that someone was "keeping an eye on you in my place."

Although expressing frustration and irritation, Sam went to see the alcoholism counselor. He told his therapist that he did not like the counselor, that she was "not as smart as you, and not very helpful," but he agreed to see her again and continued to do so for the rest of his stay. He also went to AA meetings daily and soon had stopped drinking again. On the phone, he complained to his therapist. "You treat me like I was a little kid," to which the therapist responded, "What's so bad about that? I got the feeling there that you needed a little extra outside support—a normal thing when you're away from your family, friends, and all the things that make your life the way it is." Months later, Sam came back to the topic, but with a different perspective. "I don't think I'll ever be able to thank you enough for what you did when I was away. The phone therapy was wonderful. It let me know I could hold on to you even when I wasn't with you. But your making sure that someone was watching out for me—making that connection for me, and letting me be with you and with the counselor sort of together—that was probably the most important thing anyone's ever done for me."

Sam could not articulate more clearly what exactly that experience meant to him, but my own sense was that the therapist, by providing clear, firm, and caring boundaries, supplied him with a new kind of balance between separation and connection. Further, by making it clear what her own needs were, the therapist helped Sam negotiate this balance *in relation to another*. As Benjamin (1992) has put it, this process of negotiating the tension between separation and connection is about self and other. It is not a finite negotiation with a single goal, but an ongoing process for every individual and in every relationship. The balance changes from moment to moment, day to day, year to year, depending on many different factors. In my experience, phone therapy can, when used thoughtfully and appropriately, enhance this developmental process.

REFERENCES

Benjamin, J. (1992). Recognition and destruction: an outline of subjectivity. In *Relational Perspectives in Psychoanalysis*, ed. N. J. Skolnick and S. C. Warshaw, pp. 43–60. Hillsdale, NJ: Analytic Press.

Gross, J. (1999). A long-distance tether to home: new technology binds college students and parents. *The New York Times*, November 5.

Kohut (1971). *The Analysis of the Self*. New York: International Universities Press.

Loewald, H. (1956–1957). On the therapeutic action of psychoanalysis. In *Papers on Psychoanalysis*, pp. 384–404. New Haven, CT: Yale University Press, 1980.

Mahler, M., Pine, F., and Bergman, A. (1975). *The Psychological Birth of the Human Infant*. New York: Basic Books.

Stern, D. N. (1985). *The Interpersonal World of the Infant*. New York: Basic Books.

Stolorow, R., and Lachmann, F. (1980). *Psychoanalysis of Developmental Arrests*. New York: International Universities Press.

8

When the Therapist Moves

JUDITH J. WARREN

- "But I thought I could always picture you in your office on Beverly Drive, even when I wasn't seeing you anymore. You'd be there if and when I wanted you."

- "You're going to leave me when I'm still upset with my dad, that jerk! I need you to straighten him up for me."

- "But how can I get better if you're going?"

These were just a few of the reactions I heard on first telling my patients three years ago that in a few months I would be leaving the Los Angeles area and moving to New York. Leaving my patients and the rest of my life in Los Angeles was one of the most troubling times in my life. I felt guilty about closing my practice, ending therapy with all my patients, and interrupting our relationships and our work. My practice as a whole and my individual patients were important to me. Though I tried to do all the "right things" in terms of preparing them for my departure and giving them what I believed to be appropriate referrals, I knew that my moving meant not only the end of our relationship, but also the loss of a secure place that they went to each week or every few days. It also meant losing a particular phone number by which to get in touch with me at any time. It meant deciding whom, if anyone, to continue with in therapy and having to take stock of what they had accomplished with me, what was left undone, what they appreciated about our work together, and what they were disappointed or furious or sad or scared about.

Though I didn't plan telephone therapy in advance or really think much about how the telephone might function as a long-distance umbilical cord or as a transitional object after I left my patients, it turned out to do so in a few cases that were less part of my specific plan with each patient, and more the result of initiation on their parts. Rather, my thoughts centered on how to make final closure as painless and as instructive as possible with each of my patients.

I soon began to realize, however, that phone therapy could turn out, in some instances, to be a crucial connection, particularly because the patient had been left behind. Although patients can feel abandoned even when they themselves terminate the treatment, those feelings are likely to be more intense when the therapist has interrupted the work. Telephone contact can be quite reparative in allowing patients additional time to deal directly with their therapist about feelings such as sadness, anger, jealousy, regrets, and other non-transferential issues.

Phone conversations could reinforce the fact that I cared about them. Over the years several patients had told me that they could hear me in their mind helping them when they had difficult decisions to make. By phone, my voice would actually be heard, not just remembered. For those for whom object constancy was difficult, speaking to me could be useful. Though not as good as seeing me face to face, immediate communication would not be totally lost. In the last few years people are becoming more accustomed to disembodied communication, via both the Internet and the telephone, which also makes telephone therapy more acceptable than in the past.

Telephone work can be helpful as an adjunctive tool, especially with patients one already knows well. Though these patients may yearn for face-to-face contact while speaking by phone, they at least have a mental image of how the therapist looks and may even be guessing at the therapist's expression and body language. That ability to picture the therapist while speaking on the phone may minimize the difficulty of being so far away and make the phone more of an asset and less of an obstacle than it would be if therapy were just beginning.

In each case, when someone wanted telephone sessions, I had to think about the meaning of the contact in the context of our past relationship, the present therapeutic situation, and what I thought the future would hold for us. I felt constrained by the need to work through the separation issues that were bound to emerge and also by the usual strictures about a timely termination, but I was also becoming increasingly aware that for some people brief telephone work would help ease the transition between me and the new therapist or would mitigate what might feel like an intolerably abrupt ending. The phone might even function as a safer way to express feelings too distressing or embarrassing to say in person.

In writing this chapter about telephone therapy, I have had to reexamine some of the difficult choices I faced on deciding to leave Los Angeles and move so far away. In reading other therapists' ordeals with closing their practices, and reflecting upon the experiences I went through with my own patients, I revisited the guilt and sadness I felt on knowing that leaving my patients would be very hard for them. It is difficult for most patients to end therapy, even when it is their choice or when the decision is a mutual one shared with their therapist. But here I was unilaterally leaving them!

One article I found especially helpful when guilt resurged in the process of writing this chapter was Linda Penn's, (1990)

"When the Therapist Must Leave: Forced Termination of Psychodynamic Therapy." She concludes her paper by saying that

> Although the ending may be difficult, it is helpful to remember that this is so partly because the therapeutic relationship was a meaningful one, and both therapist and patient take something of it away with them. A premature termination is not an optimal situation, but there is something to be gained from facing a less than optimal situation head-on, understanding some of its complexities, neither exaggerating nor minimizing its impact, and moving on. [p. 381]

I needed to stay in touch with the meaning for each patient about being left, as well as keeping in mind that I was not leaving to hurt them but for my own reasons. I hoped that my clarity about that would help them distinguish between this loss and other, earlier losses. According to Schwartz (1974), patients are often initially unable to differentiate between early losses and the current trauma of forced termination. That confusion frequently leads to feelings of anger, rage, and depression. If they believe themselves unworthy of love, they may believe the therapist no longer wants them and that they are being abandoned. Realistic here-and-now feelings need to be distinguished from transferential feelings, as difficult as that may be for some patients. The patients need time to sort through the variety of feelings common to forced termination so that the best possible outcome under less than ideal circumstances can occur.

As Penn (1990) indicates, some patients have an easier time expressing anger, others anxiety or sadness; still others think they are to blame for the therapist's leaving. If only they were good enough, the therapist would not leave them. No matter how skilled the therapist is, these feelings cannot all be erased. But the therapist's ability to listen to, accept, and survive all the feelings and thoughts of the patient without retaliating or being thrown off center will be calming and salutary for the patient. The therapist's acceptance of patients' ambivalent and complex affects and the exploration of them in the terminal phase should help patients to understand and tolerate their own feelings about the termination more fully. Optimally, this work can generalize to other losses and difficult interpersonal situations too. In short, this termination phase can be utilized to maximize the growth-producing and minimize the negative aspects of losing a therapist.

Nonetheless, I was worried about what my own feelings about leaving my patients would do to them. All the potentially harmful consequences of my leaving plagued me. Because I had so much else to attend to in addition to my practice, I also feared that I might not be as available to my patients as they might need. I also had my own countertransference feelings toward them, which I worried might interfere with their sorting through their feelings about my departure. Additionally, being vulnerable to guilt feelings, I worried about whether I was allowing for sufficient angry and crestfallen reactions to my leaving. To help me deal with all these feelings at this juncture, I sought supervision, which I found enormously useful and would certainly recommend even to the most experienced clinician.

CASE #1—LINDA

The week before I told all my patients that I would be leaving Los Angeles in a few months to move to New York I had the image of everyone leaving my practice immediately. That fear was not borne out. Only one of my patients decided to leave before I did. Linda was a widow who had been in weekly treatment with me for a few months, though she frequently canceled sessions due to illness. She was very anxious and lonely; her husband had died years ago, and she had ended a troubling relationship with another man about a year before she began to see me. She was distressed about being alone and talked principally about wanting a new relationship.

When I told her I was leaving, she immediately assumed I was moving to be with a man. I believe her envy of me as well as her enormous sense of renewed loss (she had also suffered the early death of her father) destroyed her ability to stay consistently with me as I tried to understand her feelings during my last months in Los Angeles. She appeared to exemplify what Schwartz (1974) discussed regarding some patients' difficulties in distinguishing between early losses and a current anticipated loss. She would cancel sessions, but wanted to talk to me by phone. She usually made good use of the phone sessions. In addition to dealing with some of her real life issues, she was able to let me know some of her feelings about my leaving, including her ambivalence about seeing me. I allowed her this enactment and also used the phone sessions to try to refer her to someone else while I encouraged her to come to my office to say goodbye.

The telephone seemed to function as a halfway house. We had some contact without her needing to drive to my office, which was difficult for her anyway as her health always seemed to be in a precarious state. It also saved her from seeing me face to face, which seemed to stir up more powerfully her conflicting feelings of envy, resentment, and longing. She came in to see me only one time, right before I left Los Angeles. That last session was poignant. She wanted to know all about my move. She wanted to show me that she could be happy for me, even though my leaving was a severe blow to her. I believe that her ability to come and say goodbye to me in person, wish me well, and accept my offer of a therapeutic referral indicated strength and resilience on her part and a real wish to look at and accept the depth of her own feelings. I also hypothesize that my acceptance of her limitations (allowing her to have phone contact without insisting that she come in to see me face to face each week) facilitated this step. It is important to keep the developmental needs of the patient in mind, rather than clinging rigidly to one right way to end therapy.

I received only one phone call from her after I moved to New York. She called about a month after I left, ostensibly to complain about the new therapist, who, from my patient's description, seemed to be doing a fine job under difficult circumstances. My main task was to help her to bring her disappointments and longings about both me and the new therapist to that new therapist. I was concerned about interfering in any way with the challenge the new therapist was facing in establishing a secure bond with this patient. Although I recognized that Linda still felt attached to me, I didn't think that additional contact was appropriate or ethical, since she now had a new therapist. My goal was to let her know I cared about her but wanted to help her deal with her loss of me with her new therapist.

CASE #2—GEORGE

Another patient I did some short-term phone work with was a young man in his twenties who initially saw me because of sporadic impotence and tremendous anger toward his father. As I got to know him, his alcohol abuse and history of poor impulse control emerged, along with tremendous shame about these issues. George had headed a middle-class "wannabe" type of gang when he was in high school. It was the only way he could lead and feel powerful. Generally he felt crippled by his well-known father's criticism of his lack of achievement. He suffered embarrassment over not measuring up to his father's achievements as well as shame about incestuous feelings toward his mother and sisters. On the one hand, George felt he could never measure up to his father's success as a singer; on the other hand, he was dismissive of his father's business acumen, claiming that his father had squandered the family's income by ostentatious behavior, such as treating everyone in his circle to fancy dinners instead of establishing financial security or ever buying a home. George was clearly both proud of his father's work and angry that his father didn't save enough so that he, George, would be "set up" for life. George's ambivalence toward his father was also revealed in how he would express anger toward him, and yet, as a farewell gift, George gave me a tape of one of his father's concerts. His wish to identify with his father was further revealed in his wanting to become his father's public relations agent as well as to bring him to a session about two weeks before I left Los Angeles. I believe he wanted his father to support him more fully, especially since I was about to leave.

During the two years that I saw him, George entered an AA program, went off welfare, started college (though he never finished his classes because he felt too inadequate), and began a new relationship with a woman, which, while tempestuous, offered him someone to care for and lessened the influence of some of his incestuous fantasies. His sexual problems also diminished. In the last year of our work together, he was doing very well in setting up a semi-autonomous business with his girlfriend. This success enabled him to feel less inferior, though he still struggled with alternating feelings of superiority and stupidity.

My work with George was interesting and complex. He often expressed anxiety about what I thought of him. Some of his worries seemed like a projection of his own harsh judgments of himself about his smoking, eating, and not exercising. His shame over what he saw as loose sexual boundaries in his family seemed to transfer to how he connected to me. Although George was an extremely responsible patient, almost always early for his appointments, very apologetic if late or if he needed to change our regular weekly meeting time, he seemed uncomfortable in my office. He sometimes found eye contact difficult and often stared down at the floor or let his eyes drift off to the pictures in my office rather than look at me. He often seemed to drift into my office and sit uncomfortably on my couch, fidgeting, as though not knowing what to do with his hands and the rest of his body. Seeing me, about the same age as his mother, appeared to stir up his unacceptable, forbidden longings. Occasionally we discussed this feature of the transference, but the feelings of shame and worry about what I would think of him made direct work on these transference feelings painful for him. Although their intensity reduced considerably over the two years of once-a-week treatment, I felt that dealing more immediately with his girlfriend and family rather than me made this area more tolerable for George. As he found out I was leaving Los Angeles and him, his oedipal issues toward both parents came to the fore.

I had given him the name of a therapist, but he didn't want to meet her until after I left Los Angeles. He called me about three weeks after I arrived in New York, on the day after his first appointment with the new therapist. He felt judged and misunderstood by her and decided not to return. He was calling me for another name. I encouraged him to talk with me about what had gone wrong for him, which he was very reluctant to do since I had made the referral. He asked me to have a few phone sessions before he spoke to anyone else. It would be too painful for him to think about another disappointment. I agreed, especially since he seemed agitated and worried about his relationship with his girlfriend. He was feeling very critical of her, and I believed that some of that anger and criticism might be meant for me, so I was willing to talk to him a few times. We set the parameters for the calls: once a week for a month. We also worked out the goals of the work: to better understand his current anger at his girlfriend and to agree to find a new therapist.

With those parameters set, George called me at the established times and struck me as able to utilize the phone sessions very effectively, even though we didn't have a history of much telephone contact. In fact, over the telephone, George seemed more vital and self-confident than he did in person. I worried about how much of this assurance was compensatory, similar to some of his feelings of grandiosity as a leader of his group in high school. But on a more positive note, I thought that my physical removal might be easing George's oedipal fantasies. After all, he had already lost me. Phone contact, though a way to hold on to me, was a poor second and very temporary. But our voice contact seemed to put George at ease. He wouldn't need to look at me. By phone, he could, for the first time, express his sadness at losing me, and was more able to evaluate the gains he had made in our work together and to assess the additional changes he wished to make for himself. I believe that as a result of having intrusive and critical parents, he could and did profit by the distance permitted by phone contact, while simultaneously receiving additional support from me to go on exploring unresolved issues in his life.

In the midst of this short-term phone therapy, I was looking for other therapists for him in Los Angeles and before our last telephone session found someone he was willing to meet with. During our final telephone hour, George indicated that he found this second therapist more acceptable and accepting and he was now ready to relinquish our relationship. I think that the phone sessions permitted him to express his feelings toward me and let go of me in a way he was not ready to do in person. This then allowed him to move on and connect with someone else without feeling judged. His anger at his girlfriend also diminished, at least for then; clearly, more work was needed with the next therapist.

Like Linda and George, most of my patients took my referrals to other therapists seriously, and before I left Los Angeles, many of them had already met with their new therapists and reported back to me about whether they would continue with them. A few patients decided to stop treatment, at least for a while, and said they would contact me in New York later if they wanted referral sources. All of them knew where I was moving. I had given them my new business address where they could write to me, as well as a phone number where they could call me. I had also sent letters explaining my move to patients who had terminated therapy with me over the previous few years. In my practice, several patients had come in and out of therapy and I wanted them to know where I was, should they try to connect with me again, rather than my just disappearing without a word.

CASE #3—RUTH

It was actually a patient whom I had not seen for several months who wanted some telephone therapy after I left Los Angeles. Ruth, 38 years of age, consulted with me originally for approximately two years starting about eight years before I left Los Angeles. Then she decided to leave treatment for a year and a half before returning to me. Ruth had endured a troubled childhood with abusive parents. She originally came to me depressed about being divorced, about unresolved issues with her parents, and about feeling stuck in her career. We worked primarily on the guilt and anger she felt toward her parents. Those feelings were exacerbated when in rapid succession they became ill and died within a few months of each other. Following considerable exploration of her relationship with both parents—her longings and disappointments and feelings of both connection and betrayal—Ruth weathered their deaths quite well and left the first phase of our work together.

She returned later to deal primarily with career issues. After she had been back with me for a few months, she was badly injured in an automobile accident. I met with her initially at the hospital and then conducted therapy by phone while she was first recovering. (Of course, phone therapy for incapacitated patients is another significant use of this mode of communication.) Ruth returned to my office within a couple of months, on crutches. She had also sustained minimal brain damage, including mild aphasia. She would begin sentences, stumble over words, and have trouble finishing them. Occasionally we had phone sessions, since she lived forty-five minutes from my office and sometimes wasn't strong enough to drive that far. When she couldn't drive yet, her driver sometimes disappointed her, so she couldn't always get to my office even when she felt up to it.

Within a year, Ruth was much improved and contemplated returning to college. As a youngster, she had attended university for only one year. Many aspects of schooling were difficult for Ruth and we spent time discussing ways to manage her work and deal with the feelings that the accident and her subsequent disabilities had brought on. She had also started dating a new man and married him about a year after her accident. This marriage was a happy one, although her husband worked long hours. She was able to tolerate his absences quite well and used those times to study and to see her women friends.

Because of her speech difficulty, talking on the telephone was not easy for Ruth. I learned considerable patience just waiting for her to find the right word rather than trying to guess what she meant or attempting to fill a word in for her. I didn't want to help her because she was yearning so much for individual achievement in an area where she now felt deficient. More than most of my other patients, she would telephone me between sessions with a question or concern about our upcoming session. Sometimes she had forgotten the time, though our schedule rarely deviated from its norm. As a result of her medical impairment, she seemed more dependent on me as a self-object whom she could idealize and aspire to be like.

She had always asked me many questions about myself, sometimes trying to catch me off guard, I felt. "What does your husband do?" "Where are your children?" I felt it less like an intrusion (though I certainly felt that also) and more like a wish to be connected with me, to bask in what she saw as my success and contentment.

While initially recovering from her accident, she questioned me more, almost like a little girl asking Mom to tell her how to dress and how to get her lunch box ready for school. I seldom answered her questions without commenting on how important it seemed to be that she know about my life and feel connected with me. She would share with me her idealizations and her wish to be like me. One important arena for these transference reactions was my clothing. She would often comment admiringly on my outfits and soon thereafter she'd be wearing something similar. Our phone conversations sometimes had a plaintive tone: "Judy, I don't remember whether we're meeting today or tomorrow." "It's tomorrow at 10 A.M." "Oh, what if I can't get there on time?" "I know you'll leave yourself plenty of time. And if you're late, we'll do the best we can with the time we have, and perhaps we can talk about whether another time would make it better for you not to have to battle with morning traffic."

Ruth had actually terminated with me about eight months before I left Los Angeles, so unlike most of my other patients, she did not have to endure being left while in the middle of therapy. But the letter that I sent to former patients brought her in. When she first called telling me she wanted to come in to say goodbye, I thought she simply wanted one session to tell me how she was doing and to find out what she could about me. It turned out that her concern about my leaving was very touching. She said "Even though I haven't seen you for quite a while and am feeling good, it's hard for me to think of you not being here on Beverly Drive anymore. When I drive down here, I won't be able to feel good knowing you're in this office and that I could call you if I want to come back again." Her wish for me as a constant presence there for her when she needed me was plain to see. At the end of the session, she asked to see me a couple of additional times before I left Los Angeles. We also discussed my referring her to another psychologist, but she didn't want or feel the need for further treatment with anyone else at that time. It was the loss of our ongoing relationship with me that troubled her and that we addressed in the last two sessions.

After I'd been in New York just a few weeks, I received my first message from Ruth saying she wanted a telephone session. She had some crisis that had just emerged, having to do with her schooling. Knowing how well she could actually cope with her college demands and having been witness to her ability to get help from her professors as well as others, I sensed that she was calling more to get additional supplies from me than for any other reason. I felt she needed to know that I still existed and cared for her. Although no longer on Beverly Drive, I was still a real person who thought about her and cared about her. By the end of the hour, she seemed satisfied that I had helped deal with the crisis and that I was still a real object to whom she could turn when she wanted to.

I heard from her again about two months later, when she was on the point of graduating from college. She was particularly worried about one class and an instructor who she felt was not giving her the help she needed. This time I thought that the call was as much about wanting me to take parental pride in her finishing college. After all, I had seen her when she first started back in school, not long after her accident. She seemed to want me to share in her good feelings, even though the manifest content of the conversation was about fear of failure. She also wanted to know how and what I was doing.

About six months after that conversation, I received a long and detailed letter from Ruth, telling me that she had just been admitted to graduate school and sharing with me an article that she had co-authored and that was about to be published. Naturally, I was delighted that her hard work had paid off. She was being rewarded and wanted me to share in her good fortune. While her parents had always praised her primarily for her good looks, I felt joy in her accomplishments. She needed to know that I was delighted in her achievements.

Ruth was a special case in a number of ways. She and I had a history of telephone contact both while she was in treatment with me and during the break in her therapy. That tradition of phone contact may have facilitated her calling me even though she knew I was far away and not planning to return to Los Angeles. The telephone had been a real lifeline for her when she couldn't get out of the house following her accident, and it remained an important link for us after I moved to New York.

Unlike her deceased parents, I was still available to her, through our phone conversations, and I was still needed to provide support and encouragement in an area of her life where she had never received it before.

DISCUSSION

The above examples show several uses of telephone therapy. The telephone functioned in one case as a more detached way to connect with a therapist about whom the patient had ambivalent feelings. When I left Los Angeles, Linda called me to complain about the new therapist but also to retain some semblance of contact until she could attach herself to that new therapist. She still needed me to unburden herself of the many hurt, angry, and disappointed feelings she carried. By telephone, I could still function that way.

With George, the telephone served as a safer way to express some longings toward me as well as disappointment and anger that I would no longer be there for him. The unseeing phone appeared to lessen the shame George felt in telling me some of his feelings in person. I believe our telephone sessions also helped diminish the internal sense of his parents' power over him. His recognition of these emotions allowed him to say goodbye to me and to move on to the next therapist. In both these cases I agree with Elkind (1995) who says "When patients have been attached to their therapists, they are usually unable to engage in a new therapeutic relationship right away. They may be unclear about what they want or they may need time to reach a sense of closure about the therapist they have lost" (p. 336). There is an assumption that patients can quickly transfer to a new therapist, with "blithe denial that their confidence in our profession may have been shaken" (p. 336). The significant bond they have created with the original therapist may need that additional telephone contact as a compromise type of connection that then allows the patient to move on when certain internal needs are met.

In the third case, with Ruth, the telephone functioned as a long connecting link allowing me to continue as an important figure who was proud of her achievements. In the face of her many losses, including her parents and her youthful body with its ability to function easily before her accident, she needed a period of ongoing, though sporadic, contact to consolidate the gains she had made while in therapy with me. I believe that my leaving Los Angeles (recall her wish for my continuous presence on Beverly Drive) even though she hadn't been in therapy with me for quite a while, was experienced as a rupture to Ruth's sense of self, which our ongoing contact by phone and mail helped to heal. She is a good example of Kohut's description of the ongoing need for selfobjects.

I realize more in retrospect even than I did three years ago while in the midst of terminating my practice in California how helpful to my patients as well as to me the additional telephone sessions were. I learned from various patients' needs, which I tried my best to attend to, that greater flexibility could be a real benefit in many ways. It also gave me additional time to think about the meaning for each individual of more contact. I saw that permitting patients additional time to express their feelings (such as abandonment, rejection, loss of a significant attachment, as well as sense of self) as a result of my leaving them was sometimes crucial. Allowing patients a transitional time before they saw a new therapist was also helpful, and the telephone was an excellent way to provide this bridge.

My patients had a lot to teach me about the various ways of saying goodbye, particularly under the duress of forced termination. They also helped me achieve a better feeling of closure as well as a link to my previous life and professional identity in California, which was very important to my sense of self. These connections turned out to be valuable for me while making the transition to a new professional life as a psychologist across the country. As mentioned earlier, it was each of these patients, of course, who initiated the contact, but I gained from the contact as well by feeling that I still had something important to provide by phone. From afar, I could furnish object constancy, a continued sense of self, or a safer container for the expression of some powerful affects.

Through various patients' wishes for continued contact, I learned much about the importance of flexibility, about individual differences, and about the power of termination. I saw that by remaining available to the needs of my patients I could simultaneously serve and set limits and as a result make their loss of me more endurable and also ease some of my pain at leaving them.

REFERENCES

Elkind, S. N. (1995). The consultant's role when the analyst terminates therapy. *American Journal of Psychoanalysis* 55(4):331–346.

Penn, L. (1990). When the therapist must leave: forced termination of psychodynamic therapy. *Professional Psychology: Research and Practice* 21(5):379–384.

Schwartz, G. (1974). Forced termination of analysis revisited. *International Review of Psycho-Analysis* 1:283–289.

9

Psychotherapy with a Patient Who Was Afraid of Seduction*

HERBERT S. STREAN

*A*gnes, an attractive 30-year-old woman, was referred to me by a physician who felt that many of Agnes's somatic difficulties had a psychological basis. Because she was suffering from acute migraine headaches, insomnia, and gastrointestinal disorders, the physician, Dr. C., concluded that Agnes needed psychotherapy. Particularly when she also shared with him that she had many phobias and compulsions, the physician was convinced that "she needed lots of therapy."

In addition, Agnes had enormous difficulty sustaining relationships with men, and in the few relationships she did have, she had serious sexual problems. An editor in a well-known publishing house, Agnes constantly felt under a great deal of stress as she conscientiously tried to meet deadlines and complete assignments.

Although I probably was influenced by Dr. C's remarks, as soon as I met Agnes I sensed that she was a very shy, inhibited woman who found it difficult to open up to me. After she spoke very haltingly and revealed next to nothing over a period of fifteen minutes, I decided to try to investigate with her

*This chapter was originally published in 1998 as "The Woman Who Did Better over the Telephone," in *When Nothing Else Works*, by Herbert S. Strean, published by Jason Aronson Inc.

what her resistance was all about. On my asking her how she felt when Dr. C. referred her to me, Agnes's face turned very red and all she could murmur was, "You come well recommended." When I tried to pursue further her feelings about the referral, Agnes embarrassedly said, "I've never done this before," and turned even redder.

I don't think Agnes was in my office more than twenty minutes when I said to myself, "This woman sounds and looks like a frightened virgin about to do it for the first time. She is terribly scared of me." Relating to her comment that she had "never done this before," I told Agnes that coming to see me could be very upsetting. She didn't know me and didn't know what she was in for. To this, she meekly said, "Dr. C. said we'll just talk here," and turned another bright red.

Not only was I feeling that Agnes appeared to be like a frightened (and perhaps angry) virgin, but when she mentioned that we'll "just talk" here, I wondered how much she was worried about being raped. She seemed terrified that some harm would befall her.

I felt that before I asked Agnes for any further information about herself, I was going to have to spend much more time trying to help her feel more comfortable talking to me. Actually, this issue was a theme throughout a good part of her therapy, but in the beginning sessions that was almost all we talked about.

For approximately six sessions, Agnes and I discussed how tough it was for her to be in my office and talk to me. While she pointed out that this was an issue in many places, she felt it most acutely while being with me. When I suggested to her that perhaps there was something about me that was making it uncomfortable for her, she became protective of me and said, "You're very patient and kind. There's nothing you're doing wrong. It's just being in a doctor's office that bothers me!"

When Agnes mentioned "being in a doctor's office," I immediately said to myself, "I bet she's worried about getting undressed, either for real or symbolically and she's frightened as hell." I knew that sharing my association would terrify her but I felt we could deal with the derivatives of "getting undressed." Therefore, I asked Agnes if she had any particular difficulty with one or more doctors at any time. After turning a bright, bright red and with her hands shaking and voice trembling, she said, "When I was 4 years old I had to go to the doctor's office often because I would get infections in my private parts. Nobody told me I would have to get undressed and it was very, very uncomfortable!"

Agnes appeared quite relieved when I made the connection between feeling forced to go to the doctor and get undressed and feeling forced to come to my office and reveal herself. Particularly when I said, "Just like it was with the doctor when nobody prepared you for what was going to happen, no one has really prepared you for me," Agnes seemed to feel somewhat supported and better understood.

Inasmuch as I had not gotten any history from Agnes and now wanted to ask her about some dimensions of the story of her life, I thought it would be helpful to reassure her beforehand. I told her that if at any point I asked her to talk about something that was uncomfortable for her, it would be a good idea to tell me she didn't want to talk about it, and we would not. With this form of preparation (different from the lack of preparation before going to the doctor or before seeing me), Agnes could begin to discuss her early and current life.

Agnes came from a big Italian family that consisted of six children. They lived in a very poor section of Brooklyn, where her father worked as a garage mechanic. According to Agnes, the parents were continually engaged in arguments. Mother tended to demean Father in front of the children and lamented her fate when he was away from home. She felt regretful that she didn't marry a more affluent, better-educated man who wasn't so coarse and crude.

Agnes tended to identify with her mother as she fought with her husband. As the oldest sibling, Agnes tended to be "mother's little helper," and often supervised her siblings. When Agnes was 14, her mother was stricken with cancer and Agnes not only "took over" the house, but became both Mother's and Father's confidante.

After her mother died, when Agnes was 15, Agnes served even more *in loco parentis* for the other children. In addition, she felt that she was in many ways acting as her father's wife, particularly when he turned to Agnes for support while mourning the loss of his wife.

When Agnes told me how much her father turned to her for solace, I wondered how much physical contact there had been between father and daughter. I had to be very careful in the way I asked Agnes about this, because she could feel as if she were being forced to reveal something she didn't want exposed. Therefore I asked her "Inasmuch as your father was very needy, did he ever hold you and cry on your shoulder?" When Agnes replied to my question, she displayed some anger for the first time, saying, "He didn't just cry on my shoulder. He kissed me on the lips! My sisters and brothers said that he acted like my lover. He made me uncomfortable and I didn't know what to do with him." Agnes then spent several sessions criticizing her father for a "form of abuse." As she did so, she became less inhibited in the sessions. By the time Agnes was in treatment about four months, she was communicating quite actively and with a much wider range of feelings. She cried, laughed, and expressed anger, hurt, and much anxiety. Since she was discharging a lot of feelings that had been under massive repression, many of her symptoms such as migraine headaches, insomnia, and gastrointestinal disorders diminished a great deal.

Though Agnes was feeling much better, she told me she was "feeling uncomfortable about feeling good," and mentioned that this had been a problem for her most of her life. As we worked on this issue in her once-a-week therapy, we learned that the problem was overdetermined. When Agnes felt good, she experienced herself as being in a "very superior" position to her siblings. It was as if she "defeated them" and won the prize of being most loved by her parents. In addition, ever since Agnes's mother died, she felt like an oedipal winner, and every time she achieved something she felt guilty about having it better than her mother, who got sick, suffered a lot, and died.

The acute problem of being both the oedipal and sibling winner was intensified because Agnes, in contrast to her siblings and parents, was a college graduate who had a prestigious job. To try to expiate her guilt for surpassing her parents and siblings, Agnes developed several defenses. First, she spent a great deal of time "taking care" of her siblings and their children. Second, she constantly gave her father and her siblings gifts of money. Third, she had a strong desire to tell the men she dated that she lived in poverty in Brooklyn, and that's where she felt most comfortable.

As Agnes was more freely sharing her feelings, history, and conflicts with me, she started to date men more often and with more comfort. After she was in treatment for about eighteen months, she was seeing one man, Dan, quite regularly. It was the closest and most enjoyable relationship with a man that she ever had.

By now Agnes could confront in therapy the specifics of her sexual problems. She found it difficult to be naked in front of a man; got an upset stomach when she was hugged, kissed, or fondled; and was often in pain when she was penetrated by the man's penis.

Together we were able to note the similarity of being uncomfortable in the nude in the present and being uncomfortable with the doctor in the past. Also, we were able to connect the anxiety in the present of being kissed with the anxiety she felt when her father kissed her on the lips. In effect, she was unconsciously turning her current suitors into father figures and feeling a lot of anxiety because her forbidden incestuous fantasies were aroused.

Reviewing her past and present and gaining insight into her conflicts helped Agnes feel a lot more comfortable with Dan and with me. Interestingly, as Agnes was gaining some mastery over her sexual and interpersonal problems, particularly as they impinged on her relationship with men, her father remarried. Agnes seemed to feel only relief and pleasure and did not express any feelings of jealousy. I noted that she became more involved with Dan and somewhat more spontaneous with me at this time.

By the time Agnes had been in treatment about two years, her life was improving in many ways. Her presenting symptoms had diminished, her life with Dan was quite happy, she was doing well on her job, and she was feeling less guilty and less involved with her father and siblings. Therefore, I was quite surprised and very disappointed when Agnes told me she was offered a position in Seattle with a different publishing company, and she wanted to take it.

Agnes stated that the idea of being apart from her family, with whom she had been too involved, was the major factor for her leaving New York, but I felt her reasons for leaving were more complicated. Although she kept repeating that she saw "cutting the cord" as a positive step, I tried to involve her in thinking about other possibilities as well. All Agnes could come

up with was the fact that she would have more status, responsibility, and money in the new job.

As I reflected more on her somewhat impulsive decision
to move to Seattle, I realized that two individuals she would
leave would be Dan and me. Inasmuch as she had not mentioned us at all, I hypothesized that continuing to be with us
may have been anxiety provoking for her.

Exploring with Agnes how it felt to say goodbye to Dan
and to me, I got nowhere. Dan was "a very nice guy but I can
do better and probably will in Seattle." As far as leaving me
was concerned, she felt I had done my job well and she was
now ready to be on her own.

Although Agnes was very reluctant to explore her feelings
about leaving Dan and me, her dreams shed quite a bit of light
on her conflict. In one dream, Dan was trying to put a wedding ring on her finger and she was squirming and fighting
him. In another dream, Dan had impregnated her and she was
arranging an abortion.

The conflicts she was having with Dan—wanting more
intimacy but fighting it because it was too incestuous—were
similar to the conflicts she was having with me. In addition to
telling me she was concerned about becoming too attached to
me, Agnes had one dream in which she made me the doctor
who was forcibly undressing her, and in another dream she
was trying to get my permission to go to Seattle and I wouldn't
give it.

I was very clear that I wanted Agnes to stay in New York
and remain in treatment with me. Yet I also knew that I did
not want to be like her dependent, demanding father who didn't
really permit her to have much autonomy. Therefore, I tried
my best to be the therapist who was "equidistant" (A. Freud
1946) and not take sides in her ambivalence. When I did tell
Agnes that one of the paramount reasons she wanted to go to

Seattle was that the closeness to Dan and me was making her uncomfortable, she agreed with me. She even went so far as to say that it was like being too involved with her father.

When I suggested to her that staying in treatment with me and talking about herself, as her dreams suggested, felt like it was combining getting undressed in front of the doctor and having sex with her father, she told me she knew she had a tendency to make me her father, and when I suggested to Agnes that it was difficult for her to explore with me why she wanted to make Dan and me her father, she also agreed with me, but it didn't have any impact on her decision.

When it became clear that Agnes was definitely going to Seattle, I asked her if she would like me to locate a therapist for her in that area. She said she wanted to see how it worked out in Seattle and then she would call me and let me know if she wanted a referral to a therapist.

After Agnes had been in Seattle about four months, she called me in New York to tell me that her family members were constantly calling to tell her that they missed her and wanted her to come back home. This was making her feel very guilty and she was considering moving back to New York. Not wanting to appear like one of her family members, and knowing of Agnes's tendency to make abrupt decisions, I suggested to her that I felt she was in a very tough position with her family and perhaps she might consider seeing a therapist in Seattle now.

Agnes was adamant about *not* seeing a therapist in Seattle. She pointed out that she knew me much better than she knew any other therapist and I knew her well, so why make a change? We could have appointments by phone.

Since I felt strongly that many dimensions of good therapy were missing when therapist and patient interact over the telephone, I was very skeptical about Agnes's proposition. However, while she was pleading her case, it occurred to me that she would probably feel protected by having no visual contact with me, and be far away yet talk to me. I concluded that it might be an interesting experiment!

I told Agnes that conducting therapy over the telephone was something I had never done except on an emergency basis and therefore I wasn't sure whether I could help her. However, I thought we might try it for a couple of months and see how it worked. Agnes seemed very pleased that I was willing to consider doing "phone therapy."

Initially, she discussed with me how difficult it was for her to be constantly "bombarded" by her father and siblings telling her in one way or another, directly and indirectly, that she should come home now. Since we had gone over before she left for Seattle how very responsible she felt for her family and guilty for having a better life than they, we were quickly able to resume our work in this area. Agnes told me that she had been having dreams of moving back to Brooklyn, but waking up in a sweat and then being relieved that she was still in Seattle.

It was obvious that the idea of moving back to Brooklyn filled Agnes with terror and I realized that the meaning of this had not yet been discussed. As we explored this it became clear that in many ways Agnes experienced moving away from her family as a hostile act. She was feeling like a fugitive and was worried that she'd be caught and punished. This insight evoked many hostile fantasies toward her family members, hostility that had been buried most of her life.

It was very liberating for Agnes to discharge murderous fantasies toward family members and have me continue to be supportive and understanding. She began really to enjoy Seattle, started to date again, and didn't feel obligated to move back to New York. However, she did feel compelled to visit her family periodically and always came to see me for as many face-to-face sessions as were available.

What I found very striking was Agnes's manner of relating to me now that she was living in Seattle. She dressed informally, spoke with more ease, and seemed much less guarded. She was able to discuss sex with less embarrassment, and expressed warm gratitude to me for helping her enjoy her life much more.

It was after treatment had been resumed for about three months that I asked Agnes in a phone session if she had noted how differently she was relating to me since she lived in Seattle. She replied in a matter-of-fact manner, saying, "Sure. You're much safer when I'm away from you. If you had a father who was too sexy and a doctor who was too sexy, you wouldn't want to be near somebody like you! This way is perfect. You can help but I don't have to worry about being undressed in front of you. You can't see me on the phone!" Agnes went on to tell me that she was still in contact with Dan and spoke to him on the phone quite regularly. As with me, she was a lot safer if she wasn't in direct face-to-face contact with him.

As I began to study my reactions to Agnes, I eventually realized how teased I felt. She was telling me how much I was helping her but also showing me she didn't want to have too much to do with me. She would show much warmth, gain insight, and be grateful when she saw me, and then take off. On the phone, she was also very pleasant to relate to, but distant. This was, of course, her way of relating to Dan and he, too, was feeling teased.

Studying my feeling of being teased by Agnes and recognizing my resentment and discomfort, I slowly began to realize that she was doing to me what she must have felt with her father, the doctor, and perhaps others—teased! I decided to first tell her how teased I felt by her and see what she would do with it. After becoming defensive and apologetic at first, she clearly showed she liked the idea. Eventually she could acknowledge that teasing me was a lot better than being teased and she could acknowledge that she wanted Dan and me to "squirm" the way she often did with her father and the doctor.

When Dan finally felt sufficiently frustrated by Agnes's teasing and broke up with her, she began to take the issue much more seriously. She then went through a long and difficult period, weighing the advantages and disadvantages of returning to New York and resuming face-to-face contact with me.

Eventually, Agnes effected a compromise. She was able to arrange a six-month change of location with the publishing company so that she could work and live in New York and see me twice a week.

When she resumed face-to-face contact, Agnes's fears returned, but only for about a month. In this round of therapy, I could discuss not only her pleasure in teasing me, but also her difficulty facing her wishes to have sexual contact with me. This was similar to her inability to face her own erotic desires toward her father and the doctor.

As Agnes could more readily face her sexual desires to seduce her father, the doctor, and me, she started to get involved with another man, Eric. Eric was several years younger than Agnes, a fact that helped her feel "less controlled" and "less intimidated" than she did with Dan. Eventually, Eric moved to Seattle with Agnes and they lived together.

When Agnes returned to Seattle with Eric, I heard from her a few times. They were planning to get married shortly and Agnes sounded extremely happy. In our last interview, she told me that there were three things I did that were most helpful to her: (1) not making her talk about anything she didn't want to talk about, (2) not making her do anything she didn't want to do, and (3) being willing to work with her on the phone. Agnes said, "When I saw that you didn't have designs on me—because you didn't object to the phone—I could then face my own problems."

I do believe that the maturational experience I offered Agnes, which helped her a great deal, was conducting telephone therapy with her. She could feel that I genuinely wanted to help her without insisting on my own preferences. Not feeling forced to submit to me and my narcissistic wishes, Agnes could better face her own wishes to seduce father figures. Had I not provided the experience of the telephone, I think Agnes would have continued to feel like a helpless victim with men and would not have matured.

REFERENCE

Freud, A. (1946). *The Ego and the Mechanisms of Defense*. New York: International Universities Press.

III

WITH PARENTS, CHILDREN, AND ADOLESCENTS

10

Use of the Telephone in Work with Parents of Children in Psychotherapy

DIANA SISKIND

*T*he telephone has a special place in child psychotherapy because it provides a vital link between the child's therapist and the child's parents. In order to fully appreciate the importance of this link we must recognize that the centrality of parents in the lives of their children is bound to extend to the treatment situation.

THE PARENTS AT THE CENTER OF THE CHILD'S LIFE AND TREATMENT

From the beginning of life a child's physical and emotional environment is created by his parents, their influence encompassing all aspects of caretaking. Within the microcosm of home, parents have absolute authority. It follows that it is the parents who make the decision to seek treatment for their child, who find a therapist, make the appointments, and bring their child to the therapist's office. Although the parents come requesting help for their child, we should not assume that the child is the one in need of help. We will not know where our help is needed until we get to know the total situation that precipitated their request. One of the very few things we can assume is that except for some rare and highly pathological

situations, the parents of any child who is troubled and unhappy are also suffering. Whether or not they realize or are
willing to acknowledge their distress, consulting a child therapist is a major action on their part. We can also be quite certain that whatever conscious attitude parents might have about
their child's treatment, their role is bound to be as key to the
child's therapy as it is to the rest of his life. And just as they
can decide that their child needs treatment, so they can change
their minds and terminate it.

The therapist is wise in recognizing and respecting the full
extent of parental power in a child's life. This recognition will
not only help her[1] in positioning herself within the family con-
stellation, but it will also help her appreciate that the other side
of parental power is that of total responsibility.

While there is a great deal of confusion and disagreement
among therapists on the relationship between the child's therapist and the child's parents, there is general agreement that it
is one that often becomes mired in rivalries. The difficulties
that arise often prevent the establishment of a working alliance
between parents and therapist, and this is a limitation that
hampers the treatment process and often leads to premature
termination.

I propose that the telephone used wisely and sensitively
by the child's therapist can go a long way toward building a
working alliance with the parents. I would like to emphasize
that I do not mean that the concrete use of the phone serves
the building of this alliance. Rather it is the therapist's use of
the telephone in response to her attunement to the *affective
states* that a parent might be experiencing when his child be-

---

1. For the sake of simplicity, the feminine pronoun will be used
when referring to the therapist, and the masculine pronoun when
referring to a child or parent.

gins an evaluation process or enters treatment proper. There are times when the parent might be feeling distraught; uncertain about what is happening, what to expect, how to respond; and eager for some contact with the therapist. At such times that parent might find having to wait several days or a week for the next face-to-face appointment with the therapist terribly taxing. By making the telephone available at such times the therapist conveys her recognition of the parent's distress; the therapist's concern for the parent thus becomes part of the field of therapeutic focus. When the therapist is motivated by such regard for a parent's psychic state, the telephone is an agent of attunement likely to reduce the parent's anxiety. When the therapist's intervention results in a diminution of parental anxiety, everyone benefits—the parent, the child, and the therapist. A more comfortable parent is usually more competent and more effective in regard to his child. And a parent who feels listened to by his child's therapist is more likely to feel that he and the therapist are allies working toward a common goal.

Before discussing the therapist's use of the telephone more fully let me briefly outline some basic differences between the treatment of children and that of adults. These differences are so obvious that they can easily be overlooked and undervalued. Understanding their impact will serve to unite reader with author and place us on common ground in entering this exploration of the relationship between child's therapist and child's parent.

SOME DIFFERENCES BETWEEN ADULT AND CHILD TREATMENT

When an adult decides to seek treatment for himself, the situation is, at least on the surface, fairly clear cut. One adult seeks another for the purpose of being helped. While this two-person arrangement does not remain static insofar as transferential and countertransferential forces expand the duet of voices to include psychic representations of past and present important objects, nonetheless, on a realistic basis, the treatment remains a process that takes place between therapist and patient. Nothing so neat exists in the treatment of children. As mentioned earlier, the parents initiate treatment for their child and play a decisive role throughout its duration regardless of the extent of their actual participation. This changes when children reach adolescence and require a more exclusive relationship with their therapist. Occasionally adolescents request treatment for themselves. But even during adolescence, treatment still has to be sanctioned and paid for by the parents, and their role in the life of their child remains active despite the adolescent's pull toward separation.

Although the initial phone call to the therapist is generally made by one of the child's parents, the recommendation for a psychotherapy consultation may originate with the child's school, pediatrician, or another person in the child's life. Whether the suggestion is initiated by parent or outsider, the implication that something is "wrong" with the child has been raised. Consequently, the process of seeking a professional opinion is always fraught with complicated feelings and reactions. In addition to the inevitable worry are such possible responses as shame; self-blame; blaming others, including the spouse; disappointment in the child; and fear of being blamed and judged by the therapist.

To complicate matters even more, there might be disagreement between the parents, or between parents and school personnel in cases of a referral being mandated under threat of the child's expulsion. When the initial phone call is made under a cloud of disagreement, the case is burdened from its inception, exacerbating all the anxiety and self-doubt that making this phone call engenders under less (obviously) charged circumstances.

It is very helpful for the child therapist to be well oriented to the drama that precedes the initial phone call. It is also important to recognize that since this first contact between these two strangers generally takes place over the telephone, neither therapist nor parent has the benefit of visual clues during their very first communication. You might ask how all this differs from the first phone call in the treatment of adults. After all, there too a drama precedes the first phone call, and there as well therapist and prospective patient cannot see each other. But there is a big difference between seeking a therapist for oneself and seeking one for a child. Parents generally have a much harder time turning their child over to another adult for psychological help than they have in securing it for themselves. They feel that they are in a better position to evaluate the quality of their own treatment than that of their child. This is not totally without logic, and when a therapist keeps in mind what a big and dangerous step this phone call might seem to a parent, the therapist is more likely to treat that initial phone call with a great deal of patience, delicacy, and tact.

THE IMPORTANCE OF THE THERAPIST'S ATTITUDE DURING THE INITIAL TELEPHONE CALL

Although the first phone call from a parent has the purpose of setting up an appointment, there are many parents who need to spend some time on the phone before feeling able to actually set a date and time. Often a parent needs to gain a sense of what the therapist is like before actually setting up an appointment. If the therapist can take the time to speak to the parent, to respond to some of his questions, and to allay some of his anxiety about the therapist's attitude toward him, this is time well spent. The therapist cannot allay a mother's or father's anxiety about the child's situation, but she can convey a calm, responsive, and respectful attitude toward the parent, and not behave as if his questions are an imposition. If the call is received at a time when the therapist is rushed, this can be explained and a call back can take place when more time is available.

The child therapist's response to a parent's initial phone call sometimes sets the stage for what is to follow. If rapport is established during that first phone call, if the parent feels the therapist's interest and concern, a very important base for the establishment of a working alliance between therapist and parent has been set in motion. At their actual face-to-face meeting this fortuitous trend will either develop further or become mired by complications typical of child treatment. Some of these complications are caused by unconscious factors. The therapist might evoke a negative transferential response in one or both parents, which in turn might evoke a countertransferential one in the therapist. This might be manifested in various ways such as, for instance, in the tone of the dialogue between parents and therapist taking on an uncomfortable, strained quality, an edge of distrust being manifested. The parents might set certain conditions regarding length of treatment, frequency of appointments, confidentiality, method of payment, and such, that the therapist can't or won't agree to. These "practical" disputes often represent masked transferential and countertransferential enactments.

When a therapist is able to observe the appearance of these negative manifestations during the first session and reflect rather than just react, there is still a chance of overcoming this inauspicious first encounter. If a level of rapport existed in the initial phone call, this can give leverage to the therapist's effort to set the session on a better course. The therapist can point out that the tone of the phone call has been replaced by a less favorable one and explore with the parents what caused this negative shift.[2]

It is useful to keep in mind that most parents have no idea of what to expect from a child therapist; their initial contacts are tantamount to entering a foreign terrain. Consequently it is prudent for a child therapist to view as part of her role introducing parents to child treatment, an aspect that has an educational component and is another departure from adult treatment. With that in mind, it is possible to view some of the questions that parents ask as an understandable response to the unfamiliar, as a wish to understand and learn. Similarly, it may be the strangeness of the therapy that provokes parents into making such conditions for treatment before the evaluation process has been completed and a decision about the need for treatment has even been made. The point is that most parents, because of their lack of experience with treatment, might not know that their requests are inappropriate. As for those who are not new to child treatment but who nonetheless impose similar conditions, we need to find out what their previous experience was like. Finally, lack of experience does not preclude the transferential issues that always play a part in this process.

If we fail to understand the vulnerability of parents who consult us about their children, we fail in a serious way. The

---

2. Once when exploring a marked change in attitude between the first phone call and the first session I learned that upon entering the waiting room the parents noticed an ash tray and were very put off by the assumption that I allowed smoking.

parents need us to be attentive to them every bit as much as their children do. Furthermore, whether their response to us is positive or negative, it is of major importance. It is as much a part of our work to find an effective way of communicating with them as it is our job to ease communication with their child.

INTRODUCING THE TELEPHONE AS A MEANS OF COMMUNICATION BETWEEN PARENT AND THERAPIST

In recent decades child psychotherapy has all but replaced child analysis, and with this change the frequency of sessions has diminished. Once- and twice-per-week appointments are now most common. This is true even during the evaluation period. Consequently, one might see a child for the first time on a Monday and not again until the next Monday. The parents may have no appointments scheduled with the therapist until the evaluation period, consisting of three or four sessions with the child, has been completed. If this is the case, and because of agency policy or managed care restrictions it usually is, the parents have no feedback from the therapist for several weeks, and the therapist gathers no information about the child's or parents' reactions to the sessions. This is one of the situations where the telephone becomes a tool of great value to both the parents and the therapist.

I always ask the parent who accompanied his child to call me in the evening of the child's first appointment to let me know how the child reacted to the session. If the child is very young and the parent was present for the session, I always ask whether the child behaved as the parent might have expected. I find this telephone conversation of great value on many counts. It confirms and elevates the interdependence of therapist and parent and underscores the collaborative aspect of our relationship. And although I focus on the child's reaction to the first session, I learn a great deal about the parent's attitude, which gives me important insight into the parent and allows me to respond in a helpful manner.

I follow this pattern of telephone contacts during the beginning phase by asking that the parent call me on the eve of the child's next appointment to let me know of any significant developments in the child's day-to-day life or in the life of the family. These phone calls allow parents to ask questions, voice concerns, and by so doing feel once again that the therapist regards them as important to the treatment process. I have been interrupted twice this morning while writing this chapter by a mother whose child is to have a first appointment tomorrow. When I met this mother for the first time last week, she was in great distress. Yet she was not particularly forthcoming during her session until the end, when I told her that what she described was not a problem without solution and that together we would figure things out. She called twice the day after our session with questions and twice more today. My accessibility has, I believe, made her feel that she is not alone. Has anyone ever tried to measure the curative power of feeling not alone?

The reader unaccustomed to the approach of planned and unplanned telephone contact might wonder about the demands this makes on the therapist. Is it not too much to work all day and then have the evening interrupted by telephone calls from anxious parents? Of course this level of availability does lengthen the hours spent working, but what a good investment of time if the child's mother and father, either or both, recognize they have found someone who is there to help them with their child. And if a call from the parents on a particular evening is not convenient, an appointment time can be set for the next day. These calls do not need to last more than a few minutes. They are mainly a way to stay in touch, to exchange information, to work together. If a few minutes don't suffice, most likely a face-to-face appointment is needed.

When this pattern of communication is established during the evaluation period, there is a good chance that when parents and therapist meet to discuss findings and recommendations, they will no longer be the strangers they were a mere few weeks before.

In addition to the usefulness of the telephone during the evaluation period I have found it of great value in short term tripartite cases involving very young children with transient developmental problems (Siskind 1997, Chapters 9 and 10). One of my goals in these cases has been to identify the problem and then to keep my role in the background and to help the mother[3] be the principal agent of change. Another way of stating this is to say that although the child's problem is the reason for ongoing contact, the mother's problem with her child becomes the focus of the work. Sometimes this approach entails having more frequent sessions with the mother than with the child and ongoing telephone contact as well.

It is important to mention that what is being discussed at present concerns the failure to master a development milestone

---

3. In the two cases referred to above it was the mother who participated in the treatment. It could, of course, have been the father, although I have found in my practice that in the case of very young children with transient problems such as eating, toilet, and sleeping problems, it is more often the mother who seeks help. (Fathers tend to think that the problem will take care of itself. See Siskind 1997, Chapter 7, for an example of a consultation regarding a sleep problem initiated by the mother, but with the solution to the problem implemented by the father.)

in an otherwise well-developing child of competent parents. Two common examples of such developmental lags are delays in toilet training and protracted sleeping problems. I consider this type of lag when it is so specific and contained to be symptomatic of something that the mother,[4] in combination with the father, has been unable to do in order to bring about the necessary change. The "something" that she has yet to do has an obvious concrete aspect to it, such as making appropriate demand on her child. But her difficulty is controlled by intra- and interpsychic forces: there is the vast territory of unconscious conflict and there is the matter of being able to attain a higher level of separateness from her child while maintaining her libidinal connection with him. Often when this type of problem arises, any negative feelings toward the child evoke intense anxiety and are defended against through reaction formation. When some of these disavowed negative affects are interpreted they become modulated, more acceptable, and are given expression through such affects as frustration, annoyance, and moderate anger.

In cases where anger to any degree has been ego dystonic, a mother needs a great deal of support in order to dare to become aware of this affect in herself. But once she is able to acknowledge her impatience with her child's sleep or toileting problem and make appropriate demands on him instead of being overly solicitous, the effect on the child's growth is often dramatic and immediate, and the effect on the mother is equally striking. To bring this about, however, the therapist needs to be attuned to the mother and readily available to her, for the dawning recognition of negative feelings toward her child is

---

4. Mother denotes primary caretaker. Either parent can, of course, be the primary caretaker. Similarly, father in this sentence refers to the mother's partner. Their positions could be reversed.

bound to be experienced as dangerous. The therapist's presence may add just enough of a sense of safety to enable the mother to take these steps, and with that in motion the mother can in turn ease the step her child must take to a manageable size.

THE ROLE OF THE THERAPIST
AS AUXILIARY EGO

I conceptualize this therapeutic role as serving as an auxiliary ego for the mother (Siskind 1997). While this is a term usually used in regard to the protective role mothers play during their children's infancy, I am stretching it to include a special role therapists on occasion need to take on.

My thinking is as follows. When an otherwise well-functioning and competent adult becomes helpless in the face of some ordinary developmental issue concerning her child, we can assume that it has a link to her own past (Benedek 1958). We can speculate that it causes a regression in the mother that renders her inadequate to do her job. The mother we meet at the beginning of the consultation process might be head of a law firm, professor at a university, a person capable of performing all manner of feats of competence, but she cannot get her 3-year-old to stay in his bed at night. When we see this we can assume she is in the throes of something that requires our unrestricted help. If this mother is told that she can call us as much as she needs to around the sleep problem, consider the significance of this offer to her. Imagine her picking up the telephone to call us when Johnny has come out of his room for the fifth time and is dancing around the living room. Perhaps she is calling because she feels helpless and needs someone to turn to. Or she is calling because she feels angry that after all the talk and self-reflection no progress has been made.

Or she is calling to say, "See, it can't be done." Whatever form the phone calls takes she thought of her therapist when in distress and this indicates her recognition that she has a partner in her troubles, and it also indicates her desire to master an aspect of parenthood that has been particularly difficult. Not feeling alone in her helplessness can have a powerful reparative impact.

Some more discussion is warranted on the question of whether this level of availability via the telephone intrudes too much on the therapist's private time. If the calls become so frequent as to become a burden to the therapist, that could be taken as an indication that the treatment plan needs to be re-evaluated, that perhaps the mother needs treatment for herself. Or it could mean that some additional face-to-face sessions are needed. But in most of these brief consultations I have found that my availability over the telephone is used productively. And whatever mild inconvenience these telephone calls might entail, the swift resolution of the problem so satisfying to the parent, and so growth promoting for the child, is also very rewarding for the therapist.

There is often the worry among therapists that allowing patients all this access to us outside the appointment time might create a harmful state of dependency in them. I suppose that if the patient were a very needy person to begin with, and the therapist took on an authoritative role and imposed advice and opinions on the patient, dependency might be encouraged. But then we would be talking about bad treatment since our job is the antithesis of an authoritarian manner and the dispensation of advice. Our role is to provide the patient with growth promoting opportunities.

And what about dependency as a concept? We have to be careful about allowing descriptive words used by the lay public to enter our diagnostic considerations. The word "dependent" is usually stated in a pejorative tone when used in reference to adults, and that tone is sometimes even extended to descriptions of fairly young children. Yet it is also recognized that the inability to express dependent feelings is a limitation in adults and children, resulting in the curtailment of intimacy, in pseudo–self-sufficiency and so forth. It becomes a murky term because value judgments so interfere with its purely descriptive meaning. In my experience as a child and adult therapist, the expression of dependent feeling in my patients of all ages, including the parents of child patients, is a mode of communicating the affective state they are experiencing at a given time. If the therapist is doing her job there is no reason to worry about promoting dependency any more than there would be in promoting any other mood, affect, or condition. Our job, after all, is to listen, learn, and join our patients in their quest for insight.

USE OF THE TELEPHONE
DURING ONGOING TREATMENT

This is a good place to move to the use of the telephone in ongoing long-term treatment of children. The cases I've mentioned so far were either at the evaluation stage, or entailed short-term intervention regarding developmental lags in otherwise well-developing children of competent parents. Now I would like to talk about the plight of parents of very disturbed children, children whose serious ego deficits make them unable to deal with the ordinary frustrations of daily life, children given to rages, tantrums, and destructive behavior, labile children who collapse under even mild stress.

The parents of children whose pathology is severe generally lead lives apart from mainstream society. Their children are socially shunned, which is a source of pain, shame, and desolation. Life at home is fraught with strain with even the most ordinary transactions like bath time or getting dressed, taking on the dimensions of a major battle. Besides the obvious despair that these parents experience, perhaps most cruel is the murderous rage that they sometimes feel toward their own child. In such situations the therapist's ready availability over the telephone can go a long way toward restoring the equilibrium of these beleaguered parents who at times are frightened by their own violent impulses toward their child.

I remember a mother who often called me when her daughter had done some unspeakably destructive deed. Because I had been so accessible to her from the first phone call, not objecting to her lengthy statement of ambivalence regarding whether to come to see me, and because my patience with her was in sharp contrast to previous therapists who wanted to settle an appointment time quickly and get off the phone, she idealized me from the beginning. I did not try to undo this elevated view of me. I understood that she needed to feel that way and that this would contribute to a solid working alliance. I realized that living with a psychotic child had tainted her in more ways than one could imagine. People in general and even intelligent and well-trained professionals assumed that her child's pathology was her fault, an attitude that was not lost on her and that confirmed her worst fears.

During one of my early exchanges with this mother she perceived in my tone respect and fondness for her child. This became to her a source of great comfort and safety. That I could think well of her child—why that was a totally novel experience, for it had never happened before and even she, the mother, could only rarely feel genuine fondness for this wild, unruly child. What happened in the course of the child's treatment was that the mother would call me whenever the child went wild and destroyed whatever was in her path.

At first the calls were the mother's desperate attempt to stop herself from hitting back at her child. It was like calling 911. But the calls were also motivated by her wish to recover her equilibrium rather than strike back, and so she called, very frequently at first. When the calls came often, two or three a day, she would describe the incident, I would listen quietly and not say much, but as I write this thirty years later I realize that I admired her calling me and that probably was conveyed to her. I would like the reader to consider how resourceful she was to call me when in despair and out of control and when she did not know what else to do. That she had found an ally was enough to calm her. And the calls came less often after awhile and eventually became a rarity. Instead she would tell me during our regular sessions about the impulse to call me after a difficult time with her child, the imagined conversation she had with me, and the calming effect it had. The call was then no longer necessary. This mother's ability to use me that way went a long way toward helping her as a parent, and making her daughter feel safer.

The treatment went well and the child made great strides, but despite good progress she could not fit herself into the world of her peers. She was, however, able to be a good student and learned to live more peacefully with her family. This was about as good an outcome as we could expect. I believe that my absolute availability to this mother was the most decisive factor in the progress of this case.

CONCLUSION

Use of the telephone in work with parents of child patients is a fine tool for exchanging information and staying in touch when that is desirable. However, that is only the practical aspect of its usefulness. The real power of telephone contact between therapist and parents comes out of the therapist's concern for the parents, for her continuous effort to understand the effect of the child's treatment on them, and out of her ongoing effort to respectfully engage them in an alliance that suits their needs. Then the use of the telephone can transcend its obvious practicality and become a metaphor for the therapist's attunement to the network of affects and connections that form the core and complexity of child treatment.

REFERENCES

Benedek, T. (1959). Parenthood as a developmental phase. *Journal of the American Psychoanalytic Association*. 7:389–341.

Siskind, D. (1997). *Working With Parents: Establishing the Essential Alliance in Psychotherapy and Consultation*. Northvale, NJ: Jason Aronson.

11

Telephones, Teens, and Therapy

MARSHA H. LEVY-WARREN

NECHAMA SORSCHER

Some believe that teenagers sprout telephones from their ears and develop talkitis as they reach puberty. Others just lament the passing of the relatively quiet, cooperative days of their children's latency years. All who know adolescents are aware of their penchant for living large portions of their home lives attached to the family phone lines. These days, they are just as likely to be online at their computers as they are to be talking on the telephone to their friends.

Why is this the case? Is it equally true throughout adolescence or do the developmental differences among early, middle, and late adolescents create different needs and wants with respect to telephone use? How are telephones potential adjuncts to the psychotherapeutic process when kids are in treatment? This chapter addresses these and other issues related to teens and telephones. It begins with a description of each of the subphases of adolescence and how telephones are seen and used by adolescents in each. It describes the ways in which telephones are often used as part of the therapeutic process for adolescents in treatment in each of the subphases and includes case anecdotes for each subphase. The chapter concludes with a discussion of how the contrasting needs of both adolescents and their parents in each of the subphases is reflected in their use of the telephone in general, and specifically, in psychotherapeutic treatment.

EARLY ADOLESCENCE

When pubertal changes urge children out of their childhood, early adolescence has arrived. The age range is about 10 to 14, and girls tend to begin sooner than boys. Their relatively androgynous bodies begin to change into more clearly gendered ones, and these once-children now-adolescents need to reevaluate who they are and who they wish to be. To this end, they look at their parents in a new way, one that more accurately takes into account who their parents are. They no longer see them as all-powerful, the way children tend to view their caregivers. This deidealization process stems from their need to be less dependent upon their parents for everyday care, and there is both inner and social pressure to move in this direction (Levy-Warren 1996). Toward this aim, they move out with intensity into the world outside the home, often forming fast friendships that are solidified through long telephone conversations.

Telephone use during this time is very significant, for it is a way that adolescents connect with their peers in the context of their home environments. Through the use of the telephone, adolescents have the opportunity to experiment with being independent while still in the safe surrounds of their families' homes. The conversations they have with their friends revolve around the most important issues in their lives: school, their social world, and their parents. These conversations permit adolescents to consolidate their views of themselves and their parents, thus aiding them in the identity formation process of this time of life.

Early adolescents usually incorporate the telephone as part of their psychotherapy. They report telephone conversations that they have had with their friends to show their therapists they are capable of conversations that are more mature than those they have in treatment. From time to time, just as they may bring a friend into the waiting room with them before a session—which gives them a way of integrating their friendships into the presentation of self that characterizes who they are in therapy—they may also ask to use the telephone to call a friend during the session itself.

During the treatment of a 12-year-old girl who had been in psychotherapy for two years, the patient frequently asked to use the telephone to talk with her peers. Most often these requests were denied; however, on an occasion in which the request was made quite urgently, the therapist decided to hand her the telephone. When the patient spoke with her classmate on the phone, the therapist was struck by how this quite young-seeming girl was relating in a sophisticated and mature fashion. The patient was very aware of the observing therapist. It was clear that she wanted to show the therapist an aspect of herself she had been unable to show directly before this moment. She was able to use the telephone to do this: it was a transitional experience, of sorts. While she could not yet behave in this fashion in direct interaction with her therapist, she could show the therapist that she was able to act this way in her relationships with her friends.

Telephone contact between sessions often revolves around crises with parents and/or friends. When messages are left on an answering machine for the therapist, the storm, more often than not, has passed once the patient is reached. There is a characteristic sense of urgency early adolescents experience that is reflected in this pattern of interaction. They call when the experience feels like an emergency; by the time the therapist calls back, all is resolved.

Both the telephone and the answering machine serve the purpose of permitting the early adolescent to have contact with the therapist on an as-needed basis. Even though the therapist may not be reached personally, the adolescent has the opportunity to touch base in a way that permits a bolstering of ego functioning that is still in a nascent stage of development.

The early adolescent's sense of urgency is also satisfied in the newest form of quick communication—being online at the computer. Many kids this age "talk" to their friends, meet new people, and share experiences through the use of email. The protection of the written word, which offers a way to experiment with new voices and new ways of being-in-the-world, is another good adjunct to the identity formation process of this time.

MIDDLE ADOLESCENCE

Where early adolescents are preoccupied with leaving childhood behind and the deidealization of their parents of childhood, middle adolescents are consumed with the world of their peers and their growing need to define themselves in terms of gender and sexuality. They are also focused on being members of groups, both those that are defined in formal terms (such as athletic teams, music ensembles, choirs) and those that are defined only in informal terms (such as manner of dress, music listened to, or patterns of friendship) (Levy-Warren 1996).

Telephone conversations of early adolescents often rehash the day and report family crises, but those of middle adolescents begin to address philosophical and cultural concerns, as well as social exchanges that involved the pairing off of peers with one another—including discussions of romance and sexual activity. Who is involved with whom, who is interested in whom, and what they do when they hang out with each other are the telephone topics of choice.

In psychotherapy, middle adolescents focus on how to establish themselves among their peers. When they are still too caught up in family matters, they tend to lag behind their friends. Here is a case in point:

Stephen was a physically mature, though rather short 16-year-old. He was a good-looking young man, with an earring in one ear, a snake tattoo on his arm, and an attitude as big as the therapist's office. He usually sauntered in, threw himself into the chair that faced the therapist, put his feet up on the ottoman, and wisecracked: "What's up, doc?" He had come into treatment at the request of his school and parents for acting belligerently with teachers and other school personnel, cutting classes, and smoking cigarettes in the school restrooms. This interchange took place after two months of once-weekly individual psychotherapy.

Stephen (begins): How's it hangin'?
Therapist: Isn't that something you'd say to a guy, or am I just out of date, as usual?
Stephen: Hey, these things are all in transition these days. Look at me, right? I'm a guy, and I've got an earring. I bet when you were young no guy would do that. But that's all retro now.
Therapist: So, you think the social distinctions between what's okay for a guy and what's okay for a girl have really broken down?
Stephen: Well, yeah . . . definitely. I mean, you know, not in my house . . . but anywhere else you look. My parents are just so out of it. They're still giving me shit about the earring. I was on the phone the other day and my father walked in. He actually said I looked

like a pansy with the earring. The guy I was talking to couldn't believe it. I mean, what's that??? A pansy?! He's from some other planet. He thinks that any guy with an earring must be gay or must want to be. Or else the guy wants to be a girl. I think he's crazy.

Therapist: Crazy?

Stephen: Out of touch, you know? No clue. Living in the seventies, or whatever . . .

Therapist: So, what *did* prompt you to get the earring?

Stephen: It's cool. I like the way it looks . . . and I like that it's cool now but didn't used to be.

Therapist: Sure makes the generational differences clearer.

Stephen: I don't care about that. I don't give a shit about what they think.

Therapist: Hey—you brought up your father's comments . . . and that it was cool to have an earring now, but didn't used to be, right? I was just thinking out loud about what you said. I didn't think it would bother you so much.

Stephen: Who said it did?

Therapist: Could have fooled me. Sure seemed like you weren't too happy about my saying what I did. But I have a feeling this whole subject—your father's views of gender and sexuality, yours, the differences, isn't the easiest thing to talk about . . . with me or anybody else.

Stephen: Hey, listen. I can talk about it all with my friends. I don't need to talk to you.

Therapist: Who said anything about need? But here we are, and we're talking about it, so why stop now? I'm certainly interested in what you have to say. I'm sure you at least have plenty you can correct me about.

Stephen: Wouldn't be hard to correct you.

Therapist: I'm all ears.

Middle adolescents like Stephen are interested in what their parents have to say, often particularly their fathers, and often particularly about sex and gender, but they are even more keenly concerned with what they see as the prevailing peer group and cultural winds with regard to these issues. Stephen's telephone friend helped him to stay grounded in his point of view about having an earring, even though he was upset by his father's comment.

Stephen is filled with distrust of adults. His somewhat exaggerated antagonism and quick reference to his father suggest that he is, in fact, still quite involved with what his parents think of him, much as early adolescents might be. He is having difficulty entering middle adolescence, where he must become his own man like his father (as a man), but also not like his father (as a separate person). He is too drawn to his parents, particularly his father and his father's view of him, to move around comfortably in the social world of his peers and adults who are not in his family. His belligerence is a defense against his sense of need for his parents, a need that feels out of line with the rest of his development and out of line with where his peers are.

Stephen needs to define his sexuality, to know who attracts him and how to pursue this attraction. He also needs to define his gender, what it means to him to be male, a man. These are the most important aspects of middle adolescent development. His preoccupation with his father's calling him a "pansy" and a "girl" is a sign of his own lack of clarity about these issues, and his being more drawn to his father's view of him than he is able to determine his own view of himself. He could juxtapose the world of his peers, with which he needs to be more engaged, and the world of his home, by having the experience of being on the telephone, talking to his friend, at the very moment that his father was criticizing him for having the earring, not being a "real" man.

In any case, Stephen—and other middle adolescents—need to pursue love and affection and define their sexuality, in large part outside their families. Family relationships are too fraught with conflict from the undercurrents of sexual feeling (i.e., the incest taboo) to offer the kind of clarity of response that adolescents require to aid them in their self-defining process. They need to feel drawn to others, pursue physical relationships with those to whom they are drawn, and feel a sense of caring to foster the development of a healthy sexuality.

Issues of control and autonomy are paramount for middle adolescents, as Stephen demonstrates. As they establish a clearer sense of who they are in relation to their families and friends, the sometimes exaggerated ways in which they attempt to assert authority tend to diminish. In the interim, they may use the telephone as a way of asserting control in their lives. They make calls according to their own schedules and in a place of their own choice. Adolescents who are particularly unsure of themselves or insecure among their peers may well find it easier to disclose intimate information on the phone without the intensity of a face-to-face encounter.

As they are struggling to balance the intense focus on their social activities with their academic and family concerns, teenagers often have somewhat chaotic lives. If they are in psychotherapy, they may use the telephone as a way of keeping contact with the therapist amid the chaos of latenesses and missed sessions. Middle adolescents, like Stephen, are often reluctant to form alliances with the therapist, who is seen as a parental figure just at the time when they are attempting to consolidate their identities in their peer group and establish themselves as separate from their families. They may use the telephone as a way to simultaneously assert their independence from the therapist and to keep a vital connection going with the therapist as they explore the often frightening world of their peers.

Middle adolescents often request phone sessions because they are having difficulty juggling the group activities essential to their development with regular therapy sessions. Therapists must carefully consider the balance of developmental needs in making decisions about whether to accede to such requests. Although adolescents may use phone sessions as a way of distancing themselves from the therapist and/or treatment, use of the telephone may also represent a compromise that ultimately serves as a lifesaver to the patient in the midst of a chaotic and overwhelming situation. The telephone also continues to be a way for adolescent patients to try out emerging features of their personalities and to reveal different aspects of themselves to their therapists, both through the reporting of telephone conversations with friends in the consulting room and in the telephone conversations with therapists when they do not come in for face-to-face contact.

Middle adolescents often spend a good deal of time in the world of cyberspace. Here, they "talk" about aspects of their sexuality and explore ways of being with regard to gender role that they often feel shy about expressing in their real life interactions. Just as therapists may learn more about who their middle adolescent patients are trying to be from hearing them speak of their telephone conversations with friends, so may therapists learn more about their patients as they describe their activities on the net.

LATE ADOLESCENCE

Early adolescents are primarily concerned with leaving childhood behind and getting used to their newly changed adolescent bodies, middle adolescents seek to establish themselves among their peers with a particular awareness of how they see themselves in terms of gender and sexuality, but late adolescents want to see themselves as individuals capable of committed intimate relationships and personally derived goals and aspirations (Levy-Warren, 1996). To this end, they spend more time one-on-one with others, both in their peer group and in the older generations. Long telephone conversations with their friends, mentors, and (even) parents about relationships and possible career choices are typical of this subphase.

Where the youngest adolescents are concerned with seeing themselves as having a past—that is, leaving childhood behind—and middle adolescents are focused very much on the here and now, late adolescents are looking to the future, trying to sort out who they are trying to be, what they want to do, what they believe in, and with whom they want to share their lives. Toward this end, there is often a reconnection with parents in a different way, one that involves these near-adult children looking at their parents more as other adults with whom they do or do not want to identify. They often look to their therapists in a similar fashion.

Late adolescents frequently must also negotiate the difficult developmental transition of leaving home to go away to college. This transition has important implications for the treatment: it may necessitate termination and transfer to a different therapist, or a shift to using the telephone for sessions while the late adolescent is away and in-office visits during vacations and summers. Making the decision about which route to take is complicated. It requires looking carefully at the way a particular patient is able to relate over the telephone; the strength of the bond between the patient and the therapist; the possibilities for private conversations while the patient is away at school, often living in a dormitory; and the relative comfort of each member of the pair in having regular telephone contact.

Some therapists find that being deprived of the visual cues in working with late adolescents compromises the treatment enormously, particularly with patients who have difficulty putting their emotions into words. Others find that there is a heightened erotic tinge to the conversations on the telephone. In these instances, finding appropriate referrals in the vicinity of the colleges their late adolescents are attending makes more sense than attempting to continue the treatment either sporadically, when the students return home, or through telephone contact that seems inadequate. These issues have to be balanced, however, with the ease with which the adolescent forms bonds. Even if the telephone contact is not as effective as it might be, if the patient is not likely to connect with another therapist, telephone contact may be the best alternative.

The following is a case in point. It illustrates the use of telephone sessions as a way to stabilize a late adolescent patient during her first semesters away at college.

Jessica's parents referred her for treatment at age 15 out of concern for her irritability, social isolation, rapid mood changes, poor grades, and temper tantrums. They described their daughter as a mercurial adolescent who demonstrated significant behavioral difficulties at home, such as oppositionalism, intense sibling rivalry, and withdrawal from all family routines. These were long-standing difficulties that began at age 2 and worsened over the years.

The therapist's diagnostic impression was that Jessica suffered from a major depression. She began once-weekly psychotherapy with Jessica, collateral parent sessions, and psychopharmacological intervention.

Jessica was an intelligent, articulate, artistic, and sensitive adolescent who was struggling to separate from her

parents and establish herself socially. Although chronologically a middle adolescent, she was frozen in early adolescence. She was inhibited by her conflicted relationship
with her parents and severe feelings of guilt related to her
younger brother, a boy with Tourette's Disorder and a host
of learning and social difficulties. The treatment focused
on helping Jessica stabilize her moods, understand her
behavior, and more directly express her pain and grief
about her younger brother's disabilities.

Collateral parent counseling emphasized Jessica's
need for appropriate limit setting and developing an understanding of her tantrums as reflecting her frustration
and guilt about her brother, as well as her conflicts
around dependency. This broadened understanding of
their daughter aided her parents in holding to the house-
hold rules more effectively. As a result, Jessica became
more tolerant of many of her brother's behaviors, and her
social relationships outside the home improved. During
the treatment, she continued to demonstrate significant
social anxiety, but was able to sustain friendships and
widen her circle of friends.

A high level of anxiety and distress marked Jessica's
application to college. She poignantly lamented having to
leave home when she had only just begun to feel positively
about her relationship with her family. Her parents appreciated her dilemma and were supportive, despite their
anxiety about her functioning and the financial stress of
college.

Before she began college, Jessica was referred to a
local therapist and her parents were encouraged to do
what they could to facilitate the referral. During her first
semester, Jessica felt overwhelmed by the workload and
had difficulty attending classes regularly and completing

homework assignments. Her social anxiety continued to interfere with forming and sustaining friendships. She often felt extremely insecure about her relationships. Despite encouragement from her parents and the therapist at home, Jessica had trouble calling the local therapist whose name she had been given to set up an appointment.

Given Jessica's level of emotional distress and academic difficulty, her therapist from home decided to establish weekly telephone sessions. She hoped to help Jessica feel more stable and to facilitate the transfer to a new therapist. Both Jessica and her parents were relieved by this decision.

These weekly telephone sessions with Jessica focused on helping her to negotiate her coursework, establish friendships, and alleviate some of her significant social and performance anxiety. They succeeded in aiding her to establish herself more securely at college, in part by providing a clear bridge between her life at home and her life away. Jessica was able to move more clearly into a late adolescent consolidation of her identity, which included ways that she was like her parents (e.g., by participating in community service work that resembled the kind of work her parents did) and ways that she was tapping her personal resources that were unlike those of her parents (e.g., teaching artistic appreciation to disadvantaged children in her college community). The therapist continued to work with her when she returned home for vacations, along with collateral parent guidance work.

Just as the use of the telephone during sessions, between sessions, and for emergency contact helps younger adolescents maintain contact with the therapist when they are feeling a sense of urgency and/or permits adolescent patients to express aspects of themselves to therapists that they might not be able to express directly to their therapists in sessions, so does telephone contact with older adolescents allow them to bridge the transition away from home by bringing "home" into their college dormitories. For adolescents like Jessica, who have not yet been able to function adequately independent of their parents and former lives, telephone contact can serve as a critical step in their growth toward living away from home.

There is no question that telephones, answering machines, and email all support adolescents in their developmental shifts. As we move into the next millennium, with new communication instruments and capacities, adolescents will undoubtedly be among the first to integrate these new devices into their ways of life. As always, adolescents' adventurousness and innovativeness will permit them to show the adult world how best to use whatever we offer them in their search for ways to be with each other and with their families and therapists.

REFERENCE

Levy-Warren, M. H. (1996). *The Adolescent Journey*. Northvale, NJ: Jason Aronson.

12

Telephone Psychotherapy with Adolescents

JOAN G. TOLCHIN

*T*he telephone has been of significant therapeutic use to psychiatrists and other mental health professionals for many years. It had its first widespread application in crisis intervention and suicide prevention (Grumet 1979). Its current uses also include follow-up of patients discharged from a psychiatric hospital (Catanzaro 1971), alcoholic rehabilitation programs (Catanzaro and Green 1970), and drug hotlines that provide information on drug rehabilitation programs and counsel patients acutely ill from street drugs (Yasser 1970). In addition, such widely divergent modalities of treatment as sex counseling ("Sex Counseling over the Telephone" 1972) and group therapy for visually impaired elderly (Evans and Jaureguy 1981) are currently available via telephone. With regard to ongoing psychotherapy, Rosenbaum (1974, 1977) described continuation of psychotherapy using the telephone necessitated by the therapist's moving to a distant city. Saul (1951) detailed a case in which regular telephone sessions helped to resolve a transference reaction that was too intense. Grumet (1979) reported on a patient for whom telephone psychotherapy became the primary and most successful modality.

It would seem that the telephone would be a natural and useful adjunct in psychotherapy with adolescents. According to an article in the *New York Times*, teenagers spend one-third of their day conversing and 13 percent of those conversations take place over the telephone (Collins 1984). Adolescence is a period of both psychological and geographic separation from the family, and study and vacations away from home are common. Kestenbaum (1978) described the use of the phone with female adolescents with separation problems. Phone contact served to make the therapist a real, available, trustworthy object during moments of separation anxiety. The author compared the reassurance afforded by the therapist's voice on the phone to the aid that a toddler in the process of achieving object constancy receives from his mother's voice.

This chapter describes several clinical uses of the telephone in psychotherapy with adolescents. In general, as Kestenbaum detailed, it is useful to let adolescent patients know that the therapist is available by phone if any significant problem arises out of the sessions, so that a supportive therapeutic alliance can develop. Even a brief phone contact can be reassuring and decrease anxiety, as in the following example of crisis intervention over the summer.

CASE EXAMPLE 1

Dorothy was an 18-year-old who was seen in brief therapy following graduation from high school. She had become acutely depressed and suicidal when her boyfriend, abruptly and without apparent reason, terminated their three-month-old relationship. She was the older of two children, extremely intelligent, gifted in art, and generally well functioning. Her parents' marriage had been stormy, and her father had divorced the mother when the patient was 5 years old and had subsequently had little to do with anyone in the family. Prior to the divorce, the father had been devoted to the patient and had spent much of his leisure time with her. Dorothy was very insightful and formed an immediate positive attachment to the therapist. She was relieved to learn that she could call if she had any suicidal thoughts or overwhelming anxieties. At the beginning of treatment, she called three or four times when she was momentarily overcome with anxiety and depression over loss of the boyfriend. The therapist's stable presence and concern reassured her. With these brief phone contacts and initially three times a week and then twice a week psychotherapy, her depression cleared. She was able to make a meaningful connection between the current rejection by her boyfriend and the abandonment and rejection by her father. She also recognized that she was especially vulnerable to loss and separation at this particular time because of her impending separation from her mother to go off to college. After two months of therapy over the summer, she successfully started college in the fall and looked forward with enthusiasm to her freshman year.

Telephone sessions can also be utilized when an adolescent patient will be away for an extended period of time, such as summer vacation. For many troubled youngsters, especially those prone to self-destructive behavior, the continuity of therapeutic sessions is very important and helps to strengthen their internal controls. Telephone therapy sessions are set up on a regular basis with a scheduled time and length. The length of a session may be that of a standard office visit. In some cases, sessions half the usual length may be more suitable, for example, if the patient has limited access to a private phone or if the patient would benefit from shorter, more frequent contacts. The following case report illustrates how telephone therapy can help to maintain continuity of treatment and prevent self-destructive behavior on the part of the patient.

CASE EXAMPLE 2

Suzie was a pretty 16-year-old high school sophomore referred for treatment one and a half months before summer vacation because of her recent involvement with a troubled youth. Heavily involved with drugs and alcohol, the boy had stolen his parents' car, run away from home, and was being sought by the police. With the support of three-times-a-week therapy, Suzie had begun to take steps to separate from him.

Suzie lived with her mother and stepfather, both highly educated professional people primarily concerned with the advancement of their careers. They denied Suzie's use of alcohol and marijuana and yet frequently encouraged her use and abuse of these substances. For example, her mother had helped Suzie obtain a false identification card so she could socialize in bars with her classmates. Despite the fact that there was little control at home, Suzie managed to be in constant conflict with her mother and stepfather.

Her parents had divorced when she was 5 years old. Her biological father and his second family lived in another state. He regularly disappointed her by rarely calling and forgetting birthdays and Christmas gifts. He was generally critical of her. Because he was having financial and marital difficulties, her father had recently canceled Suzie's regularly scheduled summer visit to his home. The patient's response to this perceived rejection was to become involved with the boyfriend, who, she said, reminded her of her father.

Suzie's family had arranged for her to spend half the summer with a cousin's family in a foreign country. Suzie anticipated even fewer limits abroad than at home. In her sessions, she ruminated with mixed feelings about the possibility of having her first sexual relationship over the summer.

The separation from her therapist and her family increased the patient's anxiety. In response to this anxiety, Suzie's behavior deteriorated further; she came to several sessions high on beer and managed between sessions to get sick on contaminated marijuana. It was clearly important that contact be continued over the summer to help her maintain her tenuous internal controls. A few sessions before Suzie was to leave for the summer, her therapist recommended that they have weekly forty-five-minute phone sessions over the vacation to maintain contact and to deal with any difficulties that might arise. "Then I won't get pregnant," Suzie responded with obvious relief. In the sessions that remained, she was calmer and stopped using drugs and alcohol.

The once-a-week, forty-five-minute telephone sessions were helpful in solidifying gains already made and in dealing with stressful incidents as they came up. On the phone, the young patient reported proudly that she was taking a strong stand against teenage use of drugs and alcohol with her cousin and friends at the vacation community.

As Kestenbaum (1978) described, the therapist for Suzie was, in addition to being a transference object, a real object providing a corrective object relationship. The parents were eager, at any cost, to have Suzie off their hands during the summer. The therapist demonstrated her concern for the girl by continued telephone contact. The need for Suzie to take responsibility for her own welfare and safety, especially in view of the parents' lack of interest, was pointed out. She found this clarification deeply moving. The telephone served as a link from the patient to the therapist that allowed her to strengthen her own controls through identification with the therapist.

One of the difficulties of telephone work noted in the literature (Catanzaro 1971, Catanzaro and Green 1970, Miller 1973) is the lack of visual and other nonverbal clues. Miller stated that depression was the most difficult mental state to evaluate over the phone and anxiety the easiest. However, the therapist can remain in good contact with the depressed patient by being highly attentive to minimal auditory cues. One can listen to the tone and strength of the patient's voice and note the length of pauses between responses. If the therapist knows the patient well, subtle nuances in the patient's voice and manner of response can convey the patient's mood. It is important when conducting telephone therapy with a depressed patient to monitor depressive symptoms closely, including suicidal ideation, with specific questions. The following case vignette illustrates the usefulness of regular phone contact with a depressed patient.

CASE EXAMPLE 3

Barbara was an 18-year-old college sophomore who had begun twice-weekly therapy eighteen months earlier for an endogenous depression connected with the breaking up of her relationship with her boyfriend. She had responded well to a six-month course of imipramine but had considerable therapeutic work to do on her low self-esteem, fears of abandonment, and envy and competitiveness with other adolescents and her four-year-younger brother. This young woman had a complicated family history. He parents' stormy marriage had ended in divorce when Barbara was 12. There had been many relocations around the country and abroad during her first twelve years because of her father's work. He was away from home for long stretches of time.

Barbara had originally planned to spend the summer after her freshman year in the city and to continue her regular therapy sessions. When her father announced his engagement and imminent marriage, Barbara precipitously decided to take a job as a counselor at an out-of-town camp. The therapist's attempts to show the girl how she was running away from dealing with the painful situation of her father's remarriage were to no avail. The therapist's opposition to this summer plan was discussed with the patient and her mother in a joint session, but both remained adamant that Barbara should have the opportunity to be a counselor in the country.

Barbara was instructed to call the therapist at any time if she was in difficulty. Regular forty-five-minute phone contacts were set up on a twice-weekly basis. By the second phone session, it was clear to the therapist that Barbara was becoming increasingly depressed, even suicidal. The responsibility of taking care of a group of young children was more pressure than the patient had anticipated. She was struggling with her own increased neediness and sense of loss connected to her father's remarriage and her distance from home. The therapist arranged for the patient to return home immediately and resume her regular therapy. Barbara was greatly relieved to have her therapist's permission to leave a situation that was becoming increasingly intolerable for her.

Barbara returned home and continued her therapeutic work in person and the suicidal ideation abated immediately. She was now much more able to recognize her despair over her father's remarriage and to begin to deal with these feelings. No medication was required for this depressive episode.

CASE EXAMPLE 4

Another example of a potential emergency that was averted by telephone therapy is the following. Sara was a 15-year-old sophomore in high school who had been in psychotherapy for two and a half years. She had come because of poor performance at school and difficulty getting along with peers. Mildly obese, she developed some anorectic symptoms a couple of months before summer vacation. She dieted excessively and had lost about twenty pounds, which resulted in a svelte and attractive figure. However, she was fearful of gaining weight again and felt the need to lose even more weight, although her menstrual periods were becoming scant and her nails were growing poorly. She reluctantly acknowledged that she had been inducing vomiting and had on a couple of occasions used laxatives for weight loss. Sara was afraid to discuss her behavior with the therapist for fear she would not be allowed to go away for the summer to work at a cherished relative's farm in the South. She was readily able to see the danger of her behavior and to stop it, and she had begun to explore the reasons underlying it. Sara and the therapist agreed to have forty-five-minute telephone sessions on a weekly basis over the summer. The patient was able to eat appropriately and even gained some weight while she was away, and there was only one further episode of laxative use. Without the regular phone contact, the therapist could never have supported the girl's decision to spend the summer away.

In addition to being useful for vacation periods, telephone psychotherapy can be a helpful modality during longer periods of separation such as the college year. Geographic distance is no barrier. In the following case, treatment was conducted during a student's junior year abroad and then continued during her senior year at an out-of-town college. When at all possible, the adolescent initiates the call for the session just as she would initiate coming to an in-person session. There are certain situations when it is more expedient for the therapist to place the call. In the following case, placing a transatlantic call from Portugal might have taken at least an hour's wait. In such instances, the therapist can arrange in advance to charge the call to a parent's charge card or to add the telephone charges onto the patient's monthly bill.

CASE EXAMPLE 5

Glenda was a 20-year-old college junior who was about to spend her junior year abroad in Lisbon. She had been seen in twice-weekly psychotherapy for eight months during her senior year in high school because of depression. The patient's father had died when she was 12 years old, and her impending graduation reevoked his loss. As this issue was explored in the therapy, Glenda was able to mourn for her father, which she had not done earlier. With her conscious mourning, the depression lifted and she was able to attend an out-of-town college and make a reasonably good adjustment. She continued to be seen in therapy over school holidays and during the summer vacation. Issues explored included her dependent relationship with her mother and her difficulty getting involved with boys.

Glenda sensed that she might need more regular therapy when she was abroad. Because of the difficulty of finding an appropriate therapist in Lisbon, it was mutually decided that she would have forty-five-minute phone sessions every three weeks and more frequent ones if necessary. After this decision was made, Glenda felt relieved and less anxious about the separation.

Glenda had an excellent capacity for insightful psychotherapeutic work. One of the first issues to arise involved her dependent relationship with her "house-mother," an intrusive, envious woman who regularly compared the patient unfavorably to previous American students who had lived with her. Glenda was readily able to make the connection between her relationship with this woman and her overly dependent relationship with her real mother. She could see that her disturbing competitive relationship with the other students was similar to that with her three-year-older brother. In response to insights from the telephone therapy, she was able to become more assertive with the housemother and more involved with her work, and she successfully completed the junior year abroad.

There are some other practical guidelines for therapists planning to utilize telephone psychotherapy. It requires a motivated patient with a basically positive working alliance with the doctor. As Sweet (1984) noted, telephone work is generally not suitable for deep fantasy analysis. However, insight work was done on the telephone with several of the cases presented above; one patient even reported a dream that was analyzed during the phone session. Rosenbaum (1974) made the point that telephone work can be a combination of uncovering and supportive work, depending on the patient.

It is important for telephone therapy that the therapist feel comfortable using the phone in this way, although—as with so many aspects of treatment—skill and ease develop with experience. Some therapists who need the stimulus of face-to-face contact with their patients may find doing telephone therapy boring and may not give it their full attention. Phone work requires the same scrupulous attentiveness as regular therapy. In addition, the therapist needs to be very active on the phone, generally by speaking more than in regular office work. Because there is no visual contact, it is only through speaking that the connection between the therapist and the patient is maintained. If the therapist is ultimately not comfortable with phone work, it is best not to do it.

Rosenbaum (1974) noted the importance of structuring the telephone therapy with a regular time, length of session, and fee for the calls so that the therapist does not feel intruded on by inconvenient calls. Telephone calls that last a few minutes do not generally require a charge, but lengthier calls that are a regular part of the treatment should be charged at the therapist's usual fee. The parents of the adolescents generally have been open and cooperative in accepting phone sessions as part of the treatment.

CONCLUSION

In general, most adolescent patients in regular treatment benefit from knowing that the therapist can be reached by phone and that their call will be returned that same day. The therapist's telephone availability helps the young patient to develop a positive working alliance. Often, only one or two test calls are made to determine the reliability of the therapist; then the doctor need only reassure the patient that the problem will be more fully discussed in their next session. If an adolescent abuses the privilege—for example, if the calls become an angry expression of the wish to disturb the therapist—the problem can be discussed and explored in a face-to-face session. Telephone psychotherapy for adolescents serves as an important and useful method in the therapeutic armamentarium for this most challenging and rewarding population.

REFERENCES

Catanzaro, R. J. (1971). Telephone therapy. *Current Psychiatric Therapy* 11:56–60.

Catanzaro, R. J., and Green, W. G. (1970). WATS telephone therapy: new follow-up technique for alcoholics. *American Journal of Psychiatry* 126:1024–1027.

Collins, G. (1984). Charting teenagers' moods and days. *New York Times*, May 21, sec. 2, p. 6.

Evans, R. L., and Jaureguy, B. M. (1981). Group therapy by phone: a cognitive behavioral program for the visually impaired elderly. *Social Work in Health Care* 7:79–90.

Grumet, G. W. (1979). Telephone therapy: a review and case report. *American Journal of Orthopsychiatry* 49:574–584.

Kestenbaum, C. (1978). Some practical considerations in the assessment and treatment of adolescent girls with separation problems. *Journal of the American Academy of Psychoanalysis* 6:353–368.

Miller, W. (1973). The telephone in outpatient psychotherapy. *American Journal of Psychotherapy* 27:15–26.

Rosenbaum, M. (1974). Continuation of psychotherapy by "long-distance" telephone. *International Journal of Psychoanalytic Psychotherapy* 3:483–495.

———— (1977). Premature interruption of psychotherapy: continuation of contact by telephone and correspondence. *American Journal of Psychiatry* 134:200–202.

Saul, L. J. (1951). A note on the telephone as a technical aid. *Psychoanalytic Quarterly* 20:287–290.

Sex counseling over the telephone. (1972). *Sexual Behavior* 2:22–25.

Sweet, A. L. (1984). *Psychotherapy by telephone.* Paper presented at a meeting of the American Academy of Psychoanalysis, Los Angeles, May.

Yasser, A. M. (1970). Treating the bad trip by telephone. *Crisis Intervention* 2:25–26.

IV

IN DIFFERENT
THERAPEUTIC
MODALITIES

13

Couples Therapy by Telephone

F. DIANE BARTH

INITIAL AMBIVALENCE
ABOUT TELEPHONE THERAPY

Although I have used the telephone as a tool for both psychotherapy and psychodynamic supervision for many years, I have
always done so with some doubts and often with at least mild
discomfort. In fact, it was not until I had an extremely meaningful telephone supervision experience with an analyst whose
expertise was in an area of special interest to me, but who was
located in a city to which I could not possibly drive for supervision, that some of my most significant questions about the
medium were erased. Still, the telephone itself remains something of a luxury and even a little bit of a mystery to me. While
many of my clients spend their workdays telecommuting, conference calling and emailing, I struggle with residues left from
the time when long distance phone calls were outrageously
expensive: for example, even in this day of "ten cents a minute"
phone calls, I continue to have a lingering sense of simultaneous guilt and rebellion when I do not hang up after three
minutes.

Habit and unfamiliarity, however, are not all that keep me
somewhat ambivalent about telephone therapy. While I have
had powerful and useful telephone sessions with some clients,

I have had others that were surprisingly disruptive to the thera-peutic work. The telephone can both create and destroy bound-aries, sometimes with serious and unexpected results. Like many therapists, I also always experience some concern about losing the nonverbal communications that I automatically and often unconsciously integrate into my work with any client. However, I have also had some important and positive experi-ences that confirm my belief that telephone therapy can be a valuable tool in some instances, as, for example, when clients are out of town, ill, in crisis on a weekend or late at night, or for some other reason unable to come in for needed sessions. The telephone is also extremely useful with some adolescents in college who have a good working relationship with their therapist and who return for in-person sessions on some holi-days, weekends, and school vacations. Similarly, I have found it to be priceless with people who, for any number of reasons, have had to move away in the middle of significant therapeu-tic work.

Not until recently, however, had I even imagined doing couples therapy on the phone. It was such an alien idea that when a couple with whom I was working requested that we continue our sessions by telephone while they were out of town for an extended period, I initially told them no. They were in a serious crisis however, and could not remain in the city to work on it. Because it was unrealistic to consider referring them to another therapist for the limited time that they would be away, I finally, although reluctantly, agreed to try to continue our work by phone. To my astonishment, the results were amazingly positive. In fact, the phone therapy was so success-ful that when a second couple made a similar request, I agreed almost eagerly. In this chapter I describe some of the ways the telephone not only allowed these couples to continue their therapy, but actually enhanced the work. Both couples found the use of the phone extremely meaningful, and I found it highly instructive.

THERAPEUTIC BENEFITS OF THE TELEPHONE

I focus specifically on ways that our work on the phone contributed to the couples' development in three related areas: (1) the ability to communicate and problem solve in the marriage, (2) difficulties both partners had using language to express and process emotions, and (3) a lack of self-awareness or capacity for self-observation on the part of both partners in each couple. One of the surprises in the experience of working with these couples on the phone was that the loss of the nonverbal cueing led to several important and fascinating insights that I believe might never have happened without this seeming handicap.

The logistics of these sessions seemed unmanageable to me at first, but both couples were in professions where telecommuting and conference calls were part of everyday life. One couple simply installed a speakerphone and sat together in the same room while they spoke to me. The other also used a speakerphone for some sessions but occasionally arranged their therapy by conference call, each of them linked from a different city. A colleague who has done occasional telephone therapy with couples told me that in one case both partners were on extensions but in the same room, one on a portable phone and the other on the room's telephone. It might be interesting to experiment with differences that occur when a couple can or cannot see one another during the session, but I was more concerned with keeping the work going than with trying different formats. My general sense was that the variations were what one might expect. The couple who were in different cities were under the same handicap and advantages as I was in terms of nonverbal cues. They also discovered that being unable to continue any discussion at the end of a session, since they both hung up at the same time I did, had both positive and negative effects. For example, they were both relieved to be able to end difficult conversations when the session was over, and they found the cooling-off time between the session and the next time they talked, even if it was five minutes later, very helpful. On the other hand, they sometimes felt that they let things slip between the cracks because they were not forced to continue to talk afterwards. Both couples quickly learned to describe nonverbal gestures and communications to me and to one another, an important activity that I will discuss more fully shortly.

The length of time of the phone work was approximately two months for each couple. One couple returned immediately to face-to-face meetings in my office, while the other took a break before resuming therapy. Sessions lasted for one hour and were held once a week. In each instance we agreed that we would view the telephone therapy as an experiment, that we would mutually evaluate the experience after the third session, and that if there were any difficulties at all prior to that evaluation, we would take time out immediately to assess the problems and decide whether or not to continue. In fact, by the third session, it was obvious in each instance that the experiment, at least to that point, was successful.

CASE EXAMPLE: HENRY AND DELORES

In order to provide an in-depth description of the issues I believe to be most pertinent to this discussion, I will focus on just one of the couples. Henry and Delores, as I will call them, were young professionals, married for nearly five years. They had met and married after a short but stormy courtship. We had worked together periodically since the birth of their child, Melissa, who was born a little over a year after their wedding. Although the presenting problem was their difficulty dealing with a physical problem detected when Melissa was born, the speed with which they had married and begun a family was indicative of the impulsive nature of their relationship. Like many couples, they had been unable to develop a stable working structure for problem solving or relaying communication to one another. The stress of Melissa's disability was more than their relationship could tolerate. They could not soothe themselves or one another, and they came to me for help in coping with the trauma and in an attempt to save their marriage.

It is hard to say what would have happened to their relationship without the unfortunate circumstances of Melissa's disability. Bright, articulate professionals in their early thirties, Delores and Henry both desperately wanted the marriage to succeed. However, although they worked hard in the therapy, they were neither self-aware nor skilled at the kind of compromise and negotiation necessary to build and maintain a good working relationship. Both had a strong sense of entitlement and feelings of victimization when their desires were not met, and each blamed the other for all difficulties in the marriage. At the same time, they were both likable, and their investment in remaining together, despite the doubts they sometimes expressed, carried them through some very difficult times.

We had worked together for about eighteen months when two events occurring nearly simultaneously led us to the telephone sessions. They had just begun to struggle with questions about whether to try to have another child. Delores in particular was verbalizing fears of the possibilities of another damaged baby. "You just don't know what can go wrong," she whispered. "I don't think I could stand the waiting, the worrying . . . and then the finding out. . . ." Henry initially stated that it was Delores's decision, but it seemed clear that he was avoiding his own ambivalence by placing the burden of responsibility on his wife.

Soon after they had begun to talk about this issue, a change in Melissa's condition required a consultation and an extended period of testing with a specialist in another part of the country. Although it was extremely difficult for them to establish a workable arrangement, they used the marital sessions prior to leaving to successfully explore their conflicts and confusion, to problem solve, and to find ways to manage the painful emotions that arose during this chaotic, disruptive, and frightening time. The final solution involved a complex arrangement of telecommuting and some actual commuting for both of them, but it also took into account the fact that Delores was the primary caregiver and Henry the primary financial support in their relationship. This system, although by no means perfect, seemed at least manageable and acceptable to them both. But even though they ostensibly tabled the discussion of a second child for the time they were away, this question had not disappeared and was clearly adding to their distress. I had begun to explore with them some of their ideas about how they were going to soothe, comfort, and support themselves, Melissa, and each other during this time. It was at this point that they proposed that we continue the couples therapy by telephone.

COMMUNICATION AND PROBLEM SOLVING

As I have noted, one of the focal points of the work with Henry and Delores was the intricately linked double area of communication and problem solving. Numerous couples therapists agree that these issues are commonly problematic in couples seeking therapy. Yet just as there are many different approaches to couples therapy in general, so too are there a number of ways of conceptualizing the work on this specific dynamic (see, for some examples, Beach et al. 1990, Gurman and Rice 1975, Martin 1994, Satir et al. 1984). My own way of working combines a number of theoretical perspectives, taking into account the narcissistic vulnerablity of each member of the couple, their capacity for self and object relatedness, and their ego strengths, as well as the dynamics and makeup of both the dyad and, when possible, the family group.

In Delores and Henry's case, I supported their individual ego strengths, such as their ability to work successfully in the professional world, and what I genuinely saw as the good job they were doing managing the psychological, emotional, and physical needs of their daughter. I attempted to explore their personal and family histories to look for patterns and relational styles, and I tried to help them develop greater sympathy and understanding for one another's perspective. However, despite great verbal acuity and above-average intelligence, Delores and Henry tended to be concrete and defensive, frequently, searching for ways to blame one another and avoid taking responsibility for any conflicts or strife between them. Especially in the early stages of the therapy and at all moments of stress, they came to sessions with a list of complaints that they angrily reported, then sat back and waited for me to pronounce judgment.

Interestingly, something about the telephone work almost immediately changed this process. To my surprise, when I suggested that it might be helpful for them to talk to me about some of the interactions that I could not see, they began explaining not only their own but one another's communications to me. I soon learned to support and encourage these explanations even if I thought I understood what they were getting at, because as they tried to make me understand, they also seemed to develop greater sensitivity to their own and each other's communications. It appeared to me that the the loss of visual cues, the very thing I had most worried about in the phone work, had in fact become an important ally. The use of the telephone seemed to spontaneously bring forth an additional step in the process, a spelling out, as it were, of material that had previously been taken for granted or lost in nonverbal messages. This shift in communication soon led to a diminished degree of hostility toward one another when messages were not immediately understood, and an increased ability to problem solve by talking about various aspects of an issue.

One example of this change occurred as Delores and Henry were describing difficulties they were having with one of the physicians with whom they were consulting about their daughter. This young doctor was giving them advice that contradicted what they had been told by their own pediatrician, and their anxiety made it extremely difficult for them to ask questions, sort out the confusing information, or seek further data on their own. They resorted to their usual way of coping with such emotionally laden problems, turning the attack onto one another. Delores complained about Henry's passivity, and he criticized her hostile, demanding attitude toward the doctors. In the past, I had frequently pointed out the defensive, destructive nature of this problem-solving style, but with little success in changing their approach. On the phone I found that I only needed to ask them a few encouraging questions, and almost without any further effort, Henry began to explain Delores's worries, and vice versa. When I pointed out how well they understood one another's anxieties, they laughed out loud and Delores said, "Maybe it's because we're really so much alike."

This joining and mutual identification, which had happened very rarely in the past, even when they were struggling to deal with the numerous doctors with whom they interacted, continued sporadically but regularly throughout the rest of the telephone work. They consistently listened to one another's comments, asked appropriate questions, and made on-target responses. Together, they developed and carried through a successful plan for speaking to the head of the medical team about their confusion. They were able to get the chief doctor to speak directly to their pediatrician and to get their many questions answered, at least to a tolerable and expectable degree. And they were able to soothe, calm, and comfort one another to a far greater extent than I had ever before seen.

USING LANGUAGE TO EXPRESS
AND PROCESS EMOTIONS

It is my sense that many of the issues that couples bring into therapy, whether they are related to poor self-esteem, difficulty with intimacy, or any other dynamics, are often exacerbated by problems that both partners have in utilizing language to process their emotions. Many of our brightest, most verbal clients turn out to use language to describe but not to actually manage, digest, or integrate their feelings. When even one member of the dyad has trouble symbolizing and dealing with affects through language, verbal communication cannot be counted on as a tool for either exploring or solving problems. The couples work, therefore, must focus not only on opening up the communications, but also on finding ways for both individuals to articulate and process painful, frightening, disturbing, or overwhelming feelings. Obviously, to accomplish this task the therapist must work carefully with both partners to make the therapy a safe enough place to risk knowing, thinking about, and sharing these emotions with one another.

Like many couples, Delores and Henry unconsciously struggled to protect themselves and their relationship from feelings that were unacceptable, intolerable, and unmanageable. Although they were both intelligent and verbal, they were, it seemed to me, unconsciously avoiding what Bollas (1987) has labeled the "unthought known." Most of these thoughts were not articulated, even internally, but because of the friction and hostility in the relationship, there was little chance for them to develop a sense of safety with one another. I hoped the therapy could become a safe place and that they would eventually develop a sense of it as a "transitional space" (Ogden 1986) where they could begin to "play" with these frightening thoughts and feelings. I struggled to establish room within the therapy for them to explore their conflicts, fears, and wishes without damaging one another, but it was an uphill battle most of the way. Since they each dealt with feelings of vulnerability by attacking the other, they were both understandably leery of exposing some of their most assailable—and least easily articulated—hopes and fears. This was an area in which I felt we were making very little headway prior to their leaving town.

Perhaps they were simply ready to make a shift, and it happened on the phone just as it would have happened in my office. Or maybe some of the other changes in their living arrangements and interactions, of which there were many, contributed to the change. Certainly the fact that they were living apart for some of the time that we were working together had an impact on them. But I also think the telephone sessions may have played some role in the shifts that occurred during this time. Whatever the cause, they were able to utilize the phone and the distance to step back and observe themselves in interaction in ways they had not done before. During the time we worked on the telephone, we were able to shift the pattern of their discussion and processing of delicate emotions on several occasions.

For example, we had often discussed a major difficulty that arose around sexual intimacy. When Henry felt close to Delores, he frequently wanted sex, but she experienced his desire as demanding, intrusive, and not genuinely loving. "He just wants me to take care of his needs," she said. When he felt tender, therefore, and hugged her, she complained, "He's going to get a hard on and want sex," and pushed him away physically while making some sort of hostile, hurtful remark. Henry then countered with angry comments about her sexual frigidity. Although we had talked about the vulnerability they each felt in these moments, with Delores feeling hurt and unloved because Henry blurred intimacy with "just wanting to relieve himself," and Henry feeling rejected and unloved "because when I love someone, I want to have sex with her," there had been few breaks in this vicious cycle.

Perhaps because they were physically separated during much of this time, Delores began one session with a new concern about their sexual activity. "I feel like there's no passion anymore. You don't seem attracted to me." Henry responded with surprise, saying, "You're usually telling me the opposite. Maybe this is part of what you've been talking about in your individual therapy" (referring to her anxiety about sexuality). Delores immediately and angrily said, "Don't put this onto me." I pointed out that they were about to embark on their usual cycle of attack and counterattack, and wondered out loud if they could step back long enough to look at what Delores's initial communication might have meant. Henry muttered, "Yeah, she's criticizing me again," and Delores started to say something, but again I intervened. I asked her if she could say what she had been feeling when she noticed that the passion was missing in her life.

She began with "feeling" words: "abandoned, hurt, angry." Because I knew on the one hand that Henry would tune out this vocabulary, and on the other that both of them had difficulty connecting to the affects implied, I encouraged her to paint a picture in words rather than to name the feelings.

"Oh," she replied. "Well, I felt like I was trapped on a broken elevator that was shooting to the bottom at a breakneck speed. I was going to die, and no one was going to be able to do anything about it."

"My God," Henry whispered. I asked him to try to say what he was thinking. "That's some image." I asked him to say what it meant to him. "I had no idea you were feeling like that—so frightened and alone . . . and in danger."

Delores sighed. I asked her to say what she was feeling. "I don't know," she began. "It seems so hard to get Henry to hear."

"Do you think he's heard you now?" I asked. She was silent for a moment, then said, "I'm nodding. I'm afraid, though. What if I trust him to hear and then he doesn't?"

This interaction was one of the first times I had ever heard them discuss a painful emotional experience without defensiveness and with some empathy. While the moment did not signal the end of the problematic interactions, it was a significant step toward understanding and relating to one another in a different, more productive manner.

SELF-AWARENESS OR A CAPACITY FOR SELF-OBSERVATION

There are obvious connections between the capacity for self-observation and the ability to explore and process emotions through language. Both Delores and Henry had difficulty in both of these areas, and the telephone work did not undo these problems. However, it provided us with a fascinating window into some of the issues and offered us an additional tool for working with these dynamics. Perhaps in large part because we were often in three different locations and therefore unable to use other cues and forms of communication, each of us became more conscious of how hard it is to talk about some of the more vague, subtle, or confusing aspects of our experience. I found myself trying to put into words my own gestures and facial expressions and became acutely aware of how many unrecognized nonverbal communications I must make in every session.

Delores and Henry, perhaps following my lead, also began to try to say things that they tended to express in body language. In the process, they began to make contact with some of those unrecognized experiences that colored all of their interactions. For example, Henry would often say, "I'm starting to hold the phone away from my head. I guess I want to tune you both out, but I really don't know why." His genuine puzzlement with his need to tune us out allowed us to begin to do some crucial work on some split-off hostility in many of Delores's communications, as well as a number of fascinating transference issues that led to some exploration of Henry's worries about becoming merged with or overwhelmed by strong women.

Interestingly, another outcome of this work was that each of them began to articulate a new sensitivity to one another's emotional state. In one instance Delores, who was in her hotel room, said to Henry, who was at home, "You sound tired. Did you eat today?" Henry sounded irritated as he replied, "Of course I ate. I'm tired because we're living an insane lifestyle." When I asked them to draw visual images of what they heard in one another's voices, Delores said she had initially heard "something gray, like sadness, maybe." Henry said he had heard "a mother nagging her child, who never gets anything right." We were able to utilize this interchange to look at a number of nonverbal cues that they give one another. I told them, truthfully, that I had not heard Henry's tiredness, and that I was impressed by Delores's acuity. I then also wondered out loud what in their interactions might lead Henry to think that Delores was nagging and critical rather than concerned or worried.

"It's always the same thing," he replied. "When a woman worries about a man, it's because she doesn't think he can take care of himself."

The discussion that followed opened up a fascinating avenue for exploration, in which we gradually teased out some of the complex and subtle ways in which the expectations they each brought with them into the relationship colored what they heard and how they reacted to one another. That the destructive, disconnecting interactions were often constructed by the two of them was never more clear than when we were able to establish that Delores, unconsciously expecting to be rejected, put out her feelings of concern with an "edge," and Henry, hearing the sharpness behind her words, interpreted it as the criticism he expected, pushed her away, and confirmed her worst fears.

THE QUESTION OF BOUNDARIES

One dynamic that became apparent during the use of the phone with both couples was the issue of intimacy and separation, or what I often refer to as boundaries in the relationship. Near the end of the telephone work, I asked Delores and Henry to tell me what they felt had been helpful and what had been harmful or at least not useful about the experience. Among other things, including missing being able to see my face as I spoke, they each commented in some way that the telephone gave them a kind of distance from the problems they were discussing. They laughingly added that they were considering trying to talk to each other on the phone even when they were in the house together because it seemed to allow them to problem solve more successfully. My own sense was that the telephone and the actual physical distance between them had provided something they had never been able to establish in their relationship: boundaries that allowed them to be both connected to yet separate from one another.

Benjamin (1992) has suggested that the attempt to regulate the ongoing tension between separation and connection is one of the basic struggles of human experience. Efforts to find an optimal balance between these poles is, to my mind, one of the keys to much strife in couples. Although we had discussed the phenomenon, and had even explored to some extent both Delores's and Henry's experiences of and worries about intimacy, this was a couple who believed that it was a bad sign for their relationship if either wanted to do something without the other. Not surprisingly, they were each frequently "sneaking" separate time, feeling guilty about it, and also feeling abandoned by the other's attempts to have some space. The telephone sessions provided us with a living sense of what could be accomplished when boundaries separated them. As Henry put it, "We actually talk better when we have some distance. We work better as a couple, too."

CONCLUSION

I recently had an opportunity to speak with a colleague who is blind about my experiences using the telephone for couples therapy. When I told him of my discovery that the phone seemed to promote the work in areas of self-observation and verbalization of nonverbal experience, he said that he had long ago found that by asking a couple to talk to him about the physical gestures, facial expressions, and interactions that he could not see, he almost automatically encouraged the development of observing egos in both partners. While my experience with this work has certainly been positive, and has in fact encouraged me to make more creative use of the phone than before, I would not suggest substituting face-to-face sessions with the telephone on an ongoing basis, but I think the lessons learned from the telephone therapy are extremely valuable. I now try to ask my clients, both in individual and couples work, to talk to me about the nonverbal gestures and expressions that I once simply added quietly to my own store of information. I encourage them to share their thoughts about my nonverbal communications, and to try to put into words what they think my movements and gestures mean. Aron (1991, 1997) and Mitchell (1997) have both emphasized the value of exploring the patient's frequently unverbalized explanation of the therapist's behavior, but the telephone work helped me to approach this process in a way I had not quite managed previously.

I would like to conclude with one last caveat. While I have gained a greater respect for the telephone as a result of this work, I think it would be a mistake to think all separations from the therapist should be automatically handled by the use of telephone therapy. A friend who is not in the field and who had a long and extremely useful therapy experience, was talking to me recently about the tremendous amount she learned after she stopped therapy. In my experience, this learning also occurs during separations, and using the phone to avoid all interruptions of the work would seriously impact the growth—including the developing knowledge that one can survive without one's therapist—that occurs for individuals and couples during separations, vacations, and time off from therapy. Each case is, of course, unique, and each situation is always changing, so I would encourage therapists to evaluate every situation carefully before deciding whether to institute phone therapy. I believe that clients should be engaged in the process of making a decision about this format, and that they should participate in anticipating possible consequences of both using and not using the telephone. And finally, clients and therapist should make ongoing evaluations of the work and be free to change their minds, instituting phone sessions even if they were not part of an original plan if they seem necessary, or ending the phone work if it appears to be producing negative consequences. Having moved into the new communications era, I believe we must remember that the telephone is yet another tool for our work and, as I learned in these fascinating sessions, it can in fact make a significant contribution to what we do. At the same time, as with any therapeutic tool, it will work best if it is carefully managed, utilized, and monitored on an ongoing basis.

REFERENCES

Aron, L. (1991). The patient's experience of the analyst's subjectivity. *Psychoanalytic Dialogues* 1:29–51.
——— (1997). *A Meeting of Minds*. Hillsdale, NJ: Analytic Press.
Beach, S. R. H., Sandeen, E. E., and O'Leary, K. D. (1990). *Depression in Marriage*. New York: Guilford.
Benjamin, J. (1992). Recognition and destruction: an outline of subjectivity. In *Relational Perspectives in Psychoanalysis*, ed. N. J. Skolnick and S. C. Warshaw, pp. 43–60. Hillsdale, NJ: Analytic Press.

Bollas, C. (1987). *The Shadow of the Object*. New York: Columbia University Press.

Gurman, A. S., and Rice, D. G., eds. (1975). *Couples in Conflict*. New York: Jason Aronson.

Martin, P. A. (1994). *A Marital Therapy Manual*. Northvale, NJ: Jason Aronson.

Mitchell, S. (1997). *Influence and Autonomy in Psychoanalysis*. Hillsdale, NJ: Analytic Press.

Ogden, T. (1986). *The Matrix of the Mind: Object Relations and the Psychoanalytic Dialogue*. Northvale, NJ: Jason Aronson.

Satir, V., Baldwin, M., and Baldwin, M. (1984). *Satir Step by Step: A Guide to Creating Change in Families*. Palo Alto, CA: Science and Behavior Books.

14

Group Therapy by Telephone

DAVID S. WILSON

*T*he opportunity to experience and evaluate group leadership by telephone was thrust upon me recently by my
neurologist. He ordered me to bed, horizontally immobile, for
"at least two weeks," as a possible remedy for the pain of spinal stenosis (the psychotherapist's frequent nemesis). This situation complicated my life. Although I was experienced and
comfortable with the prospect of conducting individual sessions by telephone, group was a new and different thing. My
first inclination was to cancel all my groups. Nonetheless, I
knew the value of continuity in analytic treatment[1] and realized that this situation was a possible preview of a much
lengthier stint of horizontal restraint if I were to undergo spinal
surgery (a distinct possibility). I therefore decided to experi-

---

1. Continuity, especially in groups, is highly desirable, as it
models for analysands the concept of responsibility as well as unconsciously providing a regular pivot around which a week can be
mentally structured. In addition, the development of the many transferences that normally evolve among all the members of the group
can be interrupted by a break in the regularity of group meetings,
whether by members or the leader. As stated by Yalom (1995), "The
more continuity between meetings, the better. A well-functioning
group continues to work through issues from one meeting to the next"
(p. 124).

ment with group therapy with me as leader on the speaker-phone. It occurred to me that group leadership by telephone might be more successful now than in the past, given recent advancements in communications and information technology. And, as Herbert Strean (1998) has said, "A good therapist is a good telephone operator" (p. 9). In any event, I thought, it would be limited to only two weeks, so I should be able to repair whatever damage might ensue later.

ANTICIPATED CONCERNS

I felt apprehensive about attempting to lead over the telephone and, in retrospect, realize that at least some of the components of this fear were the following:

1. Concern it would seem that insufficient value was being provided for the fee being charged. Undoubtedly a displacement of my own sentiments, I feared group members would feel and might actually say (as some did), "Look how inadequate he is! He's not even here in the same room with us and he still wants to be paid!"
2. The lack of all the invaluable clues that body language provides in a group setting.
3. The normal, ubiquitous human fear of the unknown.

BODY LANGUAGE LIMITATIONS

Studies of human communication have shown that words make up only about 7 percent of the total message. Thirty-eight percent of the message is conveyed by qualities of the voice, and 55 percent by body movement (MacKay et al. 1983). Although these exact percentages may be debated, personal experience has convinced me that body language is by far the most powerful component of human communication. I believe that the appreciation, study, and understanding of body language is a prime benchmark of effective psychotherapists.

This understanding helps explain the immediate and considerable difference between working with individual patients face-to-face and working with them on the couch. On the couch, we remove the 55 percent body language, thereby increasing the importance of inflection, or tone of voice, to over 84 percent. The importance of the actual words also doubles, becoming slightly more than 15 percent of the communication. As a result, the conscious component of the communication approximately doubles, helping facilitate the prime goal of psychoanalysis: to make the unconscious conscious. It is therefore not surprising that psychoanalysts perceive more rapid progress with patients on the couch than face-to-face.

An appreciation of this factor—and its major importance in group work—pre-armed me (and concerned me as well) when I was faced with the decision of whether to cancel my groups while I was bedbound, or attempt to lead them over the telephone. I concluded that, given the benefits of the couch vs. face-to-face, some version of the process could be beneficial in accelerating emotional communication in my groups. Hindsight indicates it did indeed do just that.

TELEPHONE RESISTANCES

Over the years, telephone sessions have become quite common in my practice. Most clients (individual, couple, and group) have been able to use phone sessions successfully when they were out of town, delayed, or ill. In fact, several of my individual clients actually seemed to thrive on the procedure, especially those who had moved away and embraced telephone therapy as our normal way of working. It seemed to reduce resistance significantly when I likened the phone process to the use of the couch in psychoanalysis which, I have long preached, rewards the users with "more for their money." Framing discussion this way has almost invariably resulted in patients' deciding to use the couch. In much the same way, the use of the telephone requires more of participants than the face-to-face situation but, when portrayed as a beneficial alternative, it is almost always accepted as a developmental challenge. And, while most of my groups were initially somewhat hostile to the idea, they tolerated one or more of their members on the phone increasingly well over time, especially as the quality of my telephone equipment improved. However, of the three modes of work (individual, couple, and group), group evoked the greatest resistance, as it seemed not only to demand greater attention and concentration, but also broke the flow of communication between participants more than in either individual or couple telephone work.

The acquisition of a duplex speakerphone relieved much of the tension when group patients were on the speakerphone (or "on the box" as they often called it) as overlapping dialogue was much less frequently lost.

PREPARATION

I advised each of the members of three of my four groups *by telephone* that an emergency situation necessitated my absence from the office and therefore I would be conducting the next couple of groups by phone. As well as being necessary, this way of advising them of the situation put the issue into an urgent frame and more or less demanded their cooperation. Only from the members of one group was significant resistance felt. I canceled the newest, small fourth group as I felt their transferences to me and each other were inadequately developed for experimentation.

I placed the speakerphone atop an 18-inch wooden pedestal in the center of the group circle in my office, taped the phone and power wires to the floor with duct tape and tested the system to ensure that it worked. I used a telephone line without "call waiting" to avoid interruptions. At my home (in bed), I used a 900 MHz cordless telephone with a plug-in headset, again without "call waiting," enabling my full focus on the job at hand.

After arranging with a colleague to open my group room at the regularly scheduled times, I chose one member in each group and asked him/her to turn the lights on, call me on the speakerphone when the members were assembled, and turn the lights off upon leaving. This choice proved questionable as it attached "favored person" status to the member chosen, evoking feelings of rejection among those not chosen. Fortunately, these feelings were described early in the process and were discussed and resolved before they became treatment destructive. On later occasions, I asked that the first member to arrive carry out these functions.

REACTIONS AND MODIFICATIONS
AFTER WEEK 1

At the end of their initial session, two of the three groups stated that they unanimously preferred the method over having me in the same room. The third group, chronologically my oldest group, felt abandoned and angry with me during and after their first session. However, for this first session, three long-term members were absent, with two new, rather nonverbal members and only one articulate old member present. Their opinion changed to one of equivocal approval after the second session when more long-term members were present.

Based on the reactions of the first three groups, I enlarged my telephone group roster for week two to include the fourth (new, small) group.

REACTIONS AFTER WEEK 2 (FINAL SESSIONS)

Although all groups agreed that I was more interactive and directive on the telephone than in person, after the second week I was seen as less directive than I had been during the first week's sessions.

I felt relieved and more confident at the outcome of the first week than I had been going into the experiment. Clear mental images of the groups appeared in my mind and I found myself confident in the formation of my interventions, a most reassuring feeling. As evidence that I was putting more into it, I felt more depleted at the end of each session than I would normally have been had I been physically present in the room with each group. I attribute this to the effort used to compensate for the lack of visual information I would normally use in formulating interventions, especially those bridging between members. I have found these bridging interventions[2] to be

---

2. Bridging is the group leader's use of a variety of techniques that develop interaction between group members as opposed to interaction between the leader and individual members. As conceptionalized by Ormont (1992), bridging is one of the most powerful tools available to group leaders. It strengthens emotional bonds between

critical in the development of the group as an effective, independent organism. Deprived of visual information, I had at first tended to revert more to an intense mode of individual therapy in the group setting. However, the group members, sensing more intrusion by me, worked harder in deepening their here-and-now communication, building deeper coalescence. As I appreciated this deeper emotional communication among them, I was able to correct my overworking tendency in the second session.

I had at first found myself focusing with great intensity on identifying voices by sound, as no visual or directional information was available. Consequently, at the start of the second sessions, I asked and was told the location of each of the members. This provided me with mental images of the group that were helpful in forming the bridging interventions that I used more in the second sessions.

The fourth group had only one week's experience of telephone group. But to my surprise, initial discomfort, and embarrassment, this new group stated that they preferred the process. In fact, when I returned, they asked me to lead their group by telephone from the adjacent office or the waiting room. It was clear from their comments that my presence (I am older) emphasized the generational gap between us which,

---

group members, thereby developing group coalescence. The resulting interactional skills learned by members are exportable to their outside worlds. An illustration of the opportunity for a simple bridge would exist if Mary asked the leader, "Do you think I should go to Hawaii with my new friend John?" With the history and understanding of all the members' dynamics at his fingertips, the leader would resist the impulse to answer Mary directly, then direct the question toward a particularly appropriate group member. This latter course would predictably develop increased interaction between Mary and the other group member.

when I was not physically present, they felt much less, with consequent increased freedom. When I did return and resisted leading from afar, they strongly defended their position until I suggested that we might achieve a similar effect by facing all the chairs out, to eliminate visual contact, a process variant I had often pondered. The group embraced the concept enthusiastically and several subsequent sessions were conducted in this manner. They liked the effect and, in contrast to previous meetings, they made great strides in relating to each other on an emotional level. Prior to their telephone experience, this group had found it very difficult to access any negative feelings during their session, except at me for not structuring the sessions more rigidly. They had taken little responsibility for contributions to the process during the sessions and had constantly complained that "nothing is going on." They had been impatient and demanding that I bring more people into the group "to liven it up," yet objected strongly when I suggested that maybe the thing to do was to disband the group entirely. It appears likely that they felt much more personal responsibility for making the group work when I was not physically there, and responded by revealing more of their emotional reactions to each other under the more demanding circumstances.

EQUIPMENT

Having been on the other end of speakerphones myself, I was keenly aware of the difference a duplex speakerphone makes in the quality of communication compared to more common simplex speakerphones. The latter communicate in only one direction at a time, unavoidably cutting off one or the other talker when talk occurs simultaneously at both ends. The results are always frustrating, discouraging, and anger-provoking. I knew therefore, that a duplex instrument was an almost essential component for successful group telephone work.

I did not experiment with different placements for the speakerphone as it seemed to me that the central location of the instrument was likely to be most satisfactory. The pillar upon which the speakerphone was placed is 18" high and constructed of ¾" particleboard, making a solid, flat surface under the instrument. This arrangement provides some acoustic gain for the outgoing signal over placement on a soft chair. The hard surface is preferable to direct placement on a carpeted floor as the latter will attenuate high frequency sound, which is especially undesirable for women's voices because they are normally higher in pitch and weaker than men's and therefore more frequently lost to speakerphone pickup.

All members initially reported being put off by the presence of the pillar and speakerphone, but soon seemed to acclimate to them and stopped complaining almost entirely. There were virtually no complaints during the second sessions.

DIFFERENCES IN REACTIONS AMONG THE VARIOUS GROUPS

The rather surprising variation among the groups' reactions underlines the importance of examining all the psychodynamics of each group and each individual member carefully before instituting major changes in protocol. The fact that my fourth group preferred my being on the telephone more than my other groups made me realize that I had not thought through the change as thoroughly as I should have beforehand. However, given the mandate of the situation, I was not allowed the luxury of long consideration and acquired this realization only post facto. Fortunately, no damage seems to have ensued.

In fact, the experience appears to have been a positive one for all concerned.

I believe that face-to-face contact is desirable in the early stages of therapy for both patient and therapist. It allows each to get to know and feel comfortable with the other. In the beginning stages of individual therapeutic work and in the preparation of a patient for introduction into a group, I usually employ face-to-face interaction, as it allows me to use body language to put the patient at ease. This helps most patients feel safer, allowing them to reveal more emotional history. The revelation of such material facilitates the development of transference. Except in the case of borderline or paranoid patients, whom I strive to identify from my countertransference reactions, I encourage the deepening and recognition of transference to me before introducing a patient into a group. This element of safety is essential if the relationship is to survive the inevitable strains of human interaction that is psychotherapy, whether individual or group. However, I am now convinced that group therapy facilitated by a leader on the telephone is practical. In some cases, it may actually be beneficial in developing progressive emotional communication and in accelerating group coalescence.

COMMENTS AND UNDERSTANDINGS

The favorable reaction of these groups to having the leader on a speakerphone was a surprise. Once I recovered from the initial narcissistic insult, it provided me with a wealth of psychodynamic material for discussion and analysis, both in supervision and in each of the groups.

On the telephone, I existed only as a virtual presence, obviously not a physical part of the group. This distance emphasized my older/parent/leader role, allowing the group the luxury of physical communication with each other (body language) without my participation. It engaged the children in them, enabling a degree of acting in without my being able to see it. This regression to the "what fun" or id state, facilitated group coalescence. It also gave rise to the slight pauses, laughter, and tone of voice shifts that helped me form the more frequent bridging interventions I used in these sessions. Somehow the use and separation of the telephone illuminated the parent–child role occurring between me and the group, while affording the group physical protection from me. It also made me work harder, identifying each member by sound, and forcing the formulation and timing of interventions totally in my head without visual clues. I concentrated on getting my voice up to speed in the spaces between their interaction without stepping on another group member's talk. Without my own body language to help convey meaning, I became more conscious of the importance of my verbal inflections in the communication of my mood and attitude over the telephone.

This experience has helped highlight a major danger in the process of leading a group by telephone. That danger is that, because of their isolation from the group, leaders may allow their focus to wander from their primary goal for the group, which is to facilitate progressive emotional communication *between members*, rather than *with the leader*. This sense of passivity, reinforced by the physical separation involved, can possibly cause the leader to feel removed from the emotional stream of the members' interaction. Staying mentally involved while silent and physically separated from the group demands a higher level of mental energy than when the leader is physically present.

Beneficial consequences of the process appear to be that groups both coalesce and develop their emotional communication more quickly. I would therefore approach another such necessity with optimism and confidence. In fact, the better-than-expected success of this endeavor has inspired me to establish live, visual groups on the Internet. To this end, a web site—www.groupsych.com—is under development.

POSTSCRIPT

The anticipated spinal surgery did occur. It was completely successful and I spent another two weeks horizontal, recuperating, leading my groups by telephone. The preparatory experience described above was invaluable.

REFERENCES

MacKay, M., Davis, M., and Fanning, P. (1983). *Messages: The Communication Skills Book*. Oakland, CA: Harbinger.

Ormont, L. R. (1992). *The Group Therapy Experience*. New York, St. Martin's Press.

Strean, H. (1998). *Don't Lose Your Patients*. Northvale, NJ: Jason Aronson.

Yalom, I. (1995). *The Theory and Practice of Group Psychotherapy*. New York: Basic Books.

15

Family Work by Telephone with the Hospitalized Patient

CLAIRE ROSENBERG

*T*his chapter discusses work by phone with families of hospitalized patients, exploring specific family defensive styles and cases when the continuation of treatment is in jeopardy. Family work by phone often plays a role both in holding the current frame of treatment and in diagnosing and working through the difficulties that led to hospitalization. It can also reveal family dynamics that have been repeated in the transference.

When the family is unable or unwilling to respond to a recommendation for family work on site, the telephone is a valuable resource for the clinician. Families often express geographic or financial reasons for not coming to the hospital for family work. These reasons are frequently a mask for an ambivalent alliance between family members or the patient and treatment. Sometimes the frequency of meetings prescribed seems excessive, or the contact between the parties needs titration. The family may feel ashamed, injured, or threatened by the false assumption that the hospital is trying to provide a "better family" for the patient. Hospital workers may mistakenly make the same assumption. Phone work can be an excellent tool for accommodating distance between antagonistic parties without cutting off communication altogether.

Therapists are not the only partners in treatment to offer interpretations. Patients and their relatives often generate accurate hypotheses that merit attention. The phone offers a forum for their ideas to be expressed. Ideally, a patient and his or her family will mutually agree that family work would help. This is seldom the case. What, then, makes it important to make this recommendation? The first indication is when negatively valenced communication (which can occur as active conflict or the absence of contact altogether), or self-destructive acting out by the patient threatens the continuation of treatment. When the patient or family threatens to break the frame of treatment, it may be a repetition or enactment of injuries to the original frame of family life.

Less than optimal communication (as defined by the patient, family, or treater) between family members may be due to physical separation by virtue of distant hospitalization, work or school responsibilities, or separation of adult patients from families of origin through marriage. Families are often called into treatment unexpectedly, primarily for financial support. When asked for help, they may feel lost ("What happened? I had no idea you were unhappy.") or suspicious or hurt ("Why couldn't you come to me?"). The unexpectedness of renewed contact with family members is already diagnostic of a system in which denial or disavowal may be primary defenses, both now and historically. The dependency issues reawakened by the patient's need for treatment may be far deeper than the precipitant for treatment, often moving into family biases about dependency and paranoia about going outside the family for help. Often families first find out by phone that there is a problem. Distance between family members (or closeness for that matter) is not always pathological, but it is seldom irrelevant. When a family member is close enough to the patient to be called for financial support (as is often the case for young adults), but not close enough to know there is a problem, the therapist can begin to hypothesize that there has been some distance that has interrupted the flow of knowledge between family members, but that the need for connection still exists. The refrain most often expressed in these cases is, "You only call when you need money." This may be a good working hypothesis that the family presents to the therapist and should be assumed to be true, at least in part. Phone work can use this call for funds to further explore how the relationship has come to this point. Such an expression is a clue that something is being avoided or remains unheard. It will be important to investigate whether it is the mouth of the patient or the ear of the relative, or both, that have acted as though impaired, and what protective functions the silence may serve. Such consideration helps the clinician pinpoint whether family defenses are some combination of paranoid, schizoid, avoidant, depressed, borderline, or narcissistic, and help sort out straight projections from projective identifications. Moving too quickly past the data provided by initial phone contacts may in fact serve to delay consideration of valuable working hypotheses as treatment progresses. The ideas generated by such contacts will surely come around again if nothing else interrupts treatment, but why perpetuate the cut off from the data by waiting, particularly when communication about hospitalization is being attempted? At the same time, one must remember that the data collection phase is not necessarily the time to deliver interpretations to the family. Making interpretations by phone requires that a strong alliance be in place so that parties can assess the response to an interpretation without visual cues.

Sometimes families will not consider separating at all in order for the patient to receive treatment. Other times, they will not come together. The events of separation or reconnection brought about by the need for treatment may be so intolerable to the patient or relatives that treatment may be stopped, interrupted, or otherwise sabotaged. Weddings, birthday parties, or other family gatherings may be scheduled in such a way as to place the patient in the position of having to make a choice between family and self. Commonly, family members will feel the therapist is an intruder or an adversary. Bills may not be paid. A parent may refuse to leave the side of a child in order for the child to talk to a therapist. When a patient is unable to maintain the minimum requirement of the treatment frame consistently, that is, showing up for sessions, paying the bill, or notifying the therapist of cancellations, and family members are involved in these interruptions, family work is indicated in order to preserve the treatment of the identified patient, and to understand more about the nature of the anxiety provoked that prevents the patient from pursuing independent individual treatment. Some form of separation anxiety is almost always present in a family system when the patient is unable to pursue a therapy relationship without interruptions. In such cases, the identified patient and/or family members act something out about the original frame of life provided by the family of origin.

With hospitalized patients, highly self-destructive behaviors are often the cause for interruption of treatment. The patient who threatens to end a treatment in this way often feels unattended, overlooked, or de-prioritized. Something in the transference–countertransference relationship itself may be threatening the maintenance of treatment. Such behaviors are often an indication to the therapist that the patient thinks the therapist is not enough, and this may be true. For the therapist who is unable to ask for help, or cannot manage the helplessness or anger projected into him or her by the patient, principles of confidentiality may be an excuse for the therapist's resistance to family participation, a situation more comfortable to the therapist than the patient. Keeping the family out may be the agenda of the therapist, not the patient. Similarly, when family members refuse to participate in on-site work, citing financial, geographic, or scheduling stressors, they may be passively expressing their own fears about family work, again de-prioritizing the patient. In either case, the patient may try to communicate a sense of abandonment by acting out. The thrust of the therapist's work here is not to join the family resistance by judging the quality of the patient's request for help (it's not important to decide whether the patient is being manipulative; in fact, suicidal behavior is almost always an effort to manipulate someone into a position where something more is understood), but to understand the patient's, the relatives', and possibly the therapist's resistances to communication in words. This escalation to acting out, sometimes by the patient alone, sometimes reciprocally between patient and family, and sometimes by the therapist, can often be modified with a phone intervention, providing a space to listen and talk that may feel less intrusive than on-site work, an intermediate space where further negotiation and understanding can take place without interrupting the frame of treatment.

Suicidal people are often looking for some other kind of connection when they feel their distress is ignored or denied by family members or misunderstood by therapists. The rising use of "hot lines" for individuals and telephone call-in shows provide faceless forums of communication for thousands of people daily . This same mechanism can be usefully implemented within the frame of an ongoing treatment as well. The phone provides an answer, a connection, which may allow patients and families to put feelings into words and hold treatment in place, while still maintaining a narcissistic defense against the shame of being seen as needy, avoidant, afraid, or oppositional. It may be less exposing for a patient or family member to cry or get angry on the phone, and more tolerable to hear. It may provide needed closeness and protect needed distance simultaneously, so that the suicidal patient and the narcissistically defended family or the suicidal patient and the smothering family can experience both attention and space to breathe, and enjoy a sense of differentiation rather than merger or cut-off. When geography is not an issue, or is a false issue, such an experience of safe containment will often pave the way for increased on-site participation. Working with the family by phone can be an ideal mechanism for diagnosis and working through resistance in all parties involved in the treatment of hospitalized patients.

CLINICAL VIGNETTE: TELEPHONE FAMILY
WORK AS A DIAGNOSTIC TOOL

Larry, age 19, has come into treatment for symptoms of depression. He is alcoholic and has been failing academically and socially at college. His parents are surprised and worried. They seem cooperative and acknowledge that some part of the patient's difficulties may have been caused by an interruption in the development from child to adult. They are open. In fact they introduce the idea that they may have had something to do with it, that this stall may represent some earlier failure, but they have no sense of how it happened. The patient is also unusually open to feelings, and, despite his anger and confusion, he wants to stay connected to his family and wants them to be a part of treatment. The patient's father spends a good deal of time working away from home. His schedule prohibits regular weekly meetings on site. A conference call is arranged with the patient and family therapist at the hospital, the mother and older brother at home, and the father at his office. The patient's mother volunteers to handle the logistics of connecting all three parties, a task that the family therapist would have been available to arrange. She first calls the patient and therapist (who are on one speaker phone together), and puts them on hold while she calls the father's office. There is a five-minute delay while he breaks from a meeting, and when he does come on the line he is using a speaker phone in his office. The mother and brother are on extension phones in the house, both holding receivers. The brother's phone is a portable phone. The brother and father are difficult for the patient and therapist to hear. The mother immediately tries to repeat the conversations to all parties. It's clear that this doesn't work, so the mother asks the father to pick up his receiver and asks the brother to use a different phone. At this point the conversation proceeds as follows:

> *Brother:* I don't understand why this hospital doesn't have a better way of doing this. Why do the two of you [patient and therapist] have to be on the same phone? If your technology is so old, maybe this isn't the right place for you.
>
> *Mother* (to brother): Now, now. (to patient and therapist) Will you hold a moment? (puts patient and therapist on hold)
>
> *Patient* (to therapist while they are on hold): This is so typical of my family!
>
> *Therapist* (to patient while they are on hold): Can you tell them that?
>
> *Patient:* I think so. (All lines are reconnected. All voices are clearer except for the brother. The father has

picked up his receiver, the brother remains on the portable phone.)

Patient: I was just saying this is so typical of my family.

Mother: Come on, Larry, that's not fair. (to therapist) You're putting words in his mouth.

Brother: I think you're right, Mom. We seem to be the enemy.

Father: All right now. We're wasting time. Can we just get on with it?

Patient: I hate this.

So many common hypotheses regarding family dynamics are made evident by the content, process, and sound of this fragment. By "sound" I mean not only the quality of interaction, but the actual clarity of voices, the static on the line, and the silences when waiting. Using primarily a structural family therapy approach in examining this fragment (Minuchin 1974), we note that the mother clearly has her hands full in organizing this event, something the therapist would have been happy to do. The mother is currently functioning as the "switchboard" of the family, the vehicle for connection, communication, and clarity of tone. The patient's brother, first born, remains close to the mother although on a separate, inferior instrument. The patient is coupled with the therapist, and the father is alone. Mother and brother are the couple at home. Father initially decides to join with the patient in using the speaker phone, possibly in an imagined competition with the therapist. He is brought back into the technology of the family by the mother, who, out of earshot of the patient and the therapist, brings the father into line.

The family has held the myth that it is the father's schedule that keeps them from spending time together. This phone meeting illustrates that this explanation alone is oversimplified and insufficient. The complicated difficulties the family experiences in finding a way to talk together would not have been available data to the therapist if this alternative mode of meeting had not been used. The therapist would not have the map of alliances and competitions that this rich fragment provided. For the family, the here-and-now experience on the phone of historically familiar complications allowed them a live example to work with on their hypothesis that they have something to do with the patient's problems. This incident alone provided rich material for subsequent sessions. When blame for the past seemed a dead exercise for all, this fragment provided real evidence that the impairments in family relationships were not just a matter of history, and needed some attention now. The family reorganized itself after this conversation to provide increased opportunities for talking together, including on-site work about 50 percent of the time, and the patient marked their willingness to come together as a turning point in his treatment.

The countertransference error by the therapist in asking the patient to make his (correct) interpretation to the family is worth noting. By asking the patient to deliver this interpretation, the implication to the patient was that the therapist needed his help, and this, in fact, is accurate. The weakness of the alliance between family and treater is exposed, and the patient is asked to make the link. The patient became the symptom bearer for the therapist as well as for the family. The family is right to note this as unfair, but it also allowed them to see that the therapist was as capable of isolating their younger son as they had done, and allowed them to make a choice to move to join him, rather than insist that he join them.

CLINICAL VIGNETTE: TELEPHONE FAMILY WORK AS A CLINICAL INTERVENTION TO PRESERVE THE TREATMENT FRAME

A married woman with two young children comes into treatment with ongoing, serious self-destructive behavior and suicidal ideation. Her husband and children live across the country. She manages contact with her children independently, but finds talking with her husband difficult. Conversations between them provoke anger in the husband and guilt and hopelessness in the patient. She states she misses her children, cannot tolerate her husband's anger at her absence, and can only manage these feelings by harming herself or leaving treatment to rejoin them. It's clear that they cannot meet regularly in the office because of distance, work, and child-care issues. There is some indication that the patient's symptomatic behavior began at the time of her parents' simultaneous deaths. Her husband is angry that she is so far away. A last conversation on this topic supposedly precipitates a serious overdose by the patient and raises the question of her being able to continue treatment in an unlocked unit. The family therapist offers to consult to the patient and her husband by phone.

> *Patient:* I think I have to come home. I don't think this is going to work.
> *Husband:* Why? What do you think will work? Nothing ever works.
> *Patient:* I think I have to come home and just get over it.
> *Husband:* What do you mean?
> *Patient:* I think I should just die. That would be easier for all of you.
> *Husband:* Great—that's just great. So why am I going through all of this? If you're still talking like this maybe

you *should* just come home. You can't come home though if you're going to hurt yourself. I won't put up with it. This makes me so angry. You're ruining our marriage.

Patient: I should just die.

Therapist (to husband): You're pretty angry. It may be obvious to you, but since we're new to each other, I don't want to assume I know the reason why.

Husband: Well, I think it's pretty obvious. I'm home alone with these kids I love, but I don't know where my wife went, and I can't get her back without her wanting to die.

Therapist: You think you make her want to die?

Patient: I want to die. I'm so guilty.

Therapist (to husband): This is quite a bad situation you're in.

Husband: No kidding. I feel totally helpless.

Patient: I don't want to put you in a bad situation. It would be better for everyone if I just died.

Husband: Not for me.

Therapist (to patient): If you want to help him, why do you want to hurt him by dying? Are you angry at him?

Patient (angrily): I am not angry. You're useless. (to husband) I love you.

Husband: I love you too.

Patient: I'll be all right. I'll call you later. (to therapist) You don't understand anything.

The projective material in this fragment is certainly echoed in the transference in the individual therapy. But the continuation of the treatment is threatened (either through suicide or premature termination) by the ongoing interactions between spouses in which these projections seem to be taken for truth. It is obvious that both spouses project into the other the feelings they cannot bear. The patient makes the husband into the angry one, and the husband gives his sense of isolation, helplessness, and guilt to the patient to express for him. The most minor interventions by the family therapist in the above fragment make a shift in these myths.

This is an extremely difficult case in which the dynamics cannot always be held by the patient–therapist transference. If the therapist assumes the treatment can be held in the dyad, he assumes the husband's position that a relationship with a man (her husband or her therapist) is all this patient should need to stay alive. Not therapy, husband, or children alone are enough to contain the feelings of this patient, who struggles against the accepting, mourning, and refilling the emptiness left by previous unmourned losses. If it were otherwise, she would not have had to seek inpatient help. The therapist's wisdom in using this phone intervention models that the feelings in this case can never be held alone by just two people, not therapist and patient, or husband and wife. All individuals and both dyads need and deserve support. In this tempestuous fragment, the therapist can note the hints of an early attempt by the patient and the husband to reclaim some of the projected feelings. The husband is able to say that he feels alone, and the patient is able to express anger, if not to openly acknowledge the feeling. The projective storm moves back into the relationship with the therapist, where it can be addressed in treatment. In difficult cases like this, it is inevitable that the projections of real anger, helplessness, and guilt will be felt by both the individual therapist and the family therapist. Mistakes, often fatal to treatment or the marriage if not to the patient, are made in an effort to calm the acute despair in the system by rejecting the transference, leaving it to be acted out in the world outside of treatment. Working alone in such cases is

sometimes a move by the therapist to defend against this despair. The therapist also needs not to be alone. Acknowledging the need for family work and finding a way to do it is the
therapist's empathic response to the patient, both validating
that some needs cannot be met by the patient or therapist alone
or alone in the dyad, and sitting with the patient in the reality
of her distance from her family.

CLINICAL VIGNETTE: TELEPHONE FAMILY WORK TO TITRATE AFFECT

A young woman with schizophrenia (D) comes to the hospital
for extended treatment including psychopharmacology, psychotherapy, and family work. The patient's parents visit every
weekend, following which the patient often experiences hallucinations of feeling chased and threatened. She is able to
lessen her fear by cutting herself, which chases the hallucinations away. The family enjoys an overtly warm, understanding, and nurturing relationship. The patient says she enjoys her
parents' visits. The nursing staff at the hospital has requested
some intervention with the parents by the social worker to
investigate this connection and perhaps minimize the instances
of cutting.

The parents acknowledge that they see the pattern of self-
harm following their visits. The interpretation the parents hold
is that the patient misses them when they leave and cannot
tolerate their absence. They are considering finding an apartment close to the hospital and moving there temporarily. The
patient cannot see a link between their visits and her hallucinations. They also are wondering about having an outside
consultant review the patient's current medication protocol.
According to patient and therapist, the patient has responded

well to these meds, with the self-destructive behaviors now confined to these post-weekend cuttings . In this fragment, the patient and her mother (the father is not present on this day) discuss the merits of a psychopharmacological consultation outside of the hospital.

> *Mother:* How this came about was, your father and I were at this benefit and this specialist in psychiatric drugs just offered to meet with you to discuss what might be best, and we thought that would be a good idea.
>
> *Patient:* I'd rather not. I appreciate it but I'd rather not. I think Dr. X Is doing a great job.
>
> *Mother:* Well, I think that's silly. You should take advantage of it.
>
> *Patient:* I'd rather not.
>
> *Mother:* Well, I don't understand why you don't want to get all the help you can get.
>
> *Patient:* Well, I think I'd still rather not if you don't mind.
>
> *Social Worker:* D, I hear you loud and clear, but maybe your mother isn't sure of your reasons?
>
> *Patient:* Well, I don't know. Maybe I should do it. What do you think?
>
> *Social Worker:* I've told your parents and you that I think it might be confusing for you, but that it has to be your decision.
>
> *Patient:* I'd like to think about it. Mom, what do you think I should do?
>
> *Mother:* I think we should do it. I wish you all wouldn't put these ideas in her head.
>
> *Patient:* I've gotta leave.
>
> *Social Worker:* Why?
>
> *Mother:* Oh, don't go. I can't stand it. I just can't stand this.
>
> *Patient:* I'm sorry. I just want to take a walk.

Social Worker: Is there something in the conversation that makes you want to leave?

Patient (to social worker): Do you think I should get this consultation?

Mother: (thinks D is addressing her) Yes.

Social Worker: Is that why you want to leave now? You don't know what to do?

Patient: I think so. I think it would be a good thing right now to take a walk. Mom, can I call you later?

Mother: I guess so, sure. (Patient leaves. The later nursing report takes note of the fact that the pateint remains lucid and does not cut during the night.)

Mother: What's wrong? What am I doing wrong? Doesn't every parent want what's best for their child? I think that's normal.

Social Worker: Of course it is. Sometimes D may have some ideas about what's best for her that are different from yours, and when she thinks she's in conflict with you, she may not know how to take care of herself and take care of you at the same time.

Mother: She doesn't have to take care of me. I'm as fine as I can be until she's better. I never let her see me cry (begins to cry).

This patient, whose tolerance for conflict is minimal at best, has been able to muster the strength to both disagree and find a safe way to withdraw. The mother feels abandoned and rejected—she also can't manage conflict well, and needs her daughter to be in agreement with her. Both have resorted to hiding affect in response to this fear of conflict, and the patient's capacity to overtly disagree been severely restricted. D is in a complicated position because her treaters also disagree with the parents' interest in the consultation, and thus

D is caught in a disagreement between her two "families." This mirrors the internal conflict between dependence and loneliness that the patient struggles with. This conflict is in danger of being actualized in the parents' potential creation of an "alternative hospital" if they take an apartment in town.

To date, the patient has succeeded in keeping these two families apart. The patient talks to her primary therapist or her social worker or her family or her hallucinations, but seldom to more than one at a time. She keeps the relationships dyadic, but at some cost, as it prevents intervention and interpretation of her cutting behaviors to her parents. Her appearance at this phone call is indication of some progress in tolerating more complicated relationships, but with this progress comes some risk, and the clinician, with the data from this call, is more able to see the liabilities of moving into triadic configurations where real conflict is more likely to arise and require real choice. If the treaters never provided the possibility of the phone contact, if the family never availed themselves of it, and if the patient never joined in, this liability would likely have been found in any number of other interactions. But the phone provides a less toxic, more transitional space for the patient to experiment with this configuration. The patient can begin to hear her "no" in the nonpsychotic world, and find a space to process that experience away from her parents. This has not been possible in their weekends together to date.

This phone contact initiated a process by which the patient and the mother were eventually more able to tolerate difficult interactions, using both the telephone and the social worker to titrate the intensity of the conflicts to more realistic proportions. The patient not only refused the outside consultation, but asked her parents not to rent the apartment. While this was disappointing to them, the resultant decrease in cutting behaviors made it clear that allowing boundaries between them would be important to their daughter's maturing process and to their capacity to work together as a family.

DISCUSSION AND SUMMARY

The chapter describes the value of working with families by phone as both a diagnostic and treatment option when on-site work is impractical, actively avoided, or too intense for a patient's defensive system. In the above vignettes, both the process of working by phone and the content of the conversations provide data about the impact of separation and merger fantasies on the family and treatment systems. In individual outpatient work, such data would generally be conveyed in the transference. The need for hospitalization indicates that the relationship in the transference is not sufficient to address the needs of the patient. Using the phone to understand more about these severe, usually intergenerational impairments may be the only way to derive this information. For the most part, phone work with families is an intervention to choose by default if geography is the impediment to on-site work. When intrapsychic resistance is involved, or it is too dangerous to a patient's stability, phone work may allow for insight while remaining respectful of family and patient defenses. Telephone family work in these cases may open perspectives in treatment and create the potential for less defended communications between family members.

REFERENCE

Minuchin, S. (1974). *Families and Family Therapy*. Cambridge, MA: Harvard University Press.

V

WITH
DIFFERENT
DIAGNOSTIC
DISORDERS

16

Dealing with Substance Abuse Crises by Telephone

JEROME D. LEVIN

I hate telephones. They intrude on my life and greedily gobble up any interlude in my schedule. They deprive me of museum breaks when I'm working in my city office and of swimming breaks when I'm working in my country office. They make a mockery of my desires for contemplative time and ridicule my plans to steal an hour for writing. I look at my list of calls to return and cringe. Beware of the telephone; it is a tyrant. After a day of talking and listening, some days I can't help wistfully envying the analyst in the old story of the two friends who meet after many years: "Abie, it's been so long, what's happened to you? What are you doing?" "Hymie, I've become a psychoanalyst." *"Oy vay iz mir!* How do you stand listening to *tsouris* all day long?" "Who listens?"—the last thing I want to do is to talk and listen. At one time the message on my answering machine was, "Remembering that brevity is the soul of wit, leave a message." I reluctantly changed that message when I discovered that it didn't in the least discourage those I wanted to discourage and offended those I didn't want to offend, prospective patients, for example. My acerbic answering machine message hadn't reduced the number of calls I had to return.

When we become too social, too committed to activities involving other people, my wife likes to say "schizoids should remain schizoid," a sentiment I heartily endorse. I sometimes fantasize a practice devoted exclusively to the treatment of schizoids who would neither speak nor expect to be spoken to. After ten therapy sessions I would enjoy hearing the roaring of lions or the howling of wolves, but the last thing in the world I want to hear is the human voice. Just about then the telephone rings.

Telephones exacerbate my distractibility. If I were on Ritalin I would up my dose before a telephone session. It's difficult to maintain my focus and I find myself thinking of Lacan, my least favorite psychoanalytic thinker, no doubt because of his advocacy of the short session. I'm sure that part of my feelings about the telephone derive from my gender disability, otherwise known as maleness. It is probably no accident that the vast majority of the chapter authors of this book are women. I'm not sure what that's about, but it is true that on the average, women enjoy the phone in a way few men do. Most of the successful telephone sessions I have had have been with women.

An additional reason I hate the telephone is that often I can't think of one meaningful thing to say to a patient in crisis or pseudocrisis on the other side of the line. Silence over a phone line is a very different thing than silence in a room. The latter is often productive, the former usually tense, awkward, and unproductive. When I am holding the phone in an absolute blank as the distraught mother is imploring me to tell her what to do now that her son has come home stoned for the thousandth time, I think of a colleague's story of the time his daughter woke him, saying, "Daddy, the car broke down. It's freezing out and there's no one around for miles." Her half-conscious psychiatrist father muttered into the phone, "Can you tell me more about it?" That's a reply I would like to make to the distraught mother until I remember my friend's daughter's response, "Daddy, stop that shit and come get me." One of the worst things about the phone is it doesn't give you much of a place to hide. Like it or not, you have to go get them.

Having expressed my negative transference to Bell's child and by implication to his grandchildren, the fax, the beeper (I don't do beepers) and e-mail, I feel duly bound to express the other half of my ambivalence. However reluctantly, I have to concede that the telephone has its uses in therapy and that much of my hatred of it relates more to my administrative than to my clinical duties. In fact the telephone can be a lifesaver, especially for patients struggling through the early days of sobriety. I've even had some experience with successful ongoing phone therapies, but not much. Rather, I find that brief phone sessions can get people through crises and that they can help substance-abusing patients avoid slips and maintain stable sobriety. Even more important than actual phone contact—the phone session itself—is therapeutic *availability*, the fact that the patient knows the therapist can be reached, and reached *any time*. It's the telephone that makes that possible.

You may be surprised to learn that I am a very available therapist. You can't work with substance abusers or other high-risk patients without being willing to make yourself available. This imposes a real burden on the therapist. You must be willing to check the answering machine—and you need one that you can retrieve from no matter where you are, several times a day—and to return urgent calls immediately. That sometimes means talking from less than ideal public phones and always requires the ability to think on your feet. All of this is a real intrusion in my life and, as you can tell from my opening paragraphs, it engenders real resentment. Yet, you can't do substance abuse work solo unless you can tolerate that intrusion. And one thing that facilitates tolerating it is experiencing and acknowledging your resentment. Otherwise you will act it out by not returning calls, by retaliating, or by finding other employment. The other thing you can do to make the intrusion tolerable is to limit it, to establish boundaries, however permeable, and to communicate where those boundaries lie.

I tell patients early on that I am available and I *want* them to call me if they really need to, and *I mean it*. I strongly urge you not to say that or anything like it if you don't mean it. Patients will pick up on your insincerity and either call you relentlessly to test you or not call you when they really do need to call. Either result is a disaster. Some patients need to learn to restrict their use of your availability while others need to learn to utilize it.

Although I tell patients to call me if they are afraid they will "pick up" (a drink or drug), or if they are experiencing intolerable anxiety or despair, I also convey both verbally *and* less directly, by manner and intonation, that I don't wish to be called for trivial reasons. Surprisingly few patients call frequently (or at all) and the frequency of those who do tapers off rather quickly. The idea is to convey that you truly care and that you want to be there for your patients, especially in the torment and terror of learning to live drug-free *and* that you have your own needs and your own life. More disturbed borderline patients are like small children who have difficulty accepting that their parents have their own needs. They literally don't know this. They need to be told. Less disturbed patients regress at times of great stress and become so needy that they too "forget" that their therapist has a life.

There are patients in the substance abusing population who literally have not achieved object constancy in the psychodynamic sense of being able to believe that the object is there and capable of love or caring during times of tension in the relationship or even in the Piagetian sense of securely believing that the object exists when out of sight. This may be a projection. When the patient is angry or upset with the therapist he or she may be incapable of caring for the therapist; all that good history together is wiped out and only a call can reestablish the existence of the good object. Or the patient may fear his or her hostility, envy, and hatred have destroyed the therapist (the good object) and may need to call for reassurance that this is not so. Substance abuse induces regression, and patients who were once functioning on higher developmental levels and had securely established object constancy may have regressed to a point where this is no longer so. Any and all of this can be interpreted, but such interpretation should not be delivered reflexively. Therapeutic tact and a good sense of where the patient is at should help the therapist to distinguish between situations where it is best just to be there and situations in which it is best to interpret. Remember, you can always interpret later; the premature interpretation can be off-putting and can shut the patient down. There is nothing wrong with telling the patient that you have your own needs and your own life; in fact, it is therapeutic. Many therapists are hesitant to express their own needs and that hesitancy should be explored in supervision and/or personal therapy.

I find my approach works. I get few calls, and the vast majority of those who have called should have called. Using fairly directive, didactic interventions, combined with some interpretation of, for example, the hostility behind harassing, demanding calls, I help those patients who are so impulse-ridden that they cannot accept boundaries to tolerate them. If they don't have boundaries, I do, and my willingness to talk about my boundaries helps them to establish some of their own. I find this happens rather rapidly. As firm as I am, I am equally insistent that the boundary-transgressing patient call when genuinely needy. This is a difficult discrimination for some and the therapist should give concrete examples, drawn from the

302 USE OF THE TELEPHONE IN PSYCHOTHERAPY

patient's life and circumstances, of what is and what is not an appropriate call. This less than dynamic sort of schoolmarmish work is nevertheless highly therapeutic.

The patient who is unable or unwilling to call when such a call would prevent a slip or other high-risk behavior (including suicide) is handled with a similar combination of directive, didactic, and psychodynamic interventions: "I want you to call the next time you are seriously contemplating taking a drink." "The reason you didn't call before you copped is because you were afraid the call would be effective and that talking to me would stop you from going out for heroin." "The reason you didn't call was that you feared rejection. Your parents were rarely available when you were in trouble and needed them so it was perfectly natural for you to expect I wouldn't be there for you either. It was too dangerous to find out. Better to believe I would have been there for you if you had called than to call and find out I wasn't. Such a disappointment would have been awful. Next time take a chance and call me." Exploration rather than direction or interpretation is also highly therapeutic with both types of patients, but is more effective with the telephone-shy or phobic patient: "Do you have any thoughts on why it was so hard to call me last night?"

I will try to make all this real with some case material. But first I would like to explain why substance abusers need as much access to the therapist via telephone as they do. Like most things psychical the substance abusers' need for close contact is overdetermined. The following dynamics may or may not apply in a given case, but it is not unusual to find that they all apply to the emotional condition of a particular substance abuser.

First and perhaps foremost, active substance abusers and those in early recovery tend to be developmentally regressed. That is to say their inner worlds and interpersonal relations are marked by lack of differentiation and weak integration, poor impulse control, low affect tolerance, ego weakness, poorly defined boundaries, diffuse identity, and a reliance on primitive defense mechanisms, especially splitting, denial, and projection. Insecurely established object constancy and a paucity of inner resources are part of the syndrome. This dynamic-emotional status may be the result of the substance abuse itself, in which case it is best understood as a regression, or it may have been antecedent to the substance abuse alone as deficit or fixation, in which case it is etiological of the substance abuse. Often the impoverished inner world is the outcome of a complex interaction of antecedent and consequent factors. Be that as it may, it is clear that a patient with such limited emotional resources is going to need a good deal of support and structuring from the outside and that that support must be available when it is needed.

A great many substance abusers use isolation—literally avoiding human contact to the maximum extent possible—in defense of their addiction as a result of the paranoia often secondary to substance abuse, and as an interpersonal and intrapsychic defense, particularly against feelings of rage, guilt, and shame. Paradoxically, these isolators, who hide out of fear, may have failed to develop what Winnicott (1958) calls the "capacity to be alone," so that they are caught in the dreadful trap of not being able to be part of community while not being able to be comfortably or creatively alone. For these people, the use of the telephone may be a perfect halfway house toward full participation in the human community—a connection that is not too threatening. Here the telephone and the conversation on it becomes something like a transitional object (Winnicott 1951). For the isolator, learning to use the phone to reach out for help is highly therapeutic in and of itself, quite apart from content. The twelve-step (AA type) self-help programs know this and put great emphasis on their members availing themselves of what they call "telephone therapy," contacting their fellow members for support. The telephone speaks to both sides of the defense: it allows the isolators to come out of hiding relatively easily since it engenders less fear than face-to-face contact and it replaces the substance as companion (which is what it is in one of its meanings) for those who have not developed the capacity of being alone.

Yet another aspect of the substance abusers' relationship to the substance is that of a *selfobject*. That is to say the substance abuser has developed a selfobject transference (Kohut 1977) with both mirroring and idealizing components to the substance abuse. This is a hypothesis that I have elaborated elsewhere (Levin 1987, 1991, 1995, 1999). The disruption of a selfobject transference or relationship that a move toward abstinence entails may induce profound anxiety and deep despair. The patient in early recovery, however exhilarated by his or her escape from a life-threatening addiction, is also utterly bereft of selfobject, companion, script, defense, and a deeply ingrained way of life. Any one of these may be so threatening as to set off a slip (i.e., relapse), but the loss of the selfobject relationship is particularly difficult to negotiate. The ensuing anxiety and despair may make sobriety intolerable, so it is vital that another selfobject relationship—that to the therapist— replace the one lost to the substance. The telephone facilitates this relationship. In the idealizing transference the ideal object is experienced as omniscient, omnipotent, and omnipresent. Telephone accessibility provides a simulacrum to omnipresence and the contact made assuages anxiety and provides hope as an antidote to despair. The key to treating substance abusers is to replace rum with relationship and the telephone assists this process.

Yet another reason telephone access is necessary is that the substance-abusing patient is playing with half a deck. He or she has a poisoned brain, and, not infrequently, other somatic complications. There is a Twelve-Step neologism that refers to the mental confusion and emotional turmoil of early sobriety. That word is *mokus*. When AA or NA members say that Dave or Sally is mokus they are making an onomatopoetic statement. The very sound of the word *mokus* conveys the confusion induced by a poisoned mind, of suffering from an organic brain syndrome. The fact that the Twelve-Step movement, which has vast experience in this matter, has a word for and recognizes the state of mind with which the early recovering patient must struggle says a lot about what the therapist must deal with and about the necessity of being available to the patient in that state: an availability best provided by open access to telephone therapy.

While the nonmedical therapist should never attempt to practice medicine, those in the field do acquire a good deal of knowledge about the somatic complications—enough to recognize symptoms that may be quite dangerous and to use that recognition to appropriately warn and refer. Better to have the substance abuser with a serious somatic symptom, whether from the direct toxic effect of the drug, from withdrawal, or from malnutrition (surprisingly common even in comfortably middle-class substance abusers) call you at 3:00 a.m. (since he or she probably wouldn't call anyone else) as you sleepily say, "Call 911 immediately," then to find out in the morning that your caseload has been reduced by one.

Related to the somatic complications and poisoned brain is what is known as the prolonged (or attenuated) withdrawal symptom, which is characterized by emotional lability; cognitive difficulties; and impairments in short-term memory, in sleep disturbances and in the ability to abstract. This is the neurological correlative of the psychodynamic-interpersonal regression I spoke of above. The patient is doubly damned, so to speak, by emotional regression/fixation to a primitive level of development and by neurological deficit concomitant with the substance abuse itself. As they say in AA, "Nobody is here for hangnails." Patients struggling with so much require tremendous support, including open feeding (or feeding on demand), which is what telephone access is. So characterizing active addiction and early recovery in the way I have, I do not mean to imply that substance abusers lack strength or that many do not do splendidly in recovery—they do. But it takes time, sometimes a very long time. The prolonged withdrawal symptom commonly lasts upward of a year. The Twelve-Step slogan is "It takes five years to get your marbles back and the rest of your life to use them." Here both clinical experience with substance abusers and empirical research support the folk wisdom of the Twelve-Step movement. The more we study recovery the longer it seems to take and by implication the longer telephone sessions, however short, are needed on a demand basis. I should note that the prolonged withdrawal syndrome is not the acute withdrawal syndrome that can be life threatening and should *always* be monitored under medical supervision.

Yet another reason telephone therapy is needed in early recovery is the fact that once the patient has been released from the utter slavery and compulsion of addiction that dictates his or her every move, the newfound freedom to make decisions produces tremendous anxiety. All of a sudden many things become possible and the patient is in no shape to make decisions that may profoundly alter his or her life, whether in the area of work, personal relationships, or more subtle areas requiring access to internal states. Søren Kierkegaard (1849) called the anxiety that goes with choice the "dizziness of freedom." Dizziness of freedom not only implies that decisions about basic personal and existential matters should be postponed. It also argues that the patient's anxiety about the suddenly bewildering range of options and choices is sobriety threatening and requires open contact with the therapist to help quell moments of panic, which are indeed sobriety threatening, and which arise in premature confrontation with unmanageable freedom. My clinical experience here is congruent with the Twelve-Step programs' advice to their members that they postpone decisions on these matters during the first year of recovery. The therapist's very simple intervention, "You don't have to decide that right now," during a telephone contact is often sobriety saving.

Another reason telephone access is necessary in substance abuse treatment is the simple, obvious, but often forgotten fact that drugs are dangerous. They are not only dangerous pharmacologically. Their use gets people into dangerous situations, their use is often associated with violence of many kinds, their use may lead to difficulties with the law, withdrawal can itself be dangerous, and suicide is highly correlated with substance abuse. Relapses are common and we treat active users and patients for whom abstinence is not a goal, so that imminent danger is intrinsic to substance abuse and its treatment. We cannot completely protect our patients from these dangers, nor can or should we try to live their lives for them, but we can be reachable when the patient is in danger and we can intervene appropriately, whether the intervention is advice, calling the police, talking the patient down, or interpreting the underlying dynamic of the current craziness in the patient's behavior and crisis in the patient's life. Once again, the telephone is the indispensable tool.

Substance abuse has been understood as a mistaken attempt at self-medication, a hypothesis elaborated with great subtlety and specificity by Edward Khantzian (1999). Substance abusers may be self-medicating anxiety, depression, attention deficit disorder, various personality disorders or, more rarely, psychosis, particularly paranoia. Although this self-medication may work for a while, over time it ineluctably exacerbates the very condition it is being used to treat and a vicious cycle is set up of medication of a condition caused by the medication. Nevertheless, when the self-medication is stopped, the underlying condition is now neither medicated, anesthetized by the drug, nor masked by its use, and it may be a very serious condition. That leaves the newly and sometimes not so newly recovering patient struggling both to maintain sobriety and to live with what are sometimes major emotional disorders. To do that successfully requires all the help one can get and the therapist's telephone accessibility, especially to help modulate anxiety, is absolutely necessary. Once again, the telephone session need not be long, but it must be timely.

There is a phenomenon known as *state dependent learning*, which also argues for the necessity of metaphorical, symbolic demand feeding via free access to the therapist on the phone. If you train a mouse to run a maze while it is high on some drug and then ask the mouse to run the same maze sober, the mouse can't do it. Give it cocaine or opium or alcohol or whatever drug it was on while learning the maze and lo and behold, Mickey or Minnie sails right through the maze. The learning is *state dependent*. I have argued elsewhere (Levin 1995, 1999) that something very similar happens to people, so that the recovering person has a great deal of re-learning to do. He or she literally doesn't know how to do it, whether "it" be having sex, giving a speech, or handling a feeling while sober. The newly sober person is reborn not only in the spiritual sense, but in the sense of being a child, indeed an infant, relearning to negotiate the world within and the environment without. Although I exaggerate to make a point, and state dependent learning is a partial rather than total phenomenon, it is clear that anxiety induced by the re-learning process and the anxiety of not knowing how to handle the self and the world sober threaten that sobriety. Therefore, the therapist must be available to give the "infant" guidance. Of course, the therapist should not infantilize or do for the patient what the patient can do for him- or herself, but neither should the therapist underestimate or criticize the patient's real incapacity and need for concrete guidance in early sobriety.

Martin Seligman's (1989) well-known studies of learned helplessness also argue for the therapist's accessibility on the telephone when treating substance abusers. Seligman trained dogs to escape a noxious stimulus (a shock delivered by electrifying the floor on which they stood) by jumping over a barrier. Then he pulled a really dirty trick; he electrified the floor in the escape area. The dogs jumped back over the barrier where they were shocked yet again. After a few such trials the dogs gave up and just lay there whimpering. Seligman now turned off the current, and when he turned it on again, the dogs could escape. There was now no current on the other side of the barrier. All they had to do was jump. But they didn't. They just lay there and whimpered. Seligman called this learned helplessness and argued that it was a paradigm for at least one form of human depression. He then instructed his students to drag the dogs across the barrier to the safe, unelectrified area of the floor. The learned helplessness turned out to be highly resistant to extinction and it took an average of ten trials of dragging the dogs over the barrier before they returned to spontaneous active escape behavior. Substance abusers have learned and over-learned that action is futile, whether that action be relinquishing the substances themselves, or trying to achieve while handicapped by their substance abuse. They have been shocking themselves on both sides of the barrier, so to speak, and they have learned passivity. This suggests that the substance abuse therapist needs to be highly active and directive, at least in the beginning. Many dogs have been dragged across the barrier on the telephone. The very act of calling the therapist breaks the learned helplessness quite independently of what the therapist says or does. Of course the content of the therapist's interventions (here a symbolic pulling over the barrier) has significance also. The phenomenon of the substance abusers' learned helplessness and need for the therapist's activity to counter it argues from yet another perspective that the therapist should be available on the phone in active and early recovery substance abuse treatment.

There is a strong correlation between substance abuse and suicide. In his seminal work *Suicide*, the great sociologist Emile Durkheim (1897) argued from an empirical-statistical as well as from a theoretical standpoint that suicide was strongly correlated with anomie and alienation. There are few populations that suffer more anomie and alienation than that of substance abusers. Additionally, substance abuse depresses pharmacologically and psychologically, and consequently negatively affects lifestyle. These are people who are often already depressed and attempting to self-medicate that depression. This, too, reinforces the connection between suicide and substance abuse, and a considerable number of empirical studies in the century since Durkheim's work confirm the intimate association of suicide and substance abuse. The mental confusion induced by the drugs themselves increases the suicidal risk even more. Needless to say, the telephone is an important tool in reducing this risk.

There is another risk associated with the endgame of substance abuse that therapists have not often recognized. I speak here of the point where the patient comes to believe that he or she can no longer live drunk or stoned but cannot envision a life without drugs: "I can't live with it and I can't live without it." The danger here is very great and is not only inherent in the last stage of substance abuse, but is intrinsic to early sobriety, to recovery itself. It is very real, and here the telephone can literally be lifesaving. Don't forget that the user has been fleeing intolerable feelings in the only way he or she knows, namely by substance use, and that door has now been closed, so suicide readily becomes the only viable alternative. Why, you may ask, if the danger is so great, aren't these patients hospitalized? The unfortunate answer is that with the relentless pressure of managed care it is harder and harder to get patients who are in potential danger admitted. Therefore telephone therapy in early recovery is more salient, necessary, and central to treatment than ever.

Finally, substance abuse is in itself traumatizing. It is traumatic to be out of control, it is traumatic to have the things happen to you that usually happen to substance abusers, it is traumatic to do the sort of violence to the self that substance abuse does, and there are at least a dozen other ways in which substance abuse traumatizes. The victims of trauma suffer anxiety, impulsive thinking, compulsive thinking, fixation on the trauma, rage, shame, guilt, and depression. Those traumatized by substance abuse suffer every one of these symptoms—this in addition to the antecedent childhood and adult trauma the majority of substance abusers have experienced. The consequences of traumatization dovetail and resonate with the psychodynamic and neurological conflicts, deficits, regressions, and fixations already discussed to exacerbate the active and early recovery patient's susceptibility to intolerable pain and to relapse. This, too, argues for the maximal possible strength of the holding environment the therapist seeks to build for the patient and the telephone is an intrinsic and necessary part of that holding environment.

Having made a case for telephone therapy being a necessary evil (evil for the therapist and necessary for the patient) the form of such therapy becomes the issue. As I have said, I am temperamentally averse to ongoing full telephone sessions in spite of having conducted a few such therapies successfully, but I know that others are not. Nevertheless, I cannot recommend ongoing regular telephone therapy with substance abusers as the sole modality. I've never seen it work.

The telephone too readily lends itself to deception, game-playing, minimalization, and concealment in the service of denial of the substance abuse. My experience with patients, even those with some sobriety behind them, who have moved away and wish to continue their therapy on the phone is that it doesn't work. They need the reality and intensity of face-to-face sessions. Without the intimacy of being in the same room with the therapist, these patients all too readily return to acting out of one sort or another. Part of the problem may be the failure of evocative memory so even with the reinforcement of the disembodied voice the therapist soon fades and loses potency for the patient.

On the other hand, short (meaning five- to fifteen-minute) sessions on an as-needed basis or prearranged during periods of stress are not only highly therapeutic, indeed they can be and often are lifesaving. I don't charge for these short telephone sessions; most are less than five minutes, frequently consisting of a brief exchange of a few sentences each. That does not mean that full telephone sessions should not be scheduled when for whatever reason the patient and therapist cannot meet face to face and the need is there. The "extra session" on the telephone strengthens the therapeutic alliance and facilitates recovery. Of course, in these instances the patient should be charged for a full session. Now to those examples.

Henry was sober for several years when he came to see me. His problems seemed to have little to do with his alcoholism, which had been severe but was in stable remission. Rather, he was concerned with being intensely uncomfortable with his homosexuality. Growing up in a depressed alcoholic home that was treated as a shrine for his dead older brother by his parents, Henry had all sorts of difficulties with relationships, whether at work, or in the gay world, or in therapy. We had been working on his relationship problem both within the transference and outside of it for about six months, dealing, but little other than historically, with his alcoholism, which was nicely contained by his consistent albeit somewhat timid and tepid participation with AA, when he was sent to China on an extensive business trip. An important part of his business activities was to be social. As a museum curator trying to put together a traveling exhibit he would be expected to attend banquets in which drinking was de rigueur. Suddenly his sobriety was threatened. How could he handle the banquets? We rehearsed and strategized together and made conscious the part in him that wished to drink and welcomed the banquets far from anyone he knew as situations in which "sipping a bit" could be easily rationalized. It soon became clear that valuable as this work was, it probably wasn't going to be enough to keep Henry sober on his trip. Being alone in China was too much an emotional recapitulation of being alone with his depressed parents and dead brother—the dominant "spirit" in his home—and drinking to quell the fury, sadness, shame, and guilt that had welled up in the adolescent boy struggling with an unwelcome sexuality and all the rest of the feelings he could neither repress nor accept. I suggested phone sessions.

Henry was reluctant. He didn't want to admit how much he needed me. I interpreted that trying to preserve his fragile self-esteem and less fragile, but nevertheless jeopardized, sobriety while being alone for so long in such difficult circumstances was simply too much. I went on to comment that it was not a pejorative commentary on his capacity for self-regulation to reinforce it with phone sessions with me. After much resistance, Henry agreed to prescheduled and as-needed telephone sessions. In the two months he was in China we had six prearranged half-hour sessions and several short ad hoc ones. As it turned out, we talked little about drinking. Henry's having decided in his own mind that he would return rather than drink made a real difference. What we spoke of was separation, aloneness, and the emotional abandonment by his parents after his brother's death by drowning. I asked, "Was it an accident that you almost drowned yourself in drink?" Henry's hitherto unconscious yearning for a connection to a father, and the ways in which alcohol was a pseudo-meeting of this need became another theme of our phone sessions. For the shy, rather withdrawn young man it proved easier to talk about these things over 5,000 miles than face to face, but once the ice was broken the therapy heated up and became more emotionally intense when we returned to our face-to-face sessions. The telephone had facilitated the strengthening of the fragile therapeutic alliance and made possible more in-depth work. It also kindled feelings of gratitude in Henry, since I had gone out of my way to insist on the protective structure of the telephone work. Henry felt loved without feeling so threatened by the sexualization of his yearning for a father that he needed to flee into an emotionally shallow relationship with me, or, more direly, into drinking. Although Henry felt that his sobriety was never threatened in China, I am convinced that the telephone accessibility contributed importantly to his relative ease in not drinking and that it indeed may have made his maintenance of sobriety possible. Whatever my feelings about the telephone, this work proved gratifying.

The Smiths, on the other hand, were the kind of couple whose telephone calls I dreaded. Theirs was a necessary evil, open access, unscheduled phone relationship. Larry was an alcoholic, marijuana-using manic-depressive with severe personality pathology. Drinking or high on pot he was impossible, whether as a husband or a patient. Before he achieved stable sobriety he was frequently in and out of the V.A. hospital. I was seeing him on contract for the V.A. in those days. For whatever reason, I was able to talk him down from incipient manic episodes if he hadn't gone too far and was not high on alcohol or grass. Not infrequently, that talking down was on the phone.

After his last decompensation his wife managed to get him admitted to a private psychiatric hospital with a substance abuse rehabilitation unit. After he was stabilized on the "flight deck" (AA slang for the closed ward), he was transferred for a month's stay in the substance abuse rehabilitation unit. Having had many seeds planted during his years of therapy with me, Larry got the message. He never drank or smoked pot again. However, he was always on the verge of doing so and sometimes used to threaten a relapse when he and Sally, his third wife, would fight. And fight they did. Sally was fragile, suffering extraordinarily low self-esteem and vulnerability to depression. She was prone to see offense where there was none and Larry provided too much reality-based offense.

Sally was hard to diagnose, but if I had to I would come up with a dysthymia, not infrequently associated with exacerbation into major depression, in a borderline personality with paranoid tendencies. All in all, not a marriage made in heaven. Yet these two gravely damaged people loved each other and when they weren't attacking each other they could be mutually helpful. Neither could have survived without the other. All in all a symbiosis that worked—sort of.

With Larry sober, things weren't too bad until Sally had a baby. Larry had a grown son from his first marriage and a stormy relationship with his stepdaughter from his second marriage. Although they both sincerely wanted to be good parents their resources were just too limited and the stress of having the baby set off wild screaming matches, usually ending with Sally sobbing and threatening suicide and with Larry threatening to leave or to get drunk, usually followed by his being crushed by remorse. Then would come the telephone call. First Sally would pour out her despair, begging me to stop Larry from controlling and demeaning her; then Larry would chime in with less than helpful complaints about Sally's inadequacies, which were not entirely of his imagining, forcing him to "take over." Meanwhile the baby could be heard screaming as Sally, taking the phone again, would sob, "I just can't stand it—I can't stand the baby crying and Larry screaming." I never had the slightest idea of what to say so I would sit there, holding the receiver, feeling stupid, inadequate, frustrated, and annoyed. After ten to fifteen minutes of this seeming futility they would calm down, and I would say something to this effect: "I'm glad you called out for help. You seem to be feeling calmer now so I'll see you next week as scheduled," as I hung up with relief. Not entirely honest, but the best I could come up with. The Smiths were always grateful. Just being there to listen to pacify and defuse helped. Nobody drank or drugged, nobody attempted suicide, nobody decompensated, and there was no violence. No matter how much I dreaded their calls there is no question that the calls helped them. I can't tell you that the Smiths improved much even with the more interpretive work I did in what were now couple sessions, but the combination of face-to-face and telephone therapy got them through—and through sober. That would not have been possible without the phone sessions.

Martin exemplifies another kind of telephone intervention. He was a multiple drug user, but his drug of choice was alcohol. A rather schizoid, strongly narcissistic middle-aged man whose family of origin had nicknamed him the "Baron" (he used a façade of arrogance, condescension, devaluation, and contempt for others to barely paper over an extremely fragile sense of self and an even more fragile self-esteem). An artist whose successes were intermittent and far apart, he was rageful, perpetually hurting, and chronically frustrated. In spite of these many personality problems, his developmental arrest, and primitive defenses, he managed to become stably sober as an AA member about a year before he came for therapy. He had also managed to marry a wealthy businesswoman, whom he simultaneously admired, envied, loved, and hated. She saw him as the archetypal romantic hero-artist whom she had saved from a life in the garret—or the gutter. I had no idea of how good his work might have been. He didn't really work at it during the period I knew him, but she believed in it, expecting Martin to be discovered "any day now." His wife's belief in him no doubt raised unfulfillable expectations in him, which, however gratifying his wife's support of his at best intermittent artistic efforts might have been, also set him up for crushing feelings of failure and inadequacy.

Seemingly fixated at the anal stage, Martin used language that was obsessively anal: "Blow it out your ass," "My brother [a successful corporate type Martin envied and hated] doesn't know which hand to wipe himself with," and pretty much everyone in his AA group was an "asshole." Although he went to meetings on a regular basis, Martin's contempt for AA and its members knew no bounds. Those who weren't assholes were "shits" and the whole thing smelled like a sewer. I wouldn't have bet much on his continuing sobriety.

I did what I could to shore up Martin's fragile self-esteem without encouraging unrealistic expectations, in the hope that feeling better about himself he might grow less contemptuous of others. Although there was no real therapeutic alliance, he found my encouraging his artistic activities and expressing admiration (which was sincere) for his accomplishment and courage in achieving and sustaining sobriety in spite of painful feelings gratifying, so he kept coming for treatment. I figured that as long as Martin stayed in treatment there was hope. I began to gingerly confront and interpret, suggesting that a great deal of pain and massive depression must underlie his contempt and devaluation. I kept it in the here and now, staying away from the genetic sources of his "baroncy." Even so, he couldn't tolerate much of this and I dosed my confrontations very carefully. I believe that maintaining Martin's sobriety was quite ambitious enough a goal for the moment, and Martin did stay sober.

Martin (or more accurately his wife) had a country home, which they visited weekends. Martin complained incessantly about the trip, the bugs, the landscaper who didn't show up, and his wife's wealthy, sometimes distinguished friends. Thanksgiving weekend they planned a big party and Martin, who took inordinate pride in his gourmet cooking, was preparing a feast. Of course there would be wine and cocktails before dinner. I sensed danger and tried to alert him but to no avail. He was on one of his highly emotionally invested quests for admiration of his cooking skills.

Not readily able to ask for help, Martin had never availed himself of access to me on the telephone, so phone therapy had played no role in our relationship. Late the Saturday night of Thanksgiving weekend my phone rang. It was Martin crying out and screaming in acute physical pain. As was almost predictable, he had dismissed my suggestion that the party was a danger to his sobriety and had, as he later put it, "found" himself sipping the wine he was using to cook with, the very first night he was in the country. He rationalized, Oh, it's only cooking wine, it doesn't matter." He continued to drink and things went precipitously downhill. At the party Friday night he was roaring, falling-down drunk. The party was a disaster. His wife left him there drinking and went back to the city in the morning. Martin had been drinking ever since.

As he described the excruciating abdominal pain, projectile vomiting, and the inability to straighten up he was experiencing, I guessed that Martin was having an attack of alcoholic pancreatitis, a potentially fatal complication of alcoholism. As it turned out my surmise was correct. But the relevant thing here was that he called me. Even if I was a therapist without knowledge of the medical complications of alcoholism, I would have known that this was a medical emergency and could have acted accordingly. My previously scorned invitation to call me if he needed help saved Martin's life. Because he was too drunk and too sick to help himself, I arranged for suitable medical intervention. Martin never forgave me for his having needed me and for my having "seen" him in such a condition, so therapy was at an end, an end I wasn't altogether sorry to see. But Martin was alive and had another chance to recover, a chance perhaps enhanced by his brush with death from his alcoholism. It is interesting that Martin had no previous history of somatic complications and that it had taken only a few days of drinking to bring him to death's door. His body had apparently lost its tolerance for alcohol and his drinking days would be few. For him it was probably recovery or death. This sudden decompensation—somatic, psychological, or psychotic—is not uncommon in substance abuse and is yet another reason for keeping the phone line open.

Randy was the borderline substance abuser from hell. Twenty-three and going on two, she wasn't the sort of case you hear about in analytic school: crisis-ridden, unreliable, dishonest in therapy and in life, manipulative, desperate and very, very sad. It was hard to know what to do with and for Randy. Mostly I didn't know, and stumbled from crisis to crisis keeping her afloat, more or less. The two best interventions I made in the year we worked together were: "If you treat other people the way you treat me, it's no wonder people drop you," which she managed to hear and take in although it had only a brief effect on her behavior, and "You're convinced that your problem is the pain other people inflict on you, but you don't have a chance of feeling better unless you stop inflicting the sort of pain you do on other people." Randy heard the second of these interventions and was successful in curbing her aggressive acting out for a period. My interventions sound angry, even retaliatory, but they weren't; they were actually empathic. Randy did better with confrontation than with more overtly supportive interventions. When her substance abuse, which was multiple, but mostly prescription drugs—Valium and other benzodiazepines—and alcohol weren't out of control, she was manageable. She had literary ambitions and had written some pretty decent poetry. An avid reader, she was obsessed with James Agee's *A Death in the Family*. Although it would be less than truthful to say I enjoyed her, I did like her. The telephone played a major role in our relationship from the beginning. Most of our telephone sessions were in the nature of crisis intervention, but occasionally there were calmer, longer, more interpretive ones that anchored Randy and perhaps even produced some insight.

Randy was madly, and I use the word advisedly, in love with a middle-aged alcoholic who was more or less continuously trying to end the relationship, except when he was lonely or horny. Although he sent mixed messages, my sense was that he genuinely wanted to end it. Randy was just too crazy. Several times, when he had insisted she leave his home, she had become violent and more than once the police were involved. On one occasion, Randy deliberately ran her car into a tree, cutting her head and face so that there would be a reason he would have to keep her around. She had told him another driver had forced her off the road. Who knows what the truth was, but her head and face were some mess. She was a case of what Karen Horney (1945) called "morbid dependency."

Randy insisted that she simply couldn't live without David. I interpreted the hostile, controlling aspect of her behavior, the temper tantrums over not getting her own way, the regressive, symbiotic need behind her actions phrased as, "You hope to get from David what you never got from your mother," and conveyed a dozen other confrontational, genetic, and transferential observations to her. All to no avail except for short periods of remission of her acting out, which coincided with her relative abstinence from substances. Unfortunately, Randy's "love addiction" didn't improve. Finally, with the assistance of the police, David forcibly removed her and made it clear that she was not to return. He was finally and unequivocally finished with her.

That was when I got the call about the gun. Randy called to tell me she had a gun and she was going to kill herself. I didn't know where she was, so I wasn't able to call the police. I believed her, although I knew she must have had some ambivalence about dying or she wouldn't have called. I had always used black humor with Randy; it was a language she understood. So I said, "Randy, my office is rather drab. It needs a splash of color, so would you mind shooting yourself in my office so I can get some red on my gray carpet?" Amazingly, she agreed. I paced during the half hour she took to get to the office, but then she was there gun and all. I told her she wasn't in her right mind and it was her depression, her disease that was telling her to kill herself. I insisted she go to the hospital. By then she had put the gun away, but she adamantly refused to go to the hospital. I told her that I would call 911 if she didn't go voluntarily. Randy countered with, "Call David. If he goes with me, I'll go to the hospital." The telephone again! I called David, who knew who I was, and explained why we needed him. I played on his guilt, hoping that he was not too strongly psychopathic. It worked, and within an hour Randy was happily ensconced in David's car with me following on the way to the hospital to meet my psychiatrist colleague-friend who had privileges there. The telephone again was the means of making arrangements. After some struggling with the threat of involuntary commitment Randy signed herself in. She didn't want to die. She wanted what she wanted—David—but she might very well have died if she hadn't called and reached me. Yes, the telephone is a necessary evil in substance abuse treatment.

REFERENCES

Durkheim, E. (1897). *Suicide*. Glencoe, IL: Free Press, 1951.

Horney, K. (1948). *Our Inner Conflicts*. New York: Norton.

Khantzian, E. J. (1999). *Addiction as a Human Process*. Northvale, NJ: Jason Aronson.

Kierkegaard, S. (1849). *The Concept of Dread*, trans. W. Lowrie. Princeton, NJ: Princeton University Press, 1944.

Kohut, H. (1977). *The Restoration of the Self*. New York: International Universities Press.

Levin, J. D. (1987). *Treatment of Alcoholism and Other Addictions*. Northvale, NJ: Jason Aronson.

——— (1991). *Recovery from Alcoholism: Beyond Your Wildest Dreams*. Northvale, NJ: Jason Aronson.

——— (1995). *Introduction to Alcoholism Counseling: A Bio-Psycho-Social Approach*, 2nd ed. Washington, DC: Taylor & Francis.

——— (1999). *Primer for Treating Substance Abusers*. Northvale, NJ: Jason Aronson.

Seligman, M. (1989). *Helplessness*. New York: Freeman.

Winnicott, D. W. (1951). Transitional objects and transitional phenomena. In *Through Paediatrics to Psycho-Analysis*, pp. 229–242. London: Hogarth, 1958.

——— (1958). The capacity to be alone. In *The Maturational Processes and the Facilitating Environment*, pp. 29–36. New York: International Universities Press, 1965.

17

Adjunctive Use of the Telephone in Therapy of Severe Anorexia

IRA L. MINTZ

REFERRAL

Jeanette was an 18-year-old woman with very severe anorexia nervosa. She was intensively treated as an office patient except for two brief periods of hospitalization in the very beginning of treatment before there had been an opportunity for a therapeutic alliance to develop. After the first two to three months, in spite of many difficulties and severe crises, there was little question of rehospitalization and Jeanette's treatment proceeded without interruption except for recognized vacation periods.

This case is presented to illustrate in detail the nature and therapeutic management of her illness, and to suggest that if such severe anorexia can be treated with minimal hospitalization, then perhaps the routine hospitalization of less severely ill patients deserves some reconsideration. Jeanette was treated in intensive psychoanalytic psychotherapy five times a week with no coercive procedures or behavioral modification techniques.

Jeanette was referred by another psychiatrist who had treated her for the previous five months and who had become increasingly concerned about her agitated behavior and increasing threats of suicide. At the beginning of her illness, she had seen a psychiatrist for about three months and a social worker for six weeks, and had attended a clinic for two months. Because of her age, the parents were not seen initially, but they were seen together after the fifth session when Jeanette had to be hospitalized.

FAMILY BACKGROUND

While most anorexic patients come from middle-class families, Jeanette came from a rather modest background. The father, an unsuccessful plumber, was described as a provocative, argumentative man whose work habits were erratic at best and markedly complicated by drinking, which had contributed to the loss of two previous plumbing businesses that had been financed by his brother. Jeanette felt that her father cared about her, but that he had such an inferiority complex and was so totally absorbed in his own difficulties that he couldn't pay enough attention to his children.

The mother was described as a controlling, manipulative woman who constantly fought with her husband and with Jeanette's two sisters and three older brothers. Although the father shouted at and insulted the mother, Jeanette thought that the mother was really in charge. The patient stated that her mother got her controlling ways from her own mother, who bossed her daughter around unmercifully. After the grandfather died, the grandmother spent six months of the year living with Jeanette's family and six months living with her son's family. The uncle was a wealthy man who would have preferred his mother to live in her own apartment with a companion. The grandmother would have no part of it, however, and insisted on living alternately with the two families.

The father's brother was a former policeman who ran a successful security company. When the analyst saw the patient in the mid-1960s, he was a wealthy man. This uncle paid for Jeanette's treatment. In a mixture of fondness for his relatives and a wish to demonstrate his financial success to them, he paid for all types of help for the family (e.g., camp for all six children, psychotherapy for Jeanette and two of her brothers, orthodontia for Jeanette). His largesse made the father feel demeaned, but he did not object because he could not afford to pay for such things himself.

THERAPY

Session 1

In the initial interview, Jeanette appeared very restless and agitated, was unable to sit for all of the session, and periodically got up and paced. While one could see that she must have been quite attractive before she became ill, in her current state she gave the appearance of a fluttering scarecrow. She was 5'5" and weighed 80 lbs. Her short hair was thin and dull, and hung limply about her neck. Her nose was beaklike, with its modest prominence accentuated by its thinness and by the flaring of her nostrils when she spoke. The zygomatic processes stuck out because of the lack of tissue beneath them, with darkened hollows replacing muscle mass.

She spoke in a loud, crude manner and appeared unkempt and disheveled. Her small-sized clothing hung on her sticklike frame. Her joints appeared large relative to the thin limbs emanating from them. She looked like a self-made concentration camp victim.

Her opening comments were as follows:

Look how messed up I am. . . . Let me show you how skinny
I am. It's disgusting. [Pulling up her long sleeves] Look at
my bones. I have to have something in my mouth all the
time: gum, cigarettes, candy. I chew 20 sticks of gum a day.
I don't eat regular food. . . . I stuff myself and then I vomit.
I used to weigh 110, then I went down to 70. Now I'm up
to 80. . . . I like to be with people constantly. You know, to
have my feedings. . . . I'm happy when I'm told how skinny
I am, that's how nuts I am.

Look at this. [Here she pushed down her jeans to
reveal a mass of scar tissue on her abdomen.] I get this
from burning myself with the hot-water bottle when my
stomach hurts and I'm constipated. . . . I can't stand it
when I'm constipated. I have to get it out. I take laxatives
every night, sometimes 50 or 60. . . . Then I stay up most
of the night exercising or smoking to keep up my metabolism so that I don't put on any weight. . . I do everything
to extremes. When I vomit, I jam my fingers down my
throat so hard. . . . [Here she revealed a series of long-
standing scars on the dorsum of her fingers where the
upper teeth had gashed the skin from the violence of her
thrust into her mouth.]

In her hyperactive, agitated state, she was almost oblivious to the analyst's presence and certainly was not attuned to
his responses since thus far he had had almost no opportunity
to make a comment. This was essentially the tenor of her early
therapeutic contacts. She continued, "If someone doesn't call
me, I get frustrated and act hysterical, . . . and then I go and
eat the house up. . . . I have to always be in control. . . . When
I get too frustrated, I get so depressed that I think of killing
myself. . . . I can't be alone." She suddenly looked directly at
the analyst, instead of talking to the air. "I feel that I'm not

making contact with you. I really wanted to see someone else, you know, and because his office was in W ————, he thought that it was too far. I was furious. I really liked Dr. L. [her previous analyst] very much."

The analyst asked her why her previous therapy had failed if she had liked that analyst so much. She reflected for a moment, one of the first pauses in her outpouring, and then replied, "I don't know. I was very upset when he said that he couldn't help me. . . . He was very honest though." The analyst asked her if she had felt a sense of triumph at his defeat. "No . . . well . . . I don't know. Can you help me?" The analyst replied that she was so self-destructive that she might try to wreck this treatment, too. "No, I won't do that again. . . . You're pretty smart, maybe I did do that." So ended the first interview.

Comments

At first glance, the analyst's early statements might appear intrusive, too challenging, and even precipitous. A brief explanation is in order. The analyst felt that Jeanette was so depressed and suicidal that it was important to make contact with her early, yet she treated him with indifference bordering on contempt. She made it clear that he was second rate and that she preferred the earlier analyst. She acknowledged that there was little contact between her and the current analyst. Her first response to him occurred when she was challenged as to why the last treatment had failed. Her reply, "I was very upset when he couldn't help me," suggested the hidden, defiant, negative transference so characteristic of these patients. The analyst felt that it was important to demonstrate to her that he was aware that she could also defeat him if she chose to and that he was not afraid of her manipulations through illness. That this attitude reached her momentarily was evident from her comment, "I won't do that again."

In addition, because she was so depressed and suicidal, it was necessary to attempt to establish a positive working alliance and relatively positive transference quickly in order to develop a libidinal tie to the analyst. This was not successful enough, however, and the patient subsequently had to be hospitalized, but the attempt was still necessary and, in the long run, was valid.

It is an error to wait with these patients for the transference and alliance slowly to develop, just as it is ill-advised to wait for the emergence of clear, obvious material prior to interpreting it. Anorexic patients may die before they talk because they are so self-destructive, so unused to revealing thoughts and feelings by speaking, and so prone to act out conflicts through symptoms. These patients usually have the experience in their lives of important people not listening to them or being sensitively attuned to their needs when they are well and speak normally. It was important, therefore, for Jeanette to feel that the analyst was listening very carefully and was attempting to understand her. These patients use their illness to get attention and to manipulate people. The more anxious others, including the analyst, become about a patient's threat of increasing illness, the greater the patient's tendency to exacerbate the illness in order to exercise control and achieve what are perceived to be necessary gratifications. The analyst wanted Jeanette to know that he understood this and understood her. Then she might feel that he could help her.

Sessions 2–4

The next three interviews continued in stormy fashion. Jeanette described feeling smothered by her mother, who she felt ran her life. The mother constantly told her what to do and how to do it. It had always been that way. She felt that her mother was a good person who cared about her, but couldn't stop running every aspect of her life. She constantly told her to eat. Jeanette stated that she had to get away from her mother and that she wanted to be hospitalized. She had called all the major hospitals in the area to inquire about being admitted. If the analyst didn't grant her wish for hospitalization, she wouldn't return. This was stated repeatedly, both as an imperious demand and as an infantile whine. Her grandmother kept telling her that she was killing her father, who had bleeding ulcers, and she felt guilty after each attack of bleeding.

During momentary intervals in her agitated state, she described brief elements in her childhood. As a teenager, she had overeaten and been thought of as fat by friends, who she felt had shunned her. When she was 13, she had weighed 114 lbs. In the next year, her weight had gone up to 150 lbs. She remembered disliking her sisters and most of her friends, who were thin. She became increasingly distressed following her comments about the anger toward her friends and sisters.

She again demanded hospitalization. In response to the analyst's attempts to discuss why she felt it was imperative, she again threatened to stop the treatment. When he pointed out her need to feel in control, and that she perceived any disagreement with her wish as a loss of control, she calmed down and said, "You understand about the control."

She spoke more about her turmoil and added that she "wanted to take the whole world in with my eating, . . . then I feel so guilty that I take 50 laxatives to get rid of it, . . . with the diarrhea and cramps." She again pointed to her scarred fingers and added that she masturbated every night in order to increase the pelvic muscle tone, which improved her control over defecation. She also exercised during the night and then took very cold showers to shock herself. In the fourth session, she reported taking only 30 laxatives instead of 50, and not inducing vomiting.

Comments

Jeanette's comment that she "wanted to take the whole world in with my eating" reflected the close relationship between eating and people. Anorexics deal with food the way they would like to deal with people: that is, they displace the control that they cannot achieve over people onto food. That this construct is accurate is evident in the frequent clinical episodes where frustration in a relationship, with the feeling of being helpless to control events, results either in sudden thoughts about consuming food or in an exacerbation of anorexic symptoms. These patients must gradually come to understand their difficulties and disappointments in relationships with people, especially family members.

The patient reverted to wanting to control the analyst by insisting on hospitalization. She wanted a different analyst, questioned this one's competency, and threatened to "fix" him by intensifying her starvation. She was momentarily receptive to the ideas that they could disagree but discuss their disagreement and that she could become annoyed without attempting to "fix" the analyst by starving or taking laxatives. This acceptance was followed by her associations to how guilty she felt over the hard time she was giving this analyst and had given to previous ones—she stated that they must be "nuts" to be willing to see people like her all day long.

When anorexic patients are permitted to manipulate and control the analyst and others in their life, the resultant guilt may be expiated by harsh primitive superego dictates for punishment via destructive acting out or increased symptom formation. On the other hand, if the manipulations are actively interfered with, the therapist may be seen as an extension of the controlling parents, and symptoms may become life threatening. Analysis of the behavior provides these patients with their opportunity to stop the behavior and the ability to deal with their feelings about it in a less regressive manner.

In Jeanette's case, the working alliance was evanescent, and her increasing agitation and suicidal threats required her hospitalization on the following day.

Hospitalization

In the hospital, Jeanette's regressed infantile behavior continued. She insisted on eating only low-calorie foods and also attempted to exercise excessively in order to ensure losing weight. She brought her tennis racquet to the hospital and was enraged that there were no facilities for exercise. She found that on the most modest diet, she would gain a pound or two and this increased her distress. She walked about the ward in a pair of shorts and attempted to wear an open blouse that completely exposed her breasts. She was preoccupied with her anorexia and was unwilling to talk about anything that did not pertain to it. She insisted on discussing her diet, her severe abdominal cramps, her constipation and laxative use, and her exercise requirements. She was demanding, swore and cursed, was unable to tolerate any frustration, and, on three or four occasions, "fired" her analyst, told him that the treatment was over, and threatened to sign out of the hospital against medical advice.

Medical management, including decisions about food intake, was provided by the internist. This provided careful control over her metabolic requirements and deflected any resentment about intake requirements (in order to minimize negativistic behavior in the treatment). Jeanette was told that she would not be forced to eat because she was not eating for reasons that the analyst hoped they would uncover. At the same time, the internist would provide her with enough caloric intake to prevent life-threatening conditions. When she was re-hospitalized, it was with the understanding that it was for psychiatric, not medical, reasons.

The internist never pressured or ordered Jeanette to eat, nor did he tell her what or how much to eat. Such authoritarian tactics are extremely inadvisable, as they cause the physician to be seen as a parental figure. Then patients' feelings of aggression, defiance, and negativism toward the parent are turned toward the physician, and they derive the same sadistic satisfaction in defying the doctor as they do in defying the parents. In addition, behaving in an authoritarian fashion prevents the analyst from analyzing patients' deep distrust and fear that any information they give the analyst will be used to dominate and control them. It is vital to obtain the complete cooperation and trust of patients to enable them to express fears and conflicts, and to tolerate and absorb the anxiety that emerges as they face their inner turmoil. If the physician or analyst does act authoritarian or controlling, it is very difficult later to disclaim any intention of dominating the patient. The analyst's role is to help patients understand themselves, not to tell them what to do.

In the hospital, the analyst attempted to get Jeanette to recognize that her preoccupation with the anorexia allowed her to avoid the thoughts and feelings that truly distressed her—that, in effect, the anorexia was a smoke screen for other upsetting problems. When she complained of weight gain, constipation, and cramps, the analyst pointed out that she could rid herself of these difficulties by talking about what really bothered her. Typically, she responded that nothing bothered her and that she had nothing to say. The analyst replied that she was not aware of what bothered her because she was constantly preoccupied with ideas about food, which interfered with the emergence of other thoughts into consciousness. If she thought more about her life, she would recognize some of her problems.

The other idea that the analyst attempted to discuss with her was the issue of control. He indicated that he thought it was a major problem of hers and that, reasons yet unknown, she felt out of control over the important events of her life. Consequently, she shifted the area of control to eating, which she could and did control. She attempted to exert tremendous control over everyone in the hospital and became terribly agitated and distressed when she could not do so. She acknowledged that she tried to make the analyst do all kinds of things and would explode with anger if he didn't.

This discussion, which took place repeatedly, had a number of consequences. It permitted Jeanette to relinquish some of her infantile omnipotent attitudes in the transference so that she was not constantly exploding in rageful frustration and was therefore more amenable to rational discussion and reflection. It opened a window toward the recognition and subsequent discussion of one of her major problems. Finally, it provided a link between her current behavior and her symptoms, which were discussed as regressed attempts to control aspects of her bodily function when she felt that she had lost control over her relationships with external objects.

At times, these discussions were fruitful. Mostly, however, these interchanges were met with blanket hostility and derision, skepticism, denial, ignorance, or a "blank mind." Occasionally, she would respond for brief periods, sitting quietly and reflecting on what was said and on some of her own thoughts. She would speak rationally for five minutes and then explode, deny everything that was said before, and indicate that it was all worthless, that there was no point in going on with this stupid, idiotic treatment, and that the analyst was "fired." She would then curl up in a ball, pull the blankets over her head, and terminate the interview. She repeatedly made requests to leave the hospital or to go to another hospital where behavior therapy would teach her how to eat. The following letter is a good illustration of her attitude.

Dear Doctor,

I am leaving this morning whether you like it or not, so you better sign me the hell out of here. I think your psychiatry is pure and utter bullshit and even if some of the points you make may be true, absolutely nothing is getting solved. Every patient here except me has been progressing but not with mere babble but with medication and electric shock—in other words, changing the brain. You can just about forget it with me; talking time is over. Don't waste my time, I won't waste yours. Sending me here was *your* mistake. I'll never forget you for it.

I am fucking starving now. I have been for many days. My weight has gone up. I am completely miserable. Now that you have destroyed me physically, as well as put me into deep depression, why don't you completely finish me off? My mind and feelings are still the same. I need control; I am dead without it. You killed me—you did your job and here I am in the city morgue at this hospital with all the nuts.

You can't understand my frustrations but you certainly can add to them; and you certainly have done so with great success. I hope you are as successful with all your patients—or should I say with all your victims.

When I get home I will go back to my same routine. At least I'll be able to eat and stay thin. Give up, and admit

defeat for you have failed me miserably. I know I will probably not survive for long because of malnutrition, but gaining weight on liquids and candy in the city morgue is no
fun either. At least at home I may be miserable within myself but there are people around that make me happy. Here
I sit on my ass like a dead body. My brain is dead and so
are my mouth, my eyes, my ears, my legs, my soul, and
anything else a human being is made of is buried here, too.

I'm sick of seeing you in your tweed suits, happy-go-
lucky as a lark running around with your "buddies" to your
"confidential" big shit psychiatric meetings, consultations,
dinners, ceremonials, or whatever you want to call them.
OK so give up. Sign me out. We'll give up together. I can't
stand seeing your face any longer. I don't trust you . . . I
think you are incompetent as far as anorexia is concerned.
I want to thank you for fucking up my life once more; for
taking away all my controls. But starting from tomorrow
my hell is over. Sign me out. Stay out of my room. Admit
your mistake; I should've been put in Columbia-Presbyte-
rian Hospital—and you damn well know it. Don't bother
coming in because I can't look at your face again. Depression is a hard problem to cope with and I don't need any
extras. Goodbye . . . maybe we will meet in another world
under different circumstances, . . . I'll put you through the
hell you are putting me through.

I'll expect 35 Ex-Lax at my door tomorrow. Don't give
me any more lines. I don't care to hear them. I won't give
up control so you had better quit now. I *hate* you. I honestly, honestly do.

Jeanette

P.S. I just stuffed my face and couldn't throw up. IF PARTS
OF THIS ARE IRRATIONAL AND REPETITIOUS, . . .
THEN SO IS LIFE!

If one looks beneath this angry letter, a certain involvement between patient and analyst seems evident. Jeanette
clearly indicated that she felt the analyst couldn't stand her
and wasn't interested in her. The analyst interpreted that
Jeanette felt this way toward him sometimes and that her
hostile, provocative behavior made her feel guilty and made
her fear that he would become disgusted with her, dislike her,
and stop treating her. He pointed out that she usually "fired"
him after a particularly violent outburst and that the "firing"
was in anticipation of his annoyance and abandonment of
her. Her statement "give up, and admit defeat" revealed the
depth of her anxiety and her fear that the analyst would not
understand either her testing of his resolve or the nature of
her deep problems. The analyst's calling her after one of these
outbursts, and discussing her behavior while indicating that
he could tolerate it and was not put off by it, was very reassuring to her.

There was a true threat in the letter, however. It centered
on the issue of control. At one point, she stated, "I want to thank
you . . . for taking away all my controls"; at another, "My mind
and feelings are still the same. I need control; I am dead without it." It was obvious that she felt threatened by the relationship with the analyst. This threat had a dual source. First, she
felt that a closer relationship with the analyst would result in
her being controlled by him as he learned more about her.
Second, he stood for her giving up control over food, which
was a substitute for her inability to control people. She felt that
she still needed it, and she experienced panic at its potential
loss. This again raises the question as to the advisability of
an analyst behaving in an authoritarian manner toward an
anorexic patient. Being controlled is one of her major fears.
For the analyst to attempt to regulate her eating is to verify
her greatest fear and to unwittingly repeat in the treatment

what the patient undoubtedly experienced as a child. Therefore, in an attempt to help the patient deal with conflict and early childhood trauma, the analyst retraumatizes the patient in the very way that she was originally damaged. This behavior neither encourages trust in the analyst nor provides the opportunity to analyze the patient's overwhelming fear of being controlled as expressed in the transference.

By the second week of hospitalization, Jeanette had put on four or five pounds on her minimal diet. Although she was still agitated and frequently exploded with yelling and screaming, she more frequently acknowledged that there was something that bothered her but that she did not know what it was, and that her preoccupation with the anorexic symptoms covered it up. In response to the analyst's comment that if she were willing to think and to talk her abdominal cramps and constipation would subside, she acknowledged that she was afraid of her thoughts, that she forgot what they talked about, and that she was not interested in those thoughts. At a point of anxiety, she said, "I want the anorexia again; it's better than the thoughts."

In a subsequent session, she began to reveal what some of the thoughts and fears were. She reported that that morning, when she had put on her slacks and found that they were tight across her abdomen, she had become panicky at the implication of abdominal weight gain and had sworn and become agitated. In response to the analyst's query as to what type of people complain about clothing that is tight across the abdomen, she launched into a discussion about pregnancy. The summer prior to the severe exacerbation of her anorexia, she and her boyfriend had worried about her getting pregnant. She remembered telling him that if she got pregnant she would not want to put on weight and would starve the child. She would also starve herself and behave like a child—she couldn't be a mother when she wanted to be a child. She had carefully kept this fantasy from her previous and current analysts.

After this revelation, it was possible to discuss how her preoccupation with her anorexic symptoms in part reflected a concern about pregnancy and mothering. Her preoccupation with weight and an enlarged abdomen, her morning nausea and vomiting, her daily weighing, and her amenorrhea were related to the conflict over pregnancy. Jeanette suddenly felt very frightened. Tears came into her eyes and she began to sob convulsively and reiterate her fear. She then admitted that there must be something very wrong with her. She asked if the analyst would really try to help her—she wanted to depend on him. Would he continue to see her and come tomorrow? If he would see her, she would do what he asked and stay in the hospital. Earlier in the same session, she had demanded to leave the hospital and terminate treatment. That night, the nurses reported that Jeanette ate her first normal meal.

The following day, she continued to improve and to eat more normally. She continued discussing her preoccupation with pregnancy. When she awakened, she looked at herself in the mirror before she got dressed and thought that the woman in her was returning as she saw that her abdomen and thighs were beginning to fill out. She returned to her panic over constipation and her frantic need to take laxatives to get the stools out. She had the thought that she had to get the baby out and realized that the "stool baby" inside was what frightened her. It became increasingly clear that the idea of swallowing something that gave her a fat abdomen and then expelling it was directly related to her anorexic rituals. She added that it really did not have to do with food at all. She noted feeling a calmness and tranquility that were in complete contrast to her previous wild behavior. She also acknowledged feeling that she could tolerate frustration much better. The analyst pointed out that Jeanette had tried to kill the woman in her both physically, by changing her appearance to that of a preadolescent child, and psychologically, by behaving like an infant with temper tantrums, no frustration tolerance, unreasonable behavior, and an unwillingness to deal realistically with her problems.

Jeanette continued to improve and was discharged after twelve days of hospitalization to continue her five-times-a-week office therapy. Prior to discharge, she spoke about being afraid to go home, afraid of getting her symptoms back. "I'm afraid to lose my mother. She used to baby me and care for me. Now I'll have to be grown up." This idea emerged during a discussion of how her illness permitted mother to infantilize her and Jeanette to accept it under the guise of being ill.

Jeanette stated that she felt better after her discussions with the analyst because what they talked about made sense and she was able to think about it, and also because the analyst made the image of being a little girl less appealing. "Fellows used to say, 'You look like a little girl,' and I'd say, 'I'm a woman,' but I didn't really feel that way. Now I'll have to be."

In light of the seriousness of Jeanette's illness and her rehospitalization ten days later for another week, a question may well arise as to whether her hospitalization was too short. However, it must be kept in mind that while the symptoms and behavior of anorexic and psychosomatic patients can seriously worsen very rapidly, they can improve just as rapidly. The total treatment is of long duration, but in the intermediate phase, temporary improvement in symptoms can occur quite rapidly. The problem is that it is not sustained because of continued conflicts, lack of solid ego strength and healthy defense, and persistent yearning for infantile gratifications. In general, short periods of hospitalization in conjunction with intensive analytic outpatient therapy may be helpful.

The interpretation of the conflict around pregnancy and mothering deserves some further elaboration. There are many clinicians who warn that active interpretative intervention in the acute phase of anorexia or psychosomatic illness is contraindicated and can result in accelerating the downhill course of the disease. My own feeling is that the intervention is not only warranted but crucial. The issue at question is not the intervention per se, but rather how the intervention is carried out. If it is carried out in the face of a persistent unanalyzed negative transference, then the patient undoubtedly will get worse. If, however, meaningful interpretations are made in consonance with a relatively positive transference, then the patient will improve. Nonanalytically trained psychiatrists and physicians are at a disadvantage in dealing with these aspects of the transference; as a consequence, their admonitions in the setting in which they find themselves do warrant prudent counsel. Jeanette's reaction to the discussion about the pregnancy conflict was one of anxiety, but it coexisted with a concomitant positive transference evidenced by her voiced dependency on the analyst, her desire that he continue to see her, and her willingness to adhere to his suggestions. In that setting, I felt that her temporary improvement was to be anticipated and that discharge from the hospital was warranted.

One additional point is worth noting. In dealing with the conflicts of anorexic patients, it is better to deal with those over aggression prior to those surrounding sexuality and to deal with the self-destructive aspects of the aggression before the destructive aspects. This sequence seems most amenable to these patients' strict, primitive, punitive superego, with its tendency for immediate self-punishment via symptom formation for imagined transgressions.

In Jeanette's case, the sexual conflict was dealt with first only because it emerged first and provided an opportunity to begin discussing some of her conflicts. The serious discussion of her fears of becoming pregnant interfered with her obsessional preoccupations with the anorexic symptoms and began to explain some of her behavior. The sudden undoing of anorexic symptomatology may be accompanied by a good deal of fear and anxiety, and a sudden dependence on the analyst. Bringing some of the unconscious determinants of the anorexia into conscious awareness permitted this patient greater understanding, a better sense of control, and a feeling of well being.

Rehospitalization

Ten days after discharge, Jeanette had to be rehospitalized for a week. In the interim period, she voiced considerable apprehension that she should have stayed in the hospital one week longer to solidify her desire to remain a grownup. On one occasion, she felt overwhelmed by upsetting thoughts and tried to rid herself of them by taking fourteen Dulcolax and developing stomach cramps, but still could not get rid of the painful thoughts. It is important to recognize that these patients withhold a great deal of relevant information. Sometimes it is necessary to ask about material that one suspects may be withheld. She described feeling depressed about her life; she didn't feel that she could behave like an adult. She stopped eating and complained that her analyst did not understand her and did not care as much since she had been discharged from the hospital. He used to come to see her at the hospital and now she had to drive for over an hour to see him at the office. She became increasingly disorganized and was rehospitalized.

The rehospitalization resulted in a second meeting with Jeanette's uncle. During the first hospitalization, he had introduced himself with the comment, "I'm Jeanette's uncle, you know, the one who pays the bills." At the second meeting, he was less tractable and demanded to know why the analyst had failed. Considerable time was spent dealing with him and helping him to understand the problems of anorexia. It was to his credit that he did not interject himself again during the entire course of the treatment.

In the hospital, Jeanette again began to behave in an infantile manner, with temper tantrums, swearing, exaggerated responses to minor frustrations, and attempts at running the hospital procedures. On one occasion, she was enraged that she might not be able to go home for the weekend to attend to some college courses. The analyst pointed out that she was furious in advance without attempting to determine whether it would be feasible for her to get a pass. When the analyst agreed to give her a pass, she left. She returned in an elated state and said that, from now on, she was going to work in treatment and that it was idiolic to have anorexia and to deprive herself of happiness. Instead of enjoying food, she was tearing her guts out. From now on, she was going to get better. The analyst asked her what had changed her attitude, and she stated that it was related to letting her go out on a pass: now that she trusted him more, she could believe what he said. He pointed out that it might also have been related to feeling that he listened to her and that she had some control over the events in her life. At the end of the session, she smiled at the analyst for the first time.

The analyst had to skip two days and discussed this with Jeanette beforehand. When he returned to the hospital on the third day, she appeared extremely negativistic. She had phoned the analyst's office and gone on at length about how she could not stand therapy any longer and hated the analyst. At the hospital, she stated that she was going back to stuffing herself and vomiting and to taking laxatives and that she never wanted to see the analyst again. In her ensuing temper tantrum, she appeared furious at the analyst and at herself for her infantile behavior. At the very end of the session, she provided the clue as to what had provoked the outburst: "You really don't care about me. I haven't seen you for two days."

When the analyst returned on the following morning, Jeanette was quiet and tractable. She voiced hopelessness, lack of interest in the treatment, and a feeling that the analyst had betrayed her, but she was no longer in a rage. The analyst indicated that he thought he understood what was upsetting her and why she had regressed. He pointed out that when he did not see her on those two days, she felt he really did not care about her and thus lost hope, felt overwhelmed, and regressed. He added that it seemed very important for her to feel that he did care and that she so easily could feel that he didn't. He pointed out that this represented an infantile ego position, namely, that he should be at her beck and call. This stance revealed an unwillingness to recognize that he could have other commitments and involvements in his life. They had discussed in advance the strong possibility of a negative reaction and regressive behavior on her part, but she had readily accepted the two-day absence and had made no objection.

The analyst pointed out that her intense abdominal cramps primarily represented tremendous feelings of hatred toward him that she felt unable and unwilling to accept fully and "swallow." In a sense, she had been attacking and destroying the analyst inside her (introjecting him) rather than attacking him directly with the full impact of her feelings of disappointment, frustration, and hatred. Jeanette calmed down, became more introspective, and was able to continue the session in a relatively attentive and positive manner. The marked change in her behavior was clearly the result of the analyst's transference interpretations, the hatred in the transference, pointing out the regressed infantile ego position, and indicating that she had introjected him and had attempted to destroy him in her somatizations. These transference interpretations are crucial in the early acute stage. While the usual analytic technique might require additional confirmatory evidence to fully validate the accuracy of the intervention, this luxury is not available in emergency situations and the analyst has to work on the basis of the apparent nature of the transference and experience with previous patients. This represents a difference in analytic technique and is applicable to the management of anorexic and psychosomatic conditions in general.

As the discussion continued, it was possible to indicate that her intense distress at feeling abandoned for two days must have reflected her childhood experience, which she was repeating, rather than remembering and understanding. The analyst added that the presence or absence of mother did mean life or death to the totally dependent infant or young child and that she seemed to be venting this early experience on him. In addition, a sister born thirteen months after Jeanette might have required a great deal of the mother's attention, since Jeanette had just commented on her feelings of intense jealousy toward another sick girl on the ward who was getting a great deal of attention from the nurses. She acknowledged feeling conflicted, wanting and demanding a great deal of attention from the nurses because she was sick, but also recognizing that asking them to infantilize her was not healthy.

The following day, Jeanette was cooperative, optimistic, and eager to work things out further. She commented that she had remained "mature" all day, had been eating regularly, and had not let herself slide back. She noted with a great deal of apprehension that after she had eaten well the night before, she had become very fearful and anxious.

It was possible to point out that she became fearful when she ate because she realized that through the reestablishment of a normal eating pattern, she would be closing off the anorexia, which discharged all kinds of tension; without it, she would begin to experience distressing thoughts and feelings. She readily agreed and admitted that she had begun to worry about all kinds of things and had been unable to understand the source of her recent apprehension. The analyst recalled that when she had gone home after her first hospitalization and had attempted to eat normally, she had become depressed and had had suicidal impulses. Since anorexia is so self-destructive—in a sense, a suicide in stages—it would not be surprising to recognize that when she closed it off, it might be replaced by other self-destructive impulses, including depression. As the discussion proceeded, she described increasing feelings of anxiety and apprehension, along with fear that she would be unable to cope with her problems. The analyst pointed out that this would be surprising since all her life she had been trained to think clearly and to use her intellectual ability incisively to resolve academic problems. It would be ironic indeed if she could perform so well academically and not use the very same abilities to resolve her personal problems. After this discussion, she described feeling more relaxed and confident.

It seemed clear that, in the beginning of treatment, Jeanette required frequent contact with the analyst because of her severe separation anxiety, tendency toward sudden and severe regressions, inability to tolerate reasonable frustration, lack of understanding of her problems and urge to avoid dealing with them, and building up of tension as her anorexic symptoms were closed off. In retrospect, it seemed that after discharge, daily telephone conversations with the analyst, in addition to treatment, might have prevented the decompensation and rehospitalization.

During the two periods of hospitalization, Jeanette frequently became enraged during sessions, swore and cursed at the analyst, and "terminated" the treatment. On those days, the analyst phoned Jeanette afterward, alluding to some difference of opinion during the past session and attempting to resolve it. Invariably she responded positively, talked things over, and thus prevented the feelings of guilt that she would otherwise have had when contemplating how shabbily she felt she had treated the analyst. For the analyst to call her in the face of such hostility certainly suggested to her that he cared and, moreover, that he could tolerate her hostile outbursts without retaliating and without becoming overwhelmed.

An obvious question is whether the analyst should have accepted the patient's statement that she felt the treatment was worthless, that she desired a different type of treatment, and that she wanted to end the therapeutic relationship. Some analysts, and perhaps some civil rights advocates, might have taken this patient's conscious requests at face value, ignoring the obvious unconscious pleas to the contrary. Without entering the field of legality and civil rights, but concentrating on the field of medicine, it becomes the obligation of analytically trained psychiatrists to follow their understanding of the patient's needs and to do whatever they deem best for the patient's welfare. This may include ignoring a patient's conscious statement when it is recognized that a deep unconscious attitude reflects the opposite position. The course of treatment seems to bear out this proposition.

Months 1–4: Dealing with
Anorexic Symptoms and Behavior

In the first three weeks following her second discharge from the hospital, Jeanette was seen daily and, following stressful sessions, she would talk to the analyst in the evening on the telephone. The frequent contact served to minimize her separation anxieties, foster an increased dependence on the treatment, interfere with the tendency for sudden regressions, and promote an increasing sense of trust in the analyst.

Jeanette continued to create crises and attempted to maintain her anorexic rituals. She masturbated twice a day so as to increase her metabolism and lose weight, and exercised after each meal even if she only had soup. Her numerous complaints about physical symptoms (e.g., cramps and gas) were repeatedly interpreted as representing her unconscious wish for the return of the anorexia and her unconscious desire to avoid facing her problems. At times, however, these attitudes were quite close to consciousness and Jeanette either acknowledged the interpretation or volunteered similar information herself. With much swearing and agitation, the symptoms gradually subsided. Physical symptomatology alternated with recurring statements that she could not eat, would never find out what was bothering her, and would never get well because the treatment did not work.

In one episode, when she felt more confident and trusting, she confided, '1 feel hungry now." Another time she noted: "When I eat three times a day now, the worries come out, but after I exercise, I can't think. I can't even read, or do homework." These statements represented clear clinical evidence of the defensive nature of her anorexic behavior: exercising, starving, or being mentally preoccupied with ideas about food served to prevent the emergence of psychic conflict. It also confirmed the necessity and validity of interpreting this behavior as defensive.

Jeanette became increasingly preoccupied with symptoms of constipation and again began to vomit repeatedly by putting her fingers down her throat. With considerable prodding, she finally recounted that her recent hospitalization had repeated a hospitalization exactly one year earlier for constipation. In very disturbed patients, the recognition and discussion of anniversary reaction behavior and symptomatology often provide enough understanding and insight to prevent an expanding decompensation (Mintz 1971). Jeanette went on to say that when she was very little she had been given enemas repeatedly and had hated them. She would be put in the tub and given an enema that would make her feel so full that she would defecate in the tub, all over herself. In the past two years, she had again begun to take enemas in the tub and to defecate all over herself. Her self-induced vomiting seemed to represent the same process from the other end. She related the constipation to conflict over the birth of her little sister and the desire to keep the "stool baby" inside. Concern over pregnancy in the relationship with her boyfriend had exacerbated the conflict.

In addition, the early traumatic experiences with the enemas seemed to play a considerable role in the development of anal fixations and character traits, later gastrointestinal symptomatology, and the quality of her object relationships. Certainly, issues of controlling and being controlled, and reversion to somatization, had some early roots in the relationship with mother and were connected to bowel functions.

Treatment sessions during the following month continued to be stormy. At one moment, Jeanette was quiet, tractable, and reflective, and was beginning to eat more normally. At the next, she was wild and depressed, voicing thoughts of suicide, quitting treatment, and hating the analyst. Dependence on the analyst increased. Fantasied rejections unearthed explosive diatribes. When she called the office at 6 P.M. and the analyst didn't call back until 9 P.M., she became furious, stopped eating, and accused him of complete indifference. "You know how important it is for me to hear from you."

For some time to come, Jeanette was extremely dependent on the analyst, and at the same time made inordinate demands on him. The full emergence of her insatiable dependency demands began to unfold. It was her unconscious awareness of this endless hunger and demandingness, and the anticipated rejection that they would invariably provoke, that had prompted her unwillingness to get involved in treatment in the first place. This kind of dependency had not been tolerated by parents or friends, and its various manifestations had been responded to by rejection. She had expected the same rejection from the analyst. Instead, her behavior had been interpreted and made more conscious, more understandable, and therefore more controllable.

One day Jeanette ate a sandwich for lunch and then had a normal dinner—her first in years. This was followed by feelings of panic and a bout of hysterical exercising. She then called the office seven times before the analyst got back to her. When he phoned she screamed that she quit, that she was fed up with the treatment, and that she would never get better. The analyst indicated that she was frightened partially because she felt that she was able to eat and that she could get better, but the sick part of her wanted to retain her infantile behavior, stay sick, ruin the treatment, continue to punish herself, vent hostility at the analyst for helping her get better, and avoid the worries that she would have to deal with once the anorexia no longer served as the repository of her conflicts. Many of these patients do regress in response to the inner awareness that they can get better, and it is very helpful to be able to point it out in order to interfere with the decompensation. Characteristically, Jeanette responded quickly, if temporarily, to these interpretations and quieted down. She acknowledged that she felt angry at the analyst for making her eat. The analyst hastened to point out that he could not make her eat and, furthermore, would not try to make her eat. If she ate it was because she thought about what was said and chose to eat. Her idea that the analyst was making her eat reflected both her suspicions that he was trying to control her the way that she felt others had, and her underlying wish of wanting to remain little, passive, and controlled. These comments were not made in shotgun fashion, but were presented in sequence during the ensuing discussion around her attitudes about the analyst.

Many of the negative and infantile elements in Jeanette's behavior have been discussed. The positive ones also deserve comment, as they reflect the split in her ego functioning. She had a keen intellect, and her excellent grades and academic accomplishment were not solely a result of endless drudgery. She was a leader academically and athletically. Her ability to analyze and to think incisively once she chose to do so contributed to her considerable progress in the treatment.

Jeanette began to wonder why she was eating and acting in so crazy a fashion. These reflections revealed the beginnings of an observing ego and transient moments of some insight, in contrast to earlier behavior characterized by little awareness of the pathological nature of her behavior. She acknowledged that often she felt crazy and became panicky. The analyst stated that he understood why she felt that her behavior was crazy and could recognize that anyone who behaved that way might well wonder if he or she were crazy, but that she could change her behavior whenever she chose to. It was clear that the patient was fearful that she was psychotic.

When a patient verges on panic and potential decompensation, it is important to communicate that the analyst does not share the patient's fears of her impulses and behavior, nor her fears for her sanity. If the analyst becomes anxious about the patient, then the patient feels that they both have lost control of the situation. This can result in a rapid decompensation, with a more flagrant psychosis. Discussing Jeanette's fears of craziness directly, and indicating that she could control it when she chose to, was immensely reassuring. An attitude of attentive concern is different from feeling as panicky as the patient. It can also be extremely helpful to discuss such crises with other experienced colleagues to retain one's perspective and to widen one's grasp of the situation.

The analyst asked Jeanette how she could develop any worthwhile image of herself or get involved with a man who she thought was worthwhile if she thought she was crazy or feared that he would think she was. Such confrontations resulted in increasingly realistic behavior, further serious discussion, and further involvement in the therapeutic relationship. They did not prevent subsequent regressions, however, and progress was made by climbing up the mountain, slipping back, and climbing up again, each time a little further.

In a number of sessions, as the denial of illness was further eroded, Jeanette became increasingly fearful of dying from the anorexia. In one session, she became so panicky that she insisted on an immediate appointment with the internist. To the analyst's suggestion that, if she were afraid of dying, eating might be more beneficial than an instant appointment with the internist, she blew up, stated that the analyst did not care about her, and walked out of the office saying that she never wanted to see him again. In a further discussion in the waiting room, the analyst pointed out that she was furious because she felt that he was interfering with her desire to stay sick and because she felt that she could not control him by phoning the internist from his office.

In another session, after Jeanette described having eaten normally, she kept looking over at the analyst for signs of approval. He indicated that if he approved of her eating, then she might also feel that she could frustrate him by not eating and try to control him in that fashion. If she ate and got well, it was for her benefit. She admitted that she had manipulated her previous analyst by not eating. Approving or disapproving of patients' eating habits or other behavior encourages them to displace superego attitudes onto the analyst. A comparable situation is the teenager who lets the parents worry about him and blithely goes about dangerous activities without conscious reflection on the consequences. Conversely, when Jeanette's analyst left the responsibility with her, she was able to express her own worry about her health, as opposed to making the analyst worry: "It's me that I hurt when I don't eat. I'm scared to death that I might die."

At the same time, however, part of her did wish to eat to please the analyst, obtain his approval, and be close to him. In this sense, the wish to eat could be viewed as being controlled by the analyst. In addition, the desire to be close became frightening to the degree that it was associated with a loss of identity, a feeling of being fused with the analyst, and a feeling of death.

In the next few weeks, Jeanette continued to eat more regularly and to put on weight. She reported a reversal of a previously described pattern. For the longest time she had stated that when she did not eat, she felt well, and that eating resulted in gas, stomach pains, constipation, and general discomfort. Now she noted for the first time that when she did not eat, she felt ill and experienced stomach pains that were relieved by eating. At times now, eating made her feel better. She was surprised to recognize that when she did not eat, she had trouble thinking and speaking clearly, and that this tended to subside after eating. After not eating dinner one evening, ostensibly because she was working and did not have time, she had the nagging thought that she really should have eaten, that she actually felt hungry, and that the analyst would be disappointed in her for not keeping up her half of the treatment bargain.

The reemergence of her repressed hunger sensations, her awareness that the starving clouded her thinking, her guilt and discomfort about not eating, and her feeling that something was wrong with her emaciated condition were the reverse of her previous attitudes.

She needed to talk to the analyst every day—only what he said seemed to make sense to her. Even if her friends said the same things, they would be meaningless to her. She trusted the analyst. She was extremely attached to and dependent on the treatment, saw herself as helpless, and viewed the analyst as omnipotent. Within this framework, she was able to eat, to listen to the therapist, and to counter the strong regressive pull toward illness and infantile gratifications. Primitive superego guilt and punishment were in part ameliorated through the incorporation of what was perceived to be the analyst's superego, and reality testing was enhanced by identifying with his ego functioning. The potential for sudden severe regression remained, particularly in the face of perceived disappointment in the overvalued analyst, and in the continued presence of primitive aspects of ego functioning. Ultimately, it would be vital to analyze this infantile omnipotent view of the parent-analyst but at the moment the intense relationship could be utilized to counter the regression.

Jeanette reported an infantile relationship with a girl-friend who controlled her and bossed her about. Jeanette felt helpless to cope with her. She felt that the girlfriend took advantage of her, disappointed her, and made her feel weak and inadequate, but she could do nothing. The relationship with the girlfriend repeated the relationship with the mother, as is characteristic of anorexics' peer relationships in adolescence. When she got upset with this girlfriend, she wanted to starve, but found that she was unable to do so. She then tried to get rid of the distress by "exercising like a maniac and crying hysterically, but it didn't work and it was my best way." The anorexic syndrome, initiated when she could not control an external object, was no longer effective; the conscious awareness of her conflict interfered with the previously utilized repression. Jeanette further reported how weak and unassertive she felt when it came to realistically asserting her rights. All she could do was to yell helplessly and scream in a rage like an infant. Unable to repress the conflict, and feeling helpless about resolving it, she released the full fury of her rage in the self-destructive impulse to kill herself, instead of the hated girlfriend-mother. This sequence is not atypical for anorexics or psychosomatic patients: inner awareness of the emerging depression when the aggression is no longer bound by the self-destructive psychosomatic symptoms occasionally prompts patients to develop an exacerbation of symptoms rather than to face the emerging depression.

COUNTERTRANSFERENCE

During the crucial weeks after Jeanette's second discharge from the hospital, when she was not eating properly and was constantly threatening to terminate treatment and attempting to coerce and manipulate the analyst, a subtle countertransference took place. The analyst became aware that he was calling Jeanette in the evening, instead of waiting for her to call his service. His initial rationalization that it was simpler and more expedient faded rapidly as he thought more about his concern for her welfare during the bouts of sudden irrational behavior without the protection of the hospital and his fear that she would die. This concern was unconsciously perceived by Jeanette, in whom it provoked both anxiety and an inner impulse to utilize this manipulative behavior increasingly to control the analyst.

With the more realistic change in the analyst's attitude toward Jeanette and her illness, she responded almost immediately and commented that he seemed to be behaving differently and did not seem to care as much about her.

Although analysts can he aware of their concern about a life-threatening illness, and their relative impotence in dealing with it by talking, this introspection has to be maintained constantly; otherwise, it will be eroded gradually by the patient's repeated, hostile, manipulative assaults as she relives in the transference the attempts to control the object through illness.

SYMPTOM IMPROVEMENT, EXACERBATION, AND SUBSTITUTION

In the next few weeks, Jeanette continued to improve. Her weight rose from 78 lbs. to 87 lbs. On occasion, after weighing herself, she would call up in a panic. She was frightened that she would continue to gain weight, especially after episodes of gorging when she feared that she could not stop. Bursts of exercise would follow. The impulses to starve were often dealt with by calling the analyst on the phone.

There were repeated episodes where she complained of gas, constipation, and/or nausea, usually citing the symptoms as a pretext for eating less and reverting to diet foods or starving. The symptoms were discussed as manifestations of her alleged need to remain ill, of her impulses to damage the treatment or frustrate the analyst, and of her fear of growing up. After these interpretations, her diet became more normal, exercising decreased, and symptoms lessened.

Her strong infantile attachment to her mother was dramatically illustrated in one session. The analyst stated that he would be unable to see her for the Saturday appointment because he had to be out of town. In the same session, the issue of driving to the office regularly with her mother was raised, and the analyst wondered about her not feeling comfortable driving by herself. She responded that perhaps it was time and that she would consider it. Minimal anxiety was acknowledged, and she continued discussing other subjects that bothered her.

That afternoon she called up hysterical. When the analyst returned her call that evening, she was enraged, stating that the treatment was worthless and that she was returning to her anorexia. She vowed not to eat and regressed to behaving in an infantile, hostile fashion with considerable crudeness and cursing. She appeared completely distraught and overwhelmed. She complained of stomach cramps, urges to vomit, an inability to deal with schoolwork, and depression. The analyst suggested that her turmoil might be related to his skipping the Saturday session. She calmed down and agreed to come in for the next session, where she explored further the possibility that her distress was related to the Saturday session, but was not sure. Later in the hour, the analyst suggested that she might still have some thoughts about considering driving to the session without her mother. She thought for a while and then added, "That's what it really is. When you asked me to consider coming up to the office by myself, I knew that I wasn't ready, but I was afraid to tell you." The analyst pointed out that it wasn't just that she was afraid to tell him, but rather, that if she spoke about it in the session, she would not worry about it as much and therefore would not have the excuse to hurt herself by wrecking things in the afternoon. He added that, even though she felt that she trusted him more, her attachment to her mother was still very strong. She must have felt that he was in a sense asking her to renounce the close relationship with her mother, which was available while she was ill, and at the same time advising her that he would not be able to see her on Saturday. She was reluctant to give up her mother and substitute a relationship with an inconstant analyst who would not always be there. This triggered the regression, the anger with the analyst, and the reinvolvement with the mother.

After three months in treatment, Jeanette seemed to be doing quite well. She had gained fifteen lbs. and her weight was 93 lbs. One Sunday the mother phoned, stating that the patient was wild, swearing, and threatening to kill herself. On the phone Jeanette stated that she had had a fight with her boyfriend a few days before that she had not told the analyst about. In the next session she was hostile, suspicious, and accused him of laughing at her plight. After considerable discussion, which included dealing with her negative transference, she calmed down. She spoke about how upset she felt in the relationship with her boyfriend. He was pushing her sexually, at a time when she felt that he did not care that much about her. She felt taken advantage of, used, and worthless. Although at times, and in a superficial way, she could be hostile and insulting, she was really fearful of behaving in an appropriately assertive fashion. She was unable to deal with the boyfriend and felt devastated by what she perceived as his rejection of her. When he did not call back, she felt depressed and suicidal. She spoke of impulses to starve and was reminded of an earlier boyfriend. She described how a two-year relationship with him had gradually deteriorated in her eyes. Both families were happy, however, and pushed the relationship. Her increasing unhappiness and insecurity were masked by a smiling face. She began to lose weight, recalling the thought that the boyfriend's family wouldn't want a sick girl. With a start, she realized that the previous Sunday was the one-year anniversary of her engagement to him. This recognition produced a dramatic improvement. She reported feeling better, hungry, more in control. "This time I want to eat, and get better. I couldn't understand why I was getting sick. Usually when I get sick, I want to, but this time, I did not want to."

That afternoon a hysterical phone call again revealed her fear that she was going crazy and her desire to eat, vomit, and take laxatives. She screamed that she had to "shit Tom out . . . get rid of him." The analyst suggested that she deal with and get rid of unpleasant memories by thinking about them without having to eliminate them through defecation.

In the next few sessions she elaborated on the relationship with Tom. She described how he constantly fought with her, insulted her, and argued with her friends, who hated him. He was indifferent to her anxieties during sexual relations and was not concerned if he hurt her. She remembered the first time, when it had hurt so badly that she fainted and awakened bleeding and with difficulty breathing.

It seemed evident that the anniversary of her engagement to Tom contributed an the argument with her current boyfriend in the need to relive that traumatic experience, including those aspects of the anorexic syndrome. The understanding of the anniversary nature of the behavior provided her with considerable relief.

Jeanette's eating continued to improve while her frenetic exercising tended to subside. By the end of the fourth month, she had become more interested in what was going on in the world about her. She weighed about 91 lbs. and continued to fear becoming too fat, which in her mind meant weighing 110 lbs. Her associations led to the idea that when she looked heavier, she would lose her waiflike appearance and, along with it, all the automatic attention and solicitude that she usually commanded merely by walking into a room. She would be like everyone else, would be judged equally and without special favor, and would be required to perform in mature fashion.

One night she developed a severe asthmatic attack and was rushed to the local hospital, where she was given oxygen and adrenaline. She recalled that she used to have asthmatic attacks as a child of 5, but that this was the first attack since childhood. She then looked at the analyst and accused him of causing the attack. She stated that she was no longer able to starve or exercise excessively. She couldn't stop putting on weight.

It was clear that she felt that the asthmatic attack was a substitute for the aborted anorexia. Clinical experiences with other patients reveal similar circumstances in which one psychosomatic symptom is replaced by another or alternates with phobias, depression, or self-destructive acting out. While the overt illness shifts, the underlying conflicts, defenses, identifications, and type of object relationships remain relatively unchanged.

REGRESSIVE BEHAVIOR

As the weeks progressed, starving, laxatives, and vomiting became less of a problem. They were replaced by bouts of sudden regressive behavior in which Jeanette felt that she was acting crazy. She would look at her filling-out body in the mirror, especially at what she felt was her protuberant abdomen. She reported a fantasy that there was a "baby-fetus-devil inside with horns and a tail" and that she had to get it out by vomiting or through diarrhea, but couldn't. Instead, she behaved like a devil, yelling, screaming, and throwing objects about the house in an infantile, petulant manner; the fantasy was reflected in acting out instead of in anorexic symptoma-

tology. The behavior clarified the underlying conflict and revealed the necessity for it to be analyzed after the anorexic symptomatology had subsided. She added that now she couldn't control anything. She couldn't get people to do what she wanted,
and she no longer was able to control her own body with the
starving, vomiting, laxatives, and exercises. She felt that she
had to act crazy to control the analyst and to get others to pay
attention to her, be concerned about her, and gratify her need
to be babied.

The agitated behavior persisted over the next few days,
with threats to injure herself or commit suicide. The analyst
indicated that if she really felt that she could not control herself, she would have to be rehospitalized. She countered by
berating him and accusing him of making her sick and no
longer caring about her. At the same time, she indicated how
desperately she wanted his attention. That night she phoned
and realized that it was the anniversary of the onset of her
anorexia.

After this anniversary, she calmed down somewhat, although there continued to be hysterical outbursts and temper
tantrums. One such episode was followed by a bout of bulimia,
which she compared to her previous wild, destructive behavior. She noted that both outbursts were similar: in one, she
destroyed external objects with her hands and threw them
about; in the other, she ripped foods apart and rapidly chewed
them up and destroyed them internally. The bulimia was like
a wave of destruction in which she ate five times as fast as
normal and ate to destroy, not to enjoy.

Later Therapy: Dealing with Underlying Conflicts

By the fifth month, Jeanette had put on twenty lbs. and weighed
98 lbs. She complained that now that she appeared healthy,

all kinds of demands were being made of her. When she had been sick, very little had been required of her. She knew that she had a report to finish and now the professor would tolerate no excuses. She also felt that her boyfriend was demanding more of her and no longer treated her like a helpless little waif. She could see that her worry about her weight really masked her anxiety about how she would be able to function in the world. In subsequent sessions, she stated that she would no longer go on eating binges now that she recognized that they represented outbursts of anger. She also added that she understood how much the anorexia stood for difficulties in her relations with people. She spoke again of how her previous waiflike appearance had elicited compassion from everyone without her having to say a word.

Now, however, things were different. She acknowledged how fearful she was of men. They looked at her differently now; they no longer babied her, but made sexual remarks to her instead. She realized that, as she filled out, she looked more womanly and more sexually desirable. She understood why she used to get so frightened whenever she began to put on weight and round out. She also noted that now women saw her as more of a rival and were increasingly jealous of, and competitive with, her. She even described a different attitude about sexuality. When she had been emaciated, she would have sex quickly "and get it over with." When she looked more womanly, she behaved an a more sensual manner and did not rush about so frenetically.

In the middle of the fifth month, Jeanette further clarified the nature of her object relationships, as symbolized by her attitude toward food.

I had such an urge to eat those cookies. They taste so good and I haven't had them in two years. If I eat one, I can't stop

and I'll eat the whole box. Then I'll have to vomit, so I can't
eat any. The urge is so great, just like the urge to swallow
up gratifications in relating to people . . . but I can't control
the people that way. I have better control over my relations
with people now because they won't let me behave that way
toward them. With food I can do what I want.

It was pointed out that that was what she used to try to do with
the analyst to get intense infantile gratifications from him. She
would call him and if he didn't reply instantly, she would explode, express hatred toward him, and feel that he hated her.
Jeanette had set up an all-or-nothing relationship with food,
which was rooted in her fear of losing control; furthermore,
she had made the situation as frustrating and self-destructive
as possible in order to discharge her aggression.

In the next few sessions, she revealed more about her self-
image, her low self-esteem, and the nature of her object relationships. After revealing the fear that she would never get well,
she spoke about fantasies of wanting to stay sick. In order to be
successful, she felt that she would have to trust the analyst, which
would mean "turning myself over to you. . . . that you will control me and make me better." One can see why these patients
are fearful of a close, trusting relationship. Their needs to regress to obtain infantile gratifications and to repeat the earlier
relationship with the parents require them to renounce their
independent functioning and be passively controlled and domi-
nated. This conflict is what they consciously fight and unconsciously accede to during the anorexia nervosa and its sequelae.

Jeanette's improvement continued. Her frustration tolerance increased. She developed and maintained a more realistic view of her life situation. She repeatedly spoke about the
past anorexia as crazy and said that she would never do it again.
She became more aware of bodily sensations of hunger when

she did not eat. She also noted a sense of fatigue in the late evening, which in the past had been denied.

When she experienced abdominal pains, discussion with the analyst about how they stood for an interference with her newly acquired enjoyment in eating decreased the pains markedly. She spoke about her past use of a hot-water bottle, which had burned her abdomen, and indicated that the gas inside her abdomen reminded her of a baby who suffered when greedily swallowing air with milk; the voracious swallowing of the milk was similar to her insatiable bingeing attacks.

Subsequent to meeting a young law student through one of her friends, she was unsure about accepting a second date with him because of her insecure, unstable relationships with people. She toyed with impulses to regress and to get sick. She described how difficult it was to behave appropriately. "I run from being mature. I can't think and act mature for more than three hours; then I act 'waify and infantile'."

Nine months into treatment, she reported that, on the previous evening, both of her sisters had ganged up on her and been very critical of her. She felt devastated and overwhelmed by their remarks. She felt panicky and had the thought, "I'll tell them I'm sick and I'm going into the hospital, and then they will stop." She then experienced abdominal pains. Later that evening, she cried alone in her room and then noted that the abdominal pains had subsided. She went downstairs and, in a reasonably realistic fashion, attempted to rebut her sisters' criticisms.

SEPARATION FROM THE ANALYST

A crisis developed toward the end of the first year as the analyst's summer vacation approached. Jeanette was still quite dependent, but spent most of the sessions attempting to deal with her problems. Separation anxiety was a major problem and had been discussed many, many times as it related to her social relationships, her parents, and her therapeutic contacts. In one session, she arrived very upset and agitated. Her boyfriend had not called her and had deserted her, just as the analyst planned to do. She could not get better, the treatment was worthless, and she wanted to die. Self-destructive discharge of aggressive impulses alternated with feelings of depression and preoccupations with anorexic symptoms. Although she acknowledged understanding what was happening, she felt helpless to cope with it. She stated that she didn't know what she would do if the abdominal pains persisted all during the month that the analyst was away. He pointed out that her symptoms and attitude reflected anger at the analyst for leaving on vacation and attempts to coerce him to stay or to make him feel guilty about going. The behavior persisted for almost two weeks, with repeated interpretations of her repressed resentment toward the analyst as the reason for the symptoms and depression. Finally, she responded. One week before the vacation, she walked in enraged. She screamed, "Murderer! I'm going on vacation when you get back. You can put a flower on my grave," and then walked out.

In the next session, she was more quiet and tractable, and was able to converse without screaming. She acknowledged her feelings of hatred for the analyst, but stated that she felt less violent than in the previous session. It was helpful to her that the analyst had tolerated her aggressive assault without attacking her or collapsing. She could express aggression without terrible consequences and could identify with the analyst as the recipient of it without having to fall apart. She volunteered that she had been bingeing and taking diet pills for the past four days, but that she now planned to eat regularly. She phoned the analyst each of the four weeks of his vacation. Upon his return, she described episodes of anorexic symptoms, but no major regression.

THE "THINKING STAGE"

Jeanette reported that she was out of the "anorexic stage" and into the "thinking stage." She described two earlier pathological stages: the "waif stage" and the "cute stage." When she had been really sick and emaciated, she bad been treated like a helpless waif. Everything had been done for her. "They just had to look at me, and I got sympathy." In the cute stage, she had been treated like a child. She had been encouraged, cajoled, helped along, not taken seriously, and dealt with like a little girl. "If I go over 90 lbs., they don't think cute anymore, and I have to use my personality. I have to think, and speak, and behave like an adult, not just stand there and wait to be catered to."

She commented further on her mother's continuing infantilization, which she did not mind most of the time. The mother kept offering her special foods, as if to keep the preoccupation with eating alive and active in Jeanette's thinking and behavior. She insisted on washing her clothing, combing her hair, and straightening up her room. On occasion, Jeanette resented it and told her mother that she was an adult and that the mother should stop infantilizing her. While the mother did not openly object to Jeanette's giving up the anorexia and attempting to achieve independence, she continued to foster the dependency by always wanting to be with her, by being her confidante, and by attempting to erode her relationship with the analyst.

Early in the treatment, the parents had been advised to consult a female analyst in order to help them cope with their daughter's behavior and facilitate her recovery. The mother had been going on a relatively regular basis. At this point, she refused to continue, complaining that she really would like to see a male consultant instead. It seemed evident that the mother's increasing resistance was in great part due to feeling threatened by what she perceived as the impending loss of the symbiotic tie to her daughter.

Jeanette felt equally threatened. She reported that both sisters had suddenly begun to eat and vomit secretly. This distressed her greatly, because she felt that the sisters were bidding for the mother's attention and would get closer to the mother at Jeanette's expense. She felt that her position was being eroded at a time when she still could not tolerate separating from the mother herself, let alone being separated from her by the rival sisters.

Jeanette also felt that her social life was in turmoil. If she put on weight, she would no longer be seen as cute and appealing. Left to what she felt was her deficient, inept self, she saw little chance of winning friends and influencing people. Clearly, she would be ignored, neglected, and abandoned. The treatment was responsible. Discussing these issues in great detail brought her out of regressed states, and she could view herself more realistically for brief periods. Depression and thoughts of suicide alternated with insightful periods. She implied that there would no longer be external sources of gratification and attempted to evoke it from the analyst through her helplessness and vulnerability.

At a dance, she was complimented as a beautiful woman and thought to herself, "I'm fragile . . . can't be touched . . . a statue to be admired . . . not to get close to . . . and not to be treated like a woman." The sessions interfered with her impulses to become anorexic again. Although she agreed with the general tenor of the discussions with the analyst, she developed abdominal cramps. Again, they were interpreted as anger at the interpretations and as impulses to stay sick. It was pointed out that her fear of getting close was related to impulses to be cared for, along with fears that others would find out what an infantile, immature person she was. She couldn't be accepted as an adult and feel comfortable and secure in that role, but when she gave in to her yearning to act like a child, she feared discovery of her immature thoughts and behavior. These issues were continually worked through in the transference, as well as in social contacts.

These discussions seemed to effect changes in her ego structure. She went to a restaurant with her family and got food poisoning. "I was up all night with fever, cramps, and diarrhea. I was afraid that I might die. It was just the way I felt when I took the Ex-Lax. How could I ever have done it?" She vomited from antibiotics. "It felt terrible and I was so ashamed that I vomited." She began to deal more with separation and feelings of loneliness, and found that she was more willing to tolerate and think about her sadness. She often wanted to become anorexic, but wouldn't give in to the impulse, and instead thought about why she felt that way. She no longer regressed as often, as suddenly, or as deeply. She would speak with longing about the days when she was a skinny little waif. A new, transient phobia emerged in which she was afraid to go anywhere alone. She volunteered that now that she no longer acted like a little girl, she had thoughts of being one instead. "When I was thin, I could be attached to my mother. Thin is little. Now that I'm normal, I can't."

She reported a series of dreams about dying. In one, she thought of dying, but the analyst told her, "You can't die, you have to get better." She couldn't get sick and couldn't put her finger down her throat. This dream showed the impact of the therapeutic relationship—the internalization of the analyst's attitudes and the replacement of Jeanette's own primitive superego dictates.

Another series of repetitive dreams indicated Jeanette's desire to join the mother in heaven through death; she was unable to do so and fell back to earth crying. These dreams of reunion through death were reminiscent of the ambivalence expressed in her hospital letter, where she stated that she might meet the analyst in another world.

In the second year of her treatment, Jeanette got a job in an executive training program at a department store. She reported having conflicting thoughts and feelings about her relations with her co-workers and supervisors, and about being in the business world. Initially, she felt that the other salespeople were only interested in themselves and were either indifferent to, or critical of, her. Unable to control their attitudes toward her, she contemplated returning to starving or eating strange foods so that people would pay attention to her. Momentarily, she gave in to these impulses. With increasing frequency, she thought about it instead and concluded that to give in was infantile and crazy. She resisted and contemplated the thought that she was getting better. "I'm resigned to getting better. Treatment makes you grow up." Feelings of extreme loneliness and helplessness burst on her and were followed by bouts of crying and anguish. She had no one to be with and yet felt that she could not return to anorexia. She reflected on how infantile some of her demands were and resolved to deal with them. She felt better, but still was lonely.

She realized that occasionally her supervisors criticized her unfairly; at such times, she reacted with anorexic preoccupation, despondency, or anger.

I felt so terrible about the criticism, but I didn't binge. I was very anxious and tense and I kept pacing, but I kept thinking and I controlled myself. I had fantasies of wanting to beat them up, of wanting to kick the chair as if it were they, like the fantasy isn't enough. . . . When I was young, I used to be angry at everyone who teased me and called me fat. I had all these angry fantasies of revenge, and I used to yell at everyone. Then I lost so many friends that I stopped doing it, and instead I got anorexic and I began to hurt myself.

During periods of frustration, Jeanette reported binges of stealing that seemed to replace the binges of eating. When she became upset at work, she took sweaters and other items of clothing from the store instead of becoming preoccupied with anorexic fantasies or bingeing. These impulsive episodes were invariably followed by strong feelings of guilt that encompassed not only the stealing but also eating, enjoyable vacations she had taken, and generally everything that had previously given her pleasure.

Thus, it is possible to recognize a shift in the pathological impulsive behavior, but not in the underlying orality, dependency, and voracious, greedy impulses for immediate infantile gratification. The frustration of her insatiable needs that previously had been displaced onto food and anorexic preoccupations was now displaced onto impulsive stealing. This sequence was recognized and discussed by Jeanette. After a few weeks, the stealing stopped.

She continued to use her hot-water bottle on her abdomen, ostensibly to ease the abdominal pains. Its underlying meaning slowly emerged. That she viewed the hot-water bottle as a transitional object became increasingly clear when she attempted to cope with feelings of loneliness without resorting to further episodes of bingeing or starving. When she felt very lonely at night, she took the hot-water bottle to bed with her. The hot-water bottle clearly substituted for relations with people, especially when she felt anxious about a relationship and fearful that she couldn't control it: "I don't know whether I should go out with John or eat, vomit, and go to bed with my hot-water bottle." This dilemma occurred a number of times. When she felt comfortable with her boyfriend, she did not need the hot-water bottle. She volunteered that the hot-water bottle was like a security blanket. She remembered that, in the past whenever she had a fight with her mother, she would run to use it.

Three months before the end of her treatment, she reported that she had given up the hot-water bottle. At that time, the relationship with her boyfriend had progressed very well. They had been going together for eight months and were planning to marry when he graduated from law school. Her weight was 110 lbs. and her anorexic symptoms were gone. She was still anxious in her relationships with people, but acknowledged that she preferred dealing with the problems directly rather than starving. Over the last year, she had confronted her parents more directly and with increasing success about their attempts to control her activities. Following her marriage, her husband accepted a position with a distant law firm and Jeanette was forced to terminate treatment. While the analyst felt that it would have been advisable for the treatment to continue longer, he also felt that she could work out her remaining problems on her own.

ADDENDUM

While the analyst did not hear from Jeanette following her termination, he did hear from her father and uncle every Christmas for the next five years. They reported that she was continuing to do well. With the birth of her first child, the analyst received a box of cigars from the uncle.

REFERENCE

Mintz, I. L. (1971). The anniversary reaction: a response to the unconscious sense of time. *Journal of the American Psychoanalytic Association* 19:720–734.

18

Use of the Telephone in the Treatment of Attachment Disorders

KARL HEINZ BRISCH

INTRODUCTION

The use of the telephone in psychotherapy has been neglected for a long time or considered as not applicable because the classic setting preferred face-to-face interaction between the patient and the psychotherapist. Only in recent years have more articles appeared that described the use of the telephone, the video-telephone, and the internet as media for psychotherapeutic intervention (Haas and Kobos 1996, Kaplan 1997, Rasore et al. 1997). The telephone has actually been successfully used in counseling for a long time, especially in crisis intervention (Maassen et al. 1999). The telephone has also been used in situations when psychotherapeutic settings are not accessible, or when the disorder is such that face-to-face interaction is frightening to the patient (Connell et al. 1997).

Attachment theory can be a useful background for understanding why the use of the telephone can be effective in establishing a therapeutic bond.

THE SECURE BASE CONCEPT
OF PSYCHOTHERAPY

Attachment theory (Bowlby 1969, 1973, 1980) claims that during the first year of life the infant develops an attachment relationship to his primary caregiver, which in most cases is the child's mother, but it can be any other person who interacts in a sensitive way to the child's signals. Normally there is a hierarchy along which the child addresses himself to attachment figures, with the primary one preferred in circumstances of anxiety. If that person is not available the child will address the second or third attachment figure along the hierarchy.

If the quality of attachment is secure, the child will show separation protest in the form of screaming, crying, clinging, or tracking the attachment person when this figure leaves the room. The child will search for proximity to the attachment figure and calm down once it is reestablished. In contrast, children with an insecure attachment will show no overt sign of stress on separation and will be reluctant to show their need for closeness when the caregiver comes back to pick them up. Insecure ambivalent anxious attachment behavior of the infant is characterized by such extreme forms of protest and clinging that sometimes the child literally does not allow the mother to walk away.

In the case of a secure attachment pattern the child feels safe and protected by the caregiver and can rely on the attachment figure to provide help and shelter when the infant experiences anxiety or threat, either from the outer world through physical harm or from the inner world through illness or overwhelming fantasies and anxieties.

When the child experiences security she will be able to start to explore the outer world of play objects as well as the inner world of feelings, affects, memories, and fantasies. When the attachment system is aroused because of anxiety, exploration will lessen or even come to a standstill (Ainsworth 1979, Ainsworth et al. 1969, 1978). In the first year of life the child develops an "inner working model" (IWM) of attachment as a result of numerous similar interactions with the caregiver. The IWM makes the behavior of the attachment figure predictable for the child. The caregiver will interact in a similar way whenever the attachment system is activated (Bretherton 1998). In adults the IWM is transformed into a representation of attachment. While the IWM of the child is still open for change because of secure or insecure attachment experiences with other caregivers, it becomes more stable in adulthood. Bowlby claimed that the attachment representation is never completely fixed but can be altered from secure to insecure or vice versa when the person experiences new attachment-related relationship interactions (Ainsworth 1989). This can be experienced in psychotherapy, which creates a new world of experiences when the patient comes with the expectation that his old patterns of interacting will be repeated and then undergoes a new and sometimes frightening experience if the therapist relates to him in an unexpected manner (Belsky and Nezworsky 1988, Goldberg et al. 1995).

Parental sensitivity in the interaction with the child plays an important but not exclusive part in establishing a secure base of attachment feeling that corresponds to an equivalent IWM on the representational level. Those parents or caregivers who recognize the child's signals, interpret them correctly, and react promptly and adequately will facilitate the development of a secure attachment quality (Ainsworth 1979). A similar effect is the parental capacity to verbalize with empathy the child's internal affective experience as felt by the mother or father. Those caregivers who use that form of congruent internal state talking with the child will promote a more secure base development in the relationship with their infant (Meins 1997a, b). Later on, the caregiver will help the child to use his own developing language to verbalize the internal experiences to a co-construction of a narrative and the production of his own narratives and symbolic play (Meins 1997c). Only those experiences from the interactional world that were verbalized can lead to a conscious feeling for a structured and reliable inner working model.

If the vocal rhythm matching between mother and infant is absolutely congruent, then an insecure attachment quality of the child often develops. If there are little mismatches in the vocal rhythm matching then the development of a secure attachment is more probable. And if there is gross distortion in the interaction of vocal exchange in the pre-language interaction between infant and caregiver, then insecure and even disorganized patterns of attachment can develop (Beebe and Lachmann 1994). Complete synchronicity of verbal interaction doesn't seem to be the best way for the establishment of a secure attachment. In fact, little mismatches that happen every day and that are the normal average pattern of interaction seem to be important for the development of secure attachment, whereas too much synchronic interaction can lead to a pattern of overalertness and close monitoring of the mother with irritation, ambivalence, and insecurity, expressed by clinging to the attachment figure.

ATTACHMENT DISORDERS

Attachment theory considers the secure and the insecure forms of attachment quality as adaptive patterns in the child–caregiver relationship. Insecure avoidant and insecure ambivalent patterns of attachment are not yet considered to be a form of psychopathology.

A special typology of attachment patterns on a descriptive base was developed which is more detailed than those diagnostic categories found in the *ICD* or *DSM* manuals. Seven forms of attachment disorders can be distinguished (Brisch 1999):

1. *Attachment disorder with non-attached behavior*: These patients show no signs of attachment behavior when in danger, although one would expect their attachment systems to become activated in frightening situations. They don't show a preference for a particular adult caregiver or attachment figure. They do not have a preferred attachment relationship because they did not have appropriate experiences to facilitate its development. There were multiple changes in primary caregivers, sometimes with extreme emotional deprivation.

2. *Attachment disorder with indiscriminate attachment behavior*: These patients show social promiscuity in the form of indiscriminate friendliness with strangers, whom they address with closeness without any preference. They seek comfort and nurturance from completely unfamiliar adults. Some of them run away repeatedly in the presence of the attachment figure without checking back and enter situations with risk for physical harm. They develop risk-taking behavior with accident-proneness in order to provoke caretaking behavior from the attachment figure.

3. *Attachment disorder with hypervigilant attachment behavior*: These patients are extremely frightened, even in proximity to their attachment figure, and show vig-

orous resistance to any form of separation, even of short duration. They are overwhelmed by severe distress after separation. To prevent separation they are excessively clinging and seek extreme closeness to their attachment figure. Joyful play and exploration are hindered or given up because of continuous clinging to the attachment figure.

4. *Attachment disorder with inhibited attachment behavior*: These patients show a compulsive compliance to the wishes of their attachment figure. There is no resistance or hesitation to comply with directives from the attachment figure. One can observe that they feel frightened of their attachment figure and show reluctance to play in her presence. It is astonishing that in the absence of their attachment figure they develop more open interest in play and exploration than in her presence. Some of those patients had experienced maltreatment, excessive punitiveness, and physical abuse when they were non-compliant.

5. *Attachment disorder with aggressive behavior*: These patients show a preference for a primary attachment figure and exhibit separation anxiety quite clearly, but they seek comfort and address themselves to their attachment figure with aggressive behavior. The expression of anger with verbal or physical aggression is a constitutional feature of their attachment relationship, and is far more intensive than age-appropriate non-compliance.

6. *Attachment disorder with role reversal attachment behavior*: These patients develop a pervasive pattern of inversion in their attachment relationship. They assume the role of the attachment figure toward their primary caregiver. They seek extreme proximity, with anxious

controlling and over-nurturing of the attachment figure. On separation they protest greatly because they are
terrified of losing their attachment figure who has either threatened to leave or to separate by suicide.

7. *Attachment disorder with psychosomatic symptoms*:
These patients can show either a failure to thrive as a
reaction to extreme emotional deprivation, or symptoms of excessive crying, sleep disturbances, eating
disorders or atopic eczema. Those symptoms can arise
after the caregiver's post-partum depression or post-
partum psychosis or after inconsistent emotional availability of the attachment figure, as might be experienced with drug or alcohol abuse. Anorexia nervosa
and bulimia are psychosomatic disorders stemming
from disturbances in the attachment relationship. In
those patients the psychosomatic symptom serves
as a relationship regulator mainly toward the primary
attachment figure and partially in the whole family
system.

ATTACHMENT ORIENTED PSYCHOTHERAPY

As a clinician Bowlby developed his theory from his clinical
experiences and he even tried to apply it to the psychotherapeutic treatment of patients (Bowlby 1988, Brisch 1999,
Holmes 1993, 1994, 1996). For a long time attachment theory
and research prospered in the field of developmental psychology and even in psychopathology, but didn't resonate in the
psychotherapeutic community. In the psychoanalytic societies especially, attachment theory was rejected as being too
behaviorally oriented (Bowlby 1977, 1979). Only in the last
few years has the psychotherapeutic community become in-

terested in the application of attachment theory for the treatment of patients.

Bowlby had already proposed guidelines for an attachment-oriented approach in psychotherapy. He claimed that the psychotherapist should establish a therapeutic bonding with the patient as a form of a secure attachment base. When patients approach a psychotherapist they feel anxious, overwhelmed by affects, forced into enactment, and in need for help as their psychological structure and adjustment threaten to disintegrate or break down. This is the typical situation when the attachment system is aroused to a maximum and patients seek a secure base in addressing themselves to a psychotherapist. It then depends on the sensitive reaction of the therapist to establish that secure base feeling in the form of reliable therapeutic bonding for the patient. When that bonding is accomplished, primary feelings of anxiety and fear of disintegration lessen appreciably and the patient gains psychic space for exploring his inner world of feelings, memories, and affects as well as his outer world of reality in interaction with relevant relationship figures (Bowlby 1988).

From psychotherapy research it is well known that therapeutic bonding is a powerful predictor for the successive outcome of the psychotherapeutic process (Orlinsky et al. 1994). When this bonding has been successfully established the psychotherapeutic work with distorted and disintegrated object and subject representations can begin within the process of transference and countertransference.

Real loss, separation, or any other traumatic experience, such as sexual abuse, maltreatment, torture, accidents, or overwhelming catastrophes of nature will be focused on especially and evaluated as to their real influence on psychic development. In contrast to classic psychoanalytic theory reality, not only fantasies, is emphasized in its importance as a threat to the attachment system. Fantasies and reality play an interdependent role in the process of trauma and restoration. That is why the real experience of the therapist as a sensitive attachment figure the patient can rely on is so important.

THE ATTACHMENT ORIENTED USE OF THE TELEPHONE

Most patients ask for an appointment by telephone. If their expectation is fulfilled, and they find a sensitive psychotherapist at the other end of the phone who serves as a secure base by responding adequately to the patient's signals then the patient will bond rapidly to this therapist. It is remarkable that after the first telephone contact many patients feel considerable relief of their symptoms. If a patient whose attachment system is aroused by his anxiety finds only an answering machine at the other end of the phone he might feel desperate, disappointed, and never leave a message. This can be true especially for those patients with clinging attachment disorders or those who call in an emergency situation, such as suicidal ideation. For those patients the telephone seems to be an emergency hotline that offers or suggests rapid help, but if that expectation is not answered immediately they will feel even worse than before (Haas et al. 1996). Their hope and longing to find a secure base on the other end of the phone was once more disappointed. Once again, they feel rejected or find an inaccessible or unreliable object when asking for help, just like the basic experience for their development of an insecure attachment. The telephone, which could be so useful as an easily accessible device to make contact and establish a bonding process, ends up causing an even more desperate psychological situation than before.

For patients with a clinging attachment disorder, phobias and anxiety disorders, posttraumatic stress disorders, or those with emergency calls it can be helpful in the beginning of the treatment or in situations of separation (holiday breaks, illness of the therapist) to stay in a bonding contact by telephone aside from the scheduled sessions. The therapist can bridge phases of separation by telephone appointments. While emergency calls cannot be planned or structured, it is advisable to schedule telephone contacts for patients with clinging attachment disturbances. This means that during periods of separation the therapist is more often available as a secure base than normally, but a clear schedule and an agreement about the duration of the phone call helps those patients build their psychic structure with these additional contacts with their therapist. In a later phase of the therapy it might be sufficient for the patient to leave a message on the answering machine, which becomes more or less a kind of transitional object. The transitional object typically symbolizes the therapist in separation phases; it is always available for the patient. By his own choice he can make use of the answering machine or not; he regulates closeness and distance (Winnicott 1951).

In terms of attachment theory, the patient gradually develops a more stable and secure attachment inner working model so that the actual presence or voice contact by phone is no longer necessary. Listening to the voice of the therapist on the answering machine is sufficient to calm the patient down when his anxiety is overwhelming and he needs a contact with his secure therapeutic attachment figure, in addition to the contact during the therapeutic sessions.

VIGNETTE:
CLINGING ATTACHMENT DISORDER

After the death of her mother a female patient developed a severe disorder with panic attacks. She could not stay at home alone any longer and had to be accompanied by her husband or a girlfriend to come to the outpatient department. She clung to her husband and in his absence she clung to everybody in the house without finding relief from her anxiety. During the acute panic attacks she was convinced that she was going to die suddenly, as her mother had done. She came to see me three times a week but thought that it was not enough. She also had difficulties leaving me at the end of sessions. Eventually she felt safe at home with somebody in her presence and she felt secure without panic attacks when she was in session. But traveling from far away merely for one hour to come to see me was a distance she could not cope with on her own.

She phoned me several times a day, especially before a situation of separation, such as when her husband went shopping and left her alone at home for a half hour to an hour. When she phoned me before such a shopping separation she felt secure enough to stand the absence of her husband, knowing that in a case of panic she could call him on the mobile phone as easily as she could call me.

When her symptoms got better she tried to drive to therapy on her own and used her mobile phone to call me halfway to my office in order to organize her anxieties within the framework of our relationship. I had become a secure attachment figure for her. Later on it was sufficient to have the mobile phone with her and to know that she could phone me in a possible case of emergency.

This example shows that the phone, and especially the mobile phone, can be helpful to establish and maintain contact with the therapeutic attachment figure and to diminish anxieties while relying on the available secure base of the therapy. Once the inner working model and the attachment representation have changed from insecure to more secure, the phone is no longer needed or becomes a transitional object. For many patients it is reassuring enough to have the therapist's phone number in their purse and to know that they can call him when they need him. Most of these patients never phone. However, those with severe attachment disorders need real contact by telephone, even more so when they live far from the therapist.

For those patients with a highly avoidant attachment representation, with a non-attached attachment disorder, or with an aggressive attachment disorder the telephone is an opportunity to remain in contact with a therapist over a long period of ambivalence without breaking off therapy. Normally, we would expect patients to come to our office, or to the outpatient department, or to scheduled appointments during inpatient treatment. While patients with clinging attachment disorders can't get enough appointments, those with non-attached attachment disorders avoid direct contact with the therapist. Although they long for a secure attachment figure and transfer all their hope onto the new therapist, they are afraid of the therapist at the same time. Most of these patients had traumatizing experiences with close caregiving figures during their infant development. Such experiences cause them to have a highly ambivalent or even extremely avoidant attitude toward attachment figures altogether as they fear that their relationship with their new attachment figure in the person of the therapist can become as frightening and traumatizing as have been their caregivers.

Patients with aggressive attachment disorders establish attachment relationships through verbal or nonverbal aggression. They fear that they can destroy their growing attachment base with their psychotherapist, and so they oscillate between closeness in the form of aggressive interactions with the therapist and separation and a threat to break off therapy, or else they provoke the therapist in order to get thrown out or the therapist breaks off the therapy to protect himself. For these patients the telephone is a modality that allows them to stay in contact from a distance that is so secure that they no longer fear they will attack their therapist. Verbal attacks on the phone are far less damaging and better controlled than is direct interaction when the destructive affects of those patients can become overwhelming. This is especially the case when they come close to their therapist and start to feel a kind of secure base attachment. To start treatment and to keep them in therapy using approaches that allow the use of the phone as a medium for separation while continuing contact at a greater distance is very helpful. Sometimes these patients can't even tolerate eye-to-eye contact or sit together with a therapist in the same room for any appreciable length of time. Sometimes it is a relief for them to be aware that they can't destroy the answering machine by verbal aggression. In later phases of the therapeutic process the answering machine becomes a kind of a transitional object as well, not only for soothing but mainly for containing aggressive projections.

In later phases of therapy it is important to take the messages from the answering machine and to integrate and address them during the session. Then the contents of the phone message can be worked through like a fantasy or a dream. Because the phone message is already externalized it is not as frightening as it was before it was transmitted to the machine.

VIGNETTE

A male patient who came to see me because of a narcissistic breakdown with depressive and suicidal symptomatology used to have many long conversations with friends on the phone nearly every evening and sometimes during the day. As some of these were overseas calls he spent an enormous amount of his salary to pay for them.

Because he was suicidal I wanted to see him several times a week, but after two weeks he refused to come so frequently and said that he wanted to decide how often he wanted to see me. For him "a session once in a while"—maybe one or two monthly appointments—seemed exactly right for him. It was not too frightening because there would not be too rapid a therapeutic closeness. In former days I would have insisted that he had to come several times a week, especially because of his suicidal ideation and his depressive symptoms. But taking into account the fact that his way of staying in contact was to have long phone calls but not meet face-to-face I agreed with a very uncertain feeling, not knowing if he could address to me in case of decompensation as our therapeutic bonding was at the very beginning. He seemed to be pleased that he could control our relationship and phoned me at irregular times for a short call "just to say hello" because he didn't want to disturb me. He never left a message on the answering machine. His calls gave him a very clear picture of where and when I was available to speak with him. This knowledge seemed to establish our relationship although the contents of our talks often had nothing to do with psychotherapy or even with everyday gossip or small talk. His calls lasted about one or two minutes.

Eventually he came on a more regular basis to see me twice a week in the middle phase of the therapy. He decided to sit up, especially when negative affects of hatred and disappointment came up because he felt like he might get blown away like in a hurricane. He used eye contact with me to contain those feelings during sessions and used to call me, sometimes immediately after the session, to pour out all his feelings on the answering machine. Later on, he allowed me to talk about his messages, to integrate those affects into his treatment, and to share those split-off feelings in our relationship. Thus he used the phone to establish a therapeutic relationship against the background of a very narcissistic personality disorder with extreme avoidant attachment behavior.

Some of these patients use telephone counseling services without ever coming to an appointment. They can become anonymous clients for years, with enough distance in the relationship to the counselor who is securely available by phone.

Parents with attachment disorders with psychosomatic symptoms can have highly insecure attachment representations or inner working models. Sometimes these get transferred in the form of projections onto an infant and are reenacted in the caregiver–infant interaction. Excessive crying of the infant, sleeping disorders, eating disorders, and relationship-attachment disorders can develop in the first few months of life. Often these disturbances in caregiver–infant interaction present as an emergency case when the capacity of the parents to contain their mainly negative and aggressive affects toward their infant has broken down. The pediatrician sends them to see a psychotherapist when he can no longer contain his negative countertransference.

VIGNETTE

The mother of a six-week-old infant called me feeling "at the edge" because her infant could not fall asleep. In the meantime she and her husband were exhausted. Both were walking around with the baby during the day and especially during the nights, which were even worse. Her pediatrician had called me and asked me to see this family as soon as possible because he was afraid of child maltreatment as the tension in the family system seemed ready to explode at any moment. I saw the mother with her infant, and later the father too, in the evening of the same day. Both parents seemed exhausted, depressed, and full of tension and worry about how to handle the next night when they had to put their baby to bed.

In the adult attachment interview I learned that the mother had had two traumatizing episodes of separation from her own mother because she had to be hospitalized for an operation at age 4 and after discharge she had to go to live with her grandmother because her mother had just given birth to the next sibling. She could remember how she felt an awful burning sensation in her stomach when she was separated from her mother. She reported feeling the same sensation when she puts her infant to bed and walks out of the room. When her daughter doesn't fall asleep immediately she can't remain outside the room because this terrible burning sensation in her body forces her to walk back into the room and get the infant out of bed. This is the beginning of the daily routine of walking around with the screaming baby in her arms. As I worked with the mother she began to understand the reactivation of her early separation trauma in the situations when she had to separate from her infant.

When the mother and I discussed who could give her enough security herself so that she could stand the separation from her infant she asked me if she could phone me before she was about to put her child to bed. I agreed and she phoned me in the morning, the afternoon, and the evening each time she prepared the baby for sleep. Talking on the phone about her separation anxiety helped her to relax and to understand that her feelings belonged to her history and that her feelings in the actual situation with her baby, who was ready to fall asleep, became reactivated from her history. A few times the baby fell asleep in her arms while she was on the phone talking with me.

The acutely stressful situation relaxed during the day but not at night. She needed her husband to get up with her at night and to help her to leave the baby's bedroom. During the day, this mother felt a secure base while talking to me on the phone and at night her husband reassured her that she and her infant would survive the separation.

CONCLUSION

The use of the telephone can be quite helpful to establish and to maintain a relationship, especially when severe disorders in the development of attachment are involved in the psychopathology. These attachment disorders are reenacted in the psychotherapeutic process. The phone opens up a transitional space and can serve as a transitional object to maintain the attachment relationship between patient and therapist, especially with patients with a very avoidant or very clinging enmeshed pattern of attachment disorder. In phases of a very affect-laden negative transference the phone gives the patient the ability to stay in contact with the therapist and to be distant at the same time. Telephoning eventually helps the patient become more confident about talking more openly about aggressive affects in direct contact with the therapist in sessions.

More creativity is needed in the use of modern techniques of communication such as telephones, the internet, and e-mail in the psychotherapeutic process. As therapists, we need to be open-minded while reflecting on what the unconscious message is that gets transmitted or reenacted in the process of transference and countertransference, whatever medium is used in our time.

REFERENCES

Ainsworth, M. (1979). Attachment as related to mother–infant interaction. In *Advances in the Study of Behavior*, ed. J. B. Rosenblatt, pp. 1–51. New York: Academic Press.

—— (1989). Attachments beyond infancy. *American Psychologist* 44:709–716.

Ainsworth, M., Blehar, M. C., Waters, E., and Wall, S. (1978). *Patterns of Attachment: A Psychological Study of the Strange Situation*. Hillsdale, NJ: Lawrence Erlbaum.

Ainsworth, M., Salter, D., and Witting, B. (1969). Attachment and the exploratory behavior of one-year-olds in a strange situation. In *Determinants of Infant Behavior*, ed. B. M. Foss, pp. 113–136. New York: Basic Books.

Beebe, B., and Lachmann, F. M. (1994). Representation and internalization in infancy: three principles of salience. *Psychoanalytic Psychology* 11:127–165.

Belsky, J., and Nezworsky, T., eds. (1988). *Clinical Implications of Attachment*. Hillsdale, NJ: Lawrence Erlbaum.

Bowlby, J. (1969). *Attachment and Loss. Vol. 1: Attachment*, 2nd ed. New York: Basic Books.

―――― (1973). *Attachment and Loss. Vol. 2: Separation, Anxiety and Anger*. New York: Basic Books.

―――― (1977). The making and breaking of affectional bonds: etiology and psychopathology in the light of attachment theory. *British Journal of Psychiatry* 130:201–210.

―――― (1979). Psychoanalysis as art and science. *International Review of Psycho-Analysis* 6:3–14.

―――― (1980). *Attachment and Loss. Vol. 3: Loss, Sadness and Depression*. London: Hogarth.

―――― (1988). *A Secure Base: Clinical Implications of Attachment Theory*. London: Routledge.

Bretherton, I. (1998). *The development of internal working models of attachment*. Paper presented at the Development, Structure, and Functioning of Internal Working Models Conference, Regensburg, July.

Brisch, K. H. (1999). *Bindungsstörungen—Von der Bindungtheorie zur Therapie*. Stuttgart: Klett-Cotta.

Connell, S., Sanders, M. R., and Markie-Dadds, C. (1997). Self-directed behavioral family intervention for parents of oppositional children in rural and remote areas. *Behavior Modification* 21:379–408.

Goldberg, S., Muir, R., and Kerr, J., eds. (1995). *Attachment Theory: Social, Developmental, and Clinical Perspectives*. Hillsdale, NJ: Analytic Press.

Haas, J. G., and Kobos, J. C. (1996). Psychotherapy by telephone: risks and benefits for psychologists and consumers. *Professional Psychology* 27:154–160.

Holmes, J. (1993). Attachment theory: a biological basis

for psychotherapy. *British Journal of Psychiatry* 163:430–438.

——— (1994). The clinical implications of attachment theory. *British Journal of Psychotherapy* 11:62–76.

——— (1996). *Attachment, Intimacy, Autonomy.* Northvale, NJ: Jason Aronson.

Kaplan, E. H. (1997). Telepsychotherapy: psychotherapy by telephone, videotelephone, and computer videoconferencing. *Journal of Psychotherapy Practice and Research* 6: 227–237.

Maassen, M., Groll, T., and Timmerbring, H., eds. (1999). *Mensch versteht sich nich von selbst. Telefonseelsorge zwischen Kommunikationstechnik und Therapie. (Psychotherapeutic counseling via hotline services, impact of modern communication technology, client characteristics and main features of the counseling process).* Münster: Kommunikationsoekologie.

Meins, E., ed. (1997a). Is security of attachment related to the infant's style of language acquisition? In *Security of Attachment and the Social Development of Cognition*, pp. 57–74. East Sussex, England: Psychology Press.

——— (1997b). Security of attachment and the understanding of other minds. In *Security of Attachment and the Social Development of Cognition*, pp. 111–128. East Sussex, England: Psychology Press.

——— (1997c). Symbolic play and security: A meeting of minds? In *Security of Attachment and the Social Development of Cognition*, pp. 75–92. East Sussex, England: Psychology Press.

Orlinsky, D. E., Grawe, K., and Parks, B. K. (1994). Process and outcome in psychotherapy—noch einmal. In *Handbook of Psychotherapy and Behavior Change*, 4th ed., ed.

A. E. Bergin and S. L. Garfield, pp. 270–376. New York: Wiley.

Rasore, E., Menichini, U., Moscato, F., and Luise, L. (1997). L'uso del telefono nella relazione terapeutica (The use of the telephone in the therapeutic relationship). *Neurologia Psychiatria Scienze Umane* 17:953–971.

Winnicott, D. W. (1951). Transitional objects and transitional phenomena. In *Collected Papers: Through Paediatrics to Psychoanalysis.* New York: Basic Books.

19

Use of the Telephone in Psychotherapy of the Medically Ill

HINDI T. MERMELSTEIN[*†]

*J*ust three years after Alexander Graham Bell's invention of the telephone, a report of a physician's use of the instrument to diagnose a child's cough and to reassure the child's grandmother appeared in 1879 in the *Lancet*. Since then, the telephone has become the major means of rapid access and communication between patients and physicians. It is estimated that the number of telemedicine consultations has quadrupled in the last ten years, and in primary practice today 15–20 percent of patient contact time is via the telephone. In the mental health field, telecommunications systems have been central to the development of crisis hot lines, consultations, and teaching and treatment programs to remote areas and underserved populations (Hilty et al. 1999, Knopke et al. 1979, Perlins et al. 1999, Wittson and Benschoter 1972, Zaylor 1999).

*I want to thank Dr. Jimmie Holland. She has served as my mentor and has helped shape my professional career. In addition, maybe most significantly, she has taught me to expand my therapeutic horizons in my work with the medically ill.

†An earlier version of this chapter appeared in *Psychosomatics* in 1992.

Despite the wide use of the telecommunications system in health care, there are relatively few reports of its use in psychotherapy. Saul (1951) described several cases in which the distance and separation provided by the telephone decreased the patients' fear of intimacy. Similarly, Aronson (1996) wrote about an individual who found it too anxiety provoking to express herself in the office setting but was able to interact with the psychotherapist via the telephone. Other reports of psychotherapy by telephone describe clinical situations in which either therapist or patient was absent for prolonged periods of time or, in some cases, made a permanent move to another city (Lincoln 1988, Robertiello 1972, Rosenbaum 1974). A survey of fifty psychiatrists in 1993 found that over 75 percent followed at least some patients by long-distance telephone. Yet, the events that prompted the departure from standard face-to-face therapy were exceptions to the rule, often unexpected, and initially perceived by both patient and therapist as an experiment in treatment ((Mermelstein et al. 1991).

Patients with medical illness require frequent contact with their doctors and often with mental health professionals as well. This is particularly true of individuals suffering from significant or life-threatening illnesses such as cancer. In my work as a consultation liaison psychiatrist I often evaluate and treat patients who are unable to come to the outpatient office on a regular basis because of their physical condition, because of distance, or because of psychiatric distress, which makes travel or the intimacy of face-to-face contact intolerable. For these patients, the telephone is the sole avenue for psychological counseling; likewise, it is a major therapeutic tool in working with such patients. In this chapter, I will present and discuss four cases of telephone therapy with individuals suffering from a medical illness, highlighting some of the issues that arise while using this means of conducting psychotherapy.

CASE 1

Mrs. G., a 51-year-old woman with advanced endometrial cancer was referred to psychiatry for the evaluation and treatment of anxiety about her illness. In the hospital, she complained of feeling a loss of control over her body and her life. Her husband added that she cried frequently, slept poorly, and seemed to have lost her enthusiasm for most things. On psychiatric examination, she met criteria for an adjustment disorder with depressed mood. A trial of medication and a brief course of supportive therapy were undertaken to help her deal with the poor prognosis of her disease.

Mrs. G. lived a day's drive from the hospital and returned on a monthly basis for chemotherapy. Several referrals were made to therapists closer to home but the patient never followed through on them. At the same time, she called frequently to ask for advice about her increasing feelings of depression and anxiety. During almost every call, she reminded me of how soon she would be readmitted to the hospital and of how eager she was to see me. It became clear that she was not going to transfer her psychiatric care to a local doctor. She saw me as part of the medical team that was caring for her. This added to the development of trust in our relationship. By urging her to switch therapists, I realized that I was doing her a disservice. Her illness had already destabilized her life and she needed the sense of security that continuity of medical care could provide. At the same time, she needed psychotherapeutic intervention more frequently than once a month during her brief hospital stays. I had had some limited experience with telephone therapy in the past and agreed to try telephone sessions during the weeks she remained at home. These appointments were planned with the same structure as face-to-face sessions and with a regular fee schedule. Other telephone contacts, such as urgent situations, rescheduling, and medication questions were on an as-needed basis and were done without extra fee, just as in standard therapy.

We continued treatment with this arrangement of telephone sessions once or twice a week for over six-months. When possible, the patient initiated the appointment by calling, just as if she was coming to the office. The average length of the calls was approximately thirty minutes. In our early sessions, the themes were her feelings of guilt for being sick and her dread at the loss of control that the disease caused. She mourned the loss of her future and her unfulfilled dreams. For example, when she was first diagnosed her daughter had just been accepted to college but it was unlikely that Mrs. G. would live until her graduation, which she did not. The patient had to face leaving her teenage son "unsettled." She worried that her children would not complete the plan for their lives without her to guide them.

As she neared the terminal phase of her illness, the thrust of the telephone sessions was even more on her progressively weakened state and her difficulty in dealing with her need for care. Through the positive transference that was established early in our relationship, she accepted my reassurance that it was okay to be sick and slowly give up her responsibilities. She needed frequent reassurance that it was all right to become more dependent upon her husband and others. These issues could be dealt with over the telephone.

Less easy was the assessment of her depression as her medical condition deteriorated. Without visual cues, it was hard to evaluate her general physical state and thus its contribution to her psychological state. When her voice sounded weak or when she wanted to end sessions early, I found it hard to decide whether this was due to emotional upset, pain, weakness, or fatigue. Was she still attending to her dress? If not, was she too sick, too regressed, or too depressed to do so? On several occasions, I spoke to her husband briefly to fill in the information gaps I could not get from the telephone appointments with the patient.

At our last face-to-face visit, I was shocked by her appearance. She had aged greatly, become cachectic, and looked almost moribund. As a counterphobic reaction to her increasing physical debilitation, she needed to maintain a visual facade of wellness. At that visit, she wore an excessive amount of rouge and other makeup, which gave her face a clown-like appearance. It was a surprise to see these changes because neither Mrs. G. nor her husband had mentioned them during the previous three weeks of telephone contact. One month before her death, she entered a hospital hospice program near her home. Mrs. G. chose to transfer all her care to the hospice team but asked if she could contact me if she needed additional help and support. Though I did not speak to the patient after that, her husband called from time to time for support over the four weeks until her death.

Even with its limitations, over the course of Mrs. G's therapy I became more comfortable with my decision to conduct most of it by telephone. Through our sessions I was able to offer this patient the psychosocial support and continuity of care she needed through the last phases of her illness.

CASE 2

Ms. R., a 24-year-old woman recently diagnosed with Hodgkin's disease, was referred to psychiatry because of poor compliance with recommended oncology treatment. At our first meeting, she complained of panic-like anxiety when she learned that there was a mass on her chest x-ray, "my perfection is my protection, my armor has been removed" and her worry that being near sick people would confirm that she too was ill. Intellectually she knew she had a potentially life-threatening but curable condition. However, the force of her fear of being vulnerable overshadowed her judgment and threatened to compromise her health. Through intensive psychotherapeutic support, medication, and appointment scheduling very early in the morning before the clinics opened and visiting hours began, Ms. R. was able to complete the full course of radiation therapy and begin a chemotherapy regimen.

She tolerated the treatment physically well enough to continue her usual work schedule until her hair began to fall out in chemotherapy-induced alopecia. Her panic returned and her compliance slipped. "Now not only do I know my weakness but the entire world can see it." She stopped all outside social activities, including coming to my office, and became virtually homebound. I agreed to continue psychotherapy by telephone with the hope that she could and would resume her medical treatment. Our sessions were scheduled for the same day as the oncology and treatment room visits to allow her the choice of face-to-face versus telephone contact. Midway through a course of short-term psychotherapy, which focused on her terror of feeling defenseless, she resumed chemotherapy. Gradually, she started to leave her house and attend social functions, always accompanied by a family member. Eventually she began to stop by my office to "say hello" but continued to request that the psychotherapy sessions be conducted by telephone. It was as if she needed me to function as her liaison to the world and still stay protected by maintaining the illusion of a non-vulnerable, physically healthy woman. Approximately one year after the initial evaluation, she returned to face-to-face visits, took off her wig in my office, and survived.

Ms. R.'s disease remains in full remission. She has resumed her career and we continue to work together in psychotherapy on her long-standing poor integration of her sense of self. Psychotherapy by telephone provided Ms. R. with a means to express her distress in a protected setting where the pretense of physical intactness could continue. I worried that by allowing and somewhat encouraging this agoraphobic-like behavior I was enabling her regression. Furthermore, by indirectly supporting her facade of health, I was sharing in the creation of an environment where denial and avoidance reigned rather than reality. However, Ms. R.'s adherence to the medical treatment was critical to her cure and the noncompliance put her at risk of dying from her disease. In the face of this urgent situation, I felt that a therapeutic connection that she would tolerate, even if not ideal, was indicated. I believe that the treatment course we chose was the only one Ms. R. could have worked with at the time. To this date, whenever she feels vulnerable in her professional or personal life, she has flashbacks to her alopetic self and uses emergency sessions by telephone to quell her fear.

CASE 3

Mrs. B., a 39-year-old woman with breast cancer, was referred for psychiatric evaluation at the time of her second relapse. At the initial interview, she was extremely distressed, which was appropriate to the seriousness of her medical condition. However, upon further questioning, it became clear that she had never adjusted to her illness over its five-year duration. In addition, she had signs and symptoms of a chronic depressed state, which probably predated her illness.

I agreed to see her for ongoing evaluation and supportive

treatment during her chemotherapy. At first her anxiety continued unabated, and she developed conditioned nausea and vomiting before her treatment. Any reminders of the chemotherapy could provoke these anticipatory symptoms. For example, she could no longer go out with a friend whose perfume reminded her of the smell of one of the chemotherapy drugs and nauseated her. As she began to lose her hair, she became more socially isolated and depressed. A treatment plan incorporating brief therapy and cognitive techniques, progressive relaxation, and medication helped lessen her psychiatric distress and allowed her to again enjoy her usual activities and interests.

As part of the treatment of her disease, however, she was sent to Houston for a bone marrow transplant. Though I referred her to a psychiatrist in the area who specialized in the psychological care of medically ill patients, she asked if she could continue her sessions by telephone instead of having to see a new psychiatrist in a city that was already foreign to her. In this case, it was more difficult to schedule regular sessions because of her hospitalization. We tried to speak once a week over the three months she was there. The length of the sessions varied because of her poor physical state. The major theme of our sessions was the change in her body image and her fear of being engulfed by the tubes and medication bottles that surrounded her. The goals of treatment were to support her throughout the difficult here-and-now-situation of the transplant procedure and to help her remain connected to her pre-illness self and pre-transplant world. Finally, I hoped to maintain the therapeutic relationship so that after discharge from the hospital we could continue our work together, particularly since there were many issues that remained unresolved when she left for Texas.

Once she returned to New York, she was eager to resume face-to-face contact. She told me that the telephone calls helped her feel that I cared for her no matter how sick she was or how her appearance had changed. However, because she could not see me, she had begun to feel a loss of contextual reality during our telephone sessions. At one point, she had trouble remembering what I looked like and began visualizing me as older and similar in appearance to a dear friend of hers. The long-distance treatment was difficult. I was unfamiliar with the layout of the hospital or the laminar flow rooms in which she was isolated for over two months. This added to my sense of physical and emotional distance from Mrs. B. and to concerns about how helpful I could be to this patient who was undergoing a life-threatening treatment. Concerns about how much to charge for the telephone sessions reflected my doubts about my therapeutic efficacy. Countertransference issues dealt with my fears of death and professional inadequacy. Still, the patient and I agreed that maintaining telephone contact during the period that she was away was beneficial. In fact, since her return, she continues in psychotherapy, her physical health remains good, and she is looking forward to remaining disease-free and to being a cancer survivor.

CASE 4

Mr. M., a 73-year-old man with a ten-year history of Parkinson's disease sought psychiatric help for increasing feelings of sadness. He complained that as his illness progressed he had become less mobile, and since the death of his wife, a year before the psychiatric evaluation, his social life had shrunk. Furthermore, he noted that in recent months the newspaper, his political activism, and even his grandchildren were more irritating than enjoyable. Psychotherapy had helped Mr. M. deal with the illness when it was first diagnosed and he hoped that it could help him now. On psychiatric examination, he was an alert man whose dysphoric mood and irritability were evident throughout the interview. There was no evidence for psychotic thinking or cognitive deficit or any change in his medical condition to explain his worsening depression. I thought psychotherapy that focused on his progressive illness, the isolation it caused, and the loss of his life partner would be beneficial. At Mr. M.'s request I agreed to treat him by telephone alternating with face-to-face sessions. The treatment continued for approximately two years until he moved into an assisted living facility near his daughter in another state.

In this case, there were other options for support via the visiting nurse service or agencies that served the homebound elderly in Mr. M.'s community. However, I felt that by enrolling him in the regular clinic setting, while making the necessary allowances for his disability, I was presenting to Mr. M. a model for adjustment to his progressive illness. The inclusion of telephone sessions lessened his need to ask a neighbor to drive him, which would otherwise add to his feelings of helplessness, and gave him a forum to discuss his fear of dependency. Finally, the absence of visual cues on the telephone allowed Mr. M. to imagine us as contemporaries, while during office sessions I was more likely to represent his daughter than his wife. This enhanced transferential shift was helpful in his mastery of his disability and in his working through of his grief.

DISCUSSION

These vignettes of psychotherapy with the medically ill demonstrate the use of telephone sessions as an important part of psychotherapeutic treatment. Some aspects of telephone work should be highlighted since they are relevant to this mode of psychotherapy with medically ill patients.

Psychotherapists spend a considerable amount of time on the telephone in a range of contacts with patients. Although all contact with patients (or even with others about the patient) is part of the therapeutic relationship, psychotherapy by telephone in these cases was structured just like regular psychotherapy sessions, with the difference that they were conducted over the telephone. In this mode of psychotherapeutic communication, the same therapeutic processes occurred as in standard treatment. Rosenbaum (1977) described nineteen years of continued treatment of a woman by very brief phone calls (often five minutes or less in duration) and letters. He emphasized the patient–therapist bond that grew. In the cases presented here, the content of the material discussed in telephone sessions of usual length was as important as the bond between patient and therapist. For example, the first patient's view of her therapist as an authority figure empowered the therapist to help the patient understand that it was all right to be sick. It also permitted the therapist to bolster the patient's failing ego as increasing physical debility narrowed her activities. The older man was able to borrow my youth and mobility to ward off the assaults on his self-esteem, secondary to the illness and the aging process.

Because there are no visual cues in telephone contact, the transferential representation of the therapist may be vividly apparent in the patient's visual image of the person on the other end of the telephone. The woman suffering from breast cancer who visualized her therapist's face as that of her dear long-time friend exemplifies this. In a case reported by Aronson (1996) the ready availability of the telephone and answering machine fostered the illusion of an ever-present caregiver and thereby created an environment in which the seeds of a real dyadic relationship could germinate. In a case reported by Shepard (1987), all contact during the first six months was by telephone. When patient and therapist finally met, the patient was upset to see that the therapist was the same age as the patient's daughter, whom she described as self-centered and uncaring, and not an older person like herself, as she had imagined. The patient's intense disturbance at the reality she saw probably contributed to her inability to meet face-to-face again for the remainder of the treatment. Williams and Douds (1974) noted that if patients can make of the counselor what they will, they may also be able to make of the counselor what they need.

For the individual who is unable to come into the therapist's office for physical or psychological reasons, treatment by telephone is an important and effective therapeutic tool. This may be especially true for people such as cancer patients, who are homebound because of physical disability. These individuals often feel isolated; the telephone contact helps to maintain their sense of connectedness to others, and it decreases their fears of abandonment. These effects, as well as the accessibility and immediacy of telephone communication, may be particularly helpful in the period immediately following discharge from the hospital (Catanzaro 1971, Holland and Rowland 1979, Lester 1974, Rothchild 1999). Patients are excited about going home, but are often also anxious about leaving the protection of the hospital. They are frightened about the return of disease, the loss of the readily available monitoring of the staff, and the responsibilities to be met at home. Follow-up telephone sessions reassure patients and diminish their distress, just as they do with adolescents away at school or at other trial separation periods, (Tolchin 1987). Similarly, telephone support programs during arduous or complicated treatment regimens, such as high-dose chemotherapy, have improved patients' quality of life and their overall adherence to and tolerance of the medical treatment and procedures (Alter et al. 1996, Mermelstein 1998). There have been preliminary reports suggesting that such follow-up contact by telephone improves compliance with treatment regimes and lessens the utilization of medical services (Austin et al. 1996, Infante-Rivard et al. 1988, Pollin 1996).

Another feature of the telephone is that it equalizes the power between patient and therapist. Usually the patient comes into a stranger's office. In theory, the patient is free to leave, but in reality, this is hard to do before the formal end of the session. With the telephone, patients are on their own turf and know that they can hang up. This increased sense of control may allow them to feel less guarded. For medically ill patients, whose illness has already thrust them into a dependent role and who often feel helpless, this relative empowerment during the telephone sessions may be particularly therapeutic. Several years ago I treated a young man suffering from relapsing and remitting multiple sclerosis via an early version of a videophone, a telephone machine that allows for transmission of still images as well as sound. It was our practice to exchange pictures at the opening and closing of sessions and several times in between. However, when difficult subjects were discussed and he became tearful, he would close the aperture and not exchange photo images until he felt he had reestablished a sense of emotional control. In a post-study survey, this patient commented that the ability of both therapist and patient to control the exchange equally was an improvement over standard treatment.

There may be less formality in patient–therapist interactions via the telephone. According to Grumet (1979), this facilitates the development of a parental or older sibling relationship. These roles may be particularly beneficial in crisis intervention and supportive therapy, in which the power of therapeutic suggestion, advice, and manipulation can be pivotal. A related difficulty noted by others who have reported on telephone therapy is the risk of switching to a social or conversational mode of interaction. My observation is that though this can be a problem, it seems to depend more on the individual therapist and patient, rather than on the use of the telephone as a therapeutic tool.

Another feature is the anonymity and decreased scrutiny that may allow patients with a paranoid stance or frank paranoid ideation to feel more at ease in this mode of therapeutic contact. In the case of the woman with Hodgkin's disease, it was my inability to see the signs of her ill health that decreased her feelings of exposure and lessened her panic to tolerable levels. I am currently treating a woman with chronic abdominal pain that is only partially relieved with medication. Memories from childhood were scarce until she was bedridden with a back strain. Over the telephone, with the sense of security and protective distance it can provide, she was able to recall being beaten as a child and her brother's tender ministrations afterwards. She has since been able to link the abuse with her pain behaviors as an adult and has returned to her executive position in the workplace.

The main negative features of telephone therapy are the loss of visual and nonverbal cues, which normally tell us about patients and our own responses to what is going on in therapy (Jacobs 1973). In the case of the woman with endometrial cancer, it was hard to evaluate the timbre of her voice. The significance of the parameters of a patient's voice—its tone, volume, rate, rhythm, and progression—are harder to assess in the medically ill. My inability to see the transplant patient and her environment was an obstacle to our feeling connected to each other. In an editorial by Driscoll (1992), he noted that with the telephone there was no "laying on of hands" between physicians and their patients. For the psychotherapist, face-to-face contact and the holding environment of the office may serve the same function for our patients. This very significant element in healing may be partially lost during telephone sessions.

As technology improves, the uses and applications of telemedicine and telepsychiatry have multiplied. Legal and ethical concerns and complexities have grown concomitantly. In the years ahead we hope there will be further improvements that allow for real time videocommunications to be as readily available and easy to use as an ordinary household appliance. For now, however, the telephone, an instrument within the financial and technological reach of almost everyone, can provide an accessible, effective, and much needed means of delivering psychotherapeutic intervention and support to the medically ill.

REFERENCES

Alter, C. L., Fleischman, S. B., Kornblith, A. B., et al. (1996). Supportive telephone intervention for patients receiving chemotherapy. *Psychosomatics* 37:425–431.

Aronson, J. K. (1996). The use of the telephone as a transitional space in the treatment of a severely masochistic, anorexic patient. In *Fostering Healing and Growth: A Psychoanalytic Social Work Approach*, ed. J. Edward and J. Sanville, pp. 163–178. Northvale, NJ: Jason Aronson.

Austin, J. S., Maisial, R. S., Macrina, D. M., and Hecta, L. W. (1996). Health outcome improvements in patients with systemic lupus erythematosus using two telephone counseling interventions. *Arthritis Care Research* 9:391–399.

Bucher, J. A., Houts, P. S., Glajchen, M., and Blum, D. (1998). Telephone counseling. In *Psychooncology*, ed. J. C. Holland, pp. 758–767. New York: Oxford University Press.

Catanzaro, R. (1971). Telephone therapy. *Current Psychiatric Therapy* 11:56–60.

Driscoll, C. (1992). The house calls in the electronic era. *Journal of the American Medical Association* 287:1828–1829.

Grumet, G. (1979). Telephone therapy: a review and case report. *American Journal of Orthopsychiatry* 49:574–584.

Hilty, D. M., Servis, M. E., Nesbitt, T. S., et al. (1999). The use of telemedicine to provide consultation-liaison services to the primary care settings. *Psychiatric Annals* 29:421–429.

Holland, J., and Rowland, J. (1979). Reactions to cancer treatment: assessment of emotional response to adjuvant radiotherapy as a guide to planned intervention. *Psychiatric Clinics of North America* 2:347–358.

Infante-Rivard, C., Krieger, M., Petitclerc, M., and Baumgarten, M. (1988). A telephone support service to reduce medical care use among the elderly. *Journal of the American Geriatric Society* 36:306–311.

Jacobs, T. (1973). Posture, gesture, and movement in the analyst: clues to interpretation and countertransference. *Journal of the American Psychoanalytic Association* 21:77–92.

Knopke, H. J., McDonald, E., and Siverton, J. E. (1979). A study of family practice in Wisconsin. *Journal of Family Practice* 8:151–156.

Lester, D. (1974). The unique qualities of telephone therapy. *Psychotherapy: Theory, Research, and Practice* 1:219–221.

Lester, D., and Brookcopp, G., eds. (1973). *Crisis Intervention and Counseling by Telephone*. Springfield, IL: Charles C Thomas.

Lincoln, J. (1988). Psychoanalysis by telephone. *Bulletin of the Menninger Clinic* 52:521–528.

MacKinnon, R., and Michels, R. (1970). The role of the telephone in the psychiatric interview. *Psychiatry* 33:82–93.

Mermelstein, H. T. (1998). *The telephone: a tool for our times in the psychosocial care of the medically ill.* Paper presented at the Academy of Psychosomatic Medicine, 45th annual meeting, Orlando FL.

Mermelstein, H. T., Holland, J. C., Cahan, G., and Kornblith, A. B. (1991). *The telephone: a neglected way to deliver psychotherapy.* Paper presented at the Academy of Psychosomatic Medicine, 38th annual meeting, Atlanta, GA.

Miller, W. (1973). The telephone in outpatient psychotherapy. *American Journal of Psychotherapy* 27:15–26.

Perlins, J., Collins, D., and Kaplowitz, L. (1999). Telemedicine. *Hospital Physician* 47:26–34.

Pollin, I. (1996). *The Taking Charge Program. A Trainer's Guide to Medical Crisis Counseling: A Telephone Intervention.* New York: Times Publishing.

Robertiello, R. (1972). Telephone sessions. *Psychoanalytic Review* 59:633–634.

Rosenbaum, M. (1974). Continuation of psychotherapy by "long-distance" telephone. *International Journal of Psychoanalytic Psychotherapy* 3:483–495.

——— (1977). Premature interruption of psychotherapy: continuation of contact by telephone and correspondence. *American Journal of Psychiatry* 134:200–202.

Rothchild, E. (1999). Telepsychiatry: Why do it? *Psychiatric Annals* 29:394–401.

Saul, L. (1951). A note on the telephone as a technical aid. *Psychoanalytic Quarterly* 20:287–290.

Shepard, P. (1987). Telephone therapy: an alternative to isolation. *Clinical Social Work Journal* 15:56–65.

Tolchin, J. (1987). Telephone psychotherapy with adolescents. *Adolescent Psychiatry* 21:332–341.

Williams, T., and Douds, J. (1974). The unique contribution of telephone therapy. In *Crisis Intervention and Counseling by Telephone*, ed. D. Lester and G. Brockcopp, pp. 80–82. Springfield, IL: Charles C Thomas.

Wittson, C., and Benschoter, R. (1972). Two-way television: helping the medical center reach out. *American Journal of Psychiatry* 129:136–139.

Zaylor, C. L. (1999). Adult telepsychiatry clinic's growing pains: how to treat more than 2000 patients in 7 locations. *Psychiatric Annals* 29:402–207.

VI

OTHER ISSUES

20

The Use of the Telephone for Impasse Consultations

SUE N. ELKIND

*F*or twelve years my colleagues and I have been offering a special resource to therapists and patients who are grappling with serious impasses in therapeutic relationships, impasses that jeopardize the relationship and are unresolvable within the dyad. We also offer consultation to patients and therapists who are coping with the aftermath of a ruptured therapeutic relationship.

INTERSECTING AREAS
OF PRIMARY VULNERABILITY

I understand from my experience, and that of others, that wounding of a special nature occurs in therapeutic relationships. I label this particularly difficult experience *wounding in areas of primary vulnerability*. Each of us has areas of primary vulnerability, shaped early in our lives in relationship to attachment figures or caregivers, based on the intermingling of temperament, personality, and circumstance. Manifestations of primary vulnerabilities differ from person to person, but in general they relate to the fundamental human need to preserve our sense of a cohesive self and our connection, or attachment bond, to significant others. Examples of these sensitivities, inherent in being human, include fears of betrayal, abandonment, separation, and rejection; issues of trust; or concerns about failure or success. Each of us develops defenses to protect us from falling into our areas of primary vulnerability.

Wounding in an area of primary vulnerability can occur in any relationship, particularly when the needs of each participant in the relationship conflict. I have come to regard such wounding as inevitable in therapeutic relationships. In therapy, patients come with high expectations and hopes for help. Therapists invest themselves in their patients and have a stake in the outcome of the therapy. When a therapeutic alliance forms, patients expect their therapists to understand them and to help them understand and repair wounds and deficits from their family of origin. Therapists look forward to being regarded as helpful, even while the territory of negative transference is negotiated and difficulties arise. As therapy proceeds, a strong attachment bond between patients and therapists develops, forged from the intimacy of the connection. When patients feel that their therapists, despite their knowledge of the patients, have wounded them in an area of primary vulnerability, a serious impasse can result.

In my experience, the wounding always reopens an earlier experience of traumatic wounding. A serious impasse inevitably ensues if the therapist does not grasp the full meaning to the patient of the wounding. The therapist, in the heat of the present interaction, may not recognize the transference matrix that shapes the meaning of the wounding to the patient. As a result of the patient's response to him or her, the therapist may be catapulted into an area of primary vulnerability. Even if a personal area of vulnerability is not activated, the therapist may experience a blow to his sense of a professional self. When both patient and therapist are vulnerable, the attachment bond between them is jeopardized. As we have learned from Bowlby (1988), when attachment bonds are jeopardized or lost, people experience considerable anguish.

> A feature of attachment behavior of the greatest importance clinically, and present irrespective of the age of the individual concerned, is the intensity of the emotion that accompanies it, the kind of emotion aroused depending on how the relationship between the individual attached and the attachment figure is faring. If it goes well, there is a joy and a sense of security. If it is threatened, there is jealousy, anxiety, and anger. If broken, there is grief and depression. [p. 4]

A patient who is anxious reacts to a jeopardized attachment bond with intense emotions that are apt to trigger the therapist's self-protective defenses. Both patient and therapist are then extremely vulnerable. Their energy is directed toward self-coherence and self-preservation, leaving little room for empathy for the other's point of view. This situation provides fertile ground for serious impasses that place the therapeutic relationship in jeopardy. If the therapy collapses at this point and becomes a rupture, patients are left feeling harmed by an undertaking they had hoped would be helpful and healing. Therapists are left with a sense of doubt about their capacities and the viability of their profession.

While serious impasses in therapy occur when the patient's and the therapist's primary vulnerabilities and adaptive defenses to manage the vulnerabilities intersect problematically, I have also found that another kind of impasse can occur when the patient's and the therapist's primary vulnerabilities and adaptive defenses intersect collusively and create a common blind spot. Wounding does not occur, but the therapy may be at a stalemate because patient and therapist are both invested in staying out of dangerous territory. These are the therapeutic relationships that we might call, after Freud, interminable, although I am using the word in a relational context. Even if the therapist is available, some patients, when alone in a dyad with a therapist, are unable to risk exposing what Winnicott has labeled their true self. Some patients have learned that they must set aside their needs and spontaneous reactions in order to preserve the connection to a significant attachment figure. When a consultant is in place as a safety net, both therapist and patient are freer to take risks.[1]

When I first began writing about therapeutic impasses in 1987, relational and interpersonal perspectives in psychoanalysis had not yet come to the fore. The assertions I put forth based on my experience in the role of a consultant were radical. Today the assertion that both patients and therapists inevitably have areas of primary vulnerability that are not resolved or "cured" by psychotherapy or psychoanalysis, and that serious impasses are based in the relationship rather than located in the patient alone, are far less shocking. But the idea of a consultant who intervenes directly with both patient and therapist in separate meetings, or conjointly, depending on the individual circumstances, is still a radical one.

---

1. At Austen Riggs, an inpatient setting in which patients enter into psychoanalytic therapy as frequently as five days a week in addition to being part of groups and the community as a whole, a model of consultation to therapeutic dyads has been in place for nearly twenty years. When patients enter Austen Riggs, they are given not only a therapist, but also a consultant who they are told will be available to them and to their therapist when, not if, a serious impasse arises. A series of papers by four therapists and consultants at Austen Riggs, with a discussion paper by me illustrating these consultations and their theoretical underpinnings can be found in *The American Journal of Psychoanalysis*, 1999, 59(2):101–141.

THE ROLE OF A CONSULTANT

The model of impasse consultation that my colleagues and I have been developing is intended to create a resource for both the therapist and the patient, who otherwise may remain in a relational vacuum. This model departs from the convention that the therapist obtains consultation apart from the patient and that patients will bring all their thoughts, feelings, and reactions directly to their therapist. Therapists do not routinely recommend consultation to their patients. Those who do recommend it are not thinking of themselves as potential participants with the same consultant. Patients are unlikely to think of obtaining consultation on their own. Most patients turn to friends rather than to professionals for help. Even if the idea of consultation is broached, or if they think of it on their own, patients are reluctant to seek it, reluctant to be disloyal to their therapists, even when they are wounded and angry at the therapist's behavior or attitude. A certain inertia can pervade therapist and patient, both of whom hope that the therapy will somehow improve.

With trepidation, I began providing consultation to patients. I feared that they might want to continue seeing me, that I would be perceived as the perfect therapist in contrast to their own. My experience has contradicted these fears. Patients who contact me for consultation are highly motivated to make their therapy work. Their worst fear is that the therapy will be permanently derailed. They are loyal to their therapists and eager for the therapists to receive whatever help they can. My fear that I would encounter discrepancies in the patient's and therapist's perception of the impasse has also proved groundless. I have never had a situation where the narrative of the patient and the therapist have been at odds or contradictory, regardless of the nature of the impasse, the therapist's level of skill and training, or the patient's level of functioning. Both therapist and patient make every effort to describe the therapeutic impasse accurately. They are honest and forthcoming, disclosing without hesitation behaviors that may be shameful, in the interest of preserving the therapeutic relationship.

I have found that a consultant can play a significant role as the "third" in a therapeutic relationship at risk of rupture, slowing down an escalating impasse, often removing the relationship from the brink of rupture. In order to describe the impasse, both patient and therapist are forced to reflect on it and to put it into language that another person will understand. They each must formulate an experience that is likely to have been largely unformulated. When an experience is unformulated, the accompanying affects are continually discharged without being understood (Stern 1997).[2] A consultant, by providing a separate space and relationship for each participant, enables the energy of intense affect to be garnered for a constructive purpose. If patients leave a therapy in the midst of a serious impasse, without the opportunity to put the experience into language, the entire therapy is relegated to a locked cupboard in the psyche and avoided. Patients who have good experiences in therapy take with them the positive memory of an important relationship that they can access freely, giving them a perpetually available source of replenishment. Patients who endure a ruptured termination after a wounding impasse try to avoid returning in memory to the experience. When they do return in memory, the original affects are revived in full force. Processing the painful experience with a consultant can

---

2. Stern (1997) refers to unformulated experience as "the uninterpreted form of those raw materials of conscious, reflective experience that may eventually be assigned verbal interpretations and thereby brought into articulate form" (p. 37).

be useful because the patient is compelled to use language to describe it, which means reflecting on the experience rather than being lost in it. Moreover, the patient receives from the consultant the healing balm of empathy and understanding.

The consultant provides a calming influence, holding hope for the therapist and patient that the impasse can be resolved. If the therapy is able to resume, the consultant remains a resource in the psyches of the patient and therapist to call on if unresolvable difficulties recur. Often the consultant is in a position to make helpful interpretations or assessments of the impasse. Patients who have been wounded by their therapists may be unable to receive interpretations from them while in the midst of the impasse. Even without any further intervention, the consultation can help loosen the impasse because patients appreciate their therapists' willingness to accept help from a consultant. My fear that my involvement as consultant would diminish the authority of the therapist has also proved unfounded. If anything, the patient's respect for the therapist seems to increase.

For some patients, participating in a dyad re-creates structurally a childhood experience of being helpless and trapped in a dyadic relationship with a significant attachment figure who has been experienced as traumatically abusive. I have labeled this a *structural intervention* to emphasize that the dyad has an active effect on patients just as do verbal interpretations or nonverbal actions such as body language, a smile, a handshake, or a hug. For these patients, the inclusion of a consultant can be essential in enabling therapeutic work in the dyad to proceed with increased safety.

Contrary to what might be expected, given the label of impasse consultation, my colleagues and I do not necessarily meet conjointly with patient and therapist. Paradoxically, a relational impasse is more likely to be resolved in separate meetings, although joint meetings can be useful. By meeting in a separate session with the consultant, the patient and the therapist have to access a different self than the one that has been constellated in the therapeutic relationship. In the consultant's presence, whether literally in person or through a telephone contact, the therapist and patient usually bring a less emotional self, a self that is outside the impasse talking about it and thus reflecting on it in language. This self is hopeful of being understood and helped, unlike the despairing, grieving, or rageful self that exists in the current therapy. Once patient and therapist have a different experience of self outside the stalled relationship, they are able to bring back this expanded sense of self to the therapeutic relationship. When patient and therapist feel understood, they are better able to listen to the other's point of view. The experience of being understood is a necessary precondition for being able to understand someone else.

EXPERIMENTING WITH THE TELEPHONE FOR IMPASSE CONSULTATIONS

After the publication in 1992 of my book, *Resolving Impasses in Therapeutic Relationships*, and as I continued to present my work on impasses, I began receiving requests for telephone sessions from patients and therapists in different states. I responded that I had never consulted by telephone, but I would be willing to try. Because the idea of consulting to both patient and therapist was in itself new and experimental, I had little resistance to circumventing conventional practice by using the telephone. I have never regretted this choice.

Even before I received specific long-distance requests for consultation, I had already incorporated the use of the telephone into my local, in-person consultations. I found that therapists were less able to make time to come to an in-person session than patients were. Patients are usually in more distress than therapists are (though therapists also suffer) and consequently may be more motivated to pursue in-person consultation, especially if they are self-referred. In order to consult with therapists as quickly as possible, especially when the impasse had reached a crisis, I found that I could have contact more quickly and easily by arranging a telephone session.

Perhaps I would have been more concerned about the imbalance created by meeting with patients in person and therapists by phone if my priority had not been to intervene as quickly and as efficiently as possible. However, in evaluating this imbalance now, I believe that meeting with the patient in person and the therapist by telephone has an additional and unexpected advantage of securing the essential alliance between consultant and patient. Consulting by telephone with a therapist has a collegial feel that may assuage the therapist's anxiety about relating to a consultant whom the patient chose or whom the therapist does not know from prior contact.

I have also used the telephone for as-needed contact with both patients and therapists who are in an impasse. Shorter telephone check-in times make it possible for me to keep in close contact with them to monitor their passage through the impasse and to provide timely and focused support for them. I typically schedule quarter- or half-session telephone appointments.

When patient, therapist, and consultant embark on an impasse consultation, each is highly motivated to make the consultation successful. As a result, there is a shared positive energy that sustains the endeavor when it takes place by telephone. That same energy also enables the concentrated focus on communication that tends to occur by telephone. Extended silences are not as typical as they might be in long-term therapy.

Patients and therapists, as well as the consultant, generally have a specific agenda and are focused on accomplishing this agenda during the session. I can easily take notes while consulting by telephone, providing myself with a useful record when communicating subsequently with either the therapist or the patient. Notes not only help focus my attention while on the telephone, but also serve as a record when there is a long time lapse between contacts.

My personal preference is to meet in person rather than on the telephone. This bias is most likely the result of habit, training in conventional practice, and a previously unexamined conviction that information is lost by meeting over the telephone. Earlier in my training as a therapist, I learned that therapist and patient convey who they are in their dress, demeanor and posture, facial expression, body language, and manner of making or not making eye contact. The therapist also creates a personal environment in the office that provides information to patients. I do not question these assertions; one glimpse of my special back chairs in my office immediately tells those who consult with me about an important personal priority. Yet when I focus on the information gained by telephone, I realize that there are sources of information other than visual, and that there can be advantages to the distance created by telephone contact.

In telephone contact, I attend to non-visual sources of information, including tone of voice, silences, and exclamations. Human beings are adaptable; when one sense is unavailable, others are sharpened. I suspect that the patients and therapists I talk with receive similar information about me. I also know that patients and therapists who consult with me by telephone tend to create a special place where they make the call. One woman has described making herself a cup of tea and settling herself in a chair outdoors on her patio. I sit at a desk with a notepad in a room with the doors closed. These preparations are made carefully on both sides and serve analogous functions to the patient's preparatory ritual trip to the therapist's office. What seems essential is that each participant in a telephone consultation make some effort to create a separate special place within which to focus on the interaction to come.

THE NATURE OF THE ALLIANCE FORMED IN PERSON OR BY TELEPHONE

Establishing a bond or an alliance is as fundamental to impasse consultation as it is to psychotherapy. For patients who feel rejected and unlovable in relation to their therapists, the connection to a consultant who feels and expresses positive regard for them makes a crucial difference. In considering the use of the telephone, I asked myself whether a particular kind of bond is formed in an in-person consultation session that cannot be formed by telephone. Positive regard is essential whether the consultation is conducted in person or by telephone. The specific manner of conveying this regard may differ depending on the modality, but its importance is undeniable. Two brief examples will illustrate the differences in manner of communicating. In both cases, I did not consciously plan my responses in advance.

One patient, Ms. A., was involved in an impasse with her therapist, Dr. R., that persisted for months after the therapist returned from maternity leave. She gave me the following feedback after an extended in-person consultation.

There was something else, which may sound small, but was crucial to me. At one point during our consultation, I was sitting in your office and was telling you about how much I felt Dr. R. disliked me. Before I left, you validated my perceptions, acknowledged how painful it must be, *and* you told me that in the very short time we had worked together, you found me likable. I can't tell you how powerful it was to me to hear you tell me you liked me. Coming from a family in which I felt like a pariah, it was what I always longed to hear. Of course this longing played itself out in my therapy. I was quick to interpret every gesture as a sign of disapproval and needed desperately to hear explicitly that I was likable and liked. You gave me that and it gave me a certain strength to go back to my relationship with Dr. R. and believe that this was something I could reasonably expect from her. [Elkind 1997, pp. 376–377]

I recall telling Ms. A. that I found her likable, although I had no idea that my comment would have such significance. Her feedback is a reminder that we cannot always know what aspect of our words or behavior will have an impact. We were on our way to the door to my office, chatting offhandedly after the session officially ended. On the telephone, there is no opportunity for talking after the session ends.

As an example of conveying positive regard in a telephone consultation, I think of a comment I made to a woman, Ms. N., whose consultation I will discuss in more detail later on. Ms. N. valiantly managed to stay in therapy with Dr. P., who wounded her in an area of primary vulnerability. She relied on our consultation to keep her from leaving the therapeutic relationship abruptly and looking for a different therapist. I was impressed with her capacity to stay in the relationship and struggle against her impulse to flee. At the end of one of our telephone sessions, I said to her spontaneously and emphatically, "It is an absolute pleasure to talk with you. You're so easy to help!" I probably would not have made such an emphatic positive statement to a patient I was meeting with in person for fear of being too intrusive.

I am led to the conclusion that I accomplish the same goal by different means when consulting in person or by telephone. I suspect that therapists and patients, like me, are able to adapt intuitively to the means of contact available. When the capacities for empathy, positive regard, clinical knowledge, and judgment are present and active, we use whatever vehicle is available to us. When we are in the presence of others, we might communicate empathy and positive regard via a smile or a gesture. By telephone we use other means, such as direct statements, exclamations, or tone of voice. We may have overvalued in-person meetings because we are creatures of habit, or because we dislike the isolation of telephone contact, but in reality human beings rise to the occasion when the necessity to adapt is acute or when there is an advantage to doing so.

CONSULTATION TO ASSESS WHETHER TO USE THE TELEPHONE

Even with human adaptability, there are situations in which meetings in person are essential, whether for impasse consultations or psychotherapy. Therapists must make clinical judgments about the appropriateness of the telephone just as they make judgments about other interventions. As the telephone is becoming a more common option, we need to develop means of assessing when its use is not advisable. Toward this end, I will begin with an example of a consultation that required an explicit assessment of whether the telephone was an appropriate means of working with a particular patient, both for an impasse consultation and for ongoing therapy. This vignette, like the others in this chapter, is a fictionalized composite of consultations my colleagues and I have provided.

The consultation began with a request from a therapist, Dr. M., located in another city, who had learned of my work. Dr. M. asked if I would be available to meet in person with a patient of his, Ms. B., who had reached an impasse in her marriage. Dr. M. was currently working with Ms. B. by telephone. They had met in person for several months until the patient moved out of the area because her husband accepted an employment opportunity elsewhere. Dr. M. had not heard from his patient for several years. Six months previously Ms. B. had called Dr. M. for a telephone appointment because of her marital crisis. Dr. M. hoped I might be able to use my understanding of impasses in therapeutic relationships to help with the impasse in the marriage, but he also wanted me to assess whether continuing telephone therapy made sense, given the urgent nature of the patient's problem. Perhaps Ms. B. needed a therapist in her area whom she could see in person. I agreed to meet with the patient for a consultation to determine what arrangement would best meet Ms. B.'s needs.

Ms. B. called to schedule an appointment within a day. As soon as she sat down she began to sob uncontrollably. I waited quietly. Eventually she looked up through her tears and told me she had been afraid that she would break down once she got into my office. Her next words were, "I am 39 years old and I'm afraid I want something different in my life. I'm afraid I want a child."

In the extended session that followed, I learned that Ms. B. was the oldest of four children. Her father had abandoned them when she was 10 years old, leaving her mother to fend for the family. The mother was overwhelmed and left Ms. B. in charge. Not only did Ms. B. take over the management of her younger siblings, but she tried to mother her mother as well. While the mother returned to school and gained marketable skills, Ms. B. continued to parent her younger siblings, make school lunches, and help with homework, shopping, and cleaning.

By the time Ms. B. reached college age, her mother was employed and better able to resume her responsibilities in the home. Ms. B. was able to leave home and attend college, where she met her husband. He was the first in his family to attend college and had also grown up with many responsibilities. They agreed that they did not want children. Up to now they had each done well in their employment settings and now had sufficient income to live a comfortable lifestyle.

Ms. B. told me how this arrangement suited both of them for seventeen years. But as her biological window for childbearing narrowed, she began to yearn for a baby. Torn by this yearning and by her equally powerful loving feelings for Mr. B., she did not know what to do. Mr. B. was adamant that he did not want children, nor did he want to consider marriage counseling to work on the conflict. Ms. B. had simply stopped talking to him about her wishes. Much as she tried, she could not quell the longing to have a child. She called Dr. M. for help and had been having weekly phone sessions until now, when Dr. M. asked her to meet in person with me. What was she going to do?

As our session progressed, I was convinced that Ms. B. needed to be seen in person, probably more than once a week, to deal with this conflict. I was also convinced that an impasse consultation would not be sufficient to address the conflict in the marriage. In my view, the top priority was individual therapy to help Ms. B. decide whether she wanted to have an actual child or whether she wanted to channel her maternal energy toward mothering herself symbolically. When she had telephone contact with Dr. M., Ms. B. managed to hold herself together. The telephone made it possible for her to avoid the conflict altogether, despite the urgency created by the passage of time. Sitting in my office, she found her feelings were unavoidable. I let Ms. B. know that I wanted to meet with her once more, that my tentative recommendation was that she meet with a local therapist in person, perhaps twice a week, to help her with her conflict. I obtained written permission to talk with Dr. M. and with Dr. T., the local therapist I had in mind for her. I let her know that I understood the importance of her relationship with Dr. M., and that we needed to think in terms of adding resources, not substituting or choosing *between* resources. She left my office feeling relieved and supported.

When I talked by telephone with Dr. M., I was worried that he would feel I was undermining his connection to his patient. But Dr. M. shared my concern that the telephone was not an adequate vehicle for therapy, given Ms. B.'s current needs and her tendency to compartmentalize her feelings and cope—adaptive methods in her childhood circumstances but problematic now. Neither of us wanted her ability to put aside her needs in the service of caring for others to prevent her from making a conscious choice about bearing children. We agreed that I would talk with Dr. T. about his availability to work with Ms. B. If he could be available, I would give Ms. B. the referral in my next meeting with her. I would also open a communication channel by obtaining permission from Ms. B. so that the three therapists could remain in contact with each other depending on her needs.

In the next session, Ms. B. told me she had worked hard all week and had not had much time to think about her situation. This statement confirmed my previous concern that telephone contact would make it too easy for her to avoid confronting her dilemma. I let her know I had talked with both Dr. M. and the new therapist, Dr. T., about her situation. Dr. T. was available to meet with her and had also agreed to stay in contact with Dr. M. She could meet with Dr. M. along with Dr. T. if she wanted, or she could stop seeing Dr. M. for the time being and concentrate on her sessions with Dr. T. I was assuming that she would work well with Dr. T., but if she felt Dr. T. was not right for her, I would help her find a different therapist.

Ms. B. again began to cry. Eventually she managed to tell me that she knew that she would make quicker progress in person, that it was scary but okay. She told me that her tears were not about my telling her that she needed to see a therapist in person to deal with both the impasse in her marriage and with her wish to have a child. She was crying because I had talked with both Dr. M. and Dr. T. and because the three of us planned to work with each other. The idea that the three of us were working together to help her was overwhelming. This unmothered woman for the first time in her life was experiencing maternal/paternal holding.

The transition from Dr. M. to Dr. T. was handled between the two therapists and Ms. B. continued meeting with Dr. T. I have had no further contact with either the therapists or Ms. B. I wonder from time to time what decision Ms. B. made. If she chose to have a child of her own, I wonder what happened to her marriage. While I have no answer to these questions, I continue to have a strong sense of conviction that Ms. B. needed to be in the physical presence of a therapist.

Therapists are always in the position of making assessments and judgments about what best serves their patients. These determinations are ultimately based on rational thought and intuition, as well as factors that are both conscious and unconscious. As with other issues calling for judgment, therapists need to assess consciously whether telephone communication is appropriate for a given patient at a given time or for a particular purpose.

AN EXAMPLE OF AN IMPASSE CONSULTATION
BY TELEPHONE

I will turn now to an impasse consultation conducted entirely by telephone in order to demonstrate how the telephone functioned. The therapist, Dr. P., and the patient, Ms. N., were located in another city. Dr. P. suggested that Ms. N. call for a telephone consultation because they were struggling with an impasse that was escalating rather than resolving.

Ms. N. called for an appointment and we scheduled a telephone session. In our initial session, I introduced myself and explained how impasse consultations work. As always, I felt somewhat awkward talking on the telephone to someone new, but I could tell that Ms. N. was listening to me. I asked if she had questions or concerns. She told me that she was glad Dr. P. wanted a consultation, but that she was also a bit skeptical. I let her know that I was glad she could be honest with me and hoped she would keep letting me know her feelings.

Ms. N. is a 40-year-old woman currently teaching history at a junior college. She had been seeing her therapist, Dr. P., for eight years. She originally sought therapy for depression following a divorce from her husband of fourteen years. The divorce was not her choice. Her husband initiated the divorce after becoming involved with a woman who had previously been Ms. N.'s friend. When Ms. N.'s grief and rage did not subside, and she was unable to concentrate at work, she began meeting with her therapist, Dr. P. In the beginning of the therapy, when she was struggling with suicidal impulses and needed to hold onto the therapeutic relationship as a lifeline, they began to meet three times a week with daily telephone contact in between.

Over time, with the support of the individual therapy and antidepressant medication, Ms. N. began to improve, but she continued having regular daily telephone contact with Dr. P. outside of the scheduled sessions. Eventually she needed only occasional direct contact on the telephone with Dr. P., but she continued to leave daily messages on his answering machine that ranged from one minute to ten minutes depending on her sense of need.

The serious impasse occurred when Dr. P. placed a limit on the telephone contact. He felt that Ms. N. no longer needed to leave daily messages or to speak with him by telephone. He felt he was no longer helping her by being so available. In fact, he felt he was functioning like a substitute husband and might even be keeping her from having psychological energy for new friendships outside the therapeutic relationship.

Ms. N. had a different perspective. She felt that she was trying to relinquish the telephone contact on her own. In fact, she had already begun to allow days to pass without making telephone calls. From her point of view, the primary effect of this unilateral decision on Dr. P.'s part was to pull the rug out from under her just as she was trying to feel stronger—to punish her for getting better. She felt that he was depriving her of the opportunity to stop the phone calls on her own.

By the time I intervened as consultant, the situation had become a crisis. Both of them were able to present their point of view to me in a calm manner. When they encountered each other in Dr. P.'s office, however, their emotions escalated. Ms. N. felt angry and abandoned, while Dr. P. felt frustrated and misunderstood. Ms. N. had been so upset in her previous session with Dr. P. that she had left the office saying she was not coming back, and asked him to cancel all her sessions. By the time I talked with her, she regretted her impulsive rejection of Dr. P. and was fearful that he had not saved her sessions. At the same time, she was so angry with him that she could not imagine returning to his office.

In the first telephone session, I told Ms. N. that even if she decided to stop seeing Dr. P., she would be better off having a planned ending than fleeing in a rupture. I thought that a consultation, in which I had contact with both of them, would help assess whether the therapy could get back on track. I suggested that Ms. N. leave a message for Dr. P. saying that she wanted to come in for her regular appointments. When she met with him, she could tell him that she had met with me, share what we had discussed, and see if he would be willing to talk with me. I asked her to send me a release of information to talk with Dr. P. and made a follow-up appointment with her. Knowing how anxious she was about meeting with him after having been so rageful, I asked her to leave me a message after her session, letting me know how it had gone. i could tell from her calmer tone of voice that her anxiety had lessened.

The next day I received a message from Ms. N. letting me know in a relieved tone that she had survived the session and that Dr. P. would be calling me. I began the initial telephone consultation with Dr. P. by introducing myself, then explaining the nature of the consultations I provide, and indicating ways in which a consultant might be helpful to them. Dr. P. agreed that a third person supporting the dyad would be useful. He reported that the therapeutic relationship with Ms. N. had been intense and difficult for both of them at different junctures, and that a consultant would be a valuable resource.

As in the initial session with Ms. N., I received a history and overview of the therapy from Dr. P. He was clear that he needed to implement the change in policy regarding telephone contact outside of sessions. He was convinced that the daily messages had become a habit, originally based in need, but now impeding her progress. He also acknowledged that he was feeling trapped and resentful of the time he was spending outside scheduled sessions. He regarded these feelings as further confirmation that the calls were no longer necessary.

I agreed to work with both of them around implementing this change. I shared with Dr. P. my opinion that Ms. N. was highly motivated to repair the breach and work constructively to resolve the impasse. By the end of our session, Dr. P. was clearly relieved, as if letting me know how difficult the impasse had been for him siphoned off considerable pressure and tension.

In the next few telephone sessions with Ms. N., I listened to her experience of the intervening sessions with Dr. P. I was able to talk to her about the process of negotiating conflicts of needs that occurs in all relationships. I reframed the impasse as an opportunity to practice negotiating the conflict in their needs with respect to telephone contact outside of sessions. I then speculated that the impasse might not have escalated had Dr. P. presented the policy change as having more to do with his need for fewer telephone calls outside of sessions than with making a change solely for her benefit. Ms. N. was relieved by this speculation because she was angry with Dr. P. for assuming that he knew what was best for her. From her perspective, she had her own plan in mind for reducing the telephone time.

We also discussed the power struggle over the telephone calls. I pointed out that both Dr. P. and Ms. N. were in agreement that fewer calls would be a sign of progress. Their differences centered on the reason for implementing the change and the process by which the change was established. Ms. N. wanted Dr. P. to acknowledge his personal needs and to allow her to participate in the decision. I reframed the struggle as an opportunity to practice learning to listen to the other's opinion and then asserting oneself in words, not actions.

I also helped her see herself as entering a new phase of therapy and pointed out that impasses often occur at developmental junctures when the therapist has not caught up to the patient, or vice versa. Initially, patients like Ms. N. perceive themselves as less able than their therapists, who are admired, if not idealized. As patients gain new capacities, they begin to regard their therapists in a new way, seeing their weaknesses as well as their strengths. This is an inevitable and difficult phase in any good therapy. As a consultant, I have the freedom to discuss aspects of the therapeutic relationship with the patient. The therapist, who is a source of wounding, is less likely to be heard.

When I next talked with Dr. P., he was discouraged by a setback with the patient in the previous session. I was able to support him by reminding him of the enormous progress Ms. N. had made in her work with him. Despite the severity of the impasse, she was not fragmenting or falling into depression. She was attending all her sessions and was trying to express herself in language rather than discharging affects in destructive actions. My support helped reduce Dr. P.'s anxiety and enabled him to return to sessions with Ms. N. feeling both effective and hopeful. At the same time, knowing that Dr. P. was consulting with me was reassuring to Ms. N., who was then less fearful that her therapist would give up on her altogether. Despite her anger, Ms. N. was deeply attached to him. She was learning how to tolerate the paradox of feeling both love and rage in relation to one person, an important experience in itself (Pizer 1998). I was impressed and moved when Ms. N. volunteered that she missed seeing Dr. P. as perfect, but that she also wanted him to be real.

In the next consultation session with Dr. P., we talked about the possibility of his finding ways to tell Ms. N. directly when she makes him angry or upset. Until now his efforts had been directed toward helping her modulate her affects. He was then able to take the risk of including his own affect in the sessions, knowing that I would function as a safety net. When I talked with Ms. N. after a session with Dr. P. in which he risked sharing his upset with her, she was distressed. I told her, "Dr. P. is telling you that he needs the relationship with you to be safe enough for him to say things that might make you uncomfortable, angry, or scared." There was a moment's pause, and then Ms. N. told me, "I think I understand." She went on to recognize that her ex-husband had complained during their marriage about her inability to hear his feelings.

I continued having separate sessions with each of them for the next few months. When the therapeutic relationship was back on track, I brought up with Ms. N. the prospect of ending our sessions. I told her that my preference in being a consultant is to step aside when the therapeutic relationship is working well, rather than to remain in place in an ongoing way. I would miss our sessions and wanted to arrive at a mutually agreed-upon date to stop scheduling them. In this way, we reworked the original impasse in the therapy by trying to negotiate a stopping time that worked for both of us.

DISCUSSION

I hope I have successfully conveyed the intensity and intimacy of impasse consultations even when they are conducted over the telephone between individuals who have not previously met in person. I attribute the success of these sessions to the determination of all participants to make the consultation effective and to the adaptive capacity of human beings to find ways to use whatever means are available to reach important goals.

With respect specifically to the use of the telephone for impasse consultation, the pertinent question is whether the consultant can function effectively as a "third" to the dyad by telephone. Assuming that the consultant, patient, and therapist are sufficiently motivated to adapt to the telephone, and that they are flexible enough to adapt capacities for communication, empathy, and reflection to the telephone, the determining factor becomes the quality of the alliance. If the consultant and patient and the consultant and therapist are able to form a positive alliance by telephone, the telephone can be used successfully.

A consultant also helps patients and therapists in impasses actively reflect on the experience in therapy. This active reflection can occur in person or by telephone, depending on the consultant's judgment. The process of transforming unformulated experience into language used creatively can occur in person or by telephone as long as all participants are highly motivated to do so. The telephone lends itself to focused verbal communication.

The basic ingredients for a successful consultation remain the same, whether in-person, or by telephone when in-person sessions are not possible. The consultant needs to establish a positive alliance in separate sessions with the therapist and the patient that allows them to feel basic trust, safety, understanding, and hope. The attachment bond between therapist and patient has to survive the impasse. All participants must be able to use the data at hand. With in-person sessions, the source of data will include visual cues, such as facial expression, body language, and overall appearance of each person and the environment. By telephone, the data will be comprised of auditory information, including words, silences, tone of voice, and random sounds. The data will thus differ, but the capacity to use one's empathy, intuition, knowledge of psychological theory and practice, life experience, and clinical experience in formulating the data remain the same.

In short, the telephone enables consultation for impasses in therapy to occur when in-person sessions are not possible. I have not yet had a consultation arise where I would have specifically recommended the telephone, but I can imagine a case in which I might. For example, if the patient or therapist were too upset to communicate in person, the telephone might provide the essential protection of distance. Without the same attitude of openness to exploration that enabled my colleagues and me to develop and apply the model for impasse consultation, we might never have considered the telephone as an option, given conventional assumptions. Yet my experience with both telephone and in-person consultation has demonstrated that successful consultations by telephone are possible. The telephone itself is simply one means of enabling communication. The capacities of the individuals using it are the factors that will determine its successful use.

REFERENCES

Bowlby, J. (1988). *A Secure Base: Parent–Child Attachment and Healthy Human Development*. New York: Basic Books.

Elkind, S. (1992). *Resolving Impasses in Therapeutic Relationships*. New York: Guilford.

——— (1997). Resolving impasses: including patients and supervisees in consultation. In *Psychodynamic Supervision: Perspectives of the Supervisor and Supervisee*, ed. M. Rock, pp. 361–398. Northvale, NJ: Jason Aronson.

——— (1999). Discussion of papers by Drs. Fromm, Muller, Piers, and Tillman. *American Journal of Psychoanalysis* 59(2):135–141.

Pizer, S. (1998). *Building Bridges: The Negotiation of Paradox in Psychoanalysis*. Hillsdale, NJ: Analytic Press.

Stern, D. (1997). *Unformulated Experience: From Dissociation to Imagination in Psychoanalysis*. Hillsdale, NJ: Analytic Press.

21

Legal and Ethical Issues

SYLVAN SCHAFFER

*T*he explosive expansion of the internet has correspondingly highlighted the use of the telephone in the practice of psychotherapy. It is ironic that the telephone, used in medicine for almost 125 years (Cowan 1997), has attracted new attention due to its technological sibling, the internet modem. Telephone psychotherapy, while an independent subject, is part of the general field of telemedicine and is legally and ethically similar to what is sometimes called cybertherapy or virtual psychotherapy, that is, a text-based form of psychotherapy involving the use of the internet. At the same time, there are significant differences between the use of the telephone and text-based internet therapy. Telepsychotherapy may be defined as the provision of psychotherapeutic services over the telephone to a patient in a remote location.

The primary issues that affect telepsychotherapy specifically and telemedicine in general are licensure for therapeutic contacts that cross state and national boundaries, the ethics of using such technology in lieu of face-to-face psychotherapy, reimbursement for such services, malpractice liability, the choice of forum for regulating and litigating matters related to such interjurisdictional therapeutic contacts, and issues of confidentiality and privacy.

Although this discussion focuses on the use of the telephone in psychotherapy, it is important to note that many of the laws and regulations governing the practice in this area are subsumed under the rubric of telemedicine and may include the telephone in discussions of the internet, since they use much the same technical means of transmission. Another variant on the use of the telephone is videoconferencing, a process through which the therapist can both hear and see the patient at a remote site through transmissions over telephone lines or via satellite.

The growth of telepsychotherapy and telemedicine has been rapid, widespread, and almost uncontrolled. The legal and ethical regulatory systems have been unable to match the pace of the change in technology and practice. As a result, new laws and ethics pronouncements are being drafted and approved. It is likely that the legal landscape will continue to change markedly over the next several years to meet the demands of society's greater dependence on technology in general and telemedicine specifically.

The rationale for telepsychotherapy is that the process makes treatment available to patients who live in remote areas or who are unable to travel. This is especially useful for those who are disabled, phobic, or embarrassed to come in person. In addition, the process makes it possible for experts to provide consultations to other therapists. The telephone may also make it easier for psychotherapy patients to seek help, since it may remove some of the stigma and emotional inhibitions that prevent some potential patients from seeking face-to-face help.

Before considering the licensure and jurisdictional issues of telepsychotherapy, it is important to discuss the appropriateness and ethics of providing treatment by telephone. Concerns about practitioners of medicine using telephones were raised long ago by physicians who felt that such practice undermined the profession (Reiser 1999) and could lead to substandard care (Fischer 1992). This concern could be raised for the practice of telepsychotherapy as well.

This issue was addressed in a 1997 statement by the Ethics Committee of the American Psychological Association:

> The Ethics Committee can only address the relevance of and enforce the "Ethical Principles of Psychologists and Code of Conduct." . . . The Ethics Code is not specific with regard to telephone therapy or teleconferencing or any electronically provided services as such and has no rules prohibiting such services. Complaints regarding such matters would be addressed on a case by case basis.
>
> Delivery of services by such media as telephone, teleconferencing and internet is a rapidly evolving area. This will be the subject of APA task forces and will be considered in future revision of the Ethics Code.[1]

A report by a task force on telepsychotherapy was enthusiastic about its potential but stated that nothing available in today's market can replace the face-to-face interaction of patient and health care providers. The task force also raised the concern that telepsychotherapy could lead to exploitation of the practitioners and force them to treat patients without face-to-face contact in order to reduce costs (Nickelson 1997).

The American Medical Association has also begun to address the issue of telephone advisory and referral services:

---

1. The Ethics Committee lists the following Standards of the Ethics Code which should be considered by psychologists: 1.04c; 2.01–2.10; 4.01–4.09 (especially Structuring the Relationship and Informed Consent); 5.01–5.11. Within the General Standards Section the Ethics Committee lists: 1.03; 1.04abc; 1.06; 1.07a; 125; and 3.01–3.03.

Any telephone advisory service should employ certain safeguards to prevent misuse. For example, the physician responding to the call should not make a clinical diagnosis.
Diagnosis by telephone is done without the benefit of a
physician examination or even face-to-face meeting with
the caller. Critical medical data may be unavailable to the
physician. . . . Under no circumstances should medication
be prescribed. . . . When callers are charged by the minute,
they may try to hurry their calls to limit their costs. As a
result important information may not be disclosed to the
physician. Physicians should also ensure that callers do
not incur large bills inadvertently or without understanding the billing system . . . [American Medical Association
Opinions and Standards, 5.025.]

The American Telemedicine Association has also developed telehomecare guidelines for patients and healthcare providers. These standards include the use of video visits. The
guidelines include a statement that the first and last treatment
visits must be in person (American Telemedicine Association,
www.atmeda.org). Standards for telemedicine have also been
developed for radiology (American College of Radiology 1996)
and pathology (College of American Pathologists 1995).

Standards for the ethical practice of telepsychotherapy are
still evolving and the nature of future standards will depend
to some degree on state and federal regulation and empirical
research on the effectiveness of various types of telepsychotherapy. The rapid development of the field has made research
difficult (Nickelson 1998).

The question of the effectiveness of telepsychotherapy
relates directly to the issue of professional liability for the practitioner of telepsychotherapy. The issue of malpractice for
telepsychotherapy involves fundamental questions about the

nature of the psychodiagnostic and psychotherapeutic processes. Traditional psychotherapy often involves an initial mental status examination based, in part, on visual cues such as the patient's mannerisms, eye contact, and dress. Also, in some forms of psychotherapy the personal interaction of the therapist and the patient is essential to the therapeutic process. In telepsychotherapy these factors may be minimized or absent. Does this alteration in the therapeutic process mean that the patient is not getting the full available range of diagnostic tests and therapeutic interventions and, if not, is this malpractice? To date, there is no consensus about practice standards for telepsychotherapy.

The use of telepsychotherapy raises an interesting liability dilemma for the practitioner. On the one hand, telepsychotherapy may be considered a lesser form of traditional psychotherapy and the therapist might be deemed to have practiced below the standard of the profession. On the other hand, given that telepsychotherapy provides access to other professionals and so much research and information, the failure to use telepsychotherapy might be depriving the patient of the full range of available treatment options (Kacmar 1997, Ribble-Smith and Hafner 1998).

The analysis of the telepsychotherapy liability question is based on the traditional definition of medical malpractice: Did the practitioner breach his or her duty of care to the patient? This question raises the issues of whether telepsychotherapy creates a doctor–patient relationship and then, if the relationship did exist, did the therapist breach the duty of care?

Making the malpractice analysis even more complex is the question of jurisdiction for the malpractice action (Kaar 1998). Does the psychotherapy take place in the state or nation where the therapist is located, where the patient is located, or in some form of cyberspace? This is important because it may lead to differences in the standard of care required, especially for international practice, and in the laws to be applied. Additionally it is not yet clear whether traditional liability insurance policies will cover telepsychotherapy (Granade 1995). Another issue may relate to what part of the psychotherapy has taken place over the telephone. For example, there may be a difference between primarily face-to-face psychotherapy with occasional telephone sessions, and psychotherapy totally by telephone with no face-to-face contact at all.

In addition to malpractice liability, licensed psychologists, psychiatrists, and social workers are vulnerable to complaints of unprofessional conduct made to state licensing boards and ethics committees of professional organizations and hospitals.

Practitioners of telepsychotherapy should make sure they are familiar with the latest developments and research in the field so that as they practice they will be aware of the developing standards of practice and be able to hone their skills to meet those standards. In addition, simple logic and professional judgment should guide the practitioner. For example, some practitioners have offered to provide psychological and forensic psychological evaluations over the telephone and the internet. Aside from the usual questions of validity and reliability, such practices could be challenged on the basis that the identity of the person taking the test may not be clear, and even if the identity were verified, it would not be clear that someone else was not present and providing coaching.

Mirroring the interstate and international jurisdictional issues inherent in liability issues are the complex jurisdictional issues pertaining to professional licensing. State licensure barriers are perhaps the greatest impediment to the progress of telepsychotherapy specifically and telemedicine in general. Under what is known as the police power, each state has the right to regulate the practice of medicine and related health fields by requiring that practitioners have licenses. There is currently no national psychotherapy license. Therefore a New Jersey psychologist treating a patient in Idaho, for example, might be deemed to be practicing in that state and exposing himself or herself to civil and criminal penalties in Idaho for practicing without a license. In New York, anyone who holds himself out as a professional who requires a license and does not have one, and anyone who aids and abets such a person to practice without a license, is guilty of a class E felony (New York Education Law § 6512). Kansas requires that anyone treating a patient located in Kansas must have a Kansas medical license. This would require a telemedicine practitioner to get a Kansas license (Kansas A. R. § 100-26-1).

Because states realize that the expertise of professionals in other states may benefit their citizens, there are a number of ways that states have dealt with the issue of unlicensed professionals who are engaged in telemedicine and telepsychotherapy (Telemedicine Report to Congress January 1997).

1. *Consultation exception*—Out-of-state psychiatrists may practice at the invitation of in-state licensed psychiatrists and act as advisors on a limited basis that varies from state to state (Tennessee Code Annotated § 63-6-204, Maryland Health Occupations Code Annotated § 14-302(4)). Approximately 46 states have exceptions for consultations (Center for Telemedicine Law, February 1997; Telemedicine Interstate Licensure White Paper www.arentfox.com).

2. *Endorsement*—A state may grant a license to a professional licensed in another state that has similar standards. Each state retains the power to set standards and issue licenses.

3. *Mutual recognition and reciprocity*—Two or more states may mutually recognize licensure. This method is used by the European Community and Australia (Maastricht Treaty http//europa.eu.int/cn/record/). The practitioner only needs a license in his or her home state (South Dakota Codified Laws Annotated § 36-4-19 [1996], Tennessee Code Annotated § 63-6-211(a) [1996]).

4. *Registration*—The professional would register in a state to practice part time in that state and would accept the legal jurisdiction of that state. California has taken the lead in this area.

The Federation of State Medical Boards has developed a Model Act to deal with the issues of interstate telemedicine. The Model Act would require that physicians who regularly and frequently practice interstate by electronic means have a special license issued by a state medical board. A license would not be required if the practice were less than once a month or less than 1 percent of the physician's practice. There would be an exemption for emergencies. So far, states have not adopted the Model Act.

One possibility that might address the multijurisdictional issue is the development of a national telemedicine license. Although licensure has been the exclusive preserve of the states, since telepsychotherapy is practiced over a system that comes under federal jurisdiction and since Congress may determine that there is a compelling national interest to intervene to protect consumers, there may be constitutional grounds to develop such a license. Existing mail and wire fraud laws are examples of federal regulation in this area. Such a national license might be restricted to the practice of telemedicine or might be broadened to make the license to practice more transportable.

While the practice of telemedicine raises the issue of patient privacy, it is most acute for telepsychotherapy since privacy and confidentiality are the hallmarks of psychotherapy. The threats to privacy in telepsychotherapy are both legal and technological.

In much the same way that professional licenses are governed by state law, most rules pertaining to the confidentiality and privilege of medical and psychotherapy records are similarly controlled. Therefore, different professions may or may not be covered in the same manner or the same degree in different states. If records are needed in one state, may they be subpoenaed in another state? Which state's rules govern the recording, maintaining, and releasing of patient records? These issues are not yet resolved.

Ironically, while telemedicine and telepsychotherapy have made medical skills and information available across geographic barriers, they have also increased the risk that confidential health information will be intercepted (Bashshur 1995). This has brought about the need for encoding and protecting electronic transmissions by telephone and internet (Spielberg 1998).

The federal government provides some limited protection for information privacy (Schwartz and Reidenberg 1996). One such federal statute is the Electronic Communications Privacy Act, which protected against government tapping of telephone conversations (United States Code § 2510, 1986). This statute has been updated to include other forms of digital communication and now includes e-mail (United States Code § 2510-2711, 1977). However, these protections against government intrusion may not protect information in the private sector (Whalen v Roe, 429, United States 589, 1977). Some statutes addressed health care privacy in a limited way Hodge et al. 1999). The Privacy Act of 1974 (United States Code § 552(b)

(1-3)(6), 1996), and the Americans with Disabilities Act (United States Code § 12112, 1997) control only government health data (Gostin 1995) and require employers to separate health files of employees.

Of great significance in this area is the somewhat controversial Health Insurance Portability and Accountability Act of 1996. The Congress did not meet the statute's self-imposed deadline of August 1999 to develop comprehensive medical privacy legislation. In the absence of congressional action the legislation requires the Department of Health and Human Services to issue such regulations. These proposed regulations were available for comment until February 17, 2000 (35). One aspect of this bill that has raised some concern is the possibility that in many circumstances it will abolish the need for the patient's consent before such information is released.

It therefore behooves psychologists treating patients over the telephone to use great care and discretion to preserve the confidentiality of the situation.

Another concern of psychologists doing psychotherapy on the telephone is payment for such services by third parties. Private insurers vary in their policies toward such coverage. Increasingly federal and state legislation provides coverage for certain telemedicine activities. The California Telemedicine Development Act of 1996 provides that private insurers and Medi-Cal establish a payment policy for telemedicine and allows for teleconsultation from outside the state without a license if the consultant does not have ultimate authority over the patient's care. Also, all the information transmitted over the telephone lines or other electronic means would become part of the medical record. The statute provides that the patient must consent to such treatment at its outset.

Under the Balanced Budget Act of 1997 (Human Resources 2015 § 4206, 1997) Medicare, under Part B, will often reimburse for professional consultations on telecommunications media for a beneficiary residing in a rural area designated to be a Health Professional Shortage Area (Public Health Service Act [42 United States Code 254e(a)(1)(A)]). The Health Care Financing Administration allows states to reimburse for telemedicine to Medicaid beneficiaries. To date about eleven states permit such reimbursement (www.hcfa.gov/medicaid/telelist.htm). States are provided some latitude in defining the scope of covered services within the federal requirements of efficiency, economy, and quality of care.

Given the uncertainties and risks inherent in this developing area of practice, what can a psychologist do to limit liability exposure? There are a number of risk management procedures that the psychologist can employ to greatly reduce malpractice and professional discipline risk.

1. *Training*—Psychologists need training both in general clinical issues and in issues unique to telephone psychotherapy. Many psychologists practice beyond their areas of competence. Psychologists should be aware of their limitations and move into new areas only with proper training and supervision.

2. *Written informed consent*—This is one of the least expensive but most effective methods of risk management. The patient is informed of the nature of the treatment, its guidelines, and its limitations. Issues such as, but not limited to, methods of treatment, risks, billing, and confidentiality should be included. This consent should be recorded in a manner that is later retrievable. In some situations such written consent may already be required by law.

3. *Patient screening*—One should be careful that the type of patient selected is appropriate to the therapist and

the therapeutic method. Some patients present a much higher risk and may require different interventions, such as suicidal patients.

4. *Consultation and referral*—Psychologists should not be reluctant to seek professional advice from colleagues for difficult cases and should refer patients for consultations when needed (i.e., for psychological testing, medication or neurological consultations).

5. *Maintaining treatment records*—Not only is the failure to keep records considered to be unprofessional conduct in most states and by most professional organizations, it creates greater liability risk. Records are one of the few ways psychologists can demonstrate how they diagnosed and treated a case. The failure to maintain records could seriously hamper a malpractice defense. If the psychologist wishes to tape record telephone sessions, he or she should contact an attorney about the legality of such taping and, if legal, the therapist should obtain the patient's consent.

6. *Learn about issues of fee splitting and kickbacks*—Some telephone and internet referral activities may be prohibited under certain statutes and regulations.

7. *Appropriate referral*—Refer only to qualified professionals whose background and training are known to the referring therapist.

8. *Monitoring of employees and partners*—One can be liable for the activities of subordinates and partners through vicarious liability. It is important to set up treatment protocols, train associates properly, and monitor their activities.

9. *Care in billing*—Billing for services, especially third parties such as Medicare and Medicaid, is complex. One should be aware of the various rules that may

differ from program to program and not engage in fraudulent activity in order to "help the patient." Misdiagnosing in order to get insurance coverage could lead to serious problems and prosecution.

10. *Liability insurance*—One should make sure that the telephone psychotherapy is covered and that there are appropriate limits for the coverage.

11. *Legal consultation*—Psychologists should consult with an attorney familiar with their practices to obtain the proper forms and guidance for the developing areas of practice. Psychologists should speak with their attorneys prior to taking legal action and should contact them at the earliest sign of difficulty. Often preventing a problem is much easier and less expensive than trying to fix it.

In addition to the psychotherapy that takes place by telephone, more and more psychological, psychiatric, and social work services are being offered over the internet, using both voice and text-based communication. The quality and reliability of these services are generally not regulated by any government or professional body. It is up to the consumer to protect himself or herself. The field is extremely competitive with many forms of advertising and promotions, such as psychological games, tests, information, and even the auctioning of psychotherapy services.

As with any other economic and professional system, while there will be growth pains as the field of telepsychotherapy develops, state, federal, and professional standards will gradually be developed. The electronic forms of treatment are clearly here to stay. It seems unlikely, though, that they will replace the role of face-to-face psychotherapy since so much of the therapeutic process, especially family and group therapy, is based on the interpersonal aspects of the treatment. Telephone psychotherapy will bring benefits to those who are unable to avail themselves of personal visits with mental health professionals. As the use of electronic communication increases, standards of training in such media will increase, as will the protection of confidentiality.

REFERENCES

American College of Radiology (1996). *ACR Standard for Teleradiology*. Reston, VA.

Bashshur, R. L. (1995). On the definition and evaluation of telemedicine. *Telemed Journal* 1:115–123.

College of American Pathologists (1995). *Practice of Telemedicine*. Washington, DC.

Cowan, R. S. (1997). *A Social History of American Technology*. New York: Oxford University Press.

Fischer, C. S. (1992). *America Calling: A Social History of the Telephone to 1940*. Los Angeles, CA: University of California Press.

Gostin, L. O. (1995). Health information privacy. *Cornell Law Review* 80:451–528.

Granade, P. F. (1995). Malpractice issues in the practice of telemedicine. *Telemed Journal* 1:87–89.

Hodge, J. G., Gostin, L. O., and Jacobson, P. D. (1999). Legal issues concerning electronic health information. *Journal of the American Medical Association* 282:1466–1471.

Kaar, J. F. (1998). Legal challenges to the implementation of telehealth within the United States and internationally. *Armed Forces Institute of Pathology and Legal Medicine*, pp. 32–36.

Kacmar, D. E. (1997). The impact of computerized medical literature databases on medical malpractice litigation: Time for another Helling v. Carey wake-up call? *Ohio State Law Journal* 58:617–654.

Nickelson, D. (1997). Practitioner focus. *APA Practice Directorate*, August.

————— (1998). Telehealth and the evolving health care system: strategic opportunities for professional psychology. *Professional Psychology: Research and Practice*, vol. 29.

Reiser, S. J. (1978). *Medicine and the Reign of Technology*. New York: Cambridge University Press.

Ribble-Smith, B., and Hafner, A. W. (1986). The effect of the information age on physicians' professional liability. *DePaul Law Review* 36:69–94.

Schwartz, P. M., and Reidenberg, J. E. (1996). *Data Privacy Law: A Study of United States Data Protection*. Charlottesville, VA: Michie Law Publishers.

Spielberg, A. R. (1998). On call and on-line. *Journal of the American Medical Association* 280:1353–1359.

CREDITS

The editor gratefully acknowledges permission to reprint material from the following sources:

Chapter 1, "Psychoanalysis by Telephone," by John Lindon, from *Bulletin of the Menninger Clinic* 52:521–528. Copyright © 1988 by the Menninger Foundation and used by permission of the Foundation and the author.

Chapter 2, "Telephone Analysis," by Sharon Zalusky, from *Journal of the American Psychoanalytic Association* 46(4):1221–1242. Copyright © 1998 by *Journal of the American Psychoanalytic Association* and used by permission of the American Psychoanalytic Association and the author.

Chapter 3, "Enhancement of the Therapeutic Process," by Robert H. Spiro and Luanna E. Devenis, originally titled "Telephone Therapy: Enhancement of the Therapeutic Process," in *Psychotherapy in Private Practice* 9(4):31–55. Copyright © 1991 by Haworth Press and used with their permission and that of the authors.

Chapter 12, "Telephone Psychotherapy with Adolescents," by Joan Tolchin, from *Adolescent Psychiatry*, 14:332–341. Copyright © 1987 by The University of Chicago Press and used with permission of The University of Chicago Press and the author.

INDEX